NEW NARRATIVES ON THE PEOPLING OF AMERICA

T0375099

NEW NARRATIVES
ON THE PEOPLING
OF AMERICA

Immigration, Race, and Dispossession

EDITED BY

T. ALEXANDER ALEINIKOFF

AND

ALEXANDRA DÉLANO ALONSO

JOHNS HOPKINS UNIVERSITY PRESS | *Baltimore*

This book has been brought to publication with the generous assistance of the Robert L. Warren Endowment.

Johns Hopkins University Press
2715 North Charles Street
Baltimore, Maryland 21218
www.press.jhu.edu

Library of Congress Cataloging-in-Publication Data

Names: Aleinikoff, T. Alexander (Thomas Alexander), 1952– editor. |
    Délano, Alexandra, 1979– editor.
Title: New narratives on the peopling of America : immigration, race,
    and dispossession / edited by T. Alexander Aleinikoff and Alexandra Délano Alonso.
Description: Baltimore : Johns Hopkins University Press, 2024. |
    Includes bibliographical references and index.
Identifiers: LCCN 2023028032 | ISBN 9781421448664 (paperback) |
    ISBN 9781421448671 (ebook)
Subjects: LCSH: Immigrants—United States—Social conditions. |
    Minorities—United States—Social conditions. | United States—Ethnic relations. |
    United States—Race relations. | Immigrants—United States—Literary collections. |
    Minorities—United States—Literary collections.
Classification: LCC E184.A1 N3795 2024 | DDC 305.9069120973—dc23/eng/20230630
LC record available at https://lccn.loc.gov/2023028032

A catalog record for this book is available from the British Library.

An excerpt of Clint Smith's poem "And the World Keeps Spinning" appears on
page xiv. Copyright © 2023 by Clint Smith. Published in *Above Ground* by Little, Brown
and Company. Reprinted by permission of The Gernert Company, Inc.

*Special discounts are available for bulk purchases of this book. For more information, please
contact Special Sales at specialsales@jh.edu.*

To those who tell and retell stories against erasure and exclusion,
and create new, collective narratives.

CONTENTS

For more than four centuries, debate over who should be welcomed to American shores and the terms of that welcome has been continuous. Migrants arrived as religious refugees, workers pursuing opportunity, indentured servants, family seeking to join others who came before. Millions came in chains; for more than two hundred years, slavery served as a backbone of the American economy and a stain on its national conscience. From the beginning, the Indigenous population was decimated, forcibly moved, restricted to reserved land. They and the descendants of enslaved people were denied US citizenship.

A long period of unrestricted immigration from Europe gave way to limitations based on race and nationality, which dramatically reduced the flow of migrants in the late 19th and 20th centuries. During the Great Depression, the federal government undertook a mass deportation of Mexicans; among their number were tens of thousands of US citizens.

Changes in the law eventually extended US citizenship to Native Americans, Puerto Ricans, and other residents of US territories. A great internal migration brought six million African Americans from the South to the cities of the North. In the mid-20th century, the restriction of Chinese and Japanese migrants was repealed, as was the national origin quota system that applied to European migration. Since that time, the nation has witnessed record numbers of immigrant arrivals. The foreign-born percentage of the US population is reaching a level not seen since the early 1900s. In recent decades, border enforcement has increased dramatically. Yet today, more than 10 million undocumented migrants reside in the United States.

The national discourse on immigration has become deeply polarized—and ossified. For many, the description of the United States as a "nation of immigrants" speaks to an optimistic and welcoming America; others see poorly regulated borders and demographic changes wrought by immigration as a threat to their conception of the nation.

This book provides a wide range of perspectives on the immigration narrative of the United States. Composed of twenty original chapters written by academics, journalists, artists, activists, and public intellectuals as well as two photo essays, it moves beyond traditional renderings in several ways. It is grounded on the recognition that a focus only on immigration gives an incomplete picture of who is here and how they got here; a comprehensive narrative of "the peopling" of the United States must include the stories of those who were already here when European settlers arrived, of those brought to America as enslaved persons, and of persons residing in territories and foreign nations acquired by the United States. The volume gives fuller play to revisionist accounts of the settling of the United States and puts front and center the issue of race in the construction of the American people. It also examines the role that migrant, African American, and Native American perspectives can play in the shaping of new narratives.

The issues addressed by the essays in this book are of surpassing importance today. Migration is among the top issues on the national political agenda. The new movement for racial justice has sharpened attention to the nation's unfulfilled promise of equality for non-white residents of the United States. The scope of the sovereignty of tribal governments remains a matter of contention, as does the question of statehood for Puerto Rico. Nationalist populism, globalization, transnational migrant communities, a declining US birth rate, and economic precarity for many are all part of the current US social and political context, offering a confusing array of analyses and policy recommendations.

Regrettably, the level of public discourse has not matched the saliency of the issues. We frequently seem stuck in the arguments of the past, cite data that can be shown to be wrong, and rely on stereotypes (of both the foreign-born and the native-born) that are frequently unjust to those so characterized. Important policy debates and deep cultural discussions cannot be sensibly resolved by recourse to traditional nativist tropes or the words of Emma Lazarus emblazoned on the Statue of Liberty. The goal of this volume is to improve and invigorate the discussion of the past, present, and future of the peopling of the United States.

A NOTE ABOUT THE COVER ART

red liberty

Marco Saavedra

Known originally by the Lenape people as Paggank, or "nut island," Governors Island is where the Hudson and East Rivers meet in New York Harbor and empty into the Atlantic. Where you can step into the sunset as New York City's skyline opens to river, bay, ocean, and clouds above. In the fall of 2021, I was granted a residency at the island. I had avoided painting water my whole life and now found myself surrounded by it. Unable, unwilling, to paint indoors, I carried my canvases in a shopping cart to the edge of the water and made my best effort to apply what I have learned from J. M. W. Turner, Winslow Homer, and James Whistler. And naturally also turned inward: my family is Mixteca from San Miguel Ahuehuetit-lán in Oaxaca, Mexico. Our Indigenous name translates to "cloud people" or "the land of the rain," and even when we talk it sounds like laments.

Being illegal and now a political refugee in my homeland, from my homeland, means I have had to find home in occupied Lenape territory. And also lament for the original people of these lands who now reside mainly in Oklahoma, 1,500 miles away. My family and I crossed the border illegally in 1993 and settled 2,700 miles from our ancestral village, but there is a connection in all things native. Unable to return to my native home, I must connect and cry with the native land that adopted me: "by indirections find directions out" (Shakespeare, *Hamlet*). What was here before cranes, concrete, and crosswalks? What will remain after? I have never found the Hudson River, for example, a fitting name to the body of water I grew closest to, and I find the Mohawk name Ka'nón:no more musical and true.

Everyone is from this earth, everyone is Indigenous, everyone is illegal. And in the opposing equation: your alienation from your nativity allies you with power and estranges you from your home. And it is the moral position to be an outlaw in an inhumane system. And when the waters rise, and the last bubble bursts, and our grids fail, you will not be able to hide behind bureaucracy and capital, and will have to move or die. And the American Dream will no longer be a myth but a past, a rag to wipe our tears on and move on.

So I hesitated to paint the Statue of Liberty that couldn't be avoided when I looked out at the water from the highest point on the island. The statue has always

red liberty, fall 2021, acrylic and pastel on bar mop, 16 × 19 in.

rung false and cheap to me. At Ellis Island, immigrants were denied, detained, deported. Their names were changed upon arrival. "This Fourth of July is yours, not mine. You may rejoice, I must mourn" (Frederick Douglass, "What to the Slave Is the Fourth of July?").

But I could not look away. The sun sets every day behind the statue and cloaks her in shadow, the last rays bathe her teal green into a wine-dark bloody red. And here was truth: both romantic and vicious, both engulfing and bright. To make *red liberty* (study), I applied my last acrylic paint and pastel (left over from a J. M. W. Turner study) to a flimsy rag we use to wipe the tables at my family's mutual aid restaurant, La Morada. The rag's surface is so loose and coarse that the whole statue warps with the creases, and my own violent relationship with her is also transposed. My allegiance as an illegal, Indigenous person aligns with the displaced and dispossessed:

> For every hundred people who were
> captured & enslaved, forty died before they
> ever reached the New World.
>
> . . . .
> I slide my ring finger from Senegal
> to South Carolina & feel the ocean
> separate a million families.
> (Clint Smith, "And the World Keeps Spinning")

I have been denied, detained, and deported, and judge you illegal. And bless you with illegality. To be free from the cheap web of justifications we have used to divide families and justify displacement. And as much as I want to be stateless, I cannot run away from the white canon. As was said of W. E. B. Du Bois's "The Souls of Black Folk": the work is an homage to a civilization that has largely denied it. And like Du Bois I must end all complaint with the same conclusion: "My soul wants something that's new, that's new." That newness is *allons, vamos*, let's go, *coo'o*. Is agency. Is the freedom to move, work, love, cross, return, especially when your biosphere is being destroyed. And my visa requirements are the same as all poets': "I give you myself before preaching or law. Will you give me yourself?" (Walt Whitman, "Song of the Open Road").

My ultimate identity as an artist can only create and invite others to create and protest any form of repression that commodifies and consumes us. So in my walk I turn to you, the reader, to my inner child, to my children's children, to my enemy, and to my ghosts:

> Allons! the road is before us!
>
> It is safe—I have tried it—my own feet have tried it well—be not detain'd!
> (Walt Whitman, "Song of the Open Road")

PART I

THE MAKING OF A NARRATIVE

CHAPTER 1

Toward Larger Stories

New Narratives on the Peopling of the United States of America

Alexandra Délano Alonso

I am writing under the canopy of London plane trees that so distinctly marks my Sunnyside neighborhood in Queens, New York. Once a planned community that became the home of a majority of Irish immigrants in the 1920s and 1930s, Sunnyside is now part of what makes Queens one of the most diverse counties in the United States and in the world. Home of the Matinecock, Canarsie, Jameco, and Mespeatche Indigenous peoples, today almost half of the population in this borough is foreign born, and more than 85% speak a language other than English. Described as "a 'there' without a 'there,' a cipher, a massive jigsaw puzzle: sprawling, expansive, tangled, multiform . . ." in Joseph Heathcott's essay "Queens Is the Future,"[1] it is a powerful expression of possibility and constant transformation. A "roiling, changeable, centerless borough,"[2] Queens resists and "defies ready categorization or explanation," revealing itself as a tangible expression of the openness, flexibility, and adaptability of the spaces, places, and identities we inhabit. Shaped and reshaped through the peopling of marshes, farms, trade roads, and fields by individuals from all over the world, against the fixity of political categories, borders, and lines of difference, Queens "never resolves itself into a discernible whole," and therein lies its beauty and potential. Everyone is from elsewhere, and that makes us all part of a "there without a there."[3]

My son's fourth grade class in Long Island City recently worked on a project about where they were from, that deceivingly obvious question.

They had to write and draw pictures in response to prompts that gently moved them away from geographic and political delimitations that come to mind in our usual answers. Instead, they focused on people, nature, food, moments, activities, sounds, smells, and feelings of being somewhere, a part of something:

> I am from frijoles y arroz. I am from guayabas and mangoes. I am from the trees I climb. I am from the park around the corner, from the rancho by the river, from the January snow. I am from early morning birds and grillos at night. I am from my bed, my blue pillow. I am from playing with my brother, from my feet on wet grass.

My children and I live in between two cities, two countries, two languages, two cultures, and as they grow older, they ask more questions about what that means. Do you feel more Mexican or American? Do you know more English or Spanish? Which one is better? Are we Mexican American or American Mexican? Why do people say they want to build a wall to keep Mexicans out? Why do they hate us? What does it mean to "not have papers"? Why can't Carolina and Marco just get a passport and come with us? Why is my friend Nadia's dad in Hidalgo always talking about going to Idaho? Why would he leave his daughters, and the horses, and the maíz? Will she come too? And where is my friend América's dad? Why can't he come back?

From Here and There

The three of us have the freedom and privilege of being able to travel back and forth, we have "the right papers," we have family and friends and a safe place to live in both countries, our skin is white, our curly hair light, and we speak both languages fluently enough (and with enough of an accent) that most people are taken aback when we say we're Mexican. In México, when I line up at the airport in the queue for citizens, more often than not I am told I'm on the wrong line. I decided to naturalize as a US citizen because every time I got to JFK airport with my two children, upon presenting my Mexican and their US passports, I was asked for proof that I am their mother. In New

York, when people overhear the three of us talking, they sometimes ask what language we speak. They assume we're French or Italian or Spanish or Irish and invariably say, "Oh but you don't look Mexican." When I sing along with or talk to the musicians on the #7 train in New York—who play the *corridos* and *rancheras* my mother used to teach us on the guitar growing up—they ask me why I speak Spanish so well. I tell them I'm from México. "¿De dónde?" they answer. I say, "De la ciudad de México, del DF," and they keep asking, "¿Pero de qué parte, güera?" and it feels like a test to see if I'm really from there until I say, "Soy chilanga."

We are, we can be *from here and there*. We are and can be from the flowers of jacaranda trees covering the streets of Mexico City in purple in March, and from the fallen bark of birch trees we gather from the mountains in the Hudson Valley in the autumn. We are from cider and football in November, and then *ponche* and the other *fútbol* in December. Torn between all that we love in two different places, we are often in that "Nepantla state of transition" that Gloria Anzaldúa refers to; that *in between* borders and cultures that is full of potential—"the threshold of transformation," "the place where we can accept contradiction of paradox," and also a place that can be deeply challenging and painful. Over time I've come to understand this constant crossing of borders both as a rupture and as what Anzaldúa celebrates as a state from which "direction and renewal spring forth," as "the locus of resistance . . . of implosion and explosion . . . of putting together the fragments and creating a new assemblage."[4]

America Never Was America to Me

One day my 9-year-old recited "Let America Be America Again" at the school assembly, and I asked him what line of the poem resonated the most. He paused and said, "America never was America to me." And in my son's response to Langston Hughes, I heard the raw, bitter disappointment with the fact that the freedom to explore and live out this complexity, this multiplicity of spaces, places, stories, identities that we each hold, is not, has never been, available to all.

The stubbornness of a rusted border fence against the ocean and the seagulls and the sand. The impossible contrast between the green, perfectly mowed grass, the highways, and the buildings one can see in the distance on one side, and on the other the dirt roads, the trash, and rows of unfinished houses whose backyards face the fence. A patchwork of iron and steel trying to mark a territory, a beginning and ending point for who belongs and who doesn't in the idea of the nation, the country, the United States of America. America.

I grew up with the idea of America as a continent; there was America—or, for some, the Americas (North and South)—and within it the United States *of* America. Martha Elena Venier, or "Venier," as we called our beloved writing professor at El Colegio de México, infused in us a love for our language and for accuracy of words. For every anglicism that has penetrated Spanish, she knew the perfect translation that should be used instead. Among many lessons I took from her was that the proper term to refer to people from the United States was "estadounidenses" not "americanos." We were all *americanos*, whether we were in Latin America or North America. And yet the longer I live in the United States, the clearer it becomes that this expansive notion of America as a region, a continent (or two), a people is far removed from the one expressed in the American idea of America, in the American Dream, in its exceptionalism, its individualism, and its imperialism.

As editors of this collection, Alex Aleinikoff and I have discussed many times whether to use the word "America" on its own in the title of the book. This was also debated in some of the first workshops we held with the contributing authors and other colleagues. The aim to shift the predominant, limited, colonialist narratives of immigration in the United States can begin with the title, what we recognize in the way we name a place: *New Narratives of the Peopling of the United States of America* or even further, *of Turtle Island*. Deconstructing ideas of nation-states, of borders, and of territorial sovereignty, and acknowledging histories that have been rendered invisible and silenced in that limited modern fiction requires different frames of reference, different terms, different names, vocabularies, and blank spaces to be filled. I see the depths of this possibility to think beyond simplified, assimilationist constructions of identity and nation in the urban landscape of Queens, "a habitat characterized by variations on themes, repeated and modified forms, borrowed and adapted styles, all alternating between unique and ubiquitous, quirky and quotidian."[5] I hear it in the children's responses to the "I am from" prompt. I feel it in Gloria Anzaldúa's borderlands as the space of resistance and imagination, in *Nepantla*, the indigenous cosmology of in-betweenness, in between the binaries, the extremes, the cracks. I find it again and again in the words, actions, protests, poetry, art, and ways of being expressed by those who fight for the freedom to move across borders, to be here, there, in between, here again.

My deepest understanding of what is wrong with the immigration system, how its brokenness intersects with other failed economic and political structures, and how it could change has come from listening to artists, activists, and organized communities in the United States, México, and elsewhere, say: we are undocumented, unapologetic, and unafraid. Say we are here because you were there. Say we are from here and there. Say there can be no Muslim ban on Stolen Land. Say, again, no one is free until we are all free.

Narratives as Political Horizons

The story of the "nation of immigrants," of the "American Dream," is one in which Queens is possible, but it is also a history of violence, exclusions, and contradictions. A nation, a dream, an aspiration built at the expense of Black populations, migrants, and Indigenous peoples. A history of inclusion, opportunity, and welcome for some, and also a history displacement, separation of families and loved ones, oppression, discrimination, deep trauma, and pain that tears the social fabric of communities in the countries that migrants leave and may or may not return to, as well as the communities where they arrive and settle in, temporarily or permanently.

Reading again James Baldwin's 1962 letter to his nephew on the anniversary of the emancipation—"You know, and I know, that the country is celebrating one hundred years of freedom one hundred years too soon. We cannot be free until they are free"[6]—I think of all that still hides behind the grand narrative of "liberty and justice for all," a statue of liberty with a promise denied by the detention and deportation center right next to it. The open wounds of histories unacknowledged, voices unheard, and violences that persist. The fear of facing and changing this reality. A present where so many can think only of survival in the day to day, without equal opportunities to even dream of another future. If the political horizon of "America" does not include the millions of individuals who crossed borders to arrive in "the land of the free" and live in a precarious status, the Indigenous peoples displaced over and over from their land, Black people and communities of color overpoliced and discriminated against, excluded LGBTQI communities and individuals with disabilities, then the whole of the society they are a part of cannot be free.

The home many are trying to find in the United States is, as Baldwin put it, a "burning house."[7] And where is home for you, poet Jesús I. Valles asks (chap. 8, this vol.)? Beyond a location, this poem speaks of time, of a history in which immigration laws and policies have selected "the good ones," criminalized, displaced and excluded the unwanted, a reality that is also exposed and challenged by QUEEROCRACY and Carlos Motta's *Timeline of Queer Migrations* (chap. 14, this vol.). This racialized and discriminatory migration system has closed the possibility for many in the United States to build a home in the sense that Valles's poem expresses: as a space and a time in which past, present, and future can be held, uninterrupted by forced separation, immobility and precarity.

All Nations Are Creatures of Story, Made in the Imagination

If nations and borders are creatures of story, myths, made in the imagination, then they can be erased, redrawn, remade. Following Ernest Renan, Kwame Anthony Appiah argues that what really matters in the making of nations, beyond our stories, is "the clearly expressed desire . . . and everyday commitment to governing a common life *together*" (chap. 2, this vol., p. 24). Yet, the history of immigration in the

United States shows us that the story is, in fact, deceiving, that it needs revisions, that it will continue to be written and rewritten. Moreover, the commitment to governing a common life together is not enough when there is no equal opportunity to make that life.

From its very origins, the "nation of immigrants" (a phrase popularized in 1960s, as Mae Ngai's essay documents; chap. 9, this vol.), the "country of open doors," has always been selective in who is allowed to express that desire and commitment to make a life together. Aristide Zolberg put it clearly in *A Nation by Design*: "a nation of immigrants, to be sure, but not just any immigrants."[8] Who deserves and who doesn't deserve to be in the United States has been determined by race, class, economic and political interests, gender, sexuality, and family (Vogt, chap. 13, this vol.). Alongside the construction of the idea of America, the American Dream, and the Nation of Immigrants has been a construction of Indigenous peoples as inferior, of Black people as slaves and undeserving of rights, and of many immigrants as undesirable and illegal. The existence of migrants as *impossible subjects*,[9] as deportable, disposable, illegal aliens, is explained by the political and economic interests underlying immigration policies, which have not only shaped the demographic makeup of the country but have sustained an economy and a polity that has thrived historically on the precarious status of millions of migrants and communities of color.

The impact of this system of exploitation and extraction reverberates across the Americas and beyond.[10] We cannot understand immigration and the challenges faced by those arriving in the United States without recognizing the causes of emigration in different forms of violence, extractivism, poverty, inequality, climate change, and histories of colonialism and foreign intervention in which the United States is implicated (Garcia, chap. 11, this vol.). We cannot understand the true impact of migration without looking at the communities that are left behind when someone leaves, at the families that are separated through deportation or forced return, at the tens of thousands who have died or disappeared trying to cross the border.

To remake narratives that will guide policies that recognize the right to mobility and the right to remain, we need larger stories that look beyond the United States of America. Larger stories that understand migration as a continuum of internal displacement, emigration, transit, immigration, and return.[11] Larger stories that connect the struggles of migration within structures of capitalism and white supremacy, and in relation to broader struggles of mobility, solidarity and justice (see Vogt, chap. 13, and Brown, Jones, and Dow, chap. 20, this vol.). Larger stories that shelter our big complexities and contradictions; that *contain multitudes* (see Anderson and Loredo, chap. 21, this vol, p. 380; and Patel and Agarwal, chap. 16, this vol.). Broader, complex stories that remind us that we are "part of a much larger living system that includes the water, earth, canyons, and plants" and that it is through these stories, and these places "that healing can begin," as Dakota Mace illustrates in her essay and photographs (chap. 5, this vol., p. 70).

Whiteness *Is* the National Myth

A starting point for this "national reckoning that would lead to spiritual renewal," for reparations, and for the imagining of a new country that Ta-Nehisi Coates calls for, is "the full acceptance of our collective biography and its consequences."[12]

A more complex, collective historical account of the peopling of the United States would require the willingness to complicate existing stories and longstanding symbols: "No soft-focus Lady Liberty, no voice whispering 'give me your tired, your poor' as if America is just a place of welcome. . . . America has always tried to exclude, persecute, discriminate, detain, and deport those who weren't white, always tried to keep out those who were deemed 'too poor'" (Long, chap. 6, this vol., p. 113). It means reckoning with whiteness as *the* national myth (Gest, chap. 3, this vol., p. 30), as the political calculation behind the acceptance of some immigrants and not others in order to sustain white hegemony, against the reality of demographic change and the majority-minority society that John R. Weeks describes (chap. 7, this vol.). It means reckoning with imperialism, with slavery and racism, with settler-colonialism and its legacies (Smith, chap. 4, this vol.). It means telling the histories of exclusions and inclusions and recognizing the blurry boundaries that in fact make peoples' identities and experiences against the static images of the nation (Gest, chap. 3, this vol.).

When this broader history includes those who have come or have been brought to the United States, voluntarily and involuntarily, and those who have been "crossed by the border" through annexation and conquest, as Daniel Immerwahr argues (chap. 10, this vol., p. 164), then we can also deconstruct the idea of the United States as a fixed territory, one that can be walled. The people that make the country have changed and continue to do so, and so has the place.

Centering the histories of settler-colonialism and imperialism expands the questions from borders, integration, and the need for a reform of immigration laws and policies to a broader systemic approach that addresses a larger history of violence, discrimination, racism, and exclusion. This is a call not only to deracialize, but to decolonize the history of immigration as a starting point for solidarity across different struggles.[13]

From this perspective, as many immigrant activists have claimed, achieving citizenship is not enough when US citizens are also denied rights, are discriminated against, and are killed by state institutions. The call is for a broader focus on the connections across migrant rights, indigenous rights, over-policing, gender-based violence, environmental justice, and food sovereignty. It's not only the immigration system that needs repair. As Patrick Chamoiseau puts it in *Migrant Brothers, A Poet's Declaration of Human Dignity*, "If societies, institutions, states, levels of consciousness, unprecedented intensities of communication are capable of accepting migrant catastrophes, it's because the unacceptable already thrives in their daily lives."[14]

It Makes No Sense to Assimilate into What Is

Against assimilation or integrationist frameworks that reify power hierarchies and assumptions of whiteness as superior, many excluded communities in the United States have resisted and put forward alternative visions and practices of mobility, freedom, and mutuality. Working against nationalism, against frames of hospitality and charity that maintain binaries of us/them, citizen/migrant, they are not trying to re-form the existing system or conform to its underlying and problem-atic assumptions. As Marco Saavedra has put it, "It makes no sense to assimilate into what is."[15] Through *red liberty*, he also challenges the framework of illegality in an economic and political system based on exploitation, extraction, and displacement: isn't it "the moral position to be an outlaw in an inhumane system" (Saavedra, this vol., p. xiii)? Referring to her experience of forced return to México after living un-documented most of her life in the United States, Maggie Loredo also challenges the frame of integration and re-integration that resonates across borders, asking why it is that she and her community need to accept "the state violence, gender violence, femicides, disappearance of neighbors, precarious labor conditions, lack of spaces in schools and universities, low wages, and poor *insuficiente* public health care system" that pushed her family out in the first place. "My deported and returned community will never be completely integrated into a society that does not even provide basic rights and services for most of its own citizens. We will never be integrated in a society that looks to deny our migration experience, that ignores the separation of our families, that fails to give all of us the minimum conditions we need to rebuild our lives.[16]

The challenge to the narrative of the nation of immigrants and the systems of exclusion built around it is not just to the governments and institutions that sustain it, but also to the ways in which some migrant groups themselves and the local communities they join have adopted it and are implicated in it, knowingly or not, as Dunbar-Ortiz argues.[17] Migrants have also been part of the settler-colonial project and become settlers, which creates tensions and divisions where there could other-wise be solidarity. Racism, violence, and erasure also occur among im-migrant groups and between immigrants and other communities that face exclusion and discrimination. The challenge of creating unity in struggles such as the labor solidarity across white and Black workers that W. E. B. Du Bois fought for continues today in the unions, worker centers, and organizations forging new solidarities across different groups of citizens and noncitizens.

The narratives of social movements and community organizations that make connections across struggles, from women's rights to migration, abolition, and Indigenous sovereignty has led to what Hana E. Brown, Jennifer A. Jones, and Taylor Dow describe as an emergent understanding of immigration as a civil rights and racial justice movement that is reshaping social justice struggles and "encourages us to rethink the narratives we usually tell about race, citizenship, and inclusion in the United States" (chap. 20, this vol., p. 357). Expanding the language of sanctuary, for example, and connecting it to a broader history of the Underground Railroad is evidence of this "broadening of America" that Gest calls for (chap. 3, this vol.). This is the necessary nuance and openness of narratives that allow us to build an understanding of mutuality, of the empathic imagination, and the witnessing that Allison Dorsey describes (chap. 19, this vol.): this possibility of seeing others as fully human as we see ourselves, to act compassionately, to minimize harm.

A better future, argues Dorsey, "requires that we understand the ways all our futures are intertwined" (p. 342). That means humility; it means cultivating curiosity and knowledge about other peoples' stories and experiences; it means bearing witness. Only then can more voices be added to those who are acknowledging and objecting to violence and to harm. Only then can there be "a wave of sound that reverberates and creates small fissures, tiny fractures in the structures of society, new openings for progressive change to take root" (p. 344).

Part of this work requires deconstructing, retelling, and rewriting histories, understanding and confronting "the ugly of America's history along with the good" (Dorsey, chap. 19, this vol., p. 343), from the classroom to the streets, the workplace, the media, and the political arena. Social movements past and present show that this has been and is possible. The greatest challenges to narratives of immigration that underlie policies and systems built around binaries of us/them, host/guest, citizen/noncitizen have come from the communities that show in their discourses and practices that the conditions that create forced displacement and the oppression of migrant communities are systemic and should be addressed as such, locally and trans-locally.

There are many examples of these alternative stories and lived experiences to draw from. They are present in mutual aid networks, community fridges, sanctuary spaces, community gardens, and public art spaces, especially those led by migrants and communities of color, founded on principles of reciprocity, of flourishing (Anderson and Loredo), thriving and blossoming (Dorsey) for all, against logics of deserving/undeservingness.

To Tell Larger Stories

Stitching has long been a practice storytelling, collective memory, and healing. Cinthya Santos Briones's *Migrant Herbalism* archive reinterprets the threads of ancestral knowledges and traditional medicine through the Mexican diaspora in the United States. Focusing not just on the displacement of people but also on the herbs, barks, and seeds that have migrated between the two countries, her embroideries of herbs, layered over cyanotypes "take on a political and resistance dimension" and are also "a metaphor for liberation and healing." This archive shows the importance and the need to include different generations of migrants, families, and Indigenous communities in the documentation of their personal histories and ancestral knowledges, to build collective memory in community, through oral histories, testimonios, medicinal herbs, embroidery, and art.[18]

These larger stories are already being made and remade, as Héctor Tobar shows in his beautiful account of how Latinx youth have challenged the limited categories in which they are placed; the countless ways in which they resist and create other stories against the fear, the secrecy and the violence that weigh heavily on many of their and their families' experiences: "These stories are the essence of the present-day US experience. They are the stories by which America will know itself in the unfolding century, in the decade to come and the ones that follow" (chap. 17, this vol., p. 316).

For too long, the stories, the narratives of migrants have been told by others, and the resulting policies that affect their lives have been made without their voices. The cost of doing so is high: we can see it in the one-dimensional laws that often fail to recognize the realities and experiences of migrants and their families (see Minian, chap. 12; Garcia, chap. 11; and Vogt, chap. 13, this vol.). We can see it in the torn fabric of communities and relationships, in the deep divisions in the country, and in the "hard roots of hatred" (Long, chap. 6, this vol., p. 111).

To heal these roots, the narratives (and the actions derived from them) need to not only welcome "immigrants and refugees with compassion but also address the urgent needs of ordinary US-born workers" (Milkman, chap. 15, this vol., p. 280). The task is to build an understanding that reducing inequality and improving wages, working conditions, or housing benefits the US-born and the foreign-born alike.

Any narrative that supports communities needs to include their voices as well as the land and natural materials from which these stories emerge (Mace, chap. 5; Santos Briones, chap. 18, this vol.). As Loredo and many others who have shared their stories show, they are the experts of those plots, they know the problems and solutions. If new narratives are to emerge, they must also recognize that human beings, their identities, and the places they inhabit are not static, that nothing is settled, and that transformation is constant: "The ways we narrate our lives are in constant movement, and our stories must grow and change along with us" (Anderson and Loredo, chap. 21, this vol., p. 380).[19]

A Book, a Collection of Threads

This book is an attempt to recognize the limits of existing narratives of the United States as a "nation of immigrants" and to reckon with the violent, racist, exclusionary origins of this history. It aims to understand the impact of the laws and policies that derive from supremacist, heteropatriarchal, and racist assumptions and from economic and political interests that underlie the narratives of deservingness and undeservingness that are central to US history. It offers alternative vocabularies, histories, and stories that can help us repair, rethink, remake, and thread other narratives that bring forward the resilience, the imagination, the resistance, the plurality that has existed alongside and against the predominant discourse, offering new possibilities for the present and future.

New Narratives on the Peopling of America is a multidisciplinary collection of essays and art by photographers, activists, journalists, poets, artists, writers, and scholars. We see it as a starting point, a tool to deepen conversations among a wide audience in public spaces, in museums, in classrooms at many levels, and in political debates. In addition to the publication of the book, we will create a curriculum that will accompany it and create spaces for continuing dialogue across educational, community, and art spaces. Rewriting the narratives of the United States is not just for historians, academics, or politicians to do; it is a project for all of us who have roots and seeds in this country, especially for those whose stories, whose lived realities have been ignored or left out.

The United States Are

If the United States *are* a poem, as Walt Whitman suggested in *Leaves of Grass*, in plural form (with my intentional removal of the superlative "the greatest" from his phrase[20]), then we need to remember that the words, the music, the images of each attempt to describe a place, a time, an idea, a people means something different to each person who reads them, hears them, and feels them. That their meanings change over time. That poems speak both through words and ellipses, through rhymes and dissonances. And that the lasting poems are those that hold the complexities, the in-betweens, the unknowns, the possibilities for transformation.

Notes
1. Joseph Heathcott, "Queens Is the Future," in *All the Queens Houses: An Architectural Portrait of New York's Largest and Most Diverse Borough*, ed. Rafael Herrin-Ferri (Berlin: Jovis, 2021), 10.
2. Heathcott, "Queens Is the Future," 12.

3. Heathcott, "Queens Is the Future," 11.
4. Gloria Anzaldúa, *Light in the Dark/Luz en lo Oscuro: Rewriting Identity, Spirituality, Reality* (Durham, NC: Duke University Press, 2015), 55.
5. Heathcott, "Queens Is the Future," 19
6. James Baldwin, *The Fire Next Time* (New York: Vintage International, 1993), 10.
7. Baldwin, *The Fire Next Time*, 94.
8. Aristide Zolberg, *A Nation by Design* (Cambridge, MA: Harvard University Press, 2008), 1.
9. Mae M. Ngai, *Impossible Subjects: Illegal Aliens and the Making of Modern America* (Princeton, NJ: Princeton University Press, 2014).
10. See Tanya Golash-Boza, *Deported: Immigrant Policing, Disposable Labor, and Global Capitalism* (New York: New York University Press, 2015).
11. Jill Anderson, "The Deportability Continuum as Activist Research," *Cultural Dynamics* 31, nos. 1–2 (2019): 125–39.
12. Ta-Nehisi Coates, "The Case for Reparations," *The Atlantic*, June 2014.
13. See Roxanne Dunbar-Ortiz, *Not a Nation of Immigrants: Settler Colonialism, White Supremacy, and a History of Erasure and Exclusion* (Boston: Beacon Press, 2021).
14. Patrick Chamoiseau, *Migrant Brothers, A Poet's Declaration of Human Dignity* (New Haven, CT: Yale University Press, 2018), 104.
15. Marco Saavedra, "The Mis-Education of the Migrant," in *Eclipse of Dreams: The Undocumented-led Struggle for Freedom*, ed. Pedro Santiago Martínez, Claudia Muñoz, Mariela Núñez-Janes, Stephen Pavey, Fidel Castro Rodríguez, and Marco Saavedra (Chico, CA: AK Press, 2020), 80.
16. Nin Solis and Jill Anderson, eds., *Lxs Otrxs Dreamers* (Mexico City: Blurb, 2021), 20.
17. Dunbar-Ortiz, *Not a Nation of Immigrants*.
18. *Brewing Memories*, created and facilitated by Carolina Saavedra at community gardens in the Bronx, is another example of community-led practices of collective memory and healing through medicinal herbs (see https://archivesincommon.org/workshops/).
19. See adrienne maree brown, *Emergent Strategy* (Chico, CA: AK Press, 2017).
20. Walt Whitman's original phrase in the 1855 preface of *Leaves of Grass* is "The United States themselves are essentially the greatest poem."

CHAPTER 2

Imagining an American Nation

Sharing Our Stories

Kwame Anthony Appiah

Ellis Island, that iconic place of American beginnings, is a tiny portion of the lands long occupied by Lenape people. The earliest Dutch settlers in the area began trading beaver pelts with the Lenape some four centuries ago, after arriving in 1624 across the water on the main island of Mannahatta, as the Lenape called it. That is where the idea that the Lenape "sold" that island to the Dutch comes from, something that the Canarsie chief in the customary tale was surely not empowered to do. More such "sales" followed, negotiated with other leaders of other tribes. And so Dutch people settled to farm and trade and buy those beaver pelts from the Lenape, exchanging them, among other things, for tools that made Lenape hunting and skinning more efficient.

A century earlier, the first European accounts of the area came from Giovanni da Verrazano, who sailed into the Hudson in 1524, naming the area Nouvelle-Angoulême, in honor of his patron, Francis I, King of France, who had originally been Count of Angoulême. The Dutch, ignoring this French grandiosity, named their trading post Nieuw-Amsterdam, declaring it the capital of the Dutch province of Nieuw-Nederland a year later, thus displaying a grandiosity of their own. And pretty soon their settlement included not only citizens of the Dutch Republic, but also French, German, and Scandinavian men and women, a small group of enslaved Africans, and some Jews who had come from

Brazil. Already, nearly four hundred years ago, then, the island had people from Africa, Europe, and Latin America alongside Indigenous Lenape people; already, they belonged to a diversity of Christian sects, some practiced the Jewish religion, and a few were heirs to Indigenous religious traditions of Africa and the Americas.

After Charles II, the English king, sent a force to seize the colony in 1664, he gave it to his brother, the Duke of York. Dutch settlers were permitted to stay and continue trading, however, and more people arrived from the British Isles and from Africa, the Caribbean, and Latin America. The city and the territory got its current name, "New York," from its new lord. The idea that land that was inhabited by Lenape people, perhaps for thousands of years, could be acquired and transferred between European states and their rulers was a part of that time's "common sense" that made the European settlement of these islands and the American mainland seem like the most natural thing in the world.

Our common sense about human migration and the ways in which societies and peoples come together is made, as much as anything else, by stories like these. Accounts of sales and contracts and gifts between princes lend a sort of respectable legal veneer to what were, in fact, often exercises of raw power, guided by European notions of property, in places where the original peoples had very different ideas about how to relate to the land. The chronicles of the ghosts that surround Ellis Island, where later arrivals from a wider Europe joined the American narrative, have also shaped our US common sense about how a nation comes to be peopled. What I want to suggest is that these stories matter, because, if we get them right, we can share both the United States and the wider world more rewardingly with one another.

For the truth is that, as Benedict Anderson argued, all nations are creatures of narrative, made in the imagination, not least because they are made up of people who are so numerous that they must mostly be strangers to one another.[1] Yes, of course, much that we share is real: the landscape of the continent and its islands, the Constitution and the laws, our other institutions and practices. But they unite us only because of how we *conceive* of them. The heights of Weehawken, the mighty Hudson, the great bridges over it, the magnificent tunnels beneath, the architectural landscape of the "hilly island," "Manahatta": these matter to many of us in part because we think of them *as* American and of ourselves *as* Americans. And for us *as* citizens, the Constitution matters in large measure because we think of ourselves and of one another as composing "We, the people." And that "as"—*as* Americans, *as* citizens—means that *how* we think of our countrymen and women—what ideas and ideals, what stories and concepts we bring to bear when we contemplate these places or our fundamental law—is at the heart of what connects us to them.

What unites this country, that is, is not that we are all the same, but that, first of all, so many of us think of America as ours. And that sense of possession comes from our belief that each of us has a place in a great national narrative that we are only a part of and whose complete story none of us knows, because each of us is *aware* of only a part of it. Ishmael Reed once wrote of our country, "The world is here"; and he meant that we Americans are almost as diverse in our origins and our ideas as the globe as a whole.[2] But we are all linked, despite that magnificent diversity, through our identification with one thing, America, our country, however differently we imagine it. And that identification comes, as much as anything else, from stories.

Ever since the modern nation-state was conceived in the societies of the North Atlantic, in the 18th-century conversations that made the modern world—in the age of Enlightenment, the age of Revolutions—people *in* that world have been tempted by the fantasy that each person in each nation was already in some deep way identical with every other. They have wanted to say that a nation shared something profoundly rooted in common ancestry or language or culture. Hegel taught us philosophers to call that something a Geist, a Spirit, a Consciousness. And what Hegel thought, in effect, was that you couldn't really make a nation unless you already had something deep and important in common. You could only *be* one if you already *were* one. Nothing could make you "e pluribus unum," out of many one.

The national spirit was expressed in a national culture: the language and literature of the folk, its poetry and song, its tales and myths, its music and art, whether produced by the common people or by the nation's creative geniuses. When the brothers Grimm set out to collect the German fairy tales now known around the globe, they were aiming to capture the spirit of the German people, its *Geist*. A people's folklore—the wisdom of the folk—defined the common spiritual or intellectual life of a nation. And a nation, with its shared spiritual life, was the natural unit of government. Later, but only gradually, through the end of the 19th century and into the 20th, with the rise of modern science, an idea also took hold that a nation was ideally of a single race, with a shared biology grounded in a shared ancestry, a genetic inheritance—ideas that produced the racial nationalism that we see here and around the world today.

If you think something like this, whether focused on spirit or on race, you'll want a new country to make a new people if it doesn't have one in place. Already, in 1782, John Hector St. John de Crèvecoeur wrote in his *Letters from an American Farmer* of Americans as "individuals of all nations . . . melted into a new race of men." Crèvecoeur described his new American as "an European or the descendant of an European," thus excluding people who couldn't be assimilated as white. That was an error, our founding fatal error, we now know. But he was wrong, in any case, in a deeper way, in his assumption that you couldn't have a nation without a people, a folk with a single shared spirit, an American race.

The most obvious evidence that this is wrong is the simple fact that almost every modern state began with a hodge-podge of people of diverse religions and languages and customs and ancestry and came together not by making them all the same but through a state-building project that united them while accepting they could continue to be unlike one another in lots of important ways. As late as 1893, roughly a quarter of the 30 million citizens of metropolitan France had not mastered French.[3] Similarly, as Linda Colley has argued, in the early 19th century "Britishness was superimposed over an array of internal differences in response to contact with the Other, and above all in response to conflict with the Other."[4] Since this was Britain, the Other here was mostly metropolitan France.

If "we, the people," are going to be bound together, then it's going to be the way every other nation has been: by language, law, and literature, both oral and written, by a national discourse intentionally shaped, as well as by sharing experiences. And when we speak of sharing experiences—9/11, the Kennedy assassination, the moon landing—it won't be the events themselves that we share; it'll be the stories about them that circulate among us. Americans who were alive when these things happened can talk to one another about where they were when they learned about them; they can discuss how they felt about the events and about their country at those moments; they can have conversations anchored in their different memories of the same event. And there are stories, too, to share about the long ago past of our country: the Civil War, Juneteenth, the Trail of Tears. And, once more, we can share our different—even conflicting—feelings about them because we recognize them as part of our common past.

Narratives like these have always been central to political identity: the Exodus narrative for the Israelites; Homer's tales for the Greek city-states; the *Aeneid* for a cultivated Roman elite; the story of Shaka for the Zulu nation. But there is something new in the modern world, which is that now the national stories are democratic; they connect fellow citizens to one another not in a shared subordination to gods and kings, but as participants in a common story. Modern political communities are integrated through tales in which the community itself—we, the people—is an actor; and what binds each of us to the community, and thus to each other, is our participation, through our national identity, in that action.

In these United States, people of all races, religions, and regions can and do identify with the nation in this way. But that doesn't guarantee, alas, that we are always good at identifying with each other. Because, though we Americans, *as* Americans, imagine an America that we share, we do not always share the way we imagine it.

Still, as long as each of us cares about this America, we can be connected to it by the stories about it that matter to each of us, just as our fellow citizens will care for America because of the stories that matter to each of them. Evidently, we need a shared legal framework as well—and, for the purposes of government, citizens need to have a language or two in common. Ideally, as well, the history that's taught, the stories we tell, will explain how *these* people were gathered in *this* state. Of course, the stories need to be organized around what really happened—the *res gestae*, as the philosophers of history put it. That is the only way we can have a sense of a past we have in common. But history, founded in truth, is also always composed, shaped by selection and hypothesis, and granted the different pictures of the world and the differing values of our multifarious demographic groups, that composition, selection, and hypothesis are bound to be contested. Even if we don't agree about the significance of a past fact—Thomas Jefferson's fathering of children with an enslaved woman, George Washington's address to the Hebrew congregation in Newport, Harriet Tubman's work on the Underground Railroad—we can use it to anchor our conversations with one another about our country's future, grounded as we must be in a sense of the past.

We have to accept, however, that different stories shape different senses of national identity. And political scientists such as Leonie Huddy and Alessandro del Ponte have shown that different senses of national identity can have very different political effects.[5] They have urged us to distinguish feeling warmly about the nation, for instance, from celebrating national achievements—and both from conceiving of one's nation as superior to others. National identity as *closeness*, or as *pride*, or as *chauvinism*, in their terms: each has its distinct political effects.

The diversity of national identity's effects is very evident in the current populist insurgencies around the world. As Jan-Werner Müller has argued, one key element in populism is distance from or hostility toward those within the nation who oppose the aims of "the people"—sometimes figured, in the United States, as a contrast between "real Americans," and "coastal elites."[6] Chauvinistic nationalism offers no guarantee of closeness to fellow citizens. Indeed (as Gina Gustavsson once put it), it may diminish your "willingness to share resources in general, even if the people in question are one's fellow countrymen."[7]

Similarly, pride in the nation's cultural achievements is consistent with contempt for, and distance from, many of one's fellow citizens. There have always been fans of American literature, for example, who do not care much for most Americans. After all, they say, some of them contributed nothing to the things we are proud of. But, on the other hand, celebrating the national culture doesn't preclude respect for the achievements of other nations and so does not *require* chauvinism. In fact, pride in the nation can lead to support for various cosmopolitan ideas, if the national identity is seen as connected with them—as when, for example, a Norwegian endorses participation in UN peacekeeping precisely because she takes pride in her nation's historical commitment to international peacekeeping.

The basic sense of closeness to the nation, which is an element of all three forms of national identification, could lead to support for generous immigrations laws in exactly the same way: because a tradition of accepting the "huddled masses" of the wider world, "the homeless" and the "tempest-tossed," is widely understood to be an element of our national story, American pride goes along with support for these liberal policies. But—to insist on the obvious—that works only for those of us who hold dear the stories of the peopling of our America that are filled with that generous spirit.

Still, in the end, as Ernest Renan, the great French conservative historian and patriot, argued, what really matters in making a nation, beyond our stories, is what he called "the clearly expressed desire to continue a common life."[8] What makes "us" a people, ultimately, is our everyday commitment to governing a common life *together*. The theory of democracy is that we the people—all of us—are charged as a collectivity with directing the ship of state. Democracy isn't about majorities winning and minorities losing. It's supposed to be a system in which each of us takes responsibility for contributing to our common welfare.

The challenge this poses for a liberal democracy like ours is formidable. Liberal states require a civic creed that is both potent and lean—

potent enough to give significance to citizenship, rendering us willing to make sacrifices for one another, but *lean* enough to be shared by those with different religions and ethnicities. Hegel's Romantic state could pride itself on being the expression of one folk and its primordial consciousness; our modern liberal state has to get by with a good deal less mystical mumbo-jumbo. The Romantic state rallies its citizens with a stirring cry: "One nation! One people! One destiny!" The liberal state's true anthem is: "We can work it out."

And often enough, we can. Many of us have long known here what people around the world have increasingly understood: we can stick together without a common religion or delusions of common ancestry. The truth of every modern nation is that political unity is never underwritten by some preexisting national commonality. What binds citizens together is a commitment, renewed daily, to sharing the fate of a modern state, united by its institutions, procedures, and precepts. Right now, America is being torn apart by stories that divide us, by partisan identities that make the democratic compact with its commitment to caring for every citizen unworkable. The story of America as a white nation, a Christian nation, contends with a vision of multiracial democracy. And these contesting stories are grounded in contests about what really went on as the Constitution came together and about what the Civil War and the amendments that followed it really mean. The attitudes of citizens to our noncitizen neighbors are shaped by contending stories about the ways in which the various peoples who came here joined the first nations of this continent. We debate the question of the scale and the pace of immigration and naturalization by exploring those many stories.

Today, I believe, we need to find the stories that will permit us to draw on our nonpartisan identities, as Americans, as citizens of particular communities, as members of churches and synagogues and mosques, to combat the tribalism that is undermining our democracy.

We need other things as well, naturally—some sense, for example, that our constitutional arrangements are worth respecting and holding on to even when they stand in the way of what one or the other of us wants to do. We need a willingness to see politics as more than a zero-sum game in which every policy is a win for some and a loss for others. But those things are more likely in people who have a sense that their country's story has moments of uplift. Renan argued that the celebration of our ancestors is justified because they made us who we are. And, he insisted, "An heroic past, great men, glory (I mean real glory), these are the social capital on which a national idea is founded."[9] We can no longer think that our past glory is the work only of great men. But we do need a pantheon of people we can admire, people enough of us can agree have changed our country for the better: black and white and Asian, First Peoples and the descendants of later arrivals, women and men and people who are neither, LGBTQ people, Americans of all faiths and none. A history curriculum that allows all our children to learn such stories can ground our conversations about how we want to live together; it will serve that purpose best if all Americans can, in some way, see themselves in it. And we need more than the stories of individuals: we need to know about *projects* such as the space race or the growth of the franchise or the creation of the modern city; understand *institutions* such as Hollywood and NASCAR and the National Park System; be familiar with *landscapes* "from the redwood forests to the Gulf Stream waters."

But Renan's focus on celebration, on glory, by itself, will not work to build a nation with the resilience to face the challenge of sustaining our country. We must face, too, the Middle Passage that brought the first black Americans to this continent in chains; the denial of the suffrage as the Republic began not just to blacks and women and Indigenous peoples, but to some poor white men; lynching and Chinese Exclusion; race riots and the internment of loyal Japanese Americans; the persecution of lesbians and gay men in the 1950s. In acknowledging these things, we can tell a story of our country as moving beyond them, rejecting the forms of bigotry, inequality, and second-class citizenship that produced them.

We need many stories, in short, not one vast encompassing narrative, and we do not all need to know and care about the same tales; we can coalesce if we can bring to our encounters with one another as fellows in the American constitutional experiment, shared narratives of

American people, American projects, American institutions, and American landscapes, alongside American art and American fiction, to focus our conversations. Whatever stories we tell of the peopling of this country of ours, we must hope that when these tales enter our minds and hearts, they will bring us together so we can build a nation that works not just for all of those who live here but also for all of humankind. That idea, after all, begins in an American story older than the republic, when John Winthrop, quoting the Book of Matthew, called the Massachusetts Bay Colony, a "citty upon a hill," with "the eies of all people . . . upon us.[10]

Notes

1. Benedict Anderson *Imagined Communities: Reflections on the Origins and Spread of Nationalism*, rev. ed. (London: Verso, 1991), 6–7.
2. Ishmael Reed "America: The Multinational Society," in *Writin' Is Fightin'* (New York: Atheneum, 1988), 56.
3. See Eugen Weber, "Who Sang the Marseillaise," in *My France. Politics, Culture, Myth* (Cambridge, MA: Belknap Press, 1991), 92–102.
4. Linda Colley, *Britons: Forging the Nation, 1707–1837* (London: Yale University Press, 1992), 6.
5. Leonie Huddy and Alessandro Del Ponte, *The Rise of Populism in the USA: Nationalism, Race, and American Party Politics* (New York: Routledge, 2021).
6. Jan-Werner Müller, *What Is Populism?* (Philadelphia: University of Pennsylvania Press, 2016).
7. As cited in Kwame Anthony Appiah, "An Unscientific Postscript," in *Liberal Nationalism and Its Critics: Normative and Empirical Questions*, ed. David Miller and Gina Gustavson (Oxford: Oxford University Press, 2020), 273.
8. "L'existence d'une nation est (pardonnez-moi cette métaphore) un plébiscite de tous les jours, . . ." Ernest Renan, *Qu'est-ce qu'une nation?* 2nd ed. (Paris: Calmann-Lévy, 1882), 8.
9. "Le culte des ancêtres est de tous le plus légitime; les ancêtres nous ont faits ce que nous sommes. Un passé héroïque, des grands hommes, de la gloire (j'entends de la véritable), voilà le capital social sur lequel on assied une idée nationale" (Renan, *Qu'est-ce qu'une nation?*, 7).
10. John Winthrop "A Modell of Christian Charity" (1630), *Collections of the Massachusetts Historical Society*, 3rd series (Boston: Massachusetts Historical Society, 1838), 7:31–48, https://history.hanover.edu/texts/winthmod.html.

CHAPTER 3

The Vague, Enduring Centrality of Whiteness in America

Justin Gest

In 1922 and 1923, the US Supreme Court was asked to adjudicate the eligibility of two foreign-born men for American citizenship.[1] In *Takao Ozawa v. United States*, the justices unanimously ruled that a Japanese-born man who spoke fluent English and had lived in the United States for 20 years was ineligible for naturalization because he did not qualify—and could not be construed—as a "free white person" as required under the Naturalization Act of 1906. The following year, in *United States v. Bhagat Singh Thind*, the Court held that an Indian Sikh man who identified himself as a "high caste aryan, of full Indian blood" was also racially ineligible because he did not meet the "common sense" definition of a "white person."

In the *Ozawa* decision, the Court wrote, "In all of the naturalization acts from 1790 to 1906 the privilege of naturalization was confined to white persons." The exclusion of Japanese persons and others from this understanding of whiteness had "become so well established by judicial and executive concurrence and legislative acquiescence that we should not at this late day feel at liberty to disturb it." In the *Thind* decision, the Court stated that "the term 'Aryan' has to do with linguistic, and not at all with physical, characteristics." As late as the twentieth century, the boundaries of white identity were thus formally established as the boundaries of American identity for foreigners.

In a country that was granted colonial self-governance by the British on account of its white majority, one may dismiss the Court's decision as merely affirming a centuries-old truth. However, the "white" Irish Catholics, Italians, Greeks, and Jews who were naturalized in 1906 bore little resemblance to the English Protestants who predominated in 1790. These immigrants were on the white side of America's racial divide. Was it so unthinkable that a Christian Japanese man with perfect English or an Aryan Sikh of high stature might be next? Far more remarkable and consequential for contemporary understandings of "the American people," neither Ozawa nor Thind challenged the constitutionality of the Naturalization Act's racial restrictions; they sought to be legally recognized as "white," not to end the legal superiority extended to white people.

Governments traditionally construct "the people" of their country—no matter how new the country is—as primordial in origin and long enduring, even if in different, unrecognizable forms. Institutions may change, but the people and their culture are thought to remain steadfast. National anthems solemnly croon of glory from centuries-old battlefields; national flowers symbolize the nation's indigeneity; national museums assemble artifacts to thread together narratives about the origin, tragedy, and persistence of an indomitable people.

These static national images, even those with the most historically accurate origins, are often exaggerated and cleansed of complications. The boundaries between nations of people have always been blurry. All peoples are the product of cross-national influences to some degree. And primordial stories often justify nefarious, false hierarchies of moral worth—colonialism, slavery, eugenics, and genocide. Such details are inconvenient for the assembly of a purified, virtuous national myth.

But fresh off settling the Western frontier and granting statehood to Oklahoma, Arizona, and New Mexico, the United States of 1906 or even 1922 was a nation still in progress. Americans held no illusions of primordial origins. They had always been (and in many ways remain) a patchwork of restless opportunists and pioneering prospectors, refugees and emancipated slaves once displaced by empire. American claims to the perimeter of the continent were a matter of entitlement and conquest, not indigeneity. And just as it was for colonial self-governance, the basis for this entitlement was whiteness.

A century later, the formal, legal superiority of white people has been removed from law; but social scientists and lawyers have demonstrated the enduring institutional advantages experienced by white people, and political movements are seeking greater justice in law enforcement, economic inequities, and electoral representation. As the narrative of the nation is questioned, the boundaries of whiteness—and implicitly the boundaries of America—continue to be fiercely debated. Disputes over the admission of immigrants or asylum seekers and the status of undocumented immigrants are informed by these newcomers' predominantly nonwhite, non-Protestant backgrounds and contextualized by the looming prospect of a "majority minority" society—one in which the country's non-Hispanic white people no longer hold a majority.

This future demographic milestone only makes tangible what observers of democracy have long known: precisely because the government is subject to the will of its people, the country is subject to its demographic composition. When the composition of "the people" changes, the governance and character of the country may change too. This volatility runs counter to the static national images that countries work hard to cultivate, but it has also mobilized some Americans to rethink who they are.

Even as its boundaries have shifted, "whiteness" has persistently characterized the American self-understanding. Once members of a Northern European and predominantly Protestant plantation society, Americans have come to recognize the membership of people from German, Italian, Irish, Slavic, and Middle Eastern backgrounds along with a variety of religious faiths in a high-technology democracy. But the expansion of America has taken place only with an expanded definition of whiteness. Whiteness *is* the national myth. As the United States mulls a future with a more diverse people, it will need to reconcile the nostalgia of those seeking to preserve their advantage and—as with Ozawa and Thind—reconcile some newcomers' enduring aspiration to be admitted into the country's evolving racial identity.

Majority Minority America

For a nation so conscious of racial differences, the definition of "whiteness" has been fluctuating since the inception of the United States. Early on, most citizens perceived whiteness to be limited to people of Anglo-Saxon backgrounds, but the construction of whiteness evolved to suit the needs of America's westward expansion. One of the earliest examples of this evolution of convenience took place in Texas, where President James Polk initially supported the annexation of Mexico because he believed that Mexicans' Spanish blood qualified them as "white."[2] However, as the Mexican-American War brought US soldiers south of Texas and into contact with more Mexican people, officials decided that the country was not white enough to merit annexation beyond the Rio Grande.[3]

Such contact with other ethnic groups was always what made Anglo-Saxons confront the vagaries of the social construction upon which American social relations and plantation capitalism were built. New states on the American frontier offered citizenship and land rights to the French in Louisiana, the Spanish in Florida and Mississippi, Germans in Wisconsin and Minnesota, and the Spanish of New Mexico for their whiteness alone rather than any allegiance to the nascent United States.[4] When the Oregon Territory disbursed land donations to citizens, Asian and Hawaiian immigrants were not eligible, but the mixed children of white men and Native American women were.[5] When the California Supreme Court blocked Chinese immigrants from giving evidence in court in the 1850s, it used legislative language that previously made the same distinction for Indians, concluding that both groups were of the same "Mongolian type."[6]

Questions of whiteness persisted as America diversified over the mid- and late-19th century. Millions of Irish Catholic families arrived in New York and all over the East Coast after 1845. In subsequent decades, the United States admitted millions of Germans, Italians,

Jews, and Eastern European Slavs—often referred to as "white ethnic" individuals—along with Chinese and Japanese people, all with different languages, religions, and appearances. Nearly four decades after the British Empire abolished slavery and the slave trade across its dominions, the Fifteenth Amendment declared in 1870 that no man shall be denied the right to vote on account of race, color, or previous condition of servitude—enfranchising millions of African American men who just a decade before were thought undeserving of a say in public affairs. This diversification of the American citizenry took place as global migration was also transforming the colonial and settler populations of the Caribbean, East Africa, and Oceania.

As people experienced more cross-cultural contact, eugenicist theories of racial hierarchy were popularized to justify why certain groups were being subordinated: put simply, nonwhite people were thought to be genetically incapable of self-governance. Inside the United States as elsewhere, it became clear that nativist movements such as the Know Nothings and the Ku Klux Klan did little to halt demographic change. There was a gradual realization that the Protestant, Northern European orientation of "whiteness" was unlikely to sustain a dominant majority. Already, the Democratic Party of New York City's Tammany Hall was winning elections by leveraging immigrant bloc voting.

National Life and Character

During the late 19th century, the numerical advantage and normative supremacy of the white race—as it was then constructed—was beginning to be questioned. In 1893, Australian academic Charles Pearson published *National Life and Character*, a book that prophesized decolonization and the ascendance of the "black and yellow" races. He cited the power of differential fertility rates and the way that state socialism was making white populations "stationary." He closed his work on race with an ominous prediction:

> We shall wake to find ourselves elbowed and hustled, and perhaps even thrust aside by peoples whom we looked down upon as servile, and

thought of as bound always to minister to our needs. The solitary consolation will be, that the changes have been inevitable. It has been our work to organise and create, to carry peace and law and order over the world, that others may enter in and enjoy.[7]

Soon to win the White House, Theodore Roosevelt found the prospect of a majority-minority milestone—that is, the outnumbering of white Protestants by a mix of different foreign-origin groups—alarming. In 1894 writings, Roosevelt blamed rapacious "trans-oceanic aristocracies" such as Britain and Spain for the way the trade of slaves and indentured servants altered the fragile demographics of their colonies in a manner "fatal to the white race." In contrast, he took solace from the fact that the United States and other new democratic settler states, "with the clear instinct of race selfishness, saw the race foe, and kept out the dangerous alien" by oppressing those in their midst.[8]

In an 1894 letter to Pearson, Roosevelt reassured him:

What occurs in our own Southern States at the least sign of a race war between the blacks and the whites seems to me to foreshadow what would occur on a much bigger scale if any black or yellow people should really menace the whites. An insurrectionary movement of blacks in any one of our Southern States is always abortive, and rarely takes place at all; but any manifestation of it is apt to be accompanied by some atrocity [in] the same way an Indian outbreak on the frontier would to this day mean something approaching to a war of extermination.[9]

With much of the "competition between the races reducing itself to the warfare of the cradle," Roosevelt wrote in 1897, "no race has any chance to win a great place unless it consists of good breeders as well as of good fighters."[10] Wary of the persistent proliferation and civilizational development of the darker races, Roosevelt concluded that there was a need to consolidate a broader white identity and guard the temperate zones of the earth as a "heritage for the white people."

Though Roosevelt recognized the power of restrictive immigration regulations,[11] the only way to sustain this heritage—and the Republican Party for that matter—against what was being called "race suicide"[12] would be to incrementally admit other races into the fellowship of whiteness—to assimilate them into the American creed. In his writings, Roosevelt believed that "the transmission of acquired characters" was not only possible but a strong feature "in every civilized State."[13]

This effort thereafter to redraw the color line took decades to develop in the United States but ultimately led to contemporary American conceptions of whiteness. It was a way to broaden the definition of white people enough to maintain power over what Roosevelt called the "black and yellow people" without having to incorporate the least "assimilable" among them. Even though late 19th-century white ethnic out-groups were subjected to exclusion and discrimination in northern US cities, the "white" majority began to relax these prejudices when large numbers of African Americans arrived as part of the Great Migration in the early 20th century. Intermarriage among white ethnic individuals and naturalizations among white ethnics quickly accelerated. For every standard deviation increase in the Black population of a given city, intermarriage rates among white ethnic individuals increased by 0.54 percentage points, and naturalization rates increased by 1.5 percentage points.[14] And so whiteness broadened into a new, 20th-century understanding.

If 19th-century understandings of whiteness were applied to the present moment in the United States, nonwhite minorities would comprise approximately 61% of the national population today. According to 2018 estimates by the US Census Bureau, Latinos comprised about 18% of the American population, with African Americans making up 12%, and Asians and Pacific Islanders 5%. People with predominantly Irish heritage made up 11%, people of Slavic descent 6%, Italians and Greeks 6%, and Jews, Arabs, and other Middle Easterners were about 3%. Viewed through 19th-century spectacles, the United States reached its majority minority milestone decades ago.

The modern concept of the United States as a "nation of immigrants" papers over this historical reality. It promotes America's earlier acceptance of immigrants as if it were deliberate and not conditional on a vague definition of whiteness—as if it were not at least somewhat the product of a social and political calculation to sustain white hegemony. And while the depiction of the United States as a "nation of immigrants" has since resonated with many Americans and inspired support for multiculturalist policies and antiracist movements, its pluralist message is still not pervasive enough to resolve today's fraught politics of demographic change.

Culture Wars

The broadening of whiteness that occurred during Roosevelt's era endured for many decades until the influx of new immigrants from Latin America and Asia raised the prospects of a new majority-minority milestone. Between 1980 and 2015, the number of people of Hispanic origin increased in every American state and 95% of all counties, and in three states—California, New Mexico, and Texas—the population reached majority-minority status. A fourth state, Hawai'i, has been majority minority since its annexation.[15] In the same time period, the Asian American population increased in 49 states, the African American population increased in 46 states, and there has been an across-the-board decline in the share of the country's white population.

Researchers have found that white Americans alerted to these demographic trends report greater sympathy for other white people and significantly more anger toward and fear of ethnic minorities;[16] they are less inclined toward redistributive generosity and significantly more likely to define their identity as "white" rather than as "American";[17] they express a greater relative preference to be in settings and interactions with other white people than racial minorities;[18] and they favor more exclusionary policies.[19]

While a great deal of this can be attributed to a sense of cultural threat,[20] American debates about immigration have also changed. The country is no longer seeking to settle the frontier and has implemented a thick set of legal restrictions on international migration that previously were not in effect. This has raised public expectations of control over borders but also created sharp public distinctions between legal and desirable immigrants and undocumented immigrants and others deemed undesirable. Beyond racial differences, this has hindered what might have otherwise been a proclivity to identify in today's immigrants a connection with native-born white Americans and their ancestors.

The sharp growth in the number of foreign-born people coincided independently with the late-20th-century political realignment stimulated by the civil rights movement, the decline of the manufacturing era, and the shift to a more service-oriented, high-technology global market. This economic shift weakened the wealth, status, and political clout of millions of native-born white people and thousands of labor unions—which long powered center-left and socialist parties across the transatlantic space—precisely when immigrant-origin minorities began to grow and African Americans gained new rights. In the 1990s, Democrats won a series of elections due in large part to their incremental embrace of neoliberal economics. These "third way" politics brought the center-left into greater economic agreement with their center-right counterparts, leaving future elections to be contested more on social and cultural grounds.

Debates raged over whether gay people should be permitted to serve in the military or marry, whether civilians have a right to own and carry semiautomatic weapons, and the place of prayer and religion in schools. And as the Democratic Party became increasingly associated with racial and religious minorities, Republicans also shifted debates to corner their counterparts into unpopular defenses of undocumented immigrants, refugees, asylum seekers, and Muslims, who were vilified in the aftermath of the September 11, 2001, terrorist attacks. America's polarization over immigration policy took place in this political context, amidst white people's steady loss of status.

This national discussion—oriented to mobilize Republican voters to protect traditional American values or mobilize Democratic voters to rethink them—has tested the extent of individual rights, tolerance, and empathy. Supporting further immigration or minority rights has become associated with other cultural viewpoints about the prevalence of structural racism, the legality of recreational drug use, or what constitutes national security. Each new value-driven debate has suggested another dimension of American "peoplehood" that has suddenly become subject to demographic change and the shifts in cultural beliefs that accompany it.

These debates and others have moved public discussion to matters of moral conviction and lifestyle. Rather than ideological disagreements about how to pursue *shared* values, these culture wars imply the presence of vastly different value systems that attenuate the American social fabric. State and local governments have passed laws that create different legal environments where different parts of America endorse different ways of life. Partisans moralize about the other sides' constituents until it has become conventional to perceive political counterparts to be fundamentally evil or depraved—somehow part of a different "people." As each new election poses a greater existential threat, Democrats and Republicans have stepped up efforts to delegitimize electoral victories through impeachments, claims of election fraud and tampering, and conspiracy theories.

The result is an impasse—a political stalemate and legislative paralysis amidst the racialization of American politics and the politicization of American culture. Today, most Republican voters are white, vast majorities of nonwhite racial and religious minorities support Democrats, and American elections pivot on highly symbolic identity politics. Rather than broaden their outreach to rural or white working-class constituents, the Left waits for demographic change to reach its righteous destiny. And rather than evolve with the demography of the country, the Right trades in demonstrably false narratives and contorts democratic institutions to sustain power. American politics increasingly hinge on the sustainability of the already once-broadened post-1906 concept of "white" peoplehood.

Demography as Destiny

Much as their predecessors in New York City once did, today's Democratic Party leaders wish to leverage their disproportionate support from ethnic minorities into electoral majorities. When President Barack Obama entered the White House in 2009 on the back of an electoral coalition of white urban liberals and diverse people of color, a number of Democratic consultants triumphantly pointed to projections that reliably Republican, white voters comprise a dwindling share of the American electorate. "Demography is destiny," they said at the time.

The challenge for Democrats is that many Americans remain invested in "white" peoplehood, and—even while their population share diminishes—white people still make up 70% of voters and hold outsize electoral weight because of often-racialized gerrymandering and sparsely populated, rural states' equal representation in the US Senate. Generations of people with Irish, Italian, and Slavic ancestries have relied on the "public and psychological wages" of whiteness to ensure the stability of their social standing or transition into the middle class.[21] They have long depended on the "white" racial label to secure political rights, keep treasured jobs, and remain at least one step ahead of their black coworkers on the socioeconomic ladder.[22] Poor or lower-middle-class white Americans are thought to glean "vital psychic income" from identifying with those of an upper class who happen to share similar "external characteristics."[23]

Another challenge is that demography itself is subject to the persistent vagaries of whiteness and political leaders' capacity to wield identity to build electoral coalitions. In advance of the 2000 presidential election, then–Texas Governor George W. Bush's chief strategist, Karl Rove, famously calculated that, given American (and Texan) demographics, the path to future Republican majorities was to better incorporate Latino leaders and voters into the party's constituency. With their devout religiosity, conservative social values, and interest in free markets, Latinos—he calculated—were predisposed to Republican politics if it weren't for the party's saber-rattling over immigration. Bush pitched himself as a "compassionate conservative" who cultivated Latino votes, and he would win 44% of them against then–Vice President Al Gore. Rove and the Republican Party would ultimately compromise this long-term strategy for the short-term voter mobilization provided by nativist politics in the post-9/11 era—alienating many Latinos, but also many Muslim and Asian voters, too. However, it is not hard to imagine the Republican Party, after future losses, returning to a Rove-inspired approach that seeks to embrace Latinos or to imagine a Latino Republican who espouses discriminatory views about African Americans and Muslims, exploiting prejudice among people of color. Even without these tactics, Donald Trump attracted a larger share of Latino voters in 2020 than any Republican presidential nominee since 2004.

Sociologist Richard Alba has long discounted the accuracy of majority-minority demographic projections in the United States. He expects that many Latinos and mixed-race Americans will ultimately self-identify as "white" and postpone the next majority-minority milestone. Indeed, 60% of Latinos already do. If these "white Hispanics" are counted as "white," white people are projected to remain a near-two-thirds majority in 2060.[24] A large number of such white Hispanics from South Florida and Texas's Rio Grande Valley supported Donald Trump in the 2020 election, tipping their respective states Republican despite Trump's nativism and anti-Latino policies.[25]

To some Americans, the idea that Latinos and biracial people feel welcome to join the ranks of whiteness reveals the virtuous flexibility of white American identity and its evolution to include one-time outsiders. But this notion must be exposed for the instrumental social and political calculation that it is. Consolidating the American identity around the next most assimilable group of ethnic minorities only subordinates those deemed still too different. It flatters the newest entrants in order to sustain the previous "white" majority and whiteness itself as the gateway to status. The European-origin Latinos and mixed-race Americans who accept this invitation are like the Italian, Irish, and German Americans of 100 years before. In exchange for their marginal promotion, they acquiesce to the constructed racial hierarchy of the "people" that once subordinated them.

A Democratic Challenge?

All countries periodically argue about and update their definition of "the people" in the vigorous, sometimes divisive debates that characterize a robust public sphere. Each debate requires "the people" to build new political coalitions, adapt to new ideas, and accommodate demographic change. These national discussions always alienate certain subgroups, particularly those who may be excluded from ruling majorities but who remain in the political community. That underlying sense of inclusion is essential for a nation to survive these passing debates, so democracies need to offer their constituents a "thick" sense of collective meaning, a sense of civic status, and material well-being.[26]

Still, identifying "the people" necessarily entails exclusion. In what has been called the "boundary problem," the question of how "the people" can rule can be answered only after the boundaries identifying the "people" are determined.[27] The problem is that, precisely because the "people" are thought to precede the state and transcend its different governments, the "people" are identified according to undemocratic principles that are not necessarily reflective of the current population. Even the world's most democratic states are rooted in ethno-religious, antecedent understandings of "the people" and they routinely contest their peoplehood.

Because different interests vie for power by claiming that they represent the collective will, attempts to define "the people" never really end in democratic environments. The practices of democratic politics, political scientist David Bateman writes, "constantly reopen the question of 'who are the people,' creating a fundamental tension and perhaps intractable dilemma between the requisites of stable democratic regimes, the types of politics these are likely to produce, and the questions that need to be answered by those looking to build or consolidate a democracy."[28]

But we should resist blaming frayed political relations on liberal democracy itself. Liberal democracy does not inherently entail or produce ethnic conflict. Demographic change injects uncertainty into political communities because it challenges nations that have long explained their persistence with the creed of a specific ethno-religious people to endure when their demographic composition changes and includes people they once excluded. The construction of nations as static and indigenous, therefore, has served to unify disparate subgroups into a unified "people" but also ossified concepts of "the people" in ways detrimental those nations' inevitable evolution.

The problem is that American leaders have failed to evolve the concept of "the people" and nation sufficiently to establish a bipartisan national solidarity that cuts across ethnic and religious affinities. Their social and political institutions still do not sufficiently bring together the interests of changing ethnic and religious groups. They have struggled to break down ethnic and religious hierarchies that appropriate social, economic, and political advantages to certain identities, even when this is precisely what demographic change demands. Instead, many have sought to institutionalize the boundaries of a fleeting "white" majority as the boundaries of the enduring "people."

The American Crucible

Ultimately, it is the purported and accepted whiteness of the American "people" that is the problem. By continuing to conceive of the default citizen as "white," Americans reinforce the myth that this whiteness always included all who now identify with it—as if the Irish were never demonized, as if Italians and Jews were never excluded, as if Slavs were never underestimated, and as if biracial people were never subordinated. But if Americans are not white, what can they be?

Ironically, Theodore Roosevelt had a powerful answer. Despite his susceptibility to eugenics and racial theories of supremacy, his American nationalism was defiantly civic—rather than ethnic or racial—in nature. In his narrative histories published between 1885 and 1894, Roosevelt argued that as European immigrants were assimilated, their bloodlines were being absorbed into the American body, fusing Americans into a single, pure people forged in the "crucible" of the frontier. The acts of claiming and holding land, developing it into something greater than it had been, and defending it against the forces of nature all constituted rites of passage that transformed foreigners into Americans. In Roosevelt's understanding, Americans were born through no document; they were made by their encounters with the wilderness and their development of strength, individualism, and democratic community. For Roosevelt, the white ethnicities admitted into the United States were not entitled to their American identity; it was earned.

So is American identity not earned by Latinos, Asians, and African Americans today? Is the urban wilderness of New York, Chicago, and Los Angeles no such crucible? Does the grind of modern American capitalism require any less strength or individualism? Have those who risk their lives in the US military, care for American children, and nourish American families not done enough for the democratic community? In many ways, today's social tensions reveal how Roosevelt's competing civic and racial logics remain unreconciled.

The risk of today's politics is that political parties become proxies for color. Already, nonwhite ethnicity is a strong predictor of Democratic support, and five out of six Republicans are white. It is true that demographic projections spell difficulty for Republicans. It is also true that Democrats' failure to appeal to white, religious, Middle Americans is what stands between them and victory. But, when partisanship is racialized, that spells trouble for democracy. It allows our local identities to dictate what is in the national interest. It undercuts our capacity to empathize with our fellow countrymen. It encourages us to devote ourselves to our tribe rather than our country's institutions, making us less willing to lose and more willing to break rules to win.

The best way to reverse this course is not to broaden whiteness, but to broaden America—to identify one another as equal extensions of our country's heritage, to embrace the way we are composites of the communities that surround us, to see ourselves in the eyes of others, to recognize that their struggle—and their dream—is our own.[29]

Notes

1. In fact, between 1887 and 1923, US federal courts heard 25 cases contesting the legal status of immigrants seeking citizenship.
2. Paul Frymer, *Building an American Empire: The Era of Territorial and Political Expansion* (Princeton, NJ: Princeton University Press, 2019), 19–20.
3. Frymer, *Building an American Empire*, 194.

4. Frymer, *Building an American Empire*, 18.
5. Frymer, *Building an American Empire*, 139.
6. Marilyn Lake and Henry Reynolds, *Drawing the Global Colour Line: White Man's Countries and the International Challenge of Racial Equality* (Cambridge: Cambridge University Press, 2008), 19.
7. Charles Pearson, *National Life and Character; a Forecast* (England: Macmillan and Co., 1894), 90.
8. Theodore Roosevelt, "National Life and Character," *Sewanee Review* 2, no. 3 (1894): 353–76.
9. Theodore Roosevelt to Charles Pearson, May 11, 1894, Pearson Papers, Bodleian Library, MS English letters, folios pages 187–191, d. 190, as cited in Lake and Reynolds, *Drawing the Global Colour Line*.
10. Theodore Roosevelt, "National Life and Character," in *Theodore Roosevelt, American Ideals and Other Essays Social and Political* (New York: Putnam's Sons, 1897), 293–94.
11. Roosevelt, *American Ideals*, 277.
12. Edward Ross, "The Causes of Race Superiority," *Annals of the American Academy of Political and Social Science* 18 (July 1901): 88.
13. Roosevelt, *American Ideals*, 277.
14. Vasiliki Fouka, Soumyajit Mazumder, and Marco Tabellini, "From Immigrants to Americans: Race and Assimilation during the Great Migration," IDEAS Working Paper Series from RePEc, 2018, 23–24, https://economics.mit.edu/files/15100.
15. Barrett A. Lee, Michael Martin, Stephen Matthews, and Chad Farrell, "State-Level Changes in US Racial and Ethnic Diversity, 1980 to 2015: A Universal Trend?" *Demographic Research* 37 (December 2017): 1031.
16. H. Robert Outten, Michael T. Schmitt, Daniel A. Miller, and Amber L. Garcia, "Feeling Threatened about the Future: Whites' Emotional Reactions to Anticipated Ethnic Demographic Changes," *Personality and Social Psychology Bulletin* 38, no. 1 (2012): 14–25.
17. Maria Abascal, "Us and Them: Black-White Relations in the Wake of Hispanic Population Growth," *American Sociological Review* 80, no. 4 (2015): 789–813.
18. Maureen Craig and Jennifer Richeson, "More Diverse yet Less Tolerant? How the Increasingly Diverse Racial Landscape Affects White Americans' Racial Attitudes," *Personality and Social Psychology Bulletin* 40, no. 6 (2014): 750–61.
19. Ryan Enos, "The Causal Effect of Intergroup Contact on Exclusionary Attitudes," *Proceedings of the National Academy of Sciences of the United States of America* 111, no. 10 (2014): 3699–3704.
20. Jens Hainmüller and Daniel J. Hopkins, "Public Attitudes Toward Immigration," *Annual Review of Political Science* 17 (2014): 225–49.
21. David R. Roediger, *The Wages of Whiteness: Race and the Making of the American Working Class* (London: Verso, 1991), 145; Rudolph Vecoli, "Are Italian Americans Just White Folks?" *Italian Americana* 13, no. 2 (1995): 149–61; Karen Brodkin "How Did Jews Become White Folks?" in *Race*, eds. Steven Gregory and Roger Sanjek (New Brunswick, NJ: Rutgers University Press, 1994) 86–89.

22. Roediger, *The Wages of Whiteness*, 133–36; Noel Ignatiev, *How the Irish Became White* (New York: Routledge, 1995), 96.

23. Theodore P. Wright "The Identity and Changing Status of Former Elite Minorities: The Contrasting Cases of North Indian Muslims and American WASPS," in *Rethinking Ethnicity: Majority Groups and Dominant Minorities,* ed. Eric P. Kaufmann (New York: Routledge, 2004) 36.

24. Richard Alba, *The Great Demographic Illusion: Majority, Minority, and the Changing American Mainstream* (Princeton, NJ: Princeton University Press, 2020), 64–66.

25. Jack Herrera, "Trump Didn't Win the Latino Vote in Texas. He Won the Tejano Vote," *Político*, November 17, 2020, https://www.politico.com/news/magazine/2020/11/17/trump-latinos-south-texas-tejanos-437027; Molly Hennessy-Fiske, "'We've Only Started': How Latino Support for Trump Grew in Texas Borderlands," *Los Angeles Times*, November 12, 2020, https://www.latimes.com/world-nation/story/2020-11-12/latino-support-grew-for-trump-on-the-texas-border; Mitchell Ferman, "Donald Trump Made Inroads in South Texas This Year. These Voters Explain Why," *Texas Tribune*, November 13, 2020, https://www.texastribune.org/2020/11/13/south-texas-voters-donald-trump/; Lizette Alvarez, "Trump's Gains with Florida Latinos Were Hiding in Plain Sight," *Washington Post*, November 5, 2020, https://www.washingtonpost.com/opinions/2020/11/05/how-trump-won-florida-latinos-miami-dade-cuban-americans/.

26. David Bateman, "The Dilemmas of Democratic Peoplehood," Working Paper, 2018.

27. Frederick Whelan, "Democratic Theory and the Boundary Problem," in *Liberal Democracy*, eds. J. R. Pennock and J. W. Chapman (New York: New York University Press, 1983), 13–47.

28. Bateman, "The Dilemmas of Democratic Peoplehood."

29. This chapter is a compilation of material from Justin Gest, *Majority Minority* (New York: Oxford University Press, 2022).

CHAPTER 4

A White Settler Colony or a Revolutionary People's Colony?

Narratives of America's Origins as Guides to the Peopling of the United States

Rogers M. Smith

Policies governing the peopling of the United States, as in other nations, emerge from political contests among groups favoring partly overlapping, partly clashing views of national social, economic, and political interests and ideals. Those groups conceive and articulate their interests and ideals through narratives of identity that I along with others call "stories of peoplehood."[1] These narratives offer varied answers to the question Samuel P. Huntington posed in the title to his controversial last book, *Who Are We? The Challenges to American National Identity.*[2]

As Adam Dahl has noted, Huntington's own response has proven surprisingly influential among left-leaning scholars. Dahl contends that Huntington "led the charge in reclaiming American national identity as a settler democracy."[3] In 2004, Huntington did indeed argue that "in its origins America was not a nation of immigrants, it was a society, or societies, of settlers. . . . Its origins as an Anglo-Protestant settler society have, more than anything else, profoundly and lastingly shaped American culture, institutions, historical development, and identity."[4] Dahl believes that to Huntington, this view implied that "more restrictive immigration policies" were necessary "to protect the sanctity of the founding of settler democracy" from, especially, Hispanic as well as Islamic immigrants.[5] Huntington himself was in fact more circumspect, preferring to canvass alternative paths rather than to prescribe policies.[6] Nonetheless, his anxieties about immigration were clear enough for Huntington to be called "a prophet for the Trump era," a forerunner of the immigration views expressed in Donald Trump's vision of how to "Make America Great Again."[7]

Ronald Schmidt Sr. has recently juxtaposed this "white settler colony" view of America's original identity to two others, including one he correctly assigns to me.[8] Though Schmidt finds the "white settler" account of American identity the most convincing of the three, he, like most of its other recent academic proponents, draws implications from it for policies to "people" the United States that are sharply opposed to those most assign to Huntington. Schmidt is far more favorable to welcoming diverse immigrants, to honoring the claims of Indigenous communities, and to pursuing meaningful equality for American non-white minorities through multicultural recognition and redistributive measures. On those policy questions, I am largely in Schmidt's camp, in part because it is undeniable that the United States arose out of white Protestant settler colonies that built many systems of unjust domination with severe continuing consequences that Americans must address.

Nonetheless, I believe that proponents of this "white settler colony" view on both the Left and the Right sometimes fail to grasp fully the empirical character of past and present conflicts over how to people America, because they underrate the significance of the fact that before those Anglo-Protestant settler colonies became the United States, they first became revolutionary colonies. Failure to recognize this reality can foster both misguided tactical advice for achieving a more widely beneficial politics of peopling America and deficient normative conceptions of what America should be. The burden of this chapter is to sketch why we should therefore see the United States as at its origins a "revolutionary settler colony" and to lay out the main implications of this more complex conception for understanding the historical battles and the normative aspirations that have shaped and should shape the peopling of America.[9]

The "American Creed" View

Before turning to that task, however, it is important to note a view of American identity that Huntington's 2004 book explicitly rejected, though it is one he had prominently defended in his earlier writings, especially *American Politics: The Promise of Disharmony*.[10] Schmidt begins his analysis with essentially this conception of American identity—one that is, as he argues, "dominant . . . in American public discourse."[11] Though Schmidt and I both find this view of American identity deeply misleading, it is nonetheless highly significant for understanding contests over public policies shaping the peopling of the United States, because it has been and remains for many the definitive statement of American normative ideals.

As Schmidt contends, this conception sees American identity as defined by America's "core public values."[12] It portrays those values as centered on a universalistic understanding of the principles of the Declaration of Independence, one holding that all human beings are morally equal and entitled to basic rights of life, liberty, and the pursuit of happiness, as well as to government by the consent of the governed. Huntington, following many others, termed these principles the "American Creed." He saw its elements as evolving slightly over time, but as generally including "support for liberty, democracy, majority rule, minority rights, freedom of speech and religion, and, less clearly, equality."[13] In the early 1980s, Huntington did not present immigration as a major past or present barrier to maintaining a national identity centered on this American Creed. He argued that in American history, "a bargain was struck: ethnic groups retained so long as they wished their ethnic identity, but they converted to American political values, ideals, and symbols. Adherence to the latter was the test of how 'American' one was, and it was perfectly compatible with the maintenance of ethnic culture and traditions."[14]

Two decades later, Huntington presented that bargain as breaking down, and in ways that endangered America's identity and prospects more fundamentally than he once anticipated. Criticizing his own earlier claim that "the political ideas of the American Creed have been the basis of national identity," Huntington now said that "they have been only one of several components of that identity."[15] In addition to citing my "multiple traditions" view, Huntington endorsed Michael Lind's formulation that originally American national identity was "based upon an Anglo-American Protestant nationalism that was as much racial and religious as it was political."[16] Huntington thought that beginning in the late 20th century, the adherence of Hispanic immigrants, especially, to their distinct ethnocultural traditions might be creating a "bifurcated America with two languages and two cultures," which was "fundamentally different from the America with one language and one core Anglo-Protestant culture that has existed for over three centuries."[17] As Dahl and many others have observed, Huntington did not sound happy about that difference.

Though my own preferred account of American identity also prominently features the Declaration of Independence, it stresses that there have been multiple understandings of it, and that Declaration of Independence views have been, as Huntington came to acknowledge, only some of the understandings of America that have competed historically to answer the question of "who we are."[18] Like Schmidt, I have long argued that the claim that the essence of American identity has been embrace of universalistic and egalitarian principles of rights is far too dismissive of contradictory historical realities and consequently is likely to foster misunderstandings of America's past and present, as well as excessive political complacency about continuing injustices.[19] I will not repeat those critiques here. Rather, I wish to acknowledge that Huntington's 1981 "American Creed" view, while not the "true" conception of American identity, is still a view that has been and is politically potent, though far from hegemonic, in American policy-making. Analysts should not seriously entertain it as a fundamentally accurate account, but we must always keep it in view as we try to characterize American identity more fully and assess the role that different conceptions have played and should play in American politics.

A White Protestant Patriarchal Settler Colony

Analyses of the United States as well as other nations through frames of "settler colonialism" have become ubiquitous in many disciplines, but I will confine the discussion here to some outstanding recent works in political science by Aziz Rana, Paul Frymer, and Adam Dahl.[20] Since Huntington, it is scholars like these, who see the main legacies of America's white Protestant patriarchal settler origins as things to overcome, not to preserve or revive, who have most developed "settler colonial" accounts. Their aims have been both to set the historical record straight and to chart paths toward a better future. As Dahl puts it, these writers seek "to sever constitutional thought and practice" in America from their white settler "colonial foundations" in order to advance "more inclusive and egalitarian" political projects, "decolonizing democracy" in America.[21] They pursue these shared goals in overlapping but distinct ways.

Over a decade ago, in *The Two Faces of American Freedom*, Aziz Rana sought to grasp "the lasting implications of our political origins" for "questions of settler identity," "ethnic assimilation," and "social inclusion," among other topics.[22] He contended that "American experience is best understood as a constitutional and political experiment in . . . *settler empire*," a project that intertwined "expansion, immigration, race and class" in ways that have often "undermined the very promise" of the "uniquely American ideal of freedom."[23] Rana saw the American revolutionary generation as embracing a republican conception of freedom involving "continuous popular mobilization and direct control by insiders" over major economic and political decisions, but also "Indian dispossession and the coercive use of dependent groups, most prominently slaves."[24] He recognized that "at key periods" thereafter, "reformers and social movements" sought to reconceive American freedom "without either subordination or empire." But in Rana's eyes, these efforts "atrophied" in the 20th century, placing "security at the center of political discourse" and entrenching "hierarchical forms of economic and political rule," so that empire "has become the master rather than the servant of freedom."[25]

Rana also noted that the United States was "the first example of a successful settler revolt against metropolitan rule" since European imperial expansion began in the 16th century. He stressed, however, that the "republican principles" the revolutionaries advanced to justify their cause "were not universally inclusive" and that the "basic engine" of the "republican freedom" of those included was "conquest."[26] He also maintained that the American revolutionary republicans knew that to sustain their project, they would need "new European immigrants" with easy access to full American citizenship, even as "Indians, blacks" and "Mexicans" in the United States were "denied these basic rights."[27]

Writing in 2010, Rana also stressed that American revolutionary republicanism nonetheless "gave birth to a liberating vision of collective possibility" that reformers later used to try to "create a new, universal, and nonimperial American polity," stripping "republican ideals of their oppressive roots" and making "free citizenship broadly accessible to all."[28] Unlike Huntington, Rana did not tie that vision to the Declaration of Independence, even though it invokes the consent of the government, perhaps because it does not explicitly mention, much less endorse, the republicanism that he emphasized. Rana's only reference to the declaration noted that it complained of the dangers of "Indian savages" and, less explicitly, slave insurrections.[29] He also discussed Abraham Lincoln, widely seen as championing the centrality of the declaration to American identity, only as an advocate of free labor economic ideology, and in that work he did not mention Frederick Douglass and his similar evocations of the declaration at all.[30]

Then Rana modified his views. He has argued more recently that in the early 20th century most Americans came to embrace the "American Creed" or "civic" conception of American identity that the Huntington of the 1980s endorsed.[31] In agreement with much recent scholarship, Rana has traced this shift to how, influenced by 19th-century abolitionists, Abraham Lincoln "recast the Declaration of Independence not as a long list of grievances against a distant monarch but as a promise embodied above all in the single proposition that 'all men are created equal.'"[32] However, Lincoln in Rana's view "hesitated to extend" this promise "beyond ending slavery." Frederick Douglass, in contrast, took this Declaration of Independence "creedal story to its logical conclusion."[33] Douglass in 1869 called for "the faithful application of the principle of perfect civil equality to the people of all races and of all creeds," in order to make America a "home ... not only for the negro, the mulatto and the Latin races," but for all who aspired to personal and national liberty.[34]

Though Rana has credited subsequent "creedal" or "redemptive reform" movements, built on the views of Lincoln and Douglass, with some real accomplishments, he nonetheless finds them empirically and normatively inadequate. He believes they efface rather than address or redress the nation's settler colonial origins—roots that still sustain myriad continuing inequalities, including the oppression of Indigenous peoples and denials of effective opportunities to many nonwhite Americans and immigrants.[35] For Rana, "creedal" views inevitably minimize the need for radical change through their presentations of American identity as always centered on universalistic egalitarian commitments that need only fuller realization. In contrast, Rana now appeals to a Black "revolutionary reform" political tradition that he sees as having some antecedents among more radical African Americans during the Civil War, but as especially elaborated in the ideologies of the Black Panthers and others in the 1960s and 1970s.[36]

Rana hopes that 21st-century radicals are reinvigorating this political tradition. He calls for an "anticolonial vision" that aims at "fundamental social transformation" of American racism, American power, and American political economy. In so doing, he highlights that today "it is nonwhite immigrants whose labor experience most closely mirrors that of African Americans under the old Jim Crow."[37] Consequently, the anticolonial vision Rana believes America needs must be an internationalist one that features immigrant concerns. Rana's earlier project of seeking to tear founding-era republican ideals from their oppressive roots thus appears to have given way to a call for Americans to "imagine other alternatives," and particularly to build on 20th-century African American radical traditions to enact "the structural economic and political changes that might in fact produce equal and effective freedom."[38] On this view, such freedom must not only extend to current nonwhite immigrants; it must also include receptivity to new ones, as well as concern for all those harmed by American power abroad.

Citing Rana's 2010 arguments, Paul Frymer has since shown how, from its inception, the United States sought to acquire dominion over more and more territory, but only when those territories would be peopled primarily by the sorts of white settlers who populated the original colonies.[39] However, Frymer also assigns political significance to "a small but influential and racially diverse population of radical egalitarian activists who believed in privileging the rights of all individuals and peoples" in American history. Figures such as Frederick Douglass, for example, helped to defeat schemes of African American colonization that would have heightened white demographic domination of the United States.[40]

Like Rana, Frymer notes that as the United States assumed its global leadership role after World War II, it "accentuated its role as a centerpiece of individual rights and opportunities," and he observes that it then welcomed "an unprecedented wave of immigrants" from "Mexico and Central America, as well as from Asia and Africa."[41] Frymer also maintains that nonetheless, "the idea and ideal of a nation of white settlers remains embedded in our historical understanding of the nation and in many of our modern cultural symbols and political manifestations," including the anti-immigration views of Ted Cruz and Donald Trump.[42] Frymer also notes briefly but accurately that this white settler ideal has also usually been a patriarchal view, hostile to the rights and interests of women.[43] Rather than urging any alternative vision, Frymer simply stresses that Americans have yet to resolve "how to continue to expand and endorse liberal ideals while maintaining a white settler nation," as the politics of immigration and civil rights today abundantly prove.[44]

Adam Dahl has since elaborated, even more forcefully than Rana and Frymer, how colonial dispossession of North America's Indigenous inhabitants has been and remains central to the formation and development of basic features of American democratic thought.[45] Dahl does not believe that mainstream liberal democratic thought can help to remedy this profound deficiency in American notions of peoplehood.

He argues that although a putatively democratic settler colony that has long exploited the labor of others might conceivably become more fully democratic by extending equal citizenship to all, in the case of Indigenous tribes dispossessed of their lands and their independence, such assimilative civic incorporation might well only extend the original imperial injury. Dahl contends, moreover, that American political thought not only envisioned but actively constructed the democratic people of the United States as demanding and deserving imperial expansion, so that individually and collectively, Americans would have the resources needed for egalitarian democratic citizenship among themselves.[46] As a result, the demos crafted from America's white settler origins cannot truly include or respect outsiders.

Dahl consequently interprets the American Revolution and subsequent decisions governing the peopling of America as instances in the construction of an ethnoculturally restrictive society seeking to expand its empire. He depicts the revolutionaries' cause as a quarrel between colonial settlers in North America and imperial authorities in London over whether the colonists and their communities should be fundamentally equal to other English subjects and units within the British Empire.[47] Dahl says little about the 1776 Declaration of Independence, except to note the ways it did and did not anticipate Vermont's declaration of independence from New York and Vermont's 1777 constitution, which asserted the constituent power of the people to create a new government.[48] He attends instead to the declaration of independence of the would-be State of Franklin, seeking to secede from North Carolina. He sees that declaration as more clearly expressing the core American revolutionary goal, asserting power to establish a separate, equal, and independent settler community.[49]

Dahl goes on to interpret 19th-century American leaders, including Lincoln and Walt Whitman, as settler-colonial thinkers.[50] He argues, for example, that Lincoln's free labor ideology was necessarily dependent on the government's acquisition of land for Americans to work "on their own," and he stresses, accurately, that Lincoln supported colonization for emancipated African Americans up through 1862—the point at which Dahl's discussion of Lincoln stops.[51] Unlike Rana and

Frymer, he does not accompany this analysis with consideration of how Lincoln, Douglass, and others portrayed Americans as engaged in a quest to realize the principles of the Declaration of Independence, since for Dahl, the revolution's principles aim at North American white settler independence and little more.

Dahl highlights instead the 19th-century Pequot thinker and activist William Apess, who aided the Mashpee tribe in a conflict with the Massachusetts state government by drawing up an "Indian Declaration of Independence."[52] The resolutions comprising this declaration assert that "all men are born free and equal, says the Constitution of the country" (probably referring to Article 1 of the Massachusetts Constitution, though Dahl reads this as a reference to the US Constitution, which does not contain that phrase).[53] The first resolution contends that therefore, the tribe has "the right . . . to rule ourselves."[54] Though these resolution's arguments appear to echo the natural rights opening of the 1776 Declaration of Independence, Dahl interprets them as, at most, paralleling what he sees as the American revolutionaries' key claim, that their communities were entitled to equal self-governing rights within the British Empire.[55] The denial of such self-governance to the Mashpees justified, in Dahl's reading of Apess, the "Indian Nullification" of their alleged conquest by Massachusetts and the United States.[56] He sees this nullification as crucial to how Apess "harnesses the authority of the Constitution and the Declaration" ultimately to clear space for an entirely distinct narrative of the injustice of American imperialism toward the continent's Indigenous peoples.[57]

Dahl rejects the contentions of other scholars that in so arguing, Apess used "liberal legal discourse" against the state. Citing Foucault, Dahl contends that liberal discourse, focused on social contract theories, "lacks the concept of 'conquest' in its theoretical repertoire" (an assertion made without discussing, for example, Locke's chapter entitled "Of Conquest" in the *Second Treatise of Government*).[58] Dahl concludes that the Indigenous political thought of figures such as Apess provides more resources for "decolonizing democracy" than any other American political traditions, including the republican thought and radical Black thought stressed by Rana.[59]

America as a *Revolutionary* White Settler, Protestant, and Patriarchal Colony

There is much of value in all these white settler colonial accounts of American identity and development. They help explain the powerful resistance many Americans have long shown to receiving and naturalizing nonwhite immigrants and to granting full civic equality to current inhabitants and immigrants who do not share white Protestant origins. They also help explain enduring hostility to the claims for autonomous communal existence of many Native American tribes. The white settler colonial origins of the United States are the source of those ideological traditions I have labeled "ascriptive Americanism," and they clarify why this particular array of ascriptive identities has clustered together in American political thought.[60]

The problem with these analyses is not that they are wrong but that they are incomplete. Their depictions of the origins of the United States ignore or minimize major political, economic, and ideological consequences of the late 18th-century revolution in the original 13 white settler colonies against British rule. As a result, their characterizations of subsequent American political development, including the nation's history of contestation over the peopling of the United States, omit or misconstrue important dimensions of the nation's political struggles. Those limitations also mean that Rana and Dahl, in particular, advance unnecessarily and unproductively constrained recommendations for how to combat the very real continuing injustices of American white settler colonialism today. They neglect or reject resources found in the nation's multiple ideological traditions that both redemptive and revolutionary reformers have repeatedly found invaluable, if still insufficient, for changes needed to achieve greater justice.

The heart of this disagreement is how much significance to attach to the fact that the American revolutionaries chose to open their Declaration of Independence by invoking universal "inalienable rights," derived from "Nature and Nature's God," making all persons "created equal" in key respects. This phrasing was clearly a choice. The revolutionaries heatedly debated the wisdom of adopting such language in a range of revolutionary-era documents. Some, such as John Rutledge of South Carolina, but also John Jay of New York, always feared the "subversive" potential of universalistic "rights talk" to undermine the hierarchies that characterized their white settler societies. They preferred to cast the revolutionary cause solely in terms of the rights of Englishmen, the perspective Dahl stresses.[61]

The reality, however, is that at least when it came to revolutionary rhetoric, those conservative voices lost out in the crucible of the mid-1770s. To fire up support for the dangerous and uncertain cause of revolution, advocates found it necessary to ascend above the dry doctrines of the English common law and to appeal to noble-sounding universal principles and aspirations. Innumerable historical episodes show that the choice to do so, even if largely rhetorical at the outset, gave those principles lasting though never-uncontested potency in American political thought and development.

They have nonetheless always faced opposition that has often been still more potent. Events soon proved that conservative worries about discourses of universal rights were well founded from their point of view, and American history then became in large part a tale of their often-successful resistance to change. Yet that history displays contests sometimes swinging one way, sometimes another, because leaders of the new "imagined community" of the United States frequently boasted of its commitments to equal rights for all. By doing so, they shaped the values and identities of most Americans to greater or lesser extents, enabling calls to live up to those principles to have the kind of broad popular resonance that proponents of the nation's hierarchies feared. That resonance has meant that even the most radical American voices have often found it useful to invoke the language of the Declaration of Independence to define and to defend their causes.

Still, ideas of universal rights alone have never been able to win victories. Other powerful economic and political interests, as well as other ideas, have always contributed to the limited successes that reformers have achieved over enduring interests entrenched by white settler colonialism. Yet, the evidence challenging many white settler accounts overwhelmingly shows that those seeking inclusive, egalitarian changes in policies of American peopling, as well as those opposing such changes, have regarded the ideological traditions set in train by, especially, the 1776 Declaration of Independence as formidable assets for reform efforts. As with the original American revolutionaries, moreover, reformers' reliance on those traditions, even if chiefly for tactical purposes, has inescapably influenced the goals that they and their constituencies pursue.

The examples began mushrooming in the revolutionary era itself, as those who then opposed relying on natural rights language surely knew. Massachusetts slaves unsuccessfully petitioned Massachusetts Governor Thomas Gage in 1774 to grant acknowledgment of the "natural rights to our freedoms."[62] Also in 1774, the African American poet Phyllis Wheatley wrote to her older friend Samson Occum, a Mohegan who had become a Presbyterian minister, a letter soon published in the *Connecticut Gazette*. In it she echoed the arguments of John Locke's widely read *Letter Concerning Religious Toleration*, approving Occum's call for "Negroes" to receive "their natural Rights" on the ground that "in every human Breast, God has implanted a Principle, which we call Love of Freedom; it is impatient of Oppression, and pants for Deliverance."[63]

In 1777, another Native American leader, sometimes called Corn Tassel by whites, resisted the demands of revolutionary commissioners for Cherokee lands in Tennessee through arguments that also showed great familiarity with American discourses on "the law of nature," but that expressed even more the kind of alternative Indigenous perspective Dahl rightly stresses. In addition to insisting that the Americans' own standards "are . . . against you," Corn Tassel denied that Americans could claim any "right of conquest," insisting that the Cherokees remained *a separate people*," and responding to American complaints that the native peoples did not till the ground by asking *"why the White people do not hunt and live as we do"*[64]

These invocations by African and Native Americans of the principles of freedom, equality of basic rights, and natural law that the 1776 Declaration of Independence most famously espoused admittedly did not do much to change American white settler policies. However, the incorporation into the 1780 Massachusetts Constitution of the view that "All men are born free and equal, and have certain natural, essential, and unalienable rights" proved more immediately consequential. In 1783, Chief Justice William Cushing stated in *Commonwealth v. Jennison* (Massachusetts 1783) that sentiments "more favorable to the natural rights of mankind, and to that innate desire of liberty, which heaven, without regard to complexion or shape, has planted in the human breast—have prevailed since the glorious struggle for our rights began." The embodiment of those views in Article 1 of the Massachusetts Constitution meant that "slavery is in my judgment effectively abolished ... perpetual servitude can no longer be tolerated by our government."[65] This ruling was a key development in the "first emancipation," the gradual ending of slavery in the northern states following the Revolutionary War.[66]

By ruling that enslavement was an unconstitutional violation of human freedom and equality, and through subsequent decisions treating resident African Americans as citizens, if not fully equal citizens, the Massachusetts courts made the people of the new United States less thoroughly "white settlers" than they had been in the colonial era. In these years, revolutionary leaders such as George Washington also welcomed immigrants they saw as attracted by "the Example of the Americans successfully contending in the Cause of Freedom." Washington famously promised that the "bosom of America is open to receive not only the opulent & respectable Stranger, but the oppressed & persecuted of all Nations and Religions; whom we shall welcome to a participation of all our rights & Privileges."[67]

This universalistic language notwithstanding, there is no doubt that Washington hoped "the poor, the needy, & oppressed of the Earth; and those who want Land" would "resort to the fertile plains of our Western Country, to the second Land of promise," and assist in the advance of the Americans' white settler empire, at the expense of Indigenous peoples.[68] Yet just as the rhetoric of the Declaration of Independence aided egalitarian causes far more radical than those embraced by the American founders, so the expansive statements by Washington and other early American leaders of welcome toward immigrants, linked to the nation's founding commitments to rights and freedoms, have proven a resilient resource in subsequent immigration and naturalization debates.

The Jeffersonian Albert Gallatin, for example, countered Federalist contentions in 1793 that his election to the US Senate was void because he had not been a naturalized citizen for nine years by citing the Declaration of Independence and its complaints against British barriers to expatriation from one country and naturalization in another.[69] Gallatin did not then prevail, but he soon returned to Washington as a member of the House of Representatives and went on to become Secretary of the Treasury. The Jeffersonians and Federalists fought for the next decade over how many years of residency should precede naturalization, advancing positions that clearly reflected calculations of partisan advantage, but also contrasting conceptions of American identity and appropriate policies for its peopling.[70]

As the new nation became established, moreover, a wide variety of groups who felt they were at least as oppressed in the American republic as the white settler colonists had been repeatedly turned to the language of the now-venerated Declaration of Independence to articulate their grievances and aspirations. In 1829, the New York Working Man's Party promulgated "The Working Men's Declaration of Independence," championing the "natural and inalienable rights" of "one class of a community" against "other classes" who denied them a "station of equality."[71] In the first issue of the *Liberator* in 1831, William Lloyd Garrison thundered that the principle "maintained in the American Declaration of Independence, 'that all men are created equal, and endowed by their Creator with certain inalienable rights'" required "the immediate enfranchisement of our slave population."[72] In 1834, the Boston Trades' Union announced that "we hold that all men are created free and equal, endowed by their Creator with certain unalienable rights," and that "laws which have a tendency to raise any peculiar class above their fellow citizens, by granting special privileges," violate those rights.[73] In 1848, the feminist Seneca Falls "Declaration of Sentiments" held it to be "self-evident" that "all men and women are created equal" and "endowed by their Creator with certain inalienable rights," which included the franchise for women.[74]

Rana is nonetheless right that Abraham Lincoln and the new Republican Party, building on the arguments of anti-slavery constitutionalists including Lysander Spooner and Frederick Douglass, did the most to establish the view that the Constitution was an instrument to realize the principles of the Declaration of Independence for "all people, of all colors, everywhere."[75] That view became Huntington's "Creedal" account of American identity—a genealogy that by itself shows that, contrary to its self-presentation, this view is not the "true," original, unchanging core of American identity, but rather one that gained elaboration and acceptance only as the antebellum era proceeded.

As it did so, it influenced views on major public policies. Notably for issues of American peopling, Lincoln thought it compelled opposition to the powerful anti-immigrant Know-Nothing movement of the 1850s, which attracted so many of his fellow Whigs. Lincoln believed that those nativists falsely read the declaration to hold that "all men are created equal, except negroes and foreigners and Catholics."[76] Democrats such as party pamphleteer Henry E. Riell similarly contended that the Know-Nothings were wrong because America was "destined, both politically and physically, to be the free asylum for the oppressed and distressed of the universal world" that Washington had promised.[77] Opposed by these Declaration of Independence–based arguments as well as by political and economic interests favorable to European immigration, and after some brief success in electing officeholders, the Know-Nothings failed to achieve their restrictive goals.

Still more importantly, the Union's victory in the Civil War enabled Lincoln's Republicans, after his assassination, to adopt the Thirteenth, Fourteenth, and Fifteenth Amendments. They collectively embedded the view that the Constitution aimed to secure for all the basic rights of the Declaration of Independence more firmly, though still not unequivocally, into that document. These momentous developments did not mean that the United States ceased to pursue white settler objectives. In 1879, Chief Joseph of the Nez Perce tribe, recently forced to resettle on reservations, wrote in the *North American Review* that whites and the tribes could become "one people" if Indians were granted "equal rights"—including rights to choose their teachers, to practice their religions, and to "think and act and talk" for themselves.[78] However, in the decades that followed, the dispossession of Native American lands from the tribes only accelerated.[79]

Similarly, on other issues of the peopling of the United States, efforts to invoke the Declaration of Independence for more inclusive and egalitarian policies continued in the late 19th century, but often failed. Tennessee Republican William Moore opposed the Chinese Exclusion Act by contending that such a racist measure "by the United States, the recognized champion of human rights—the nation of all others in the world whose chief pride and glory it has been to truly boast of being known and recognized everywhere as the home of the free, the asylum of the oppressed, the land where all men, of all climes, all colors, all conditions, all nationalities, are welcome to come and go at will . . . is one that does so much violence to my own sense of justice that I cannot . . . consent to aid in establishing it."[80] Restrictionists derided his view as "utopian" and "absurd," and Chinese exclusion prevailed. Another great opponent of race-based immigration restrictions, Massachusetts Senator George Hoar later denounced proposals to deny constitutional rights to the inhabitants of the territories acquired in the Spanish-American War. Hoar contended, "You will have to enlarge the doctrines of the Declaration of Independence . . . before you find your right to buy and sell that people like sheep," even "for all this wealth, all this glory, all this empire."[81] He, too, saw his arguments rejected.

Those defeats are among the mountains of evidence that millions of Americans have never accepted compliance with the "American Creed," derived from the Declaration of Independence, as definitive of American identity. Attention to the legacies of America's revolutionary origins is most important for grasping American struggles, not American successes, though it is wrong to insist that no successes have ever occurred. Famously, Martin Luther King Jr. repeatedly turned to the "inalienable rights" proclaimed in the Declaration of Independence to justify his calls for national actions for racial equality, including in his March on Washington speech, which helped set the political stage for the 1964 Civil Rights Act and the 1965 Voting Rights Act.[82] Also in 1965, civil rights groups such as the NAACP as well as President Lyndon Johnson championed the repeal of the race-based national quota system for immigrants by contending, as Johnson put it, that those restrictions violated "the basic principles of American democracy" rooted in the declaration, making them "un-American in the highest sense."[83] Like others, I have argued that Cold War pressures combined with civil rights protests to make those immigration reforms appear to be in the political and economic interests of many national elite actors. The new policies were not due to Declaration of Independence ideals alone. These changes came, moreover, accompanied by erroneous assurances that the demographics of the nation would not alter much, so that again, reforms achieved greater egalitarian inclusiveness, but without any full repudiation of America's white settler traditions of national identity.[84]

Yet there is no reason to dismiss the judgments of the advocates of these measures that the declaration's language was invaluable for winning support, nor any basis to assume that its invocation did not reflect any of their core commitments. The evidence is to the contrary. In the contestation that has always characterized American life, reliance on the universalistic rights principles of the declaration has been consistently used to combat white Christian patriarchal settler policies—and not only by those whom Rana calls "redemptive reformers." The Black Panthers' 10-Point Platform and Program in 1966 urged the courts to follow the Fourteenth Amendment. It ended by quoting the opening paragraphs of the Declaration of Independence in full, contending that they justified a plebiscite, to be supervised by the United Nations, "to be held throughout the black colony . . . for the purpose of determining the will of black people as to their national destiny."[85] The Panthers thereby combined the rhetoric and substance of radical critiques of white settler colonialism with that of the declaration, judging it helpful to their cause. To turn to radical African American thought therefore involves in part turning to the nation's revolutionary Declaration of Independence traditions, not away from them.

Today, movements for egalitarian transformation, such as Black Lives Matter, usually stress still more than the Panthers did that struggles against oppression must be intersectional, recognizing the multiple systems of race, class, gender, sexuality, and other forms of discrimination, subordination, and exploitation that many see as stemming from America's white settler origins and European imperialism more broadly. Nonetheless, linkages of these causes to the declaration's promise of recognizing rights to diverse pursuits of happiness for all persist. Indeed, when in 1986 sociologist Patricia Hill Collins published "Learning from the Outsider Within," an important text for theorizing on intersectionality, she cited an 1893 speech by the Black feminist educator Anna Julia Cooper as an example of the insights that Black feminist thought had into "the interlocking nature of oppression."[86] Cooper had argued that "not till race, color, sex and condition are seen as accidents . . . not till the universal title of humanity to life, liberty, and the pursuit of happiness is conceded to be inalienable to all; not till then is woman's lesson taught and woman's cause won—not the white woman's nor the black woman's, nor the red woman's, but the cause of every man and woman who has writhed silently under a mighty wrong."[87]

Similarly, journalist Nikole Hannah-Jones was the chief architect of the *New York Times*' 1619 Project, which enraged conservatives by stressing America's origins as a society reliant on African enslavement from its early days onward. Yet when she went on to argue for a broad-ranging reparations agenda in the spirit of the Black Lives Matter movement, Hannah-Jones described America as "a nation built on the espoused ideals of inalienable, universal rights," and she contended that "if we are to live up to the magnificent ideals upon which we were founded, we must do what is just."[88] In sum, it is neither historically accurate nor true to the practices and professed ideals of even America's "revolutionary reformers" to dismiss the value of anti-white settler invocations of the Declaration of Independence and the traditions of American identity that appeal to it. America was indeed born from a set of white Christian settler colonies of the British Empire, but its revolution against that empire, though limited, provided ammunition for assaults on imperial legacies that have since won vital victories, even if they have never come to dominate the former settler nation.

Conclusion

Many recent white settler accounts minimize those historical and political realities, largely by ignoring the kinds of evidence provided here. Dahl's few references to the Declaration of Independence do not mention its natural rights arguments. He treats Lincoln only as an advocate of land acquisition for whites and colonization for African Americans, omitting Lincoln's shift to advocacy for voting rights for Black veterans and for educated Blacks. Dahl does not mention Frederick Douglass or, still more pertinently, Indigenous figures such as Chief Joseph at all. Rana does recognize Lincoln and Douglass as major contributors to a tradition calling for realization of the principles of the declaration for everyone, but he treats Lincoln as concerned only with slavery, neglecting his opposition to nativism and his (admittedly limited) endorsements of women's rights, including voting rights. Rana discusses the 1966 Black Panther Party Platform and Program without mentioning its culminating reliance on the Declaration of Independence.[89] Schmidt rightly contends that the arguments that my co-authors and I have advanced have failed in turn to elaborate the larger imperial structures shaping the origins of American racial hierarchies. This is indeed a major contribution of recent white settler analyses. Schmidt agrees, however, that there is "no lack of historical documentation" that the "universalistic language of freedom, equality and consent" in the declaration "have inspired racially egalitarian reformers throughout much of the nation's history."[90]

The point, however, is not to affirm the Declaration of Independence view as the "right" view of American identity in comparison to an emphasis on the nation's white settler origins. It is instead to assert the greater accuracy of a multiple traditions account and to insist that opponents in many policy conflicts in American life, including those central to the peopling of America, have drawn on diverse combinations of those multiple traditions. Proponents of receptive immigration policies have usually argued that America should be an asylum for lovers of freedom and human rights, regardless of their races or religions. Champions of immigration restrictions have instead appealed to America as fundamentally a Northern European–descended Christian nation. In clashes over not only rights of entry but also the rights of admitted immigrants, the claims of Indigenous peoples, the permissibility of minority religions, the requirements of civic education, and many more issues, some have built on America's white settler origins to argue for restrictions, while others have used its revolutionary origins to argue for greater and more egalitarian inclusiveness. Nowhere has this American structure of ideological conflict been more prominent than in the nation's long and so often dismal history of struggles for equality of Americans of color.

Let me stress that although I see the Declaration of Independence tradition of Lincoln and Douglass as the best of the mainstream American political traditions and as one that has aided the achievement of important reforms, it has certainly not been sufficient to achieve justice in America or the world. Even its contemporary political champions, such as Joe Biden, now acknowledge that "racism, nativism, fear, and demonization" have been as central to American experience as the Declaration of Independence ideals and that the success of the latter "is never assured."[91] Not only has the United States never shed many of the systemic inequalities born of its white Christian patriarchal settler origins; those origins resound today in many policies of the Trump movement, including immigration restrictions, which Desmond King and I have labeled "white protectionism."[92]

Yet much of both analytical and political value is lost if we see mainstream American political thought, politics, and policies simply as expressive of white settler colonialism and little else. We fail to convey accurately the substance and the extent of the contests over the peopling of America and other policies that have defined American identity and shaped American political development, far more than any single tradition. Still more seriously, we may well also underestimate the potential to build political coalitions for change by identifying supportive elements in early America's revolutionary traditions, as well as in the often intertwined anticolonial thought advanced then and since by African American, Native American, and other significant voices. If we insist on stressing only the ways those traditions differ, seeking to harden their opposition instead of exploring creative syntheses, we may heighten the danger of political defeat for all reform efforts. We risk handing the future development of US policies over to those who read the lessons of America's white settler origins not in the way most contemporary academics do, but in the grimly restrictive, exclusionary ways that, sadly, Samuel P. Huntington came to do.

Notes

1. Rogers M. Smith, *Political Peoplehood: The Roles of Values, Interests, and Identities* (Chicago: University of Chicago Press, 2015).
2. Samuel P. Huntington, *Who Are We? The Challenges to American National Identity* (New York: Simon & Schuster, 2004).
3. Adam Dahl, *Empire of the People: Settler Colonialism and the Foundations of Modern Democratic Though*t (Lawrence: University Press of Kansas, 2018), 185.
4. Huntington, *Who Are We?*, 39.
5. Dahl, *Empire of the People*, 185–86.
6. Huntington, *Who Are We?*, 171–82, 324.
7. Carlos Lozada, "Samuel Huntington, a Prophet for the Trump Era," *Washington Post*, July 18, 2017, https://www.washingtonpost.com/news/book-party/wp/2017/07/18/samuel-huntington-a-prophet-for-the-trump-era/.
8. Ronald Schmidt Sr., *Interpreting Racial Politics in the United States* (New York: Routledge, 2021).
9. This argument is an elaboration of the "multiple traditions/racial orders" views that Schmidt rightly attributes to me and critiques thoughtfully in ways that others may well find more persuasive than I do. This chapter, however, responds only indirectly to those critiques.
10. Samuel P. Huntington, *American Politics: The Promise of Disharmony* (Cambridge, MA: Harvard University Press, 1981).
11. Huntington, *American Politics*, 30.
12. Huntington, *American Politics*, 30.
13. Huntington, *American Politics*, 18.
14. Huntington, *American Politics*, 27.
15. Huntington, *Who Are We?*, 46–47.
16. Huntington, *American Politics*, 49. Huntington cited Rogers M. Smith, "Beyond Tocqueville, Myrdal, and Hartz: The Multiple Traditions in America," *American Political Science Review* 87, no. 3 (1993): 549–66.
17. Huntington, *Who Are We?*, 324.

18. Rogers M. Smith, *That Is Not Who We Are! Populism and Peoplehood* (New Haven, CT: Yale University Press, 2020).
19. Smith, "Beyond Tocqueville, Myrdal, and Hartz"; Schmidt, *Interpreting Racial Politics*, 43.
20. See Aziz Rana, *The Two Faces of American Freedom* (Cambridge, MA: Harvard University Press, 2010); Paul Frymer, *Building an American Empire: The Era of Territorial and Political Expansion* (Princeton, NJ: Princeton University Press, 2017); Dahl, *Empire of the People*.
21. Dahl, *Empire of the People*, 186–87.
22. Rana, *Two Faces*, 2.
23. Rana, *Two Faces*, 3 (emphasis in the original).
24. Rana, *Two Faces*, 3.
25. Rana, *Two Faces*, 3–4.
26. Rana, *Two Faces*, 11–12.
27. Rana, *Two Faces*, 12–13.
28. Rana, *Two Faces*, 14.
29. Rana, *Two Faces*, 96.
30. Rana, *Two Faces*, 173, 186, 265, 318.
31. Aziz Rana, *The Two Faces of American Freedom*, 2nd ed. (Cambridge, MA: Harvard University Press, 2014), 268.
32. See Aziz Rana, "Race and the American Creed: Recovering Black Radicalism," *n + 1* 24 (Winter 2014), https://nplusonemag.com/issue-24/politics/race-and-the-american-creed/; Rana, *Two Faces*, 2nd ed., 270.
33. Rana, "American Creed."
34. Rana, "American Creed."
35. Rana, *Two Faces*, 2nd ed., 268, 277.
36. Rana, *Two Faces*, 2nd ed., 271, 277–86.
37. Rana, "American Creed."
38. Rana, *Two Faces*, 2nd ed., 288.
39. Frymer, *Building an American Empire*.
40. Frymer, *Building an American Empire*, 18, 261–62.
41. Frymer, *Building an American Empire*, 279.
42. Frymer, *Building an American Empire*, 281.
43. Frymer, *Building an American Empire*, 278–79.
44. Frymer, *Building an American Empire*, 281.
45. Dahl, *Empire of the People*, 6.
46. Dahl, *Empire of the People*, 9–11.
47. Dahl, *Empire of the People*, 29–34.
48. Dahl, *Empire of the People*, 51–54.
49. Dahl, *Empire of the People*, 61–63.
50. Dahl, *Empire of the People*, 135–53.
51. Dahl, *Empire of the People*, 135–39.
52. Dahl, *Empire of the People*, 162.
53. Dahl, *Empire of the People*, 162.

54. Dahl, *Empire of the People*, 162.

55. Dahl, *Empire of the People*, 163.

56. Dahl, *Empire of the People*, 163–64.

57. Dahl, *Empire of the People*, 172, 176–83.

58. Dahl, *Empire of the People*, 158. See John Locke, *Two Treatises of Government* (1689), ed. Peter Laslett (New York: Cambridge University Press, 1963), 431–44.

59. Dahl, *Empire of the People*, 187.

60. Rogers M. Smith, *Civic Ideals: Conflicting Visions of Citizenship in U.S. History* (New Haven, CT: Yale University Press, 1997).

61. Daniel T. Rodgers, *Contested Truths: Keywords in American Politics since Independence* (New York: Basic Books, 1987), 46, 52–57; Richard R. Beeman, *Our Lives, Our Fortunes, and Our Sacred Honor: The Forging of American Independence, 1774–1776* (New York: Basic Books, 2013), 116–18, 139.

62. Keith E. Whittington, *American Political Thought: Readings and Materials* (New York: Oxford University Press, 2017), 52.

63. Isaac Kramnick and Theodore J. Lowi, eds., *American Political Thought: A Norton Anthology*, 2nd ed. (New York: W. W. Norton, 2018), 244.

64. Whittington, *American Political Thought*, 149–50 (emphasis in the original).

65. *Proceedings of the Massachusetts Historical Society* (Boston: Massachusetts Historical Society, 1874–1875), 13:293–94, https://www.jstor.org/stable/25079475.

66. See Arthur Zilversmit, *The First Emancipation: The Abolition of Slavery in the North* (Chicago: University of Chicago Press, 1967).

67. George Washington, "To the Members of the Volunteer Associations and Other Inhabitants of the Kingdom of Ireland Who Have Lately Arrived in the City of New York" (1783), Founders Online, https://founders.archives.gov/documents /Washington/99-01-02-12127.

68. George Washington, "To David Humphreys" (1785), Founders Online, https:// founders.archives.gov/documents/Washington/04-03-02-0142.

69. Smith, *Civic Ideals*, 160.

70. Smith, *Civic Ideals*, 153–63.

71. Philip S. Foner, ed., *We the Other People: Alternative Declarations of Independence by Labor Groups, Farmers, Women's Rights Advocates, Socialists, and Blacks, 1829–1975* (Urbana: University of Illinois Press, 1976), 48.

72. Clarence L. Ver Steeg and Richard Hofstadter, eds., *Great Issues in American History: From Settlement to Revolution, 1584–1776* (New York: Vintage, 1969), 321–22.

73. Foner, *We the Other People*, 53.

74. Foner, *We the Other People*, 78–79.

75. Smith, *Not Who We Are!*, 107.

76. Smith, *Civic Ideals*, 211.

77. Moses Rischin, ed., *Immigration and the American Tradition* (Indianapolis: Bobbs-Merrill, 1976), 93.

78. Isaac Kramnick and Theodore J. Lowi, *American Political Thought: A Norton Anthology* (New York: W. W. Norton, 2008), 939–40.

79. Frymer, *American Empire*, 264–65.

80. Cited in Smith, *Civic Ideals*, 360.

81. George F. Hoar, "Reply to Beveridge," January 9, 1900, *Congressional Record* 56, 1st Session: 712.

82. Martin Luther King Jr., "I Have a Dream" (1963), in *From Many, One: Readings in American Political and Social Thought*, ed. Richard C. Sinopoli (Washington, DC: Georgetown University Press, 1997), 305.

83. Lyndon B. Johnson, "Remarks on the Signing of the Immigration Bill" (1966), in *Public Papers of the President: Lyndon B. Johnson*, vol. 2 (Washington, DC: Government Printing Office, 1966), 1038.

84. Desmond S. King and Rogers M. Smith, *Still a House Divided: Race and Politics in Obama's America* (Princeton, NJ: Princeton University Press, 2011), 238–40.

85. Judith Clavir Albert and Steward Edward Albert, eds., *The Sixties Papers: Documents of a Rebellious Decade* (New York: Praeger, 1984), 159–64.

86. Patricia Hill Collins, "Learning from the Outsider Within: The Sociological Significance of Black Feminist Thought," *Social Problems* 33, no. 6 (1986): S21.

87. Collins, "Learning from the Outsider Within," S21.

88. Nikole Hannah-Jones, "What Is Owed," *New York Times Magazine*, June 30, 2020, https://www.nytimes.com/interactive/2020/06/24/magazine/reparations-slavery .html?.

89. Rana, *Two Faces*, 2nd ed., 284.

90. Schmidt, *Interpreting Racial Politics*, 43–44.

91. President Joseph R. Biden Jr., "Inaugural Address," White House (January 20, 2021), https://www.whitehouse.gov/briefing-room/speeches-remarks/2021/01/20 /inaugural-address-by-president-joseph-r-biden-jr/.

92. Rogers M. Smith and Desmond King, "White Protectionism in America," *Perspectives on Politics* 19, no. 2 (2021): 460–78.

CHAPTER 5

Dahodiyinii (Sacred Places)

Dakota Mace

The vastness of Dinétah (the Diné homeland) is rich with the narratives that exist within the landscape. We hold a close relationship to our home, and each area has sacred significance and places of stories. We visit these places to connect to our ancestors and connect with the powers of the land. Through these interrelated places, we never forget that we exist within a larger story, one that is part of a much larger living system that includes the water, earth, canyons, and plants. It is through these places that healing can begin.

Hwéeldi (Bosque Redondo) is the site that was the final stop in what was known as the Long Walk for the Diné, a painful removal of my ancestors from their home. Hwéeldi is the Diné name for Fort Sumner, located in central New Mexico. It is a place of extreme hardship, where many of my Diné ancestors were imprisoned from 1864 to 1868. During this period, many Diné perished and were unable to return to their home, and the only existing photographs erased our identity, romanticizing our pain. The stories remembered come from the elders, and each story was passed on from one generation to the next. Many of these stories and the history of Hwéeldi were omitted from US history books, furthering the effects of colonialism. While the stories existed, many elders chose not to tell them, believing that further harm can come from these memories. The photo series in this chapter provides the platform for carefully using photography and oral narratives to offer healing for those who came before us and future generations.

While the stories of Hwéeldi are withheld and responses to such death and violence are not to be taken lightly, there is a need to carry these stories of resilience. Each photograph represents the lost stories of our ancestors who don't exist in the minimal records kept within Fort Sumner. As has happened with the COVID pandemic, many of the individuals lost are represented only by numbers. Our stories open up opportunities to see our history as a continuum of our traditions and culture. While the Long Walk to Hwéeldi happened more than 100 years ago, it still with us, and we must remember what happened. This has held true throughout the COVID pandemic, which has caused the second most significant loss of Diné life. Through the memories of our home, we are able to persevere and continue our traditions and stories. This moment in our history, the Long Walk, defined a new era of sovereignty, one of resilience and survival, and reminds us of the struggles for the rights of our land, natural resources, and freedom.

It wasn't until the passing of the American Indian Religious Freedom Act in 1978 that my own people were allowed to practice our ceremonies, collect sacred materials, and visit our sacred sites, which existed long before the birth of our nation. This is just one reminder of how very recently the freedom of spiritual practices of the Americas' Indigenous people was allowed and the trauma that resulted from its prior history. Through the camera, traditionally seen as an oppressive weapon, I challenge documentation of Indigenous people by decolonizing the violent visual history of colonialism. Through my photography, I provide the opportunity to heal and allow the land and its natural materials to tell our stories.

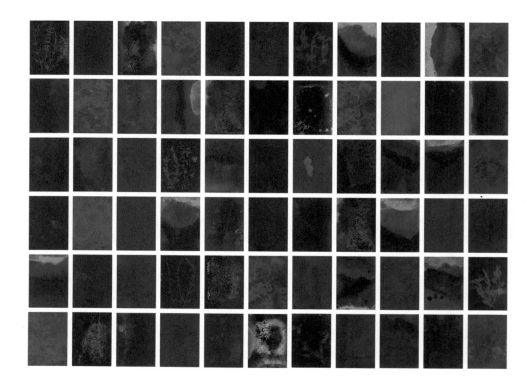

This project honors the importance of land and natural materials. It is believed that to understand the Diné, you must place yourself into the world of Diné tradition. Art is essential to our beliefs and is a lifeline to our culture, land, and the histories that are a part of our identity. Tradition forms a line between one generation to the next.

I have created small-scale cyanotype prints of abstracted locations seen as sacred for the Diné along the trail to Bosque Redondo. I allow the landscape to create the photograph; the earth produces abstract forms of the memories that it holds. Each cyanotype is made to remember my ancestors, who went unnamed or unrecognized. Their identity is embedded within the land itself.

Hwéeldi is the Diné name for Fort Sumner, located in central New Mexico and pictured on the left. On the right is a cyanotype made on the grounds of Ft. Sumner. It is a place of extreme hardship where many of my Diné ancestors were imprisoned from 1864 to 1868. It is estimated that 2,000 Dine died walking this route.

I take an indigenized approach to storytelling, collapsing the past, present, and future. While the Long Walk happened to Hwéeldi more than 100 years ago, it is still with us, and we must remember what happened.

I asked each person I interviewed to select a memory, object, or landscape that has become a place of healing—a Sacred Place.

Chester Otero is a Diné elder from Torreon, New Mexico. He is my great uncle, my grandmother's older brother. The sacred memory he chose to offer was the only photograph he has of his mother. Within the Diné culture, our identity and kinship are passed down from our mothers. We introduce ourselves by our mother's clan, and we, as children, take their family name. Diné women are the center of the family; they are the keepers of our ancestral teachings.

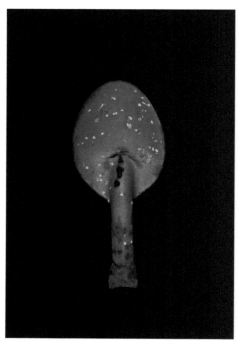

This is Joe Mace, a Diné elder from Ojo Encino, New Mexico. He's my grandfather and was the main Diné translator for the project. He is deeply connected to the communities surrounding Torreon, New Mexico, and works to provide outreach for Diné youth on their culture and identity.

This piece represents my grandfather's childhood, one of hardship and continued survival. The spoon on the right is a remnant of his childhood home, a place that today is controlled by the Bureau of Land Management. On the left is the only existing photograph of Joe as a young man. It was taken in front of Fort Wingate, the residential boarding school he attended for four years. Fort Wingate is notorious for being the starting point for the forced removal of the Diné during the Long Walk to Bosque Redondo. This led to the loss of culture and language and the historical trauma that still affects many Diné people today.

This is Elsa Otero. She was born in 1948 in Torreon, New Mexico.

This photograph of Elsa at a residential boarding school is a scan of a scan, with her name written on it in a ballpoint pen. The quality of the image contradicts how precious it is since it is the only photo she has of herself as a child.

In the background are cyanotypes created near Elsa's home, where details, such as those in her photo, have been layered and obscured. The deterioration of this piece represents the US government's repeated attempts to eliminate Diné ways of life through residential boarding schools, Christian missionaries, and forced assimilation.

Chapter One

I was born on September 17th 1935 In McKinley County, State of New Mexico, I was the first one in the Lewis family there 12 of us boys & 4 sisters, but now only 4 of us left 1 b. 3 of my Sisters, My Mother who Ruth Pinto Lewis & dad Ignacio Lewis Jr. They are both Passed away. My Aunt told me When I was about 3 months old my mom got really sick she can't walk, so mom got newly to feed me, My Grandma & Grandpa start feed me by bottle, they use Coca Cola bottle using the lamb Nipple, buying Pet Milk which cost about 3 cents a can that time, the Store is Milan away to Sterd Life Traly Pst, one @ Torreon 10 miles away they used to ride horses or wagon to get grocery, every thing was Cheap, by the time I'm about 11 yrs old helping mom with sheep, Goat taking sheep out to water well. Some times when I get tired I ride the mom or billy goat, notice the weather was dry and hot. the water well was 4 miles away lots of people waiting to the well to have their livestock drink Lots of horses, Donkeys, Very few Cattle my great father have some Cows So is 2 more people, people get their water & take water from spring @ ojo encino, some time using rain water or from well, there lots of sheep, goats, My grandma & my father. Yes, has about 2 thousand head of Sheep, maybe more, (2) donkey. So in my great father has about 500 Sheep plus 40 goats, 25 head of horses, 6 Donkeys, 30 Cows I go with my grand father to gather the Cattle, Mama star like ahea, riding green broke 4 yrs old Colts some back. My father told me to ride the green broke Colts to Run drive Cattle with the Colt they get tried, and so he went like gentle horse.

Herbert Lewis is from Rincon Marcus, New Mexico, close to Torreon. He was born in 1935. Herbert's mother told him that he was born in McKinley County but didn't know the exact location due to a lack of records. Herbert wasn't officially recognized by the United States until later in his life. He was treated as if he was an immigrant on his ancestral land.

For this project, we spoke in Navajo; however, he felt more comfortable writing in English and wanted to write his story down as his contribution for a sacred object. He shared his biography—the story of his birth and early life with the hopes that his children, who don't speak Navajo, could read it.

Herbert had a hard childhood. Families moved seasonally, and he herded sheep for his paternal grandmother from November to June at a camp in the desert. He often didn't have enough to eat and would either sneak food or take game hunted by the sheepdogs. Finally, he ran away and made it back to his maternal grandfather's home. His grandfather was well off; he had many sheep and cattle. While there, he was told to go to a residential boarding school to learn how to write, read, and understand English—that this would benefit him in the future.

This is another piece made by Herbert Lewis's memories. He was married to his wife, Ruth, for 59 years before her death in 2018. She often looked out the window at this tree in their yard. The cyanotype was made from the earth near that exact location, and the deep cochineal red signifies the importance of this color to Diné people. It is a color used in our medicines and used to protect those who are traveling.

While on the Long Walk, many Diné would seek shelter under juniper trees, like the one pictured here, and share stories beneath them. These stories were often prayers offered to lives lost.

This is a photograph I took of my brother, Chionte, on the left. Earlier this year we lost our father, my stepfather, who is pictured in the archival photo on the right as a baby with his father. For my brother, this project was an opportunity to learn about his culture and language but also a chance to heal. In Diné culture, it is important to spend time with the land in order to find Hózhó, or balance.

Throughout this project, Chionte and I talked about the generational trauma that stems from centuries of colonialism and the toxic masculinity that history has produced. For Diné people to heal we need to find a way back to who we are, our beliefs and culture and our beliefs in our Diné women.

Helen Nez is an elder from Blue Gap, Arizona, situated in the center of Navajo Nation. She was born in 1938 and is related to me through my maternal clan, Redhouse.

On the left, the cyanotype features wildflowers growing near her home. These are among the few plants that have survived in that area, which has been mined for uranium since 1944. Much like the flower, Helen continues to persevere, even as each of the flowers represents one of Helen's 11 children who died from exposure to uranium.

Diné women are taught that they are sacred. Through their hands, they carry their children, pick traditional plants, tend to livestock, and perform ceremonies. You can see Helen's history etched within her hands and her silver jewelry—a true matriarch preserving her culture and homeland, and protecting her family.

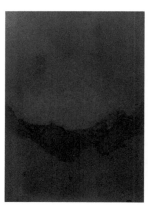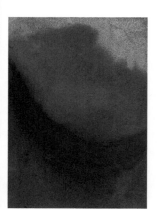

Louise Badoni was born in 1943 in Blue Gap, Arizona. She is related to me through my maternal clan, Redhouse.

Louise is seated in her yard, where she is often surrounded by her children and grandchildren, who listen to her stories about the creation of our people, the importance of family, and the continuation of our traditions. For Louise, these gatherings are special times because very few Diné children come together this way anymore.

The cyanotypes were created near her home, and the wind created these abstracted images. For us, the land is our record keeper, giving us the knowledge and strength to carry on our traditions. If you listen carefully, you can hear the stories of our ancestors being carried across the land.

This is another memory from my grandfather, Joe Mace. Like many Native Americans, he served in the US Army, and on the left he is pictured while stationed at Fort Huachuca, Arizona in 1972. On the right, the US flag is flying at Fort Sumner, formerly known as Bosque Redondo.

Today, the fort is a tourist destination, though it remains a place of deep sorrow for the Diné. The exhibits tell the story of how the US Army used scorched-earth policies to forcibly remove the Diné people from their homelands and bring them to this inhospitable location. This was a pivotal part of the history of the American West, and many Diné died during the 300 mile walk. During their internment, my ancestors were prevented from practicing our ceremonies, singing our songs, and even speaking our language. This oppression by the US government forever changed the way we would live and reshaped our culture.

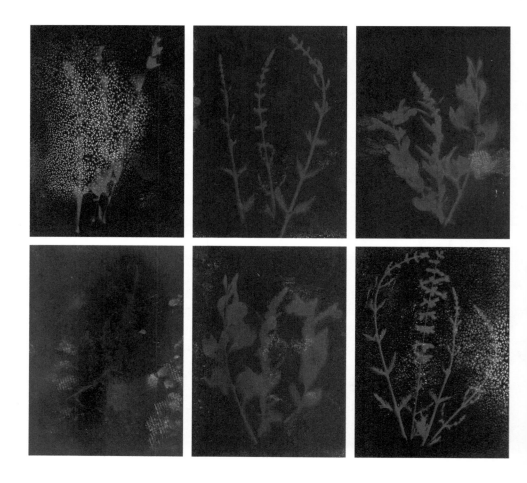

In this cyanotype, I selected plants and flowers along the route of the Long Walk to represent the lost stories of our ancestors, stories that were never recorded. Many elders chose not to share their memories, believing that they could create further harm. Despite cultural taboos, there is a need to carry forward these stories of resilience.

It wasn't until the passing of the American Indian Religious Freedom Act in 1978 that my own people were allowed the freedom to practice our ceremonies, collect sacred materials, and visit our sacred sites that have existed long before the birth of the United States. This is just one reminder of how very recently it was that America's Indigenous people were granted this most basic freedom guaranteed by the Constitution.

Through the camera, traditionally seen as an oppressive weapon, I challenge the documentation of Indigenous people by decolonizing the violent visual history of colonialism. Through my photography, I provide the opportunity to heal and allow the land and its natural materials to tell our stories.

CHAPTER 6

American Immigrant

Katy Long

The everyday experiences of immigration don't reside in any grand narrative. Immigrants' memories are made in the cataloguing of small differences, the unexpected presence or absence of mundane things. When I talk about what it is like to be an English immigrant in San Francisco in the early 21st century, I talk about the absurdity of checkbooks still existing and the infamy of private health insurance and the way the firefighters wave to small children from their trucks—*trucks*, not engines—like local celebrities. I talk about the way language changes, transfiguring trousers into pants and pavements into sidewalks. To be an American immigrant—wherever you are from—is to code switch, always, to find yourself rushing to catch up to a culture you don't quite speak fluently and then turning back to see the culture you are losing behind you. *Where did you come from originally?* The answer, wherever you came from, is the same: *not here.*

All immigration is a lesson in loss.[1] But there are also moments when to be an American immigrant is to fall in love. This is how I feel when I talk about the way the California light catches the ocean spray when you speed south out of the city on Highway 1, or the beauty to be found in the fog that marches on the city most summer evenings, an implacable advancing army, or the sheer scale of the California redwood trees that stretch all the way to the stars.

The poetry is easy. It's easy to fall in love with a place, with a home rooted in geography. Immigrants have been falling in love with San Francisco since they first started rushing here in search of gold, writing stories about a West Coast paradise, a "land of perpetual spring."[2] But America? America is an imagined community. America is an idea. So how do you come to understand your place as an immigrant in an idea as complicated, as ambitious, and as flawed as the United States of America?

For a country that invented itself just 250 years ago, the history of the United States of America is overwhelmingly a history of injustice: slavery, genocide, displacement, exclusion, imperialism, racism, poverty, inequality. America is a lesson in double-think: freedom paired with slavery, the land of opportunity a place of systemic discrimination, soaring ideal set against harsh reality. What are we immigrants to make of this? How does this become *our* history?

After all, *I* am not an American. I am seven years an immigrant—and it felt possible to say, at least at when I arrived, that some of this history was not my burden. As a newly arrived immigrant—even when you are not forced into the shadows by the xenophobia and racism and disdain that immigrants of color or without money or papers often face—you are allowed, even encouraged, to sit still on the sidelines. I bore witness to the elections of President Trump in November 2016 without feeling entirely responsible. I could not vote. In 2016, it was easy to pull away, to say that this was not my history, my bigotry, my president.

But when immigrants stay, they find themselves building some kind of American life regardless of their intentions. Today, I am the mother of two small blue-eyed American boys. I am rooted here now. I find myself one more voice in an immigrant chorus. *No, I am not an American—but my children are.* Their future demands I reckon with America's history and find my place in its story.

This is why I find myself asking, again and again, just how immigration fits into the stories America likes to tell about itself—how immigration fits into the histories that run below those stories, hidden currents of truth. *Immigration*, mind you, not just immigrants, for the history of those arriving can't be told apart from the history of those who were already here. This is not a Hollywood script. Saccharine-soaked, sepia-tinted nostalgia should not mask the fact that US immigration history is at least as much about exclusion as it is about welcome. Not just in the past, either: parts of this story must be told in the present tense. This is a country with a border wall 30 feet high; armed police seizing parents at dawn; children in cages. Oscar Handlin and JFK might have been right—immigrants *are* America[3]—but these outrages against strangers are America, too.

In the long COVID pandemic months of 2020, I taught myself to knit. Though the results were at best a triumph of creative effort over skill, I found comfort in the rhythm, looping the wool around the needles, pulling them—*click!*—sharply back. I liked too, that when I noticed a slip—a dropped stitch, a miscounted purl—I could follow the threads backward, eventually unraveling the error. What I very quickly learned was that I could not ignore these mistakes, for then the entire project would run away from me, breaking into a disordered mess.

As with knitting, so with history. Before we can build a new American history of immigration, I think we need first to assess the flaws in the old one: the elisions, omissions, revisions. This was part of the reason why I set out, in the spring of 2018, to travel overland from San Francisco to New York. I wanted to write my own history of immigrant America.[4] I wanted this history to be something that lived and breathed beyond archives and museum cases and the other dusty places where history is often kept. What follows are four stories from that journey that might provide a foundation for a new American history. These are the stories of Jamestown's Poles, New Orleans' Haitians, San Francisco's Chinese, and Los Angeles' Chicanos.

Readers might ask, with some justification, why *these* stories? One answer is about framing. I chose this collection of stories in part to address the traditional idea of America as a "composite" nation, with each story corresponding to one of white, Black, Asian and Latino experiences of migration. These categories have long framed ideas of American identity: think of Diego Rivera painting his *Four Races* mural in 1930s America. Here, I want to contribute to the process of deconstructing these archetypes, by showing just how complicated the experiences of migration and belonging are, how they defy such easy categorization. However another part of my answer is that the curator of any exhibit has enormous powers—both of commission and of omission—and does not make choices in a political or social vacuum. In this chapter, these stories—the stories I chose—all speak in some way to my own preoccupations in trying to create *my* "American" identity. What we chose to remember is always self-selective, reflecting as much the storyteller as the truth of any story told. National myths are one example of this—but an alternative storyline, including this one, also has an editor, something it is important to acknowledge.

Jamestown, Virginia

First stop: Jamestown, Virginia. For over a century, Jamestown has been feted by establishment voices as "the place where America began." Jamestown was where, in 1607, Captain John Smith and 104 Englishmen established the first permanent settlement in the lands that would become first Virginia and then the United States.[5] The *New York Times Magazine*'s 1619 Project has helped to reframe Jamestown as the setting for a much more tragic story, the place where Africans were first sold into slavery on American soil.[6] But there's a third Jamestown story we should tell. It's a story that sits, sometimes uneasily, in the spaces between "white colonist" and "Black slave" identities: the story of Jamestown's immigrants.[7]

Unlike the pilgrims who would land at Plymouth Rock in 1620, Jamestown's first arrivals did not see their New World adventure in religious terms, but in financial ones. Jamestown was a money-making venture, backed by London's leading merchants, who were betting on the possibility of future American riches.

But there was a problem. Seventeenth-century Jamestown had a skills shortage: English laborers were not familiar with old-growth forests; nor were they experts in viniculture, silk-farming, or glass-making. The solution was clear: the colonists should import foreigners—immigrants—to get the job done. In 1608, a group of eight Polish and

"Dutchmen" workers arrived in the colony, recruited by the settlers as specialist tradesmen.[8]

These workers were recruited in part for their expertise in producing lumber, potash, and other goods from raw materials. But these skills were also matched by their reputation for being willing to work—like so many migrant laborers—for what Sir Walter Raleigh had called in 1585 "small wages."[9] Eventually, other migrants joined the Poles and Dutchmen, also recruited for their specialist skills. Italians were hired to make glass; Frenchmen to instruct English colonists in how to cultivate vines and silkworms.[10]

The total number of immigrant workers in early Jamestown at any one time was never very high—perhaps at most a few dozen among a population numbering a few hundred[11]—but their skilled contributions to the fledgling settlement were essential. The significance of these contributions should not be lost four centuries later: immigrant labor built the place where America began.

Yet many of the foreign arrivals in Jamestown felt exploited. Perhaps as many as half of all immigrants arrived as indentured laborers, who, in return for the Virginia Company paying for their passage, found themselves bound to work in service for a number of years, after which they could supposedly aspire to join the landowning classes. The terms of this servitude were often exacting, and the Poles erupted into anger when, on the completion of their contracts, they found themselves *still* barred from owning land in the colony. They were told that because they were not English, they could never own land or become "denizens" under Virginian law—a category halfway between citizen and alien, roughly equivalent to a green card holder today.[12]

So this Jamestown story is not only a story about how immigrants were there at the political beginnings of the prototype government that would provide a blueprint for what developed into today's United States of America: it is also a story about how immigrants were discriminated against from that very beginning. The English wanted to exclude their foreign workers from full membership of their fledgling community.

The foreign workers, however, had other ideas. In the summer of 1619, the Poles put down their tools, demanding that the Virginia Company meet their demand for the right to vote and to own land as equal Virginians. On July 21, 1619, the Virginia Company of London recorded that "upon some dispute of the Polonians resident in Virginia, it was now agreed (notwithstanding any former order to the contrary) that they shall be enfranchised, and made as free as any inhabitant there whatsoever."[13] In an early victory for immigrant rights, the strikers won.

In the end, the Poles were not excluded because of their ethnicity or language. But their membership in the Virginia commonwealth was not automatic. To write in anachronisms, the immigrants had to show they were "twice as good." Worse was to follow. Just weeks after the Polish workers won their right to the franchise, the first African slave ships arrived in Jamestown: "About the last of August came a Dutch Man of warre that sold us 20 Negars."[14] Thus, Jamestown teaches us another lesson: from the very beginning, it is impossible to write well about American immigration without also writing about race.

New Orleans, Louisiana

I move south: New Orleans. The brightly colored houses and wrought iron balconies are instantly recognizable, wrapped with strings of plastic beads leftover from Mardi Gras. There is music everywhere: I dance down the streets. *Laissez les bons temps rouler.*

New Orleans's soul belongs to the Caribbean. And the history of immigration in New Orleans is inextricably tied up with the story of a Caribbean slave revolution. To understand this, you must first turn the map upside down. In its early years, New Orleans—a colonial backwater, founded by the French in 1699, but ruled by the Spanish after 1762—faced south, toward the rich sugar and slave islands dotting the Caribbean Sea. New Orleans was a satellite city of the tiny island of Saint-Domingue, the jewel in the French colonial crown. But then, in 1791, Saint-Domingue's slaves—inspired by the French Revolutionary promise of *liberté, égalité et fraternité* and the decision in Paris to grant full citizenship to free persons of color—revolted against their French colonial masters. Thirteen years of bloody war and insurrection followed.[15] Ultimately, the self-liberated slaves—collaborating with some of the free people of color on the island—defeated Napoleon and won freedom for the Republic of Haiti.[16]

America's slave-owning elites were terrified that Caribbean contagion might spread and lead to all-out racial war in their newly independent nation. But if the specter of racial annihilation haunted Americans' dreams, the more immediate question was how to respond to thousands of *white* French refugees from Saint-Domingue, who arrived in American ports accompanied by their slaves. This was America's first refugee crisis. Panic was compounded when the refugees' ships arrived carrying not only exiles but yellow fever. Five thousand died in Philadelphia in the summer of 1793 as the epidemic swept through the city.[17]

White American sympathy for the plight of the white Saint-Domingue refugees—many of whom had witnessed brutal violence, and whose property had been seized, plundered, and often burnt to the ground—was therefore tempered by fear of what might accompany these refugees, particularly those who arrived with slaves who might spread revolutionary doctrine. Left unchecked, Haiti's rebellion might spread, not only bringing disease, but also disorder, and destruction of their own precariously maintained racial hierarchy.

As a result, an instinct to let in the victims of the Haitian revolutionaries (rebels whom Thomas Jefferson called "cannibals of the terrible republic") conflicted with an instinct for self-preservation.[18] For this reason, a number of Southern slave states *voluntarily closed* their slave markets in the wake of the Haitian Revolution. The largest American slave market of all, in South Carolina, closed altogether in 1792: the militia were sent to the ports to *prevent* slave ships from landing.[19]

The slave trade could be dealt with as a matter of commerce. But many of Haiti's rebels—and many of the would-be refugees—were not slaves but *free* persons of color. These *affranchis* had been able to purchase their freedom under French law. Their very existence was proof that the American equation of color and freedom was not as absolute as many white Americans wanted to believe. Here is another history lesson, one that stretches wider than America. Immigrants—especially when they are refugees—often disrupt the settled order of things, reminding us that "how things are" is not always "how they are" *elsewhere.*

Southern states—determined to protect their slave economies—enacted the first American travel bans. In 1793, Georgia barred the entry of free people of color from the West Indies; South Carolina followed suit in 1794, North Carolina in 1795, Maryland in 1797. In 1820, Missouri attempted to join the Union under a constitution that expressly forbid free Blacks from entering.[20] These state-level bans initially faced outward, as slave states sought to assert their rights to secure their borders from the dangerous foreign revolutionaries. But over time the right to refuse free Black immigrants entry expanded to cover existing free populations of color moving between states, too. States passed laws permitting their deportation and expulsion, which prohibited their own free Black residents from returning should they travel beyond state lines. In 1859, Arkansas passed legislation that required *its* free population of color to choose between expulsion and reenslavement. Although never enforced, nearly all of Arkansas's free Black population fled the state.[21]

Back in the 1790s, European powers continued to play out political conflicts on a Caribbean chessboard. The largest number of Saint-Domingue's refugees had in fact not traveled northward to America, but settled in Cuba, hoping to rebuild their plantations on the island. They remained there for a decade, but in 1809—angered by Emperor Napoleon's encroachments on Spanish sovereignty in Europe—Spain passed a decree expelling these French colonists. Exiled once more, over 9,000 of these second-wave refugees made their way to New Orleans in the course of just 12 months.[22]

Until then, New Orleans's total population was only 10,000. The refugees' arrival doubled the size of the city almost overnight. One-third of these new arrivals were white, one-third were enslaved, and one-third were free persons of color.[23] The result was not just a population explosion but a significant demographic shift. Previously only about one in ten of New Orleans' residents was a previously free person of color; now the figure was one in four.[24]

Haiti's Revolution did not just bring new people to New Orleans. It also ushered in a new era of American political control. The city itself became officially American when Thomas Jefferson capitalized on Napoleon's retreat to complete the Louisiana Purchase in 1803.[25] So how did the newly American city's residents respond to the upheaval caused by a rush of traumatized new arrivals in 1809? Perhaps unsurprisingly, Francophone New Orleans was initially extremely sympathetic to the plight of white exiles, with French-language newspapers writing in emotional terms about the horrors faced by white refugees and their bravery in seeking to reestablish themselves in Louisiana.[26] Thanks to the Louisiana Purchase, the other major group immigrants arriving in New Orleans in the first decade of the 19th century were Anglophone Americans, arriving from the East to establish themselves in the new US territory. So the rapid influx of French-speakers from Cuba was a bulwark against the Americanization of New Orleans.

But for exactly the same reason, the Americans in New Orleans resented the arrival of these refugees who would set back their *American* immigration project. The secretary of the governor of Louisiana, W. B. Robertson, wrote that the arrival of these Francophone exiles would "prevent us, for many years to come, from considering this in heart and sentiment an American country." There were also suspicions that these French citizens would form a fifth column inside the US Republic by remaining loyal to Napoleon Bonaparte.[27]

All this reflected the fact that white identity politics in New Orleans in 1809 was complicated by competing ideas of who was "foreign" and who "belonged." White, French-speaking exiles were constantly suspected of being Bonapartists by American authorities. It was only when the British invaded Louisiana in 1814 that the foreigners' loyalty to the American cause was proven beyond doubt: historians estimate that about one-third of the veterans who fought in the campaign against the British were in fact refugees from Saint-Domingue. As the French consul wrote then to his relatives two days before the Battle of New Orleans in January 1815: "Nationalities no longer count: we are all Americans."[28]

At least, we are all *white* Americans. The question of how to deal with the *other* Haitian refugees—free persons of color—was less easily answered. By 1809, under the threat of fine or immediate deportation, New Orleans authorities required any free Black émigrés arriving in the city to register their entry with city officials. Black males over the age of 15 were also required to post a bond that would guarantee both their good behavior while in New Orleans and their prompt and permanent departure should they stray. Yet even at the height of the Haitian crisis, the mayor of New Orleans reported that only 64 men had complied and registered with city officials. Many young men claimed to be underage in order to evade the requirements. Nearly half of the free persons of color arriving in 1809 were recorded to be children, a significantly higher proportion than among either the white or slave population arriving from Haiti. Many more free Black men promised to return to the authorities at a later date bringing with them proof of freedom or a security to be lodged against their imminent departure— only to disappear and continue to live in New Orleans' shadows, as undocumented Haitian migrants.

Inevitably, the imposition of immigration controls helped fuel the business of people smuggling. By 1808 the notorious pirate Jean Lafitte—a figure beloved by New Orleans's tour guides[29]—had established himself on the island of Baratasria, a costal settlement just west of the Mississippi River. Lafitte's main business was black market smuggling, although he increasingly engaged in supplementary piracy, and many of the men who joined him in his attacks upon Caribbean shipping were Haitian refugees. Barataria's residents in 1810 also included at least 800 free Black veterans of the Haitian revolution. Immigration laws intended to eradicate the problem of free Blacks in America had brought about real white slaveholder's worst fears: the presence, just beyond the border, of an uncontrolled group of armed Black men.[30]

The history of Haitians in New Orleans tears down another pervasive American immigration myth. Immigration controls were not late additions to American politics. America's "golden doors" weren't open to the world until the 1870s. The Haitian Revolution set off a race-based immigration panic that resulted in the passing of America's first immigration bans. Seeking to keep people out is at least as foundational to the United States as welcoming people in.

San Francisco, California

Forward to the late 19th century. Everyone thinks of Ellis Island when they think of American immigration during these decades: huddled masses arriving at the Lower East Side of Manhattan. But there are other histories that complicate the story. That's why I turn back towards San Francisco, the city I call home. One hundred years ago, San Francisco was the beating heart of a nativist movement intent on driving the "yellow peril" of Asian immigration from American shores altogether. Crowds 10,000 strong gathered regularly outside city hall to demand that the Chinese be sent home.[31]

The Chinese arrived in California—along with the rest of the world—in the frantic years after 1848, when gold was discovered in the Sierra foothills. Within a few years, one in every four of the men digging in California's gold fields was Chinese, joining a rainbow cast of Chileans, Peruvians, Mexicans, Germans, and Italians, who were all dreaming of striking a fortune.

However, as competition in the gold fields intensified, prejudice hardened; white American miners sought to drive away foreign competition. In 1850, California, newly admitted to the United States, passed a foreign miners' tax that required all non-Americans working claims in California to pay $20 a month.[32] In any case, by the 1860s most of the gold was exhausted.

The building of the transcontinental railroad bought the Chinese another decade of toleration—the "Big Four" capitalists needed cheap indentured labor.[33] But in the 1870s recession arrived. The Workingmen's Party of California, established in 1877, salted progressive working-class politics with virulent anti-Chinese racism. Every speech that Denis Kearney delivered ended with the same familiar cadence: "The Chinese Must Go!"[34]

Natives forcing out newcomers: there's a familiar narrative. Except Kearney, an Irishman, had arrived in the United States only a decade before. Most of the crowd listening to him were also Irish immigrants—a group who, in the 1870s, often weren't considered "white" enough for America's establishment to count them as "true Americans," even if they officially held citizenship. But recession had left tens of thousands of immigrants—Chinese and Irish—competing for scarce jobs. Kearney's response to this—and to the exclusion and discrimination that the Irish continued to suffer at the hands of Anglo-Americans—was to stoke Asian hatred. Tie another knot binding the history of American immigration policy to American racism.

In 1882, the federal government responded to public agitation by passing the 1882 Chinese Exclusion Act. This law barred new Chinese laborers from migrating to the United States and prohibited the naturalization of those already there. Put in place for 10 years in the first instance, the bar was made permanent in 1902. By this point, even legal Chinese residents of the United States were required to carry identity papers at all times.[35] Finally, in 1924—at the same time as the National Origin Acts drastically reduced immigration from Europe—the US government placed a total bar on Asian immigration.[36]

This story of Chinese exclusion isn't just about discrimination and prohibition. It's about resistance and resilience—about the way immigrants have shaped the meaning of America even as America has fought to exclude them. Faced with a ban, the Chinese community organized and fundraised; it hired sympathetic counsel; identified test cases. Between 1882 and 1905, the Chinese in California alone brought more than 10,000 cases against the federal government. This number is even more staggering when you consider that the total Chinese population in the United States was only about 100,000. The sheer volume of *habeas corpus* cases lodged brought the California courts to a standstill, until Congress passed harsher, more exclusionary laws that made finding legal grounds for admission to the United States far more difficult.[37]

If you want to know what makes an American, you need to know the history of this resistance. In particular, you need to know the story of Wong Kim Ark, a Chinese man who ran afoul of the exclusion laws when he attempted to re-enter the United States after making a visit to China. But unlike previous petitioners who had lost their cases, Wong Kim Ark was American-born. In a landmark 1898 judgment, the Supreme Court declared him to be a US citizen. In doing so, the Court judged the

Fourteenth Amendment to grant citizenship to children born on American soil—regardless of their ethnicity or the citizenship status of their parents.[38] In the century since, this ruling has made Americans of tens of millions of immigrants' children—including my sons.

Los Angeles, California

Now I head south, joining the traffic on the 101. Los Angeles's freeways are infamous, but in the very heart of LA there is a street—Olvera Street—that is car-free. And in the city that invented Americana, Olvera Street is (at least in pre-pandemic times) filled with street stalls hawking Mexican trinkets, *calaveras* and Catrinas. It is exactly that dissonance—that sense that Olvera Street is atypical, out of place, exotic—that explains why Olvera Street deserves a place in this new history of immigrant America.[39]

To the side of Olvera Street, a bronze plaque marks the spot where in 1781 el Pueblo de Nuestra Señora la Reina de los Ángeles was founded by 22 adult *pobladores* and their 22 children, sent north to California by the Spanish king. Only two of those original LA settlers were white. The rest were mestizos; mulattos; *indios y negros*. Mexicans. The plaque commemorating their arrival is a reminder that from the moment of its birth, Los Angeles' story has always been one about Mexican immigration. In fact, there were no restrictions on Mexican immigration to the United State *at all* until 1917, when literacy tests and head taxes were imposed despite the strenuous objections of the Southwest's agricultural businesses. Mexico—in fact the entire Western Hemisphere—was exempted from the United States' infamous National Quotas Act of 1924.[40] If America's immigration history can be told as a series of contradictions, here is another to add to the list: in the same decades that no Asian could legally enter the country—and almost no Italians, Poles, Greeks, Russians, or other southern and eastern Europeans either—Latinos were still able cross the border largely unchecked. This is in part because the Mexican workforce was so essential to so many American businesses, and in part because Mexicans were viewed as seasonal workers, not would-be Americans.

Yet this idea of Mexicans as temporary—as not-Americans—took an ugly turn in the late 1920s. Because, of course, many Mexicans did not return home, not least because, in California and Arizona and Texas, there were always Mexicans, decades before there were Americans. Another lesson in our American immigration history: sometimes it is the borders that move, not the people.[41] Olvera Street, branching north from the plaza, was at the center of the Los Angeles *pueblito* that in just 200 years grew into a megacity. For a century the plaza remained central to city life. But by the 1920s, the neighborhood was dilapidated, the buildings decayed. Olvera Street was a barrio where new immigrants hustled. It was home not only to Mexicans but to Italian and Chinese newcomers. The unemployed massed in the plaza. Radicals such as Emma Goldman and Sun Yat-Sen spoke there.

Even as Olvera Street fell into disrepair, Mexican immigration to the "Sonora Town" neighborhood rose sharply. Civil War and poverty pushed Mexicans to leave their homes, while American businesses—riding the economic boom of the mid-1920s—depended on immigrant labor, and almost the only place that immigrant labor could legally come from after the 1924 Immigration Act was Mexico. Then the American economy collapsed.

Xenophobia and anti-immigrant nativism were already part of mainstream American politics by 1929, but the Wall Street crash accelerated racist public policy as a response to the Great Depression. In time-honored fashion, President Herbert Hoover called for migrant deportations in order to protect "American jobs for real Americans."[42] Across the United States, Mexicans were harassed back over the border. To facilitate these removals, a new racial category was created for the 1930 US census: "Mexican."[43] At least 400,000 and up to 2 million Mexicans were forcibly removed from the United States between 1929 and 1936. Here's the kicker: at least 60% of those "Mexicans" were American citizens by birth.[44]

Olvera Street was at the center of this storm. The Los Angeles Police Department enthusiastically pursued a "repatriation" policy, raiding the city's Mexican *barrios* and indiscriminately rounding up residents and visitors for deportation. Frightened residents would hide in the basements of the buildings surrounding Olvera Street. Women would emerge to find their husbands deported. The American government has never apologized for the million Mexican "repatriations" it initiated in a decade of betrayal—a misnaming that masks the gravity of the crime, because the "repatriations" were also American expulsions.[45]

This history alone would make Olvera Street an important memorial to the dark side of America's immigration history. But the history of Olvera St is more complicated still. That's because when you visit today, you find yourself standing in a colorful, noisy, kitsch version of an imaginary Mexico. There are cafés called "Mr. Churro" and "Juanita's"; there are (in non-COVID times) a hundred vendors selling sombreros and skeletons. The impression is of something romanticized, invented, Disneyfied. But don't look away: the invention of Olvera Street is the point.

It's no accident that the Olvera Street you see today resembles the "authentic" "Old Mexico" that has only ever existed in white America's imagination. The maker of this "Mexican village" at the heart of Los Angeles was a wealthy, white American socialite, Christine Sterling. Sterling successfully campaigned against the planned demolition of Olvera Street's old adobes by promising to turn Olvera Street into a Mexican fiesta. The *LA Times* wrote op-eds in support of her project— and the sheriff's department provided prison labor. A reimagined Olvera Street opened to American tourists on Easter Sunday 1930. In that same year, over 100,000 Mexican-Americans were forcibly removed from the United States, including some residents of Olvera Street.[46]

This is why Olvera Street matters. It matters because Olvera Street is the physical connection between those two sentences, a place that reminds us that the practice of eating tacos while deporting Mexicans is not new. It's an immigration story that echoes painfully in the here and now, an American story that asks us not only "What do we remember?" but also "What happens next?"

Immigrants' History

Four vignettes from a road trip do not an immigration history make. I could tell you 100 more such stories—from the Trump-voting descendants of Oklahoma's dust-bowl refugees in California's Central Valley, through the refugee workers in Texas' meat-packing plants, to the story of Sunnyside Plantation in Arkansas where 100 years ago Mary Grace Humiston, the first female special assistant US district attorney, went undercover to investigate the exploitation of indentured Sicilian laborers. I could tell you stories about sheltering in a thunderstorm in a Springfield, Missouri, Laotian restaurant; the same afternoon we drove past a whole avenue of Confederate flags. I could tell you that the most "American" man I met on my journey owned a mobile phone store in Nashville and sat on his desk with a frame photo of an AK-47 behind him on the wall, telling me how he loved BBQ and fast cars and heavy metal and his wife. Then he logged onto Facebook to show me photos of his birthplace—a Kurdish refugee camp in Turkey. In every corner of the United States, look hard enough, and you will find an American immigration story, the contradictions writ large: inclusion and exclusion, opportunity and exploitation, the hard roots of hatred and the promise of belonging.

But these are just stories. How do you string them together into something more, weaving them into a national history that both acknowledges the immigrants who became Americans, and those who were barred and excluded and humiliated in the pursuit of a white America?

This much is certain: you cannot teach the history of immigration in the United States without reaching into the history of race and racism. From Jamestown in 1619 through to the present, race has always permeated US immigration policy. White immigrants have always been broadly welcomed to the United States—although tracing the label of "white" through American immigration history underlines just how much the whole idea of "white" has always been about power and not skin tone.[47]

Yet it would be dangerous to collapse the history of immigration into a history of race in America. As a white, English-speaking resident of the United States, I have lost count of the times I have been told I am "not really" an immigrant. To dispute my immigrant status, however, not only speaks to the ways in which mainstream America still equates race with belonging (particularly when contrasted with a parallel insistence that the fifth-generation Chinese American must be from somewhere else "originally"), but also denies a part of who I am. I am *not* an American: I am an immigrant. I know about homesickness, about the bureaucracy of visa applications, about raising my children in a culture that is not my own. An American history of immigration has to capture this lived experience of belonging elsewhere: the everyday, domestic reality of immigrants' lives.

But nor should we write immigration history as if it is just about suffering, endurance, assimilation. Too often immigrants' lives have been lived in the shadows, families inching their way to acceptance. Even when we celebrate the achievements of immigrants—and their children—we too often tell these stories as morality plays, framed as the triumph of "model minorities," an apolitical assimilation. Telling immigration history like this robs the narrative of its political power and fails to acknowledge the ways in which immigrants have shaped not only their own stories, but this country. Immigrants fought for their place in the United State of America from the very beginning: so let us tell a story in which there are immigrant heroes and allies, loudly protesting xenophobia and bigotry. This is not just stylistic: history is much easier to relate to—especially for children and teenagers—when the story is about dynamic individuals and dramatic confrontation. I want my kindergartener to wear a t-shirt printed with Won Kim Ark's face, because I want him to believe in a story about America in which immigrants are agents of change.

Any worthwhile history of American immigration will be controversial. It will need to interrogate not just the idea but the geography of America, reminding America's citizens that the United States was not a fixed entity for the first 100 years of its existence. For the first half of the 19th century, white Americans were the immigrants in territories belonging first to Spain and then to Mexico. In many cases they were illegal immigrants, arriving without papers and taking land to which they were not legally entitled.[48] An American immigration story in which white Americans are the illegal immigrants unmoors the history we thought we knew from our expected reference points. It opens up the possibility that there are other stories to tell, stories that aren't the history we thought we already knew.

America's Future

So what makes an American? I am still not sure I know the answer. But on January 20, 2021—the day of President Joe Biden's inauguration—I opened my laptop, navigated to the United States Citizenship and Immigration service website, and began to fill out form N-400: Application for Naturalization. A little over a year later I became a citizen, the COVID-era ceremony lasting all of five minutes before I was ushered out of the building holding a naturalization certificate and a tiny American flag.

Am I an American now? Every immigrant will tell you that papers aren't the same thing as belonging. And every immigrant will tell you that there's always loss in new beginnings. To become an immigrant is to leave another life behind at the moment of departure—and then to lose it again and again. But I also think there's a bravery and an independence in every immigrant's story that speaks to what politicians and patriots often tell us are "quintessentially American values."

This is why the history of American immigration I think we should tell is one in which the faults of America's imagined community are laid bare. I want no soft-focus Lady Liberty, no voice whispering "give me your tired, your poor," as if America is just a place of welcome.[49] Let our new American narrative instead begin with a reckoning—for it is long overdue. America has always tried to exclude, persecute, discriminate, detain, and deport those who weren't white. American has always tried to keep out those who were deemed "too poor."

This is the past we inherit. And I believe we help to repair it, stitch by stitch, every time we don't just settle for easy answers, but instead ask hard questions and tell complicated stories about borders and bigotry, about entitlement and citizenship and justice. So let us begin our new American narrative by agreeing upon this foundational truth: America's immigration history is as much about exclusion as it is about inclusion. There should be shame in that; but there need not be despair.

After all, history also tells us that America's immigrants have always been the mothers of reinvention. Immigrants gave us America: blue jeans and video games, hot dogs and Budweiser, the Fourteenth Amendment. The United States has always been shaped by the immigrants who came "expecting us to be better than we are"—and who stayed despite the deception. Immigrants, after all, are optimists. And just like those other famous optimists—Americans—they keep believing (despite all evidence to the contrary) that when you tell the story right, sometimes hope and history rhyme.[50]

Notes

1. See, for example, Gary Younge, "As Migrants We Leave Home in Search of a Future, but We Lose the Past," *The Guardian*, March 24, 2015, https://www .theguardian.com/commentisfree/2015/mar/24/migrants-leave-home-future-past -borders.
2. Lansford W. Hastings, *The Emigrants' Guide to Oregon and California* (Cincinnati: George Conclin, 1845).
3. Oscar Handlin, *The Uprooted: The Epic Story of the Great Migrations that Made the American People* (Philadelphia: University of Pennsylvania Press, 2002); John F. Kennedy and Robert F. Kennedy, *A Nation of Immigrants* (New York: Harper & Row, 1964).
4. Some of the material collected during this journey can be read at Helen Dempster, Charlie Zajicek, Tom Alwyn, and Katy Long, "American Journeys," ODI, https:// odi.org/en/about/features/american-journeys/.
5. There are many histories of Jamestown. See, for example, Robert Appelbaum and John Wood Sweet, eds., *Envisioning an English Empire: Jamestown and the Making of the North Atlantic World* (Philadelphia, University of Pennsylvania Press, 2012).
6. "The 1619 Project," *New York Times Magazine*, August 14, 2019, https://www .nytimes.com/interactive/2019/08/14/magazine/1619-america-slavery.html.
7. As the Powhatan would have been quick to point out 400 years ago, everyone arriving in boats from Europe was an immigrant—they were arriving to occupy lands inhabited by others. But the English understood Jamestown to be an English place, and I use the word "immigrants" here to refer to those who arrived voluntarily in the colony but who were seen and understood themselves to be "foreign" in this context.

   The "immigrant" story is not the only narrative that falls outside the "Black" and "white" stories of Jamestown. When the English arrived, they encountered the Powhatan, Algonquin-speaking group with some 30 tribes, numbering about 14,000 persons. Not only did this Powhatan engage in extensive trade with the

English, they were quickly ensnared in the nascent capitalist economy and increasingly used by the English as forced slave labor.

8. Richard Orli, "The Identity of the 1608 Jamestown Craftsmen," *Polish American Studies* 65, no. 2 (2008): 17–26, 18; interview with Dr. James Horn, April 18, 2018.

9. Sir Walter Raleigh, as cited in Orli, "1608 Jamestown Craftsmen," 18.

10. Horn, interview.

11. It is extremely difficult to calculate just how many foreign (i.e., non-English) immigrants arrived in Jamestown or what proportion of the total population they made up. Foreign passengers were often not logged by name on ship manifests. The phenomenal mortality rate also makes demographic calculation very difficult: in the winter of 1609, known as the "starving time" the population dropped from 500 to 60 in 6 months; by 1625, the population had recovered to 1,200—but at least 6,000 colonists had sailed to Jamestown during this time. What is clear is that there were immigrants from at least a dozen non-English European nations present in Jamestown in the first two decades of the colony's settlement and that their work as skilled artisans meant they had real value to the Virginia Company. See Bill Warder, "'From Forraine Parts': Non-English Europeans at Jamestown, 1607–1625," Historic Jamestown Fact Sheets, US National Park Service (2017).

12. For more on denizens and denization during this period, see Daniel Statt, "The Birthright of an Englishman: The Practice of Naturalization and Denization of Immigrants under the Later Stuarts and Early Hanoverians," *Proceedings of the Huguenot Society of Great Britain and Ireland* 25, no. 1 (1989): 61–74.

13. "Abstract of the Proceedings of the Virginia Company of London" (July 21, 1619), in *Collections of the Virginia Historical Society*, Volume 7 (Richmond: Virginia Historical Society, 1888), 17.

14. John Smith, *The Generall Historie of Virginia. New England and the Summer Isles* (1607), UNC-Chapel Hill Libraries, https://docsouth.unc.edu/southlit/smith/smith.html.

15. The history of the Haitian Revolution is extremely complex. For an accessible overview in podcast format, see Michael Duncan, *Revolutions* Podcast, Series 4: Saint-Domingue (2015). For general academic overviews, see Jeremy Popkin, *You Are All Free: The Haitian Revolution and the Abolition of Slavery* (Cambridge: Cambridge University Press, 2010); Malik Ghachem, *The Old Regime and the Haitian Revolution* (Cambridge: Cambridge University Press, 2012).

16. Haiti's refugees were not the first to arrive in Louisiana. In 1755, the British expelled some 11,000 Acadians from Eastern Canada. Deported back to France, many were recruited by the Spanish to populate Louisiana in the 1760s.

17. See Gary B Nash, "Reverberations of Haiti in the American North: Black Saint Dominguans in Philadelphia," *Pennsylvania History: A Journal of Mid-Atlantic Studies* 65 (1998): 44–73; Nicholas Foreman, "The History of the United States' First Refugee Crisis," *The Smithsonian* 5 (January 2016).

18. "Thomas Jefferson to Aaron Burr," February 11, 1799, quoted in Tim Matthewson, "Jefferson and Haiti," *Journal of Southern History* 61, no. 2 (1995): 209–48, 217. See also Joan Dayan, "A Few Stories about Haiti, or, Stigma Revisited," *Research in African Literatures* 35, no. 2 (2004): 157–72.

19. South Carolina reopened its ports to the slave trade in 1803.

20. Gerald L. Neuman, "The Lost Century of American Immigration Law (1776–1875)," *Columbia Law Review* 93, no. 8 (December 1993): 1833–1901, 1866–70.

21. Guy Lancaster, "'They Are Not Wanted': The Extirpation of African Americans from Baxter County, Arkansas," *Arkansas Historical Quarterly* 69, no. 1 (2010): 28–43.

22. Paul F. Lachance, "The 1809 Immigration of Saint-Domingue Refugees to New Orleans: Reception, Integration and Impact," *Louisiana History: The Journal of the Louisiana Historical Association* 29, no. 2 (1988): 109–41.

23. On the question of how slaves were disembarked in New Orleans in 1809, despite the recent ban on importation of slaves passed by the US Congress, see Rebecca J. Scott, "Paper Thin: Freedom and Re-Enslavement in the Diaspora of the Haitian Revolution," *Law and History Review* 29, no. 4 (2011): 1061–87, 1071–73.

24. Lachance, "Saint-Domingue Refugees."

25. See also Daniel Immerwahr, chap. 10, this vol.

26. Lachance, " Saint-Domingue Refugees."

27. Lachance, " Saint-Domingue Refugees."

28. "Anne-Louis Toussard, 6 January 1815," in Thomas N. Ingersoll, *Mammon and Manon in Early New Orleans: The First Slave Society in the Deep South, 1718–1819* (Knoxville: University of Tennessee Press, 1999), 245.

29. Lafitte's Blacksmith Bar, at 941 Bourbon St, is one of the most photographed buildings in the city.

30. In fact, despite the fears of the Louisiana governor, William Claiborne, the Barataria militia played a key role in assisting General Andrew Jackson at the Battle of New Orleans. Lafitte was consequently granted a free pardon in February 1815, a month after Jackson's victory. See Robert C. Vogel, "Jean Laffite, the Baratarians, and the Battle of New Orleans: A Reappraisal," *Louisiana History: The Journal of the Louisiana Historical Association* 41, no. 3 (2000): 261–76.

31. For accounts of this movement, see, for example, Elmer Sandmeyer, *The Anti-Chinese Movement in California* (Chicago: University of Illinois Press, 1991).

32. Mark Kanazawa, "Immigration, Exclusion, and Taxation: Anti-Chinese Legislation in Gold Rush California," *Journal of Economic History* 65, no. 3 (2005): 779–805.

33. The "Big Four"—Collis Huntington, Leland Stanford, Charles Crocker, and Mark Hopkins—were Northern Californian businessmen who funded the Central Pacific Railroad.

34. Michael Kazin, "Trump and American Populism: Old Whine, New Bottles," *Foreign Affairs* 95 (2016): 17.

35. An Act to Execute Certain Treaty Stipulations Relating to Chinese, 47th Congress, 22 Stat. 58, Chap. 126 (May 6, 1882).

36. Immigration Act of 1924, 68th Congress, 43 Stat. 153, Chap. 190, 153–69.

37. Christian G. Fritz, "A Nineteenth Century 'Habeas Corpus Mill': The Chinese before the Federal Courts in California," *American Journal of Legal History* 32, no. 4 (1988): 347–72.

38. United States v. Wong Kim Ark, 169 U.S. 649 (1898). It should be noted that the Fourteenth Amendment continued to be held to exclude Native Americans; this was changed by the 1924 Indian Citizenship Act.

39. See William D. Estrada, "Los Angeles' Old Plaza and Olvera Street: Imagined and Contested Space," *Western Folklore* 58, no. 2 (1999): 107–29. See also "Welcome to Olvera Street," https://www.olvera-street.com.

40. See Mark Reisler, "Always the Laborer, Never the Citizen: Anglo Perceptions of the Mexican Immigrant During the 1920s," *Pacific Historical Review* 45, no. 2 (1976): 231–54.

41. See Daniel Immerwahr, chap. 10, this vol.

42. Delia Fernández, "Mexican Repatriation, 1930–1935," in *50 Events that Shaped Latino History: An Encyclopedia of the American Mosaic*, ed. Lilia Fernández (Santa Barbara, CA: Greenwood, 2018), 329–44.

43. Jennifer Hochschild and Brenna Powell, "Racial Reorganization and the United States Census 1850–1930: Mulattoes, Half-Breeds, Mixed Parentage, Hindoos, and the Mexican Race," *Studies in American Political Development* 22, no. 1 (2008): 59–96.

44. Francisco E., Balderrama and Raymond Rodríguez, *Decade of Betrayal: Mexican Repatriation in the 1930s* (Albuquerque: University of New Mexico Press, 2006).

45. Balderrama and Rodríguez, *Decade of Betrayal*.

46. "Welcome to Olvera Street"; interview with Abelardo de la Peña, Jr., LA Plaza de Cultura y Artes, March 8, 2018.

47. See Justin Gest, chap. 3, this vol.

48. See José Angel Hernández, *Mexican American Colonization during the Nineteenth Century: A History of the US-Mexico Borderlands* (New York: Cambridge University Press, 2012).

49. Emma Lazarus, "The New Colossus" (1883), https://www.poetryfoundation.org/poems/46550/the-new-colossus.

50. Seamus Heaney, *The Cure at Troy: A Version of Sophocles' Philoctetes*, rev. ed. (New York: Farrar, Straus and Giroux, 1991).

CHAPTER 7

The Future Is a Foreign Country

We'll Do Things Differently There

John R. Weeks

In 1967, the British novelist Leslie Poles Hartley taught us that "the past is a foreign country; they do things differently there."[1] Population change and all that goes with it is an integral part of creating a present that seems foreign by comparison to the past, and it will create a future that will make today seem strange to those who look back on it a few decades from now. American society is intimately bound up in both the global and the local demographic changes that, in particular, shape the patterns of immigration to the United States, shape the reaction to immigrants coming here, and then shape the local, national, and global communities. In this chapter I review how past demographic transitions in the world shaped who we are as a nation, and then I discuss what the current demographic trends suggest the future will look like.

Why Do We Care About Migration?

Like most animal species, humans tend to be suspicious of strangers (an attitude often described by the Greek term "xenophobia"). History provides thousands of examples why this is so, as strangers may be people who want to take your land or other possessions or even kill you and your family members. At the same time, strangers may be viewed as inferior beings who are not worthy of equal treatment, leading to what we now call "racism." Strangers come in all shapes and sizes, however, so it is not easy to make a blanket statement about how we will react. We might invite some right in to join us for dinner, while others will be summarily sent away.

History suggests that the more people with whom we interact who are "different" from us, the more likely we are to soften our feelings and be more accepting. Rather than familiarity breeding contempt, familiarity actually tends to breed comfort. This is borne out by two recent examples: the 2016 presidential election in the United States and the 2016 Brexit vote in the United Kingdom. A major part of Donald Trump's campaign was based on anti-immigrant rhetoric, and yet the states in which he got the lowest percentage of votes were states with the highest percentage of immigrants. In the United Kingdom, the Brexit movement was based heavily on the notion that the nation was being taken over by Eastern European immigrants, and the counties with the highest percentage of votes for leaving the European Union were places with the lowest percentage of immigrants.

So, if familiarity breeds comfort with immigrants, where are the most comfortable places in the United States? Figure 7.1 shows the percentage of the population that is foreign-born in each state in the continental United States. It is obvious that there is a lot of geographic variability in the location of the foreign-born. The top states on the list are California (28%), New York (24%), New Jersey (23%), Florida (21%), Nevada (21%), Texas (18%), Massachusetts (17%), Maryland (16%), and the District of Columbia (16%). In general, the edges of the country are more likely to have immigrants than the interior.

Now, let us look at a variable known to be associated with anti-immigrant sentiment—voting for Donald Trump. How did that vary by state in the 2016 election? Figure 7.2 shows that the pattern is essentially reversed from that in Figure 7.1. The coastal states were less likely to vote for Trump than were the states in the middle of the country.

A frequently offered reason for the fear of immigrants as stoked by the Trump campaign is that immigrants are likely to take jobs away

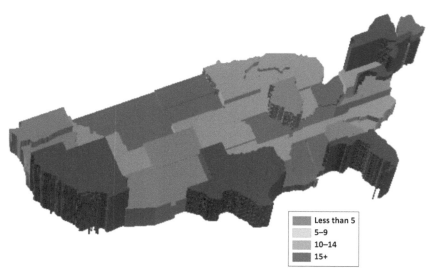

Figure 7.1. Foreign-born US population, by state, 2016 (in percentages)

Source: Adapted from John R. Weeks, *Population: An Introduction to Concepts and Issues*, 13th ed. (Boston: Cengage, 2020), figure 6.1.

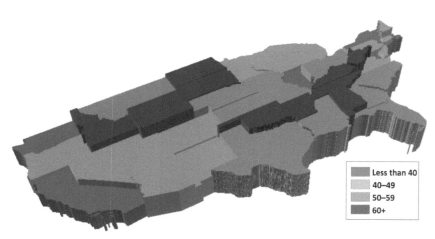

Figure 7.2. Popular vote for Donald J. Trump in the 2016 US presidential election (in percentages)

from the native-born. The evidence suggests that, to the contrary, immigrants tend to help promote economic growth and thus create jobs, rather than the other way around.[2] So, why have jobs gone missing in the industrial heartland? They have gone to less-well-paid workers in other countries. This new pattern of globalization is a consequence of post–World War II population growth in developing countries, which is a result of the global spread of death control technology. This most notably lowered infant and child death rates, and rates of population growth truly exploded before fertility levels could be brought under control. The resulting youth bulge brought a demand for jobs that was met especially in Asia, where there was an emphasis on educating the burgeoning youth population. Cheaper workers continue to vie with American and European workers for jobs, albeit a lot of new jobs have been created in the process.

The other recent example of fear of immigrants driving big political decisions was, as I noted above, the Brexit vote in the United Kingdom. It was well known that the flood of immigrants to the United Kingdom, especially from eastern Europe, was pushing people toward wanting out of the EU. But ahead of the vote, an analysis showed that the support for Brexit (based on likelihood to vote for the UK Independence Party—UKIP) was strongest in those areas with the fewest immigrants, largely in the northern and western counties, and weakest in the southeast counties, where most immigrants live.[3]

Comfort with others allows us to learn from them, and they from us, shifting the cultural milieu in the process. This has happened over and over again throughout the history of the world, including in the United States. Keep in mind that every inch of the Western Hemisphere has been inhabited by one group of migrants after another, including the Indigenous populations, who arrived first, but originated in Asia, whose inhabitants had of course originated in Africa. This is not to downplay the devastation wrought on these populations by the eventual arrival of Europeans, but it is a reminder that human society has always been on the move, although of course it is now a lot easier to move than ever before. Added to that is the fact that there are vastly more of us than ever before.

Although we live in a world on the move, it is nonetheless true that most people do not move. Migration has no known biological components in the way that mortality and fertility do. We accept the idea that humans have an innate sense of and attachment to place that may transcend rational decision-making about the desirability of staying in one place or moving to another. At the same time, migration is an important societal force because it has the potential to profoundly alter a community or an entire country within a short time. In-migration and out-migration can increase or decrease population size, respectively, far more quickly than either mortality or fertility can. And even if the number of in-migrants just equals the number of out-migrants, the flow of people in and out will affect the social and economic structure of a community.

The Past Is a Foreign Country

The past is very clearly a foreign country, which is why the future will also be so different. A quick glance at Table 7.1 shows you the changes in the population of the United States between 1910 and 2020. Population change and all that goes with it is an integral part of creating a present that seems foreign by comparison to the past, and it will create a future that will make today seem strange to those who look back on it several decades from now. Although the population of the United States grew considerably during those 110 years, from 92 million in 1910 to 330 million in 2020, it did not keep pace with overall world population growth and so accounted for a slightly smaller fraction of the world's population in 2020 than it had in 1910. Mortality levels dropped substantially over the century, leading to a truly amazing 28-year rise in life expectancy, from 52 for females in 1910 to 80 in 2020.

Fertility also declined, although by world standards fertility in the United States was already fairly low in 1910 (3.5 children per woman). Still, the drop from 3.5 to 1.6 clearly makes a huge difference in the composition of families. Americans rearranged themselves geographically within the country over that century, and their westward movement is exemplified by the change in the fraction of the population living in

California, from only 3% in 1910 to 12% in 2020. Consider that in 1910 Los Angeles had slightly fewer people than Buffalo, New York, but in 2020, Los Angeles was 16 times more populous than Buffalo.

In the latter part of the 20th century, much of that growth in Los Angeles was fueled by immigrants from Mexico and Central America, but over the course of the century the composition of international immigrants shifted substantially. In the decade following the 1900 census, there were about 123,000 Mexican immigrants to the United States, compared with 1.2 million Italian immigrants in the same time period. By contrast, in the decade following the 2010 census, the numbers were essentially reversed, with 35,000 Italian immigrants and at least 1.7 million legal Mexican immigrants.

Yet, as strange as it might seem in an era when there is so much talk about immigrants, the data in Table 7.1 show that the foreign-born population actually represented a greater fraction of the nation in 1910 than it did a century later. That has a lot to do with the array of

Table 7.1 The Past Is a Foreign Country

	1910	2020
World population (billions)	1.8	7.8
US population (millions)	92	331
US percentage of world total	5.1	4.2
US female life expectancy	52	80
Children per US woman	3.5	1.6
Persons per US household	4.4	2.6
US population in California	3%	12%
Population of Buffalo, NY, compared to Los Angeles	Buffalo was more populous	LA was 16 times more populous
Urban population	46%	82%
Population under 15	32%	18%
Population 65+	4%	17%
Number of passenger cars	450,000	287 million
High school graduates among those 25 and older	~10%	90%
Immigrants from Italy (1900–1909); (2010–2019)	1.2 million	35,000
Immigrants from Mexico (1900–1909); (2010–2019)	123,000	1.7 million (legal immigrants)
Foreign-born population	14.7%	13.6%

Sources: US Census Bureau (various dates); US Department of Homeland Security (various dates); Population Reference Bureau, *World Population Data Sheet 2021*, Washington, DC, 2021.

immigration restrictions imposed over the years. Let's briefly review that bit of history.

Historical Background of Migration and Immigration Laws

At the time of the country's founding, the evidence (admittedly scant) suggests that the foreign-born population was actually quite small. The majority of early immigrants were from Britain, but the Irish Potato Famine in the 1840s led to a massive migration of the Irish into the United States, pushing the proportion of the foreign-born up to nearly 10%, as can be seen in Figure 7.3.

The flow ebbed during the Civil War, although it was during that period that Congress passed the Immigration Act of 1864, which established a commissioner of immigration within the State Department.[4] This legislation correctly assumed that after the war the pace of immigration would resume. The opening up of new land in the United States in the middle of the 19th century coincided with a variety of political and economic problems in Europe, and that helped to generate a great deal of labor migration to the United States. Immigration to the United

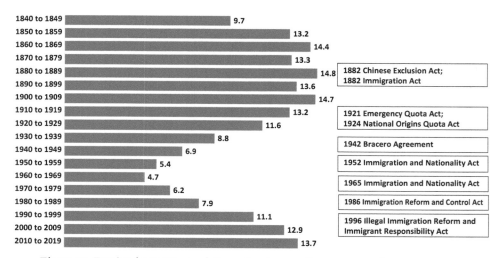

Figure 7.3. Foreign-born US population, 1840 to 2019 (in percentages)
Source: Adapted from John R. Weeks, *Population: An Introduction to Concepts and Issues,* 13th ed. (Boston: Cengage, 2020), figure 6.4.

States during the second half of the 19th century was dominated by people arriving from northern and western Europe (beginning with England, Ireland, Scotland, Sweden, and Denmark, then stretching to the south and east to draw immigrants from Germany, especially).

Economic expansion also brought migrants from Asia, and the United States responded in 1882 with two sets of immigration restrictions. The first of these was the Chinese Exclusion Act of 1882. The discovery of gold in California had prompted a demand for labor—for railroad building and farming—that had been met in part by the migration of indentured Chinese laborers. In 1869, however, after the completion of the transcontinental railroad, American workers moved West more readily, and the Chinese showed up in the East on several occasions as strikebreakers. Resentment against the Chinese built to the point that in 1882 Congress was willing to break a recently signed treaty with China and suspend Chinese immigration for 10 years. But Congress was not through for the year. The 1882 Immigration Act levied a head tax of 50 cents on each immigrant, no matter where they came from, and blocked the entry of so-called idiots, lunatics, convicts, and persons likely to become public charges.[5]

The Chinese Exclusion Act was challenged unsuccessfully in the courts and, over time, restrictions on the Chinese, even those already residing in the United States, were tightened (indeed, the Chinese Exclusion Act passed in 1882 was not repealed until 1942). The exclusion of the Chinese led to an increase in Japanese immigration in the 1880s and 1890s, but by the turn of the century hostility was building against them, too (the Japanese Exclusion Act was passed in 1924), and against several other immigrant groups.

By the late 19th and early 20th centuries, the immigrants from northern and western Europe were being augmented by people from southern and eastern Europe (Spain and Italy, then stretching farther east to Poland and Russia). In 1890, 86% of all foreign-born persons in the United States were of European origin, but only 2% were from southern Europe—almost exclusively Italy. Only 30 years later, in 1920, it was still true that 86% of the foreign-born were Europeans, but 14% were southern Europeans—a sevenfold increase.

Immigration to the United States (and Canada) reached a peak in the first decade of the 20th century, when 1.6 million entered Canada and nearly nine million entered the United States, accounting for more than 1 in 10 of all Americans at that time. This represents one of the most massive population shifts in history. Compared to the United States, European wages were low and unemployment rates high. Economies were very weak in some of the less developed areas of southern and eastern Europe. Eastern Europe was also undergoing tremendous social and political instability, and the Russian pogrom against Jews caused many people to flee the region.

In a series of laws in the 1920s, Congress imposed for the first time a numeric limit on immigration. The National Origins Quota, put in place in 1929, based immigration numbers on the percentage of each nationality group in the United States in 1790 (the first US Census) and then traced "the additions to that number of subsequent immigration."[6] The net effect of these calculations was to greatly reduce the number of southern Europeans, especially Italians and Greeks, who could legally enter the United States, since there had been very few of them counted in the 1790 census.

The McCarran-Walter Act (the Immigration and Nationality Act of 1952) retained the system of national origin quotas while adding to it a system of preferences based largely on occupation.[7] The act permitted up to 50% of the visas from each country to be taken by highly skilled persons whose services were urgently needed. Relatives of American citizens were ranked next, followed by people with no salable skills and no relatives who were citizens of the United States. Thus, the freedom of migration into the United States was severely restricted, even from those countries with an advantage according to the national origins quota system.

The Immigration and Naturalization Act (INA) of 1965 ended the nearly half-century of national origins as the principal determinant of who could enter this country from non–Western Hemisphere nations. Although the criterion of national origins is gone, restrictions on the numbers of immigrants remain, including a limit on immigrants from Western Hemisphere as well as non–Western Hemisphere nations. A system of preference was retained but modified to give relatives of American citizens a first crack at immigration. Parents of US citizens could migrate regardless of the quota. A subsequent amendment to the INA includes the requirement that occupational preference applicants provide a certification by the US Labor Department that their skills are required in the United States. Another amendment to the law dictates that parents of US citizens have highest priority only if their child is at least 21 years old. The intent of that change was to eliminate what many people believed to be a fairly frequent ploy of a pregnant woman entering the country illegally, bearing her child in the United States (the child then being a US citizen), and then applying for citizenship on the basis of being a parent of a US citizen. Although there is little evidence to suggest that pregnant women now routinely cross the border illegally to have babies, there are many undocumented immigrant women in the United States who get pregnant and have a baby. These children are sometimes referred to as "anchor babies" because they provide an "anchor" for the family in the United States once the child becomes an adult.

Recent Immigration Trends

Since the change in immigration legislation in the 1960s (including its various amendments over time), European immigrants to the United States have been replaced almost completely by those from Latin America (especially Mexico, but more recently from Guatemala, Honduras, and El Salvador), Asia (especially China, India, and the Philippines, as well as Vietnam and South Korea), and increasingly Africa. The annual number of legal permanent immigrants peaked in 2006, at 1.2 million.

Migration between Mexico and the United States represents the largest sustained flow of migrant workers over the last several decades, although it also took a hit with the global recession starting in 2007 and has diminished significantly since then both because the birth rate in Mexico has dropped nearly to replacement level and because the Mexican economy is now better able than in the past to absorb new entrants into the labor force (Figure 7.4). In fact, immigrants from

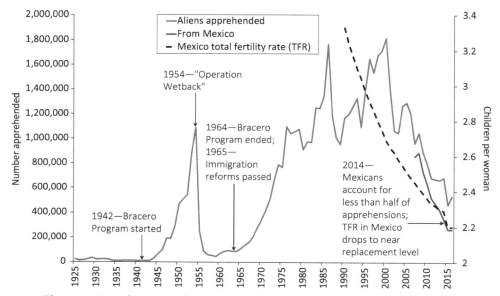

Figure 7.4. Apprehensions of undocumented immigrants, 1925–2015.
Source: Adapted from John R. Weeks, *Population: An Introduction to Concepts and Issues*, 13th ed. (Boston: Cengage, 2020), 275.

Mexico are no longer the largest group from any given country into the United States. The number of legal immigrants has been surpassed by those from China and India, and the number of undocumented immigrants from Mexico has dropped precipitously since the beginning of the 21st century.[8] Data from the US Census Bureau on the foreign-born population point to the shifts in immigration trends, as noted in an article from the *New York Times*:

> The Census Bureau's figures for 2017 confirm a major shift in who is coming to the United States. For years, newcomers tended to be from Latin America, but a Brookings Institution analysis of that data shows that 41 percent of the people who said they arrived since 2010 came from Asia. Just 39 percent were from Latin America. About 45 percent were college educated, the analysis found, compared with about 30 percent of those who came between 2000 and 2009. "This is quite different from what we had thought," said William H. Frey, the senior demographer at

the Brookings Institution who conducted the analysis. "We think of immigrants as being low-skilled workers from Latin America, but for recent arrivals that's much less the case. People from Asia have overtaken people from Latin America."[9]

Not all immigrants are legal permanent residents, of course. Many are undocumented (in legal terms, having a "lack of legal status"). In the United States there were an estimated 10.5 million undocumented immigrants (the US government uses "undocumented," "unauthorized," and "illegal" to describe this population) in 2017, but that number was lower than the peak of 12.2 million in 2007.[10] Mexico represents the single largest source of immigrants (legal and undocumented) to the United States, with the 12 million immigrants from Mexico accounting for about 1 in 4 immigrants. Less than half (45%) of the immigrants from Mexico are undocumented, according to estimates prepared by the Pew Research Center in Washington, DC, but they account for about half of the country's undocumented immigrant population, which in turn accounts for almost one-fourth of the foreign-born population.

Migration from Mexico to the United States began in earnest early in the 20th century, increasing especially in the 1920s and 1930s. That flow was then halted by a combination of the Great Depression and the concomitant discrimination against immigrants that surfaced during this period, leading to massive deportations of many immigrants (legal and otherwise), including many from Mexico.

Labor shortages in agriculture during World War II, however, led to a renewed invitation for Mexican workers to migrate to the United States. In 1942, the United States signed a treaty with the government of Mexico to create a system of contract labor whereby Mexican laborers (*braceros*—literally those who work with their arms) would enter the United States for a specified period of time to work. After the war ended, the bracero program remained in place, but it was not until the early 1950s that the number of Mexican contract workers began to increase noticeably,[11] as can be seen in Figure 7.4. By the mid-1950s, the contract workers had been joined by many undocumented immigrants from Mexico, and the United States reacted in 1954 by deporting more than a million Mexicans (some later found to be US citizens) in what was called "Operation Wetback."

The bracero program was ended formally in 1964, and in 1965 the new immigration act, which ended the national origins quota system, also put a numerical limit on the number of legal immigrants to the United States from countries in the Western Hemisphere. Neither action noticeably slowed the migration from Mexico, which was by then well entrenched because there was and still is a demand for immigrant labor. However, both of these government actions did jointly conspire to increase the number of immigrants classified as illegal or undocumented.[12] This is a critical point with respect to undocumented immigration from Mexico. The flow from Mexico to the United States began because workers were needed and the government agreed to provide them with temporary work visas. Since the 1960s, however, the labor supply has continued to be needed, but the government has been less willing to provide documentation for the immigrants, so they "enter without inspection." In other words, the flow of immigrant workers continued, but it came to be defined as illegal.

I should point out that there are two primary ways by which a person becomes an undocumented immigrant. Entering the country without inspection is the obvious way, but a person may also enter the country with a tourist or other visa and then overstay the visa. For example, you may arrive with a student visa, attend college in the United States, and then decide not to return home, at which point you become an illegal immigrant. Almost two-thirds (62%) of undocumented immigrants coming into the United States in 2016 were visa overstayers, and that pattern has prevailed for several years.[13]

The 1965 Immigration Act opened the door to migration in a way that will define the future demographic trends in the United States. You can see in Figure 7.5, in a graph put together by the Migration Information Source in Washington, DC, that the foreign-born population (including both legal and undocumented immigrants) has jumped tremendously since 1965, pushing the percentage of foreign-born back to a level very close to where the country was in 1890.

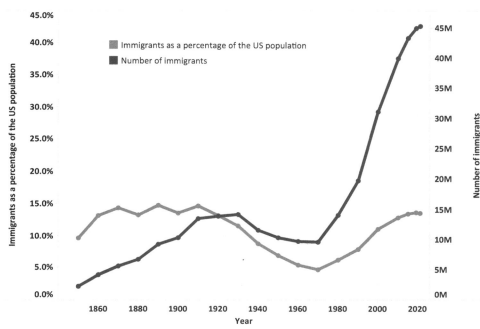

Figure 7.5. Number of immigrants and their share of the total US population, 1850–2021

The Future Is a Foreign Country

It is common to hear that the demographic future of the United States is "majority minority." However, this claim is based on a whole set of complicated assumptions about how people identify themselves. That is a moving target, partly because of the influence of immigrants and then their children and subsequent generations, and partly because social change routinely redefines people's sense of themselves and others.

On an everyday basis, a person's identity tends to be based on the concepts of race and ethnicity. The US Census Bureau asks two questions to allow people to report their race/ethnicity. The first of these is about "race" and the second is about your identity as "Hispanic." Over time, however, the Census Bureau has kept adding more detailed categories of "race" to which people can respond in the decennial census and the various other census surveys, including the American Community

Survey and Current Population Survey. Of special note is that people are able to check more than one box, encouraging a recognition of diversity. In the 2020 US Census, 10.2% of all 331 million respondents indicated that they identified with two or more races. This was more than 4 times higher than the 2.3% in the 2010 Census. Analysis of data from people who have taken genetic ancestry tests like those offered by Ancestry.com suggests that at least some of the rise in multiracial identification comes from greater knowledge that people have about their own genetic background.[14]

Despite increasing diversity, it was nonetheless the case that 90% of Americans indicated that they identified themselves with only one race, and the clear majority of them (69%) said they were white. Overall, that meant that in 2020, 62% of Americans considered themselves to be "white alone" with respect to race. This was, of course, a fairly substantial drop from 50 years prior to that, when 89% of the population was white—when "white" was not yet thought of as an ethnic category.[15] Interpreting this gets a bit more complicated when we take Hispanic ethnicity into account.

A person of "Hispanic, Latino, or Spanish" origin is defined as one who is "of Cuban, Mexican, Puerto Rican, South or Central American, or other Spanish culture or origin regardless of race." The relatively "indeterminate" concept of Hispanic is often confusing to those arriving in the United States from those origin countries,[16] because it is not used anywhere outside of the United States and was not asked of everyone on the US Census until 1980. Immigrants from Nicaragua, for example, will find themselves identified officially as Hispanic, while having a high probability of being thought of unofficially as Mexican or more generally as Latino/a (or Latinx), even though they are likely to think of themselves as "Nicaraguans." The majority of Hispanics in the United States are indeed from Mexico, and despite the discrimination that they have faced over time, they are less discriminated against than Blacks. "Mexican Americans intermarry much more than do Blacks, live in less segregated areas, and face less labor market discrimination. . . . In this sense, racial boundaries for Mexican Americans are clearly less rigid than for African Americans."[17]

In the 2020 census, 19% of the American population identified as Hispanic, but 65% of them also identified their race as "White alone." The second most common race response for Hispanics was "Other race," which was checked by 35% of Hispanics, reflecting their confusion about the race question. A little less than 2% of Hispanics considered their race to be "Black or African American," and so in real-life situations they might identify themselves as either Hispanic or Black, depending upon the context. Is it appropriate to essentially force Hispanics into a single race/ethnic category of "Hispanic" while ignoring their separate race designation? As Dowell Myers and Morris Levy have argued: "At different moments the same person, such as an African American who is also Hispanic, might wish to be categorized with all African Americans or, alternatively, with all Hispanics. For some purposes, it clearly is desirable to count all people of a race rather than just the non-Hispanic remainder."[18]

In the 21st century, the racial and ethnic changes have become so substantial that Anthony Perez and Charles Hirschman refer to the phenomenon of "emerging American identities,"[19] while William Frey labels it a "diversity explosion,"[20] and Richard Alba calls it the "great demographic illusion.[21] The "diversity explosion" has also created what we might call a "diversity confusion or illusion," because the data collected by the government can be organized in several different ways, each of which tells a somewhat different story,[22] and also because diversity is not just a function of "race" or "ethnicity" but also your social and geographic background, as I noted previously with respect to the foreign-born population residing in the United States.

On an everyday basis people are conscious of ethnicity in a broader context than found in the census questions on race and ethnicity. The concept here is your ancestry—where did you come from? Although this question is not asked on the long form of the census, it is incorporated into the ongoing American Community Survey. Data from the 2019 survey show that 84% of people responded to the ancestry question, and the origin most often mentioned (9.1%) was "German." The next most common response was "African-American" (7.7%), followed by "Mexican" (7.2%). There were 20 million people who responded that their ancestry was "Irish" (6.3% of the total), which is pretty remarkable when you consider that there are fewer than 5 million people living in Ireland, and not even all of them are Irish.

The fact that Irish and Italian are among the top 10 ancestries listed by Americans on the Census Bureau's American Community Survey is a testament to how societies can change, since both groups were heavily discriminated against when they first arrived in the United States in the 19th century. To be sure, a genuine concern in the widespread use of the racial/ethnic categories discussed above is that they tend to reify the concept of race—that different groups are inherently different—and in some ways this is how the eugenics movement of the early 20th century lives on. In the future can we just talk about "us" (meaning everyone) instead of the conversation so often being about "us" and "them"?

How Will the Future Be Different?

We obviously cannot predict the future, but demographic trends can at least give us a sense of what our society will look like, and from that we can try to deduce societal responses. For example, even if we shut off all immigration as of today, the racial/ethnic diversity of the country will be different in the future than it is now, because of the fact that past immigration has already made younger groups racially more diverse than older groups. As the younger groups age, the demographic composition of the United States will shift. You can see this in Table 7.2.

Table 7.2 The Racial/Ethnic Composition of the 2017 US Population by Age Group (in percentages)

Age group	Hispanic	Non-Hispanic white	Non-Hispanic Black	Non-Hispanic American Indian or Alaska Native	Non-Hispanic Asian/Pacific Islander	Non-Hispanic Other
0–19	25	51	14	1	5	5
20–39	21	55	14	1	7	3
40–59	16	63	12	1	6	2
60+	9	75	10	1	5	1
All ages	18	61	12	1	6	3

Source: Steven Ruggles, Sarah Flood, Ronald Goeken, Josiah Grover, Erin Meyer, Jose Pacas, and Matthew Sobek. *Integrated Public Use Microdata Series: Version 8.0* [dataset]. Minneapolis: University of Minnesota, 2018. http://doi.org/10.18128/D010.V8.0.

At the same time, the percentage of foreign-born varies by age in a somewhat different pattern, as you can see in Figure 7.6. This is due partly to changes in migration laws and in the patterns of un-documented immigration, as well as to the fact that immigrants tend to be younger adults of reproductive age whose children are then born in the United States. This latter phenomenon is, of course, a major contributor to diversity at the younger ages, and then those people age through time, creating more diversity at each successive age.

The rise in the percentage of foreign-born among the Generation Xers is, of course, a result of the 1965 changes to the immigration laws,

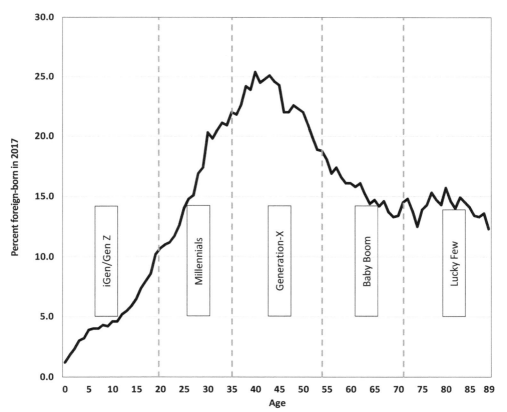

Figure 7.6. Foreign-born US population by age (in percentages)
Source: IPUMS data for the 2019 ACS

in combination with the age pattern of immigrants, which you can see in Figure 7.7.

So, you can see that the future will be different in terms of race, ethnicity, and percentage of foreign-born by age, even if we experience no further immigration. Of course, we almost certainly will continue to have immigrants, and the US Census Bureau has built that into its latest set of projections, which go all the way out to the year 2060. Its basic assumptions are that the population of the United States will increase from our current 331 million to 404 million between now and 2060, through a combination of more people aging and dying, babies

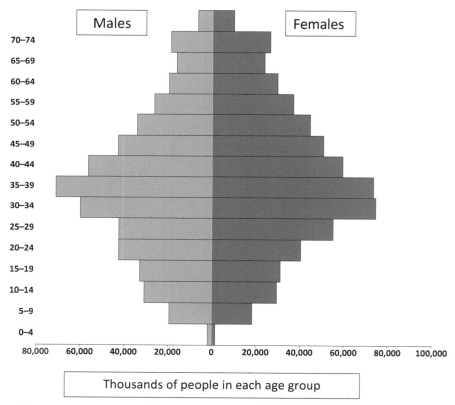

Figure 7.7. Age structure of legal immigrants to the United States

Source: Adapted from John R. Weeks, *Population: An Introduction to Concepts and Issues*, 13th ed. (Boston: Cengage, 2020), figure 8.7.

Figure 7.8. Total fertility rate estimated, 2015–2020
Source: Adapted from John R. Weeks, *Population: An Introduction to Concepts and Issues*, 13th ed. (Boston: Cengage, 2020), figure 5.1.

being born (albeit fewer per woman, but a disproportionate share to immigrant mothers), and a continuous stream of about 1 million immigrants per year. Overall, this leads to a projected modest increase in the overall percentage of the population that is foreign-born, from the current level of 14% to 17% in 2060.[23]

Where will people be coming from? It is notable that there are projected increases in the percentage of the population that is of African and of Asian origin. We can understand that best by looking at where the populations of the world are growing most quickly and thus where the pressure to migrate will be strongest. Africa and Asia are the places with the highest fertility rates and thus the greatest pressure on younger populations. You can see this in Figure 7.8.

Conclusion

The future is likely to be one with a continued flow of immigrants, including from places that do not currently send us a lot. The main lesson here is that the more of the "others" we know, the greater our likelihood of accepting them. As the United States becomes increasingly urban and older, communities face extinction without new faces.

Those new faces will come from abroad, and as they make their way into the "heartland," the face and politics of America will almost certainly change. Not without a fuss, I expect, but change, nonetheless.

At the same time, we should keep in mind that immigrants are being incorporated more successfully in the United States than the media attention to this issue might suggest. A 2019 issue of the *Economist* summed it up this way:

> By most measures, immigrants in the United States are integrating as well as ever. Their unemployment rate is a negligible 3.5%, lower than for the native-born. Only half of first-generation immigrants speak English "very well," but by the second-generation English dominates even among Hispanics, who are surrounded by other Spanish-speakers. Only 6% of second-generation speak mostly Spanish. By the fourth generation, half of those with Hispanic forebears are so well integrated that they no longer identify as Hispanic.[24]

This is backed up especially by the research of Rubén Rumbaut and his colleagues.[25] It reminds us that over the last century the Irish became "white," as did Italians and Puerto Ricans.[26] In recent years it has become commonplace for a taco truck to be the preferred way to feed people at a special occasion. We are doing things differently than we used to, and that will continue into the future, as the demographics of the country continue to evolve.

Acknowledgments

Portions of this chapter are adapted from John R. Weeks, *Population: An Introduction to Concepts and Issues*, 13th ed. (Boston: Cengage, 2020). Many thanks to Alex Aleinikoff for helpful comments on an earlier draft.

Notes

1. L. P. Hartley, *The Go-Between* (New York: Stein and Day, 1967).
2. For a review, see Abhijit V. Banerjee and Esther Duflo, *Good Economics for Hard Times* (New York: Public Affairs, 2019).

3. Lawrence Dodds and Raziye Akkoe, "Mapped: Where Is UKIP's Support Strongest? Where There Are No Immigrants," *The Telegraph*, April 17, 2015, https://www.telegraph.co.uk/news/politics/ukip/11539388/Mapped-where-is-Ukips-support-strongest-Where-there-are-no-immigrants.html.

4. Migration Policy Institute, *Major US Immigration Laws, 1790-Present* (2013), https://www.migrationpolicy.org/research/timeline-1790.

5. US Immigration and Naturalization Service, *An Immigrant Nation: United States Regulation of Immigration, 1798–1991* (Washington, DC: Government Printing Office, 1991).

6. See Robert A. Divine, *American Immigration Policy, 1924–1952* (New Haven, CT: Yale University Press, 1957); Alejandro Portes and Rubén G. Rumbaut, *Immigrant America: A Portrait*, 4th ed. (Berkeley: University of California Press, 2014).

7. Charles B. Keely, "Effects of the Immigration Act of 1965 on Selected Population Characteristics of Immigrants to the United States," *Demography* 8, no. 2 (May 1971): 157–70.

8. Ana Gonzalez-Barrera and Jens Manuel Krogstad, "What We Know about Illegal Immigration from Mexico," Pew Research Center, June 28, 2019, http://www.pewresearch.org/fact-tank/2018/12/03/what-we-know-about-illegal-immigration-from-mexico/.

9. Sabrina Tavernise, "U.S. Has Highest Share of Foreign-Born Since1910, with More Coming from Asia," *New York Times*, September 13, 2018, https://www.nytimes.com/2018/09/13/us/census-foreign-population.html.

10. Jynnah Radford and Luis Noe-Bustamante, "Facts on U.S. Immigrants, 2017: Statistical Portrait of the Foreign-Born Population in the United States," Pew Research Center, June 3, 2019, https://www.pewresearch.org/hispanic/2019/06/03/facts-on-u-s-immigrants-2017-data/.

11. Garcia y Griego, M., J. R. Weeks, and R. Ham-Chande, "Mexico," in *Handbook on International Migration*, ed. W. J. Serow, C. B. Nam, D. F. Sly, and R. H. Weller (New York: Greenwood Press, 1990).

12. US Immigration, *An Immigrant Nation*.

13. Robert Warren, "U.S. Undocumented Population Continued to Fall from 2016 to 2017, and Visa Overstays Significantly Exceeded Illegal Crossings for the Seventh Consecutive Year," Center for Migration Studies, January 16, 2019, http://cmsny.org/publications/essay-2017-undocumented-and-overstays/.

14. Sasha Shen Johre, Aliya Saperstein, and Jill A. Hollenbach, "Measuring Race and Ancestry in the Age of Genetic Testing," *Demography* 58, no. 3 (June 2021): 785–810.

15. Pamela Perry, "White Means Never Having to Say You're Ethnic: White Youth and the Construction of 'Cultureless' Identities," *Journal of Contemporary Ethnography* 30, no. 1 (2001): 56–91.

16. José Enrique Idler, *Officially Hispanic: Classification Policy and Identity* (Lanham, MD: Rowman and Littlefield, 2007); Mark Hugo Lopez, Jens Manuel Krogstad, and Jeffrey S. Passel, "Who Is Hispanic?" Pew Research Center, September 15, 2022, https://www.pewresearch.org/fact-tank/2019/11/11/who-is-hispanic/.

17. Edward E. Telles and Vilma Ortiz, *Generations of Exclusion: Mexican Americans, Assimilation, and Race* (New York: Russell Sage Foundation, 2008), 264.

18. Dowell Myers and Morris Levy, "Racial Population Projections and Reactions to Alternative News Accounts of Growing Diversity," *Annals of the American Academy of Political and Social Science* 677, no. 1 (2018): 218.

19. Anthony Perez and Charles Hirschman, "The Changing Racial and Ethnic Composition of the US Population: Emerging American Identities," *Population and Development Review* 35, no. 1 (2009): 1–51.

20. William Frey, *Diversity Explosion: How New Racial Demographics Are Remaking America* (Washington, DC: Brookings Institution Press, 2018).

21. Richard Alba, *The Great Demographic Illusion* (Princeton, NJ: Princeton University Press, 2020).

22. Kenneth Prewitt, "The Census Race Classification: Is It Doing Its Job?" *Annals of the American Academy of Political and Social Science* 677, no. 1 (2018): 8–24.

23. Jonathan Vespa, Lauren Medina, and David M. Armstrong, "Demographic Turning Points for the United States: Population Projections for 2020 to 2060," in US Census Bureau, *Current Population Reports: Population Estimates and Projections* (Washington, DC, 2020).

24. "Special Report: Migration," *The Economist*, November 14, 2019, 9, https://www.economist.com/special-report/2019-11-16.

25. See Ruben G. Rumbaut, Douglas S. Massey, and Frank D. Bean, "Linguistic Life Expectancies: Immigrant Language Retention in Southern California," *Population and Development Review* 32, no. 3 (2006); 447–60; see also Portes and Rumbaut, *Immigrant America*; Cynthia Feliciano and Ruben G. Rumbaut, "Varieties of Ethnic Self-Identities: Children of Immigrants in Middle Adulthood," *RSF: The Russell Sage Foundation Journal of the Social Sciences* 4, no. 3 (2018): 26–46.

26. Mara Loveman and Jeronimo O. Muniz, "How Puerto Rico Became White: Boundary Dynamics and Intercensus Racial Reclassification," *American Sociological Review* 72, no. 6 (2007): 915–39.

CHAPTER 8

And Jesús, Where Is Home for You?

Jesús I. Valles

"And Jesús, where is home for you?"
                    is a place question
        I only have time answers for &
time is a question of everybody left that place
        is a lie because there are still those we left then
is a Chinese Exclusionary Act becomes the blueprint for
        the hurt, how to best turn a people into a plague
is years later, Ronald Reagan signs a Simpson-Mazzoli act is
        Haitian blood shut out is three million people sin visas
is a pregnant mami, happy-fat rose-cheek lady is
        a belly full of promised green card is a bridge crossed
is a bridge burnt when she births the paper
        baby in Juárez is a Mexican & illegally crossed baby
is a wetback if it can't make that pretty mouth sound
        is a tongue shaped coup & all the little teeth
is a way to pass the time which is a place is
        a 1996 Clinton hand signing a law
is the Illegal Immigration Reform and Immigrant
        Responsibility Act is a pinche mamada
is another way to say You are not welcome is
        a brutal brick in Obama's DREAM Act

is another way to say Wait. Just wait. Just. Wait. is
	another way to say, No, not them. We meant the good ones.
is we couldn't all go to abuelito's funeral, sin papeles death is
	like that is sometimes all I want to do is die, too
is the spirit of the law means all that parchment is haunted is
	a ghost is the only way we can get out or in
is it would be some bullshit if the next life had checkpoints is
	the thing I hated about Coco & Beetlejuice
is even the dead can't avoid bureaucracy & is
	the refusal of any god that asks for proof I lived a sin
is a notice to appear, is an order for deportation is
	an Executive Order & and Executive Order
is a way to kill a people whose only home is a time is
	a way of saying it might be best to ask me
"When is home for you?" & I would show you every ugly
	time thing living inside me.

PART II

BEYOND A "NATION OF IMMIGRANTS"

CHAPTER 9

A Nation of Immigrants

A Short History of an Idea

Mae Ngai

The idea that America is a nation of immigrants is relatively new, born in the post–World War II period and popularized, perhaps most famously, by John F. Kennedy. In 1958 Kennedy, then senator from Massachusetts and himself the descendant of an Irish immigrant, published a little book titled *Nation of Immigrants*. The book promoted a historical narrative that the United States is, and has always been, a nation of immigrants, and celebrated the achievements of Americans of foreign birth, such as Carl Schurz, Andrew Carnegie, Samuel Gompers, and Albert Einstein.

The purpose of the book was to advocate for immigration reform legislation in Congress. As senator, Kennedy had sponsored bills to ease restrictions on foreign adoptions, and he co-sponsored the Lehman-Humphrey bills that would have repealed the national origin quotas. Those quotas, in place since 1924, explicitly and grossly discriminated against immigrants from southern and eastern Europe. Great Britain, for example, enjoyed an annual quota of 34,000, and Germany, 51,000, which were left mostly unused; Italy's quota, in contrast, was 5,800, Hungary's, 473, and that of Greece, 100. The national origin quotas were the triumph of two decades of nativist agitation against the so-called new immigrants—Jews, Italians, Slavs—whose labor had powered the industrialization and urbanization of the United States, but whose presence offended native-white elites and skilled workers on grounds of cultural difference and economic competition.[1]

As president, Kennedy sponsored an immigration bill that repealed the national origin quotas. After his assassination, Lyndon Johnson took up the bill, which ultimately Congress passed as the Hart-Celler Immigration and Nationality Act of 1965. In the run-up to the 1965 act, Kennedy's book was reissued, with an introduction by the late president's brother, Robert Kennedy. In 2008 the book was again published, this time with an introduction by Senator Edward Kennedy, who himself championed immigration reform during the first decade of the twenty-first century.[2]

A Nation of Immigrants tells a simple story about "continuous waves" of immigration since the colonial era and the contributions of immigrants to the building of the nation—contributions they made as farmers, workers, and consumers; as scientists, artists, and writers. Each successive wave faced difficulty and hardship, and occasionally discrimination, but each eventually climbed the ladder of socioeconomic mobility and realized the American Dream. This narrative is familiar to all of us. But it was a new idea in the post–World War II era.

A Nation of Immigrants was first published as a modest pamphlet, of just 40 pages, of which 15 were devoted to an analysis of policy and recommendations for reform. The second edition, published in 1964, was enlarged to 160 pages. The text was the same, with some interesting, subtle revisions. The original section on "Waves of Immigration" was divided into two chapters, one on "The Pre-Revolutionary Forces" and the second on "The Post-Revolutionary Forces," in effect establishing a periodization divided by the American revolution. Those of us who study and teach immigration history would find this periodization strange. But it accomplished two things. First, by noting the early Dutch, French, Huguenot, Swedish, Irish, German, and other settlers, alongside the English, it downplayed the role of the latter and rewrote European empire-building as diverse immigrations (although it barely mentioned Spain's conquest of Florida and the Southwest). Second, by placing all subsequent immigrations into one "post-revolutionary" chapter, it emphasized continuity and made immigrants who came at the turn of the 20th century—those targeted by the national origin quotas—only the latest wave of immigrants in a long succession of waves.

Perhaps not surprisingly, *A Nation of Immigrants* focused entirely on European immigrants. That there was no discussion of Mexican or Asian immigrations reflected the conventional thinking that they were temporary migrants, birds of passage and sojourners. One paragraph discussed the Chinese Exclusion Act, calling it an exception to the historical practice of nondiscrimination. The picture gallery of notable immigrants in the second edition included just one person who was not a European, the Japanese scientist Hideyo Noguchi.

The second edition continued to erase Mexicans and other Latinos from immigration history. But it did give the Chinese more attention, perhaps owing to Cold War politics. Since the text itself could not be changed, the editors included Chinese in an expanded glossy photo insert, with several photographs and references in the captions. The captions themselves in the photo section constituted a mini-narrative. A reader who might peruse without reading the book itself (a common enough practice) might come away with an understanding that Chinese held a respected place in immigration history.

The third edition of the book, issued in 2008, tackled the erasure of Latino immigration, but indirectly—by adding a map and appendices on chronology, major legislation since 1965, and a bibliography, all of which incorporated Mexican, Puerto Rican, Cuban, and other Latinx migrations. Senator Edward Kennedy's introduction did not mention Latinos explicitly but highlighted the need to legalize the undocumented population. Nevertheless, readers of the book in 2008 would have been struck by the contrast between the contemporary resonance of the introduction and appendices and the text's plainly outmoded Eurocentrism.

Kennedy's *Nation of Immigrants* was the direct product of the post–World War II liberal movement to repeal the national origin quotas. The Anti-Defamation League of B'nai B'rith had proposed to the senator that he author a short book on the subject, in order to assist immigration reform efforts. Throughout the 1950s and 1960s the ADL published scores of books and pamphlets, many commissioned to academics, which aimed to combat not just antisemitism but racism, nativism, and religious intolerance in general. One gets a sense of the project from the titles of ADL's various publications: *Civil Rights and Minorities* (1956), *Negro American Intelligence* (1964), *Privacy and Prejudice: Religious Discrimination in Social Clubs* (1962); *Prejudiced—How Do People Get That Way?* (1959).[3]

These efforts were characteristic of the belief held by many postwar liberals and social scientists that prejudice was born of ignorance and could be resolved with education and persuasion. Francis Brown, a sociologist, explained at the time that "the whole problem of minorities must be approached from the point of view of modifying basic attitudes. The first step," he added, "is knowledge of and appreciation for the contribution of each group."[4]

When the ADL pitched the idea for *Nation of Immigrants* to Senator Kennedy, it proposed an outline that was prepared by Arthur Mann, then a young history professor at Smith College. Mann was the first PhD student of Oscar Handlin at Harvard. Handlin, born in Brooklyn in 1915 to Russian immigrants, was one of the first American Jews to hold a full professorship at Harvard. Handlin founded the field of American immigration as an academic historical inquiry, and he was the first to study immigrants as subjects—as historical actors—rather than as objects—that is, as problems for study. He was also active in postwar liberal causes. He wrote several books for the ADL and was a leading voice in immigration reform matters.[5]

And indeed, Kennedy's *Nation of Immigrants* quotes the famous first lines of Handlin's 1952 Pulitzer Prize–winning book, *The Uprooted*: "Once I thought to write a history of the immigrants in America. Then I discovered that the immigrants *were* American history."

But Kennedy (or more likely, his anonymous staff writers) drew from Handlin only in a partial and superficial way. Handlin's view was not merely celebratory; in fact, he believed immigration history had already moved beyond the compensatory stage to yield larger lessons about American national development. His claim that "the immigrants *were* American history" actually carried a double meaning—the familiar one about immigration waves and heritages, but also his theory that the alienation and eventual assimilation of immigrants exemplified the more general process of Americans' transition to modernity. Handlin bore an ultimate faith in assimilation and modernity but was also, and perhaps more, interested in the "tragic depths" of experience that accompanied America's "progress and growth," which were known to immigrants and native-born alike: the move from countryside to city, the breakup of village or small-town life, the transformation of the family, the alienation of factory work and the city.[6] His work echoed that of the sociologists of the interwar period, especially those at the University of Chicago—Robert E. Park, Louis Wirth, and others—who were interested in the nature of ethno-racial relations as an integral part of modern urban and industrial life.[7]

Notably, Handlin believed that institutions of American civil society, including immigrant-ethnic groups' voluntary associations and newspapers, promoted assimilation. Here, Handlin drew from a consensus view in postwar American political science that emphasized that the United States' robust civil society was the lynchpin of democracy and individual freedom, which accounted for the relatively small footprint of the central state.[8] Historians have since rejected Handlin's thesis that European migrants in the late 19th and early 20th centuries were premodern peasants who lived outside of capitalist market relations, and scholars no longer subscribe to Handlin's normative assumptions about assimilation.[9] My point is to situate Handlin's interpretation of immigration history in the context of midcentury social science thinking about modernity and democracy.

Kennedy may have agreed with Handlin's analysis, but he did not emphasize it. Nor did he absorb the complexities of immigration history suggested by Mann's outline. The purpose of A Nation of Immigrants was to mobilize a general audience to support immigration law reform. Kennedy opted to write a more celebratory history of inclusion and contribution that exalted a simplistic teleology of assimilation. He was inattentive to the "tragic depths" of experience that accompanied the transition to modernity, about which Handlin wrote so poignantly.

Both Handlin and Kennedy's thinking exemplified the racial liberalism of the times, an outlook toward racial reform most famously captured by Gunnar Myrdal in *An American Dilemma*, the epic study of American race relations underwritten by the Carnegie Foundation and published in 1944. In that book Myrdal wrote, "This country has a national theory, if not a consistent practice, of freedom and equality for all. What America is constantly reaching for is democracy at home and abroad. The main trend in its history is the gradual realization of the American Creed."[10] That view established what the scholar Nikhil Singh aptly described as "the rhetorical framework in which the liberal, perfectionist emphasis upon racial reform . . . is something that is paradoxically always already accomplished, and something that is never quite complete."[11]

Handlin and Kennedy articulated the exceptionalism of the American Creed in a Cold War frame. *A Nation of Immigrants*, and the reform legislation that it promoted, was preoccupied with the image of American democracy abroad. Like Jim Crow segregation, the national origin quota system harmed the United States' reputation in its global fight against communism. The geopolitical stakes were particularly high in southern Europe and Asia, where immigration quotas were especially low. Domestically, American Jews, Italian Americans, and other European ethnics who were experiencing unprecedented socioeconomic mobility in the postwar years, were less interested in actually increasing immigration from their ancestral countries than they were in eliminating that which symbolized their historical discrimination. So the 1965 Immigration Act was written more as a symbolic reform than a substantive change in policy. While repealing the national origin quotas, it maintained a low overall numerical ceiling with restrictive quotas for all countries.[12] Upon its passage, Handlin himself remarked, "The change in our immigration law will have only minor quantitative significance. Revision is important as a matter of principle."[13]

Handlin's writings on immigration reform always emphasized symbolic themes and objectives. Throughout the 1950s and early 1960s he wrote opinion essays for *Commentary*, a liberal Jewish periodical, that stressed a politics of inclusion for Euro-American ethnics. The national origin quotas "cast the slur of inferiority," he wrote, "upon all those whose grandfathers would have been reckoned fit, under these laws, for admission to the United States. . . . The Italian American has the right to be heard [on matters of national interest] *as* an Italian American. The quotas implicitly pass a judgment upon his own place in the United States."[14]

Handlin exercised profound influence over the conceptualization of immigration reform, serving as consultant to President Harry Truman's immigration commission and to Senator Herbert Lehman (D-NY), the major sponsor of the immigration reform bills in the 1950s that eventually passed, culminating in the passage of the Hart-Celler Act of 1965. Handlin wrote essays on immigration history for both, including critiques of the national origins quota law, its consequences for American inclusion and citizenship, and a prescription for reform based on equal quotas for all countries. Oscar Handlin bears the unusual distinction of a historian who wrote the historiography of the 1965 immigration act at the time of its making.[15]

If the Hart-Celler Act of 1965 reflected a confluence of foreign policy and domestic interests in symbolic reform, Handlin was less concerned with foreign policy than he was in fulfilling the assimilation promise of American history. In addition to his writings on immigration reform, he wrote about the paradoxes of identity for American Jews, whose religiosity seemed to wane in proportion to their degree of assimilation, and wrestled the differences between European ethnic groups and racial minorities (Blacks, Puerto Ricans, and Chinese). He was not a conservative Cold War warrior: he opposed McCarthyism and defended civil liberties; his commitments for immigration reform were animated by antipathy to the anti-communist McCarran-Walter Immigration and Nationality Act of 1952, which added national security provisions to the national origins system. Nevertheless, the Cold War shaped the exceptionalist narrative of American society written by Handlin and other historians and social scientists. Although they pushed hard against the old-line white supremacists who were obstacles to Black civil rights and immigration reform, the liberals' vision was ultimately limited and contained by the US nation-state. The emphasis on symbolic reform, articulated in a politics of recognition and formulations of abstract equality, advanced the foreign-policy agenda without requiring a deeper reckoning with class and racial inequalities that immigration policy had historically produced.[16]

The liberal nationalism of Handlin and Kennedy was at a considerable remove from a more progressive and cosmopolitan trend of liberal pluralism in American politics that flourished in the 1930s and 1940s. Two writers, Louis Adamic and Carey McWilliams, exemplified that trend. Adamic, a Slovenian immigrant, was a popular author of many books, most notably the best-selling *Nation of Nations* (1944), and editor of *Common Ground*, a culturally pluralist magazine dedicated to publishing diverse American voices. McWilliams was a native-born white American lawyer and journalist who advocated for minority and immigrant groups. He served as director for the State of California's Division of Immigration and Housing (1938–1942) and was a defense lawyer in the "Sleepy Lagoon" LA murder case involving twelve Chicano youth.

Adamic was born in 1898 in the village of Carniola, in what is now Slovenia (then part of the Austro-Hungarian Empire). As a boy, he had listened to the stories of emigrants who had returned home and was awestruck that ordinary workmen "could make pots of money in a short time, acquire immense holdings, wear a white collar, . . . and eat white bread, soup, and meat on weekdays as well as Sundays."[17] He left Slovenia for the United States when he was 15 years old; he served in the army in World War I, with posts in Panama, Louisiana, and Honolulu. After the war he moved to Los Angeles and worked in construction and then as clerk in the pilot house in the port of San Pedro, which had an ethnic Croatian fishing community. There he expanded on his writing for periodicals and met McWilliams.

McWilliams was a recent arrival to Los Angeles from Denver and, like Adamic, a journalist and avid observer of the great Los Angeles boom of the 1920s. Adamic and McWilliams forged a friendship based on a shared identity as "American enthusiasts [who] yet, in different ways, felt alienated from the mainstream of American life."[18] It is no accident that Adamic's and McWilliams's views formed in Southern California, far from the stuffy hierarchies of Ivy League universities and Washington politics. Los Angeles bespoke that which was new. Almost everyone came from somewhere else; everyone was on the make. McWilliams described the city as the staging ground of an "accelerated reenactment" of the "saga of frontier growth and westward expansion."[19] Adamic saw in Los Angeles a microcosm of America's development: "Los Angeles is America. A jungle," he wrote. "Los Angeles grew up suddenly, planlessly, under the stimuli of the adventurous spirit of millions of people and the profit motive. . . . Inferior as well as superior plants and trees flourish for a time, then both succumb to chaos and decay. They must give way to new plants pushing up from below, and so on. This is freedom under democracy. Jungle Democracy!"[20]

In California and in America, Adamic was struck by the ordinariness of "physical freedom unimaginable in the Old World. At the same time, however," he continued, "I saw that this vast and free land was crisscrossed with cultural walls sheltering snipers, bearing ill-considered posters, casting shadows, keeping men from the other, preventing the full flowering of life."[21] Adamic saw that immigrants' lives were ruled by "haphazardness, chaos, violence and accident," which he attributed to the complexities of freedom, democracy, individualism, and capitalism that defined the "fantastic [United] States."[22]

By the 1930s Adamic was a national figure, publishing two well-received books and frequent essays in *Harper's* and other periodicals. He became editor of the *Foreign Language Information Service*, a newsletter for and about immigrants, and its successor, *Common Ground*, funded by the Carnegie Corporation to promote pluralism. In 1936 Adamic arranged for moving the bronze plaque inscribed with Emma Lazarus's poem, "The New Colossus," to the front entrance to the Statue of Liberty. The poem, written in 1886 for an art auction to raise money for constructing the pedestal of the statue, fell into obscurity until 1903, when a friend commissioned the plaque; however, its placement on the second floor of the pedestal left it largely unseen. It was not until Adamic moved the plaque and drew attention to the poem that the Statue of Liberty assumed its identity as America's welcome to immigrants.[23]

If Adamic believed that immigrants found refuge and freedom in America, he soon developed a more daring idea: that immigrants would change the country, and for the better. In his view, immigrants held the "promise of a possible spiritual and intellectual awakening and flowering of America," whereas the early American stock was "emotionally, spiritually and intellectually flat, for generations . . . pickled in the sour juices of Puritanism, or dried over the sacrificial fires on the altars dedicated to the great god Work."[24] When he wrote *Nation of Nations*, he had concluded that

> the fallacy [of American history as an Anglo-Saxon nation] [was] diffused throughout our national life and thought . . . like a fog rolling about, spreading everywhere. . . . What was desired ultimately . . . was a reorientation of the American state of mind . . . a reevaluation of facts in the American Story so that Immigration might cease to be a footnote . . . and become a main subject in the text, so that each group in our population would be seen as a necessary and integral thread. . . . The pattern of America is all of a piece; it is a blend of cultures. . . . Diversity itself is the pattern, is the stuff and color of the fabric.[25]

Adamic's pluralism differed from that of Handlin's and Kennedy's in some important respects. They all bore faith in the exceptional promise of American democracy, but "nation of nations" and "nation of immigrants" signaled different patterns of national identity. Whereas Adamic saw immigration injecting new life into national complacency, Handlin and Kennedy emphasized immigrants' absorption into the mainstream.

Adamic also considered the so-called Negro Problem a "national question," the term of art among the communist Left to refer to the right of self-determination for oppressed national minorities. He considered racism against Blacks and immigrants to come from the same fount of white Anglo-Saxon superiority and capitalist exploitation. As editor of *Common Ground* (1940–1941), Adamic published articles about racism and racial issues, including essays by Langston Hughes and other

African American writers. He quit the magazine, after editing just six issues, over differences with the publisher, Read Lewis, who disapproved of the relative decline in articles about European immigrants and ethnic groups.[26] The differences between Adamic and Lewis foretold a divide between "ethnicity" (for Europeans) and "race" (for Blacks, Latinas/os, and Asians) that would emerge among social scientists in the 1960s.

Carey McWilliams similarly increasingly emphasized the conditions of African Americans and other non-European minority groups as central to the problem of American democracy. Again, his views were undoubtedly shaped by his experience in California, where Asians and Mexicans were prominent in the working class, especially in agriculture, and as targets of racial discrimination and exclusion. McWilliams's *Factories in the Field* (1939) was a best-selling exposé of California agriculture as a new type, "large scale, intensive, diversified, mechanized," controlled by monopolies and dependent on "cheap labor [from] China, Japan, the Philippines, Puerto Rico, Mexico, the Deep South, and Europe." McWilliams cited an unbroken line of continuity of "theft, fraud, violence, and exploitation" in the patterns of ownership and control in California agriculture dating to the feudalistic Spanish colonial period—an indictment of the ongoing history of settler colonialism in the American West.[27] By the early 1940s McWilliams was arguing that the problem of America's "colored minorities" was more urgent and consequential than that of European ethnics, who he believed were assimilating, which was a nod to their proximity to whiteness. He understood, too, that the reversal of Reconstruction and the promise of democracy for African Americans had foreclosed the possibility of equality for all other racial groups. McWilliams noted, for example, that the Asian exclusionists in California believed the "unsolved Negro problem in the South [was] a warning . . . against a policy to admit further 'colored' people to the United States."[28]

Both Adamic and McWilliams believed that World War II was a wake-up call to the exigencies of decolonization that linked anti-racism domestically and internationally. McWilliams considered the Western attitude of civilizational and racial superiority to be "debunked not only by modern science but the tangible achievements of the so-called backward peoples."[29] Adamic similarly noted that "the unfavorably situated peoples all over the world ... are stirring and heaving toward self-improvement, toward industrialization and higher productivity, toward uniting with one another in common causes of self-realization and development. I am afraid that some of our jingos will presently again begin to talk of the 'yellow peril,' while it seems to me that the chief danger actually exists within the white people—within ourselves."[30]

These connections—between immigrants and racial minorities, between nativism and racism, and between democracy and decolonization—were attenuated, if not absent, in the "nation of immigrants" discourse promoted by Handlin and Kennedy. To be fair, postwar liberals supported civil rights for African Americans and often marched with Dr. Martin Luther King Jr. in the South. But they viewed ethnicity and race as separate concepts, which led to comparisons that were sometimes invidious, such as the "culture of poverty" thesis of social scientists Oscar Lewis, Nathan Glazer, and Daniel Patrick Moynihan. And, of course, the international dimension shifted from anti-colonialism to anti-communism.[31]

In 1951 Oscar Handlin published *The Uprooted*, for which he would win the Pulitzer Prize. Carey McWilliams moved to New York to become editor of *The Nation*, a post he held until 1975. Louis Adamic died from a gunshot wound at his home in New Jersey. It was never determined if he died by suicide or murder; but McWilliams wrote that Adamic had been depressed over a failed marriage, the McCarthyite witch hunt, and the intensification of the Cold War, which affected relations with Yugoslavia, the nation he had embraced as his home country.[32] All three were powerful voices that advocated for the recognition and equality of immigrants and their descendants. Adamic and McWilliams were marginalized with the advent of the Cold War and McCarthyism, along with other internationalists such as W. E. B. DuBois and Paul Robeson. Adamic opposed all ideological affiliations, and McWilliams was not a member of the Communist Party, though he was a sympathizer, a so-called fellow traveler. Handlin's was a narrower, nationalistic view, which prevailed as an expression of racial liberal-ism that was both encouraged and contained by the Cold War.[33]

A Nation of Immigrants has bequeathed to us a nationalistic interpre-tation that has been hard to shake, even as new paradigms emerged in immigration history. The post-Handlin generation of immigration his-torians rejected the idea of assimilation and theorized ethnicity as an "invention" that negotiated between cultural persistence and adapta-tion. It viewed ethnic formation as the product of a dynamic interaction between immigrants and the host society, not a one-way assimilation into Anglo cultural norms. They reprised Adamic's view that the pat-tern of American history was diversity. But their view remained US-centric and left unchallenged the idea of migration as a unidirectional phenomenon.[34] It would take another generation of historians to write about Chicano, Latinx, and Asian immigrations, reframe the study of American immigration in the context of colonialism and race, and open the way for transnational histories.[35]

"Nation of immigrants" has always been a slogan tied to immigra-tion reform, and so it is taken up again in our own time. It routinely shows up on placards at protest rallies; the Anti-Defamation League issued a fourth edition of the book in 2018 on the occasion of its 60th anniversary and as a rebuke to the Trump administration's assault on immigrant rights. In the introduction to the latest edition, Joe Ken-nedy III, at the time a member of Congress (D-MA), reiterated a version of the wave theory and its message that today's immigrants are, in their essential characteristics, like all others who came before, each group a confirmation of America's success.[36] But the approach is am-bivalent and misleading—it obscures other dynamics of American his-tory that are not properly explained as immigrations—that is, settler colonialism, conquest and removal of indigenous peoples, slavery, and the acquisition of colonies.[37]

More useful than a simple succession of waves, the arrival of new-comers in the context of the major periods of American history might be more profitable to consider. Migration held different meanings dur-ing the periods of colonial settlement (1619–1790) and national ex-pansion (1820s–1880s) and during the two great episodes of mass immigration at the turn of the 20th century and again at the turn of the 21st century. During the first two periods, Europeans furthered the aims of colonialism, native dispossession, and continental expansion. They called themselves settlers, pioneers, and colonists, not immigrants. They did not envision themselves entering an already existing society but as replicating, indeed perfecting, that of the Old World in the New. The Irish and Chinese who came in the mid-19th century were exceptional cases, considered to be nonwhites and uncivilized. In the late 19th and early 20th century, newcomers from Europe—now explicitly called immigrants—provided labor for America's industrialization and urbanization. In our own time, immigrants are again important figures in the great structural changes of the domestic and global economy, this time as service and other low-waged workers in a landscape dominated by finance at one end and service industries at the other, with a shrinking manufacturing sector.

What should become of "nation of immigrants"? As a concept, I believe it represents a flawed narrative of history and therefore should be jettisoned. It is more appropriate to think about the "peopling" of America. Native American scholar Jodi Byrd offers the categories "indigenous," "colonists," and "arrivants," the latter a broad category that includes those who arrived in the aftermath of settler colonialism, including both enslaved Africans and immigrants.[38] "Nation of nations," Louis Adamic's view of a national culture built on diversity was more progressive than Handlin's view of assimilation at midcentury. But reading Adamic now, one is struck by its optimistic spirit and its inattention to legal and material structures that reproduce racism and discrimination.

As a slogan for immigrant reform, "nation of immigrants" has the same the flaws as the concept does for history. It is rightly criticized by Indigenous people and African Americans, who reject the subsumption of their histories by a singular national immigration narrative. In the interests of a more honest, nuanced, and accurate historical narrative, and in solidarity with all peoples who been racialized and othered by white supremacy, immigrant reformers and activists should stop using it. Today's immigrant rights organizations do not display the slogan. The New York Immigration Coalition's webpage highlights "Equal Rights" as its core principle.[39] Make the Road, an advocacy and activist group, takes its name from a poem by Antonio Machado, "Searcher, there is no road. We make the road by walking," which conveys the activism of history-making.[40] United We Dream, the organization born of the DACA/Dreamers movement, likewise tells a story in its name.[41] There are many ways to get a message about immigration history, immigrant rights, and immigration reform across without rehearsing that which is outworn and inadequate to the challenges of our time.

Notes

1. On national origin quotas, see Mae Ngai, *Impossible Subjects: Illegal Aliens and the Making of Modern America* (Princeton, NJ: Princeton University Press, 2014, 2004), chap. 1.
2. John F. Kennedy, *A Nation of Immigrants* (New York: Anti-Defamation League of B'nai B'rith, 1958); 2nd ed. (New York: ADL and Random House, 1964); 3rd ed. (New York: ADL and Random House, 2008).
3. Selected titles published by Anti-Defamation League of B'nai B'rith include Paul Hartman, *Civil Rights and Minorities* (1956); Thomas F. Pettigrew, *Negro American Intelligence* (1964); William Van Til, *Privacy and Prejudice: Religious Discrimination in Social Clubs* (1962); William Van Til, *Prejudiced—How Do People Get That Way?* (1959); Oscar Handlin, *Danger in Discord* (1949); Oscar Handlin, *Out of Many: A Study Guide to Cultural Pluralism in the United States* (1964).
4. See Stuart Svonkin, *Jews against Prejudice: American Jews and the Fight for Civil Liberties* (New York: Columbia University Press, 1997). Quote from Francis J. Brown Jr. and Joseph S. Roucek, eds., *One America: The History, Contributions, and Present Problems of our Racial and National Minorities*, rev. ed. (New York: Prentice Hall, 1946), 622. On the evolution of ethno-racial group consciousness in the postwar period and implications for liberal democracy, see David Hollinger, *Post-Ethnic America* (New York: Basic Books, 1994); Nikhil Pal Singh, *Black Is a Country* (Cambridge, MA: Harvard University Press, 2004).
5. Oscar Handlin wrote *Danger in Discord*, about antisemitism (1949), *American Jews: Their Story* (1958), and *Out of Many*, on cultural pluralism (1964) for the ADL, in addition to many other books and essays on immigration and ethnic history and cultural and religious pluralism, among them *Adventure in Freedom* (New York: McGraw Hill, 1954); *Chance or Destiny* (Boston: Little, Brown, 1954); *Race and Nationality in American Life* (Boston: Little, Brown, 1957); *Immigration as a Factor in American History* (Englewood Cliffs, NJ: Prentice Hall, 1959); *The Newcomers: Negroes and Puerto Ricans in a Changing Metropolis* (Cambridge, MA: Harvard

University Press, 1959); *The American People in the Twentieth Century* (Boston: Beacon, 1963); *Children of the Uprooted* (New York: Braziller, 1966); *A Pictorial History of Immigration* (New York: Crown, 1972).

6. Oscar Handlin, "Immigration in American Life: A Reappraisal," in *Immigration in American History: Essays in Honor of Theodore Blegen*, ed. Henry Steele Commager (Minneapolis: University of Minnesota Press, 1961), 24.

7. Most influential was Robert Park's theory of the "race relations cycle," which moved from conflict to competition, accommodation, and assimilation. Robert E. Park, *Introduction to the Science of Sociology* (Chicago: University of Chicago Press, 1921); Robert E. Park, Ernest W. Burgess, and Frederick D. McKenzie, *The City* (Chicago: University of Chicago Press, 1925); Louis Wirth, *The Ghetto* (Chicago: University of Chicago Press, 1928); Paul C. Siu, *The Chinese Laundryman: A Study in Social Isolation* (New York: New York University Press, 1987). See also Emory S. Bogardus, "A Race-Relations Cycle," *American Journal of Sociology* 35, no. 4 (January 1930): 812–17; Henry Yu, *Thinking Orientals: Migration, Contact, and Exoticism in Modern America* (New York: Oxford University Press, 2001); William I. Thomas and Florian Zanecki, *The Polish Peasant in Europe and America* (Boston: Richard G. Badger/Gorham Press, 1918).

8. Handlin, *The Uprooted*; see also Oscar Handlin, "Group Life within the American Pattern: Its Scope and Its Limits," *Commentary* 8 (November 1949): 411–17.

9. John Bodnar, *The Transplanted: A History of Immigrants in Urban America* (Bloomington: University of Indiana Press, 1985); Kathleen Neils Conzen, David A. Gerber, Ewa Morawska, George E. Pozzetta, and Rudolph J. Vecoli, "The Invention of Ethnicity: A Perspective from the U.S.A." *Journal of American Ethnic History* 12, no. 1 (Fall 1992): 3–41; Russell A. Kazal, "Revisiting Assimilation: The Rise, Fall, and Reappraisal of a Concept in American Ethnic History," *American Historical Review* 100, no. 2 (April 1992): 437–71; Richard Alba and Victor Nee, *Remaking the American Mainstream: Assimilation and Contemporary Immigration* (Cambridge, MA: Harvard University Press, 2003). On assimilation as part of postwar normative immigration theory and the intellectual and practical pressures on it in the 1960s, see chapter 2.

10. Gunnar Myrdal, *An American Dilemma: The Negro Problem and Modern Democracy*, 2 vols. [1944] (New York: McGraw Hill, 1964), 3.

11. Nikhil Pal Singh, "Culture/Wars: Recoding Empire in an Age of Democracy," *American Quarterly* 50, no. 3 (September 1998): 487.

12. In fact, the 1965 act was more restrictive than previous laws because it not only kept a low overall ceiling but also imposed numerical quotas on the countries of the Western Hemisphere, where none had existed before. Congress replaced the national origin quotas with a distribution that limited every country's immigration to 7% of the total, or 20,000, a gesture of "equality" that resonated with the civil rights ethos of the time. Congress did not anticipate the increases in immigration from Asia and Latin America, including unprecedented undocumented entries from Mexico. Ngai, *Impossible Subjects*, chap. 7.

13. Oscar Handlin, "Americanizing Our Immigration Laws," *Holiday* 39 (January 1966): 8–13.

14. Oscar Handlin, "The Immigration Fight Has Only Begun: Lessons of the McCarran-Walter Setback," *Commentary* 14 (July 1952): 6 (emphasis in original).

15. Ngai, *Impossible Subjects*, 240.

16. Mary Dudziak similarly critiques "cold war civil rights" pursued by Kennedy and the 1964 Civil Rights Act, which emphasized formal equality over substantive equality. Mary Dudziak, *Cold War Civil Rights: Race and the Image of American Democracy* (Princeton, NJ: Princeton University Press, 2000). See also Jessica Lee's work on the rise of Italian American ethnic politics in the mid-20th century, which focused on cultural identity at the expense of material or class-related issues. Jessica H. Lee, "'To the Seventh Generation': Italians and the Creation of an American Political Identity, 1921–1948" (PhD diss., Columbia University, 2016). Handlin himself moved increasingly to the Right beginning in the 1960s; he wrote *The Distortion of America* in 1961, critiquing the seduction of communism among American liberals, and was one of 14 scholars who wrote a report for the Freedom House Foreign Affairs Institute defending the U.S. war in Vietnam.

17. Louis Adamic, *Laughing in the Jungle* (New York: Harper & Brothers, 1932), 5.

18. Carey McWilliams, *The Education of Carey McWilliams* (New York: Simon & Schuster, 1979), 177.

19. McWilliams, *Education*, 42.

20. Adamic, *Laughing in the Jungle*, 219–20.

21. Louis Adamic, *Nation of Nations* (New York: Harper & Brothers, 1945), 3–5.

22. Adamic, *Laughing in the Jungle*, 324.

23. Adamic, *Laughing in the Jungle*; Louis Adamic, *Dynamite: The Story of Class Violence in America* (New York: Viking Press, 1931). Although we associate Lazarus's poem about the "huddled masses yearning to breathe free" with the meaning of the Statue of Liberty, the statue was originally intended to honor the emancipation of America's slaves. When it was completed in 1886, it bore the mantle of the republicanism shared by the United States and France. See "The Statue of Liberty," The Statue of Liberty-Ellis Island Foundation (2021), https://www.statueofliberty.org/statue-of-liberty/overview-history/.

24. Adamic, *Laughing in the Jungle*, 325.

25. Adamic, *Nation of Nations*, 5–6.

26. "Common Ground (Magazine)," Densho Encyclopedia, July 14, 2020, https://encyclopedia.densho.org/Common_Ground_(magazine)/.

27. Carey McWilliams, *Factories in the Field: The Story of Migratory Farm Labor in California* (Boston: Little, Brown, 1939), 5–8.

28. Carey McWilliams, *Brothers under the Skin* (Boston: Little, Brown, 1943), 8–9, 165, 268.

29. McWilliams, *Brothers*, 18.

30. Louis Adamic, Ernest Colwell, Harley McNair, and Robert Redfield, "Peace as a World Race Problem," radio roundtable discussion by the University of Chicago and National Broadcasting Company, August 20, 1944.

31. Oscar Lewis, *La Vida: A Puerto Rican Family in the Culture of Poverty—San Juan and New York* (New York: Random House, 1966); Nathan Glazer and Daniel F.

Moynihan, *Beyond the Melting Pot: The Negroes, Puerto Ricans, Jews, Italians, and Irish of New York City*, 2nd ed. (Cambridge, MA: MIT Press, 1970); Daniel P. Moynihan, *The Negro Family—The Case for Action* (Washington, DC: US Government Printing Office/Department of Labor, 1965).

32. McWilliams, *Education of Carey McWilliams*, 178–79.

33. On the demise of progressive and internationalist politics in the late 1940s, see Penny Von Eschen, *Race against Empire: Black Americans and Anti-Colonialism, 1937–1957* (Ithaca, NY: Cornell University Press, 1997); Singh, *Black Is a Country*.

34. Conzen et al., "The Invention of Ethnicity."

35. George J. Sanchez, "Race, Nation, and Culture in Recent Immigration Studies," *Journal of American Ethnic Studies* 18, no. 4 (Summer 1999): 66–84. For exemplary transnational migration histories, see Madeline Yuan-Yin Hsu, *Dreaming of Gold, Dreaming of Home: Transnationalism and Migration between the United States and South China, 1882–1943* (Palo Alto, CA: Stanford University Press, 2000); Eiichiro Azuma, *Between Two Empires: Race, History, and Transnationalism in Japanese America* (New York: Oxford University Press, 2003); Catherine Ceniza Choy, *Empire of Care: Nursing and Migration in Filipino American History* (Durham, NC: Duke University Press, 2003); Kornel Chang, *Pacific Connections: The Making of the U.S.-Canadian Borderlands* (Berkeley: University of California Press, 2012); Ana Minian, *Undocumented Lives: The Untold Story of Mexican Migration* (Cambridge, MA: Harvard University Press, 2018); Deborah Cohen, *Braceros: Migrant Citizens and Transnational Subjects in the Postwar United States and Mexico* (Chapel Hill, NC: University of North Carolina Press, 2011); Mireya Loza, *Defiant Braceros: How Migrant Workers Fought for Racial, Sexual, and Political Freedom* (Chapel Hill: University of North Carolina Press, 2016); Julie M. Weise, *Corazón de Dixie: Mexicanos in the U.S. South since 1910* (Chapel Hill: University of North Carolina Press, 2015).

36. John F. Kennedy, *A Nation of Immigrants*, updated ed. (New York: HarperCollins Publishers, Perennial Classics, 2018).

37. See Immerwahr, chap. 10, and Smith, chap. 4, this vol.

38. Jodi Byrd, *The Transit of Empire: Indigenous Critiques of Colonialism* (Minneapolis: University of Minnesota Press, 2011).

39. New York Immigration Coalition (2022), https://www.nyic.org/.

40. Make the Road New York (2022), https://maketheroadny.org/our-model/.

41. United We Dream (2022), https://unitedwedream.org/.

CHAPTER 10

The Border Crossed Us

Taking the Measure of a Migrating Country

Daniel Immerwahr

On March 31, 1917, more than 25,000 people became US nationals at the same time. It was an emotional moment; the *New York Times* reported many in the crowd weeping at the sight of the Stars and Stripes.[1] It was also an unusual moment, as the 25,000 new nationals weren't migrants. They hadn't crossed US borders or even moved at all. Rather, the United States had paid Denmark $25 million to buy the Danish West Indies, and they were part of the deal. The US Virgin Islands—the new name of their colony—was now a territory of the United States.

We usually assume, in speaking of migration, that there are two sorts of people in the United States: the native-born and the newcomers. Members of the first group, who make up the majority of the population, have citizenship by birthright. Members of the second, today numbering more than 40 million, are not all citizens. But they have a different claim on the country: they opted for it. They are "Americans by choice," "dreamers" who crossed a border "seeking a better life," as the peppy titles of recent books put it.[2]

What we don't always appreciate is that, in the course of US history, there has been another route by which people have ended up in the country, which is annexation. It is not just people who have moved; borders have, too. US borders, in fact, have danced across North America, the Caribbean, the Arctic, and the Pacific, enclosing people like the US Virgin Islanders. Only rarely did the annexed populations have a say in this. Most were absorbed into the country involuntarily, by conquest or by sale from one empire to another. The slogan of Mexican American activists captures this well: "We didn't cross the border. The border crossed us."

We don't have a ready language for the involuntary inhabitants brought into the United States this way. The words we usually use to refer to the non-native-born all imply some form of movement: "migrants," "immigrants," "newcomers," "refugees," "asylum seekers," or perhaps, going back farther, "pioneers," "settlers," and "captives." Often—with the important exception of enslaved or trafficked people—the stories we tell about such individuals emphasize their great desire or need to move. In these stories, the United States is a torch of prosperity and freedom, and the people of the world are drawn to it.

The word that best captures the plight of those crossed by the border, by contrast, is one that doesn't always arise in discussions of US history: "colonized." It's a contentious word because there's a long history of US leaders insisting that their country is a republic, not an empire. Yet there's an even longer history of the United States expanding by annexing foreign lands. The country at its founding stretched from present-day Maine to Georgia, from the Atlantic to the Mississippi. This was a large domain, yet it amounted to less than a quarter of the area that the United States claimed at its peak in the twentieth century. The other three quarters came by war or purchase. In other words, by colonizing.[3]

How many people were fenced within the United States when its boundaries advanced? The numbers in Table 10.1 are pulled from official censuses and supplemented in a few instances by scholars' population estimates. Despite their to-the-last-digit appearance of precision, they are approximations and in some cases undercounts, most suffering badly from the United States' lack of interest in counting its nonwhite populations throughout the 19th and early 20th centuries. Nevertheless, they give a rough sense.

Using these figures, we can safely say that between nine and ten million people have acquired US nationality via colonization. There are

Table 10.1 Populations of Annexed Regions
at the Time of US Annexation

Louisiana Territory, 1803	102,375
Florida, 1819	35,000
Mexican lands, including Texas, 1845–1854	285,000
Oregon Territory, 1846	13,000
Alaska, 1867	33,000
Hawai'i, 1898	154,001
Philippines, 1899	7,635,426
Guam, 1899	9,000
Puerto Rico, 1899	953,243
American Samoa, 1900	6,100
US Virgin Islands, 1917	26,051
Northern Marianas, 1986	32,270
Total Population	**9,284,466**

two things worth noting about that. The first is the sheer size of that number. More people were annexed into the United States than comprised its original settler population upon independence from Britain (3 to 4 million), and more came into the country via annexation than by the African slave trade (less than 500,000).[4] From 1820, the first year immigration data are available, to the end of the 19th century, colonization supplied about half as many permanent residents as immigration did.[5] In other words, in that period two out of every three people who came to reside in the United States crossed a border, and the third was crossed by one.

A second thing to note is the source of those people. The United States fought for and bought many bits of land, but in terms of population its largest acquisitions were the Philippines and Puerto Rico, both won in an 1898 war against Spain, during which the United States also annexed Guam and the non-Spanish lands of Hawai'i and American Samoa. When students in the United States are taught the history of their country's expansion, their attention is typically drawn to the Louisiana Purchase and the 1846–1848 war with Mexico, both of which added enormous amounts of acreage to the country, which eventually became states. But in terms of adding people, the 1898 war was the true centerpiece, accounting for roughly 95% of the annexed populations—and for territories that never became states.

Of course, Table 10.1 notes only the initial populations in the newly added lands. Those populations grew. The three most-populous states today—California, Texas, and Florida—were all annexed lands, and in each the population is more than a quarter Latino. The overseas territories grew in population, too, and at their peak around World War II, they encompassed nearly 19 million colonized subjects. At that time, if you lived in the United States, there was a one-in-eight chance you were living in an overseas territory. The United States at that time contained more colonized people than it did Black people or immigrants.[6]

And that counts only formally annexed territories. The United States also occupied foreign countries, establishing temporary jurisdiction over them without officially making them part of the country. Its most famous occupations followed wars: Cuba in 1898, Japan and parts of Germany in 1945, and Iraq in 2003. Although Washington still treated occupied areas as foreign, the line could be blurred, as when the US government established a US postal service at domestic rates in Cuba or included the Panama Canal Zone in the US census. If we count the occupied territories, at the end of World War II there were around 135 million people living under US jurisdiction overseas. Significantly, that was more than the 132 million people living on the US mainland. If you looked up and saw the Stars and Stripes in late 1945, in other words, you probably weren't seeing it because you lived in a state. You were more likely seeing it because your country was occupied or colonized.[7]

That 135-million-strong empire didn't last long, though, because the United States shifted to another form of power projection. Today, the footprint of US territorial power abroad mainly takes the form of military bases: hundreds of small zones of semi-sovereignty over which the United States claims jurisdiction. The most developed bases came to resemble "little Americas." By the start of the 21st century, Guantánamo Bay, which the United States had "leased" from Cuba since 1903 (Cuba has for decades tried to end this lease), contained a shopping mall, a McDonald's, a Baskin-Robbins, a Boy Scout contingent, a

Star Trek fan club, and a golf course. Today, there are some 750 US bases in territories and foreign countries.[8]

The United States prides itself on being a republic, a land of citizens rather than subjects. But there are currently two important formal constraints on citizenship. The first is on the border crossers: people entering the country have faced hurdles, sometimes impossibly high, to becoming citizens. The second is on the border crossed.

Border-crossed peoples were on rocky legal terrain from the start. Native Americans did not, as a rule, become citizens of the United States upon being enclosed within its borders. In fact, the Constitution specifically excluded "Indians not taxed" from the polity for the apportionment of representation—the only people to be so treated.[9] The Fourteenth Amendment, ratified in 1868, granted citizenship to anyone born in the United States with the exception of Native Americans in tribes. In the early 20th century, another carve-out came with a set of Supreme Court rulings collectively known as the "Insular Cases." The Court ruled in those cases that the Constitution fully applied to only *part* of the United States, to the "incorporated" land. The country also contained "unincorporated" territories—including all of the colonies seized from Spain—where the Constitution did not fully apply. As one justice explained the logic, the Constitution was the "supreme law of the land," but the unincorporated territories were "not part of the 'land.'"[10]

The result was to turn the United States into legally partitioned space, divided into a constitutionally governed zone and an extraconstitutional zone. That is why, even today, if you are born in American Samoa, you are a US national but not a citizen, despite American Samoa having been "American" for well over a century.

There's a colloquial term for people denied standard civil rights: second-class citizens. In the case of colonial subjects, their citizenship—when they've had it—has been literally second class, in that it's a different type of citizenship. Because the Supreme Court has never ruled that the Fourteenth Amendment covers the inhabitants of the unincorporated territories, they've lacked constitutional citizenship. Instead, they have had at most statutory citizenship, granted by Congress, a legislative body in which they have no effective representation. But because statutory citizenship is not backstopped by the Constitution, it can be rescinded by a congressional majority.

Often, citizenship for annexed peoples came late, if at all. Puerto Ricans became citizens in 1917, Native Americans in 1924 (some were already citizens by special legislation), US Virgin Islanders in 1927, and Guamanians in 1950. Filipinos were never made citizens before gaining independence in 1946, and American Samoans to this day have no birthright to citizenship.

It is not an accident that the US nationals who have been denied citizenship or granted only statutory citizenship have been largely—at least in the eyes of lawmakers—nonwhite. The history of annexation, like the history of immigration, has been one of careful racial curation. Until 1898, decisions about where US borders should go were explicitly governed by an exclusionary logic. Generally, US leaders sought to annex as much land as they could without bringing too many more nonwhite people into the country.[11] Around 1898, one influential argument against annexing large territories was the fear that new annexations would inject too many nonwhites into the union. Policy-makers overcame this objection by protecting white rule in a different way: they annexed those territories but restricted rights and representation in them—and blocked them from becoming states.

Part of the United States but disenfranchised and not quite "American" in the eyes of its leaders, the people of the post-1898 territories suffered serious hardships. It's no accident that the largest mass shooting by police happened in the colonies: the 1937 Ponce Massacre in Puerto Rico, in which more than 150 were wounded. The worst military massacre took place in them, too: the Bud Dajo massacre in the Philippines, which killed hundreds and possibly more than a thousand.[12] The bloodiest war on US soil was not the Civil War, as is commonly assumed. The 1899–1913 war to suppress Philippine independence and the Second World War in the Philippines both appear to have killed more people.[13] Such was life in the "back room" of the

United States, as the president of the Philippine commonwealth Manuel Quezon put it.[14]

In all this, the border-crossed people of the United States have much in common with the border-crossing ones. But there are important differences. One has to do with legality. Some migrants to the United States enter or remain in violation of the law, and their lack of documentation puts them in a precarious and dangerous position. In the case of annexed peoples, questions of legality arise in a different way. The chief legal question with respect to annexation is whether the *United States* broke the law. This possibility has attended annexations since the first, the Louisiana Purchase, which Thomas Jefferson himself acknowledged went "beyond the Constitution."[15] The United States' first overseas acquisitions, a set of uninhabited "guano islands" valued for the nitrate-rich fertilizer they possessed, met with a challenge that rose to the Supreme Court.[16] To this day, sovereignty activists maintain that the US acquisition of Hawai'i violated international law and that Hawai'i is not part of the United States but rather illegally occupied by it.

Hawai'i's incorporation into the United States came over the strong objection of Native Hawaiians, who bombarded the authorities with anti-annexation petitions.[17] When the United States annexed the Philippines, it could fully establish civilian rule there only after fighting for 14 years against an armed independence movement that, at least at the start of the war, appears to have commanded strong popular support. This is another difference between the border-crossers and the bordered-crossed: colonized populations by and large did not choose the United States. Only in Texas and the Northern Mariana Islands was annexation put to a popular vote, and in Texas that vote was restricted to white men. Thus, of the roughly 9.3 million who joined the country via annexation, less than 200,000—around 2%—did so via a vote. It is not a coincidence that, of the tiny number who got to choose annexation, the majority were white.

Migrants to the United States have met by and large three fates: in, out, or in between. In other words, they've been legally included via official status and perhaps citizenship, they've left or been deported, or they've remained in the United States without documentation. We can use the same schema to think about the three trajectories for the places that have, via annexation, become territories of the United States. Some have become states (in), others have gained independence (out), and still others remain indefinitely as territories, persisting in a sort of legal gray zone (in between).

The willingness of the United States, from the start, to welcome territories into the union as states on an equal footing with existing states is noteworthy. Not only was this a country open to incorporating new people, but it was also one open to incorporating new places. In other empires, territories often remained subordinate without any expectation that they'd achieve the political status enjoyed by the metropole. But with the Northwest Ordinance of 1787 and a series of similar laws following it, US lawmakers established a process by which territories could become states, sometimes in less than a decade. This was a sign that the United States represented a new kind of politics, republican rather than imperial.

Still, there were caveats. Until territories gained statehood, the federal government held absolute power over them. The Northwest Ordinance recommended population thresholds at which the territories would gain internal representative government and then statehood, but these thresholds weren't binding; Congress could (and did) hold territories back or admit them early. "In effect," wrote James Monroe, who drafted the Northwest Ordinance, it established "colonial government" in the territories, akin to the kind that had governed the 13 colonies before their independence.[18] And it is remarkable how long the federal government held its territories in that form of colonial government. On the mainland, the average time from annexation to statehood was 45 years.[19]

The map in Figure 10.1 hints at the source of the delay. The territories that lingered were the ones with large and enduring Native populations. The column of territories springing from the top of Texas, all of which took more than 50 years to become states, were carved out of Indian Territory (also called Indian Country), an enormous zone that

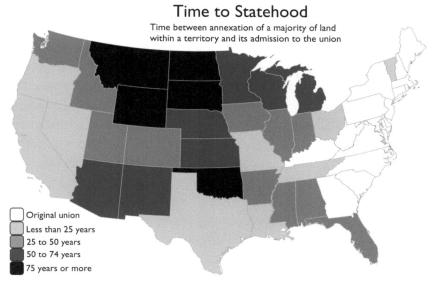

Time to Statehood

Time between annexation of a majority of land within a territory and its admission to the union

- Original union
- Less than 25 years
- 25 to 50 years
- 50 to 74 years
- 75 years or more

Figure 10.1. Time from annexation to US statehood

initially covered 46% of the United States' area.[20] Oklahoma, the Dakotas, and places like them stayed territories so long not because they were empty, waiting for enough people to form a government, but rather because they were inhabited by Native polities. The magic dust sprinkled on territories to turn them into states was white settlement, and the territories that moved most quickly into the union were the ones in which settlers most quickly outnumbered Indigenous people. This explains why California, which filled quickly with settlers due to its gold rush and saw mass murders of Native peoples, became a state in two years whereas Oklahoma, long reserved for Indians, remained a territory for more than a century.

It also explains the fate of the overseas territories. The colonies that seemed most amenable to settlement campaigns by whites from the US mainland were Alaska and Hawai'i, the only overseas lands that the Supreme Court ruled "incorporated." Still, they never saw as much white migration as expected; at the end of the Second World War, Alaska was still half Native, and whites were an outright minority in Hawai'i. So both remained territories for quite a while: 92 years in Alaska's case, 61 years in Hawai'i's.

It was only during the Cold War, when their subordinated status became a vulnerability on the world stage, that Alaska and Hawai'i joined the union. Moscow made much of the fact that the United States, for all its boasting about freedom and democracy, still had large colonies. US Congress finally made them states in 1959, overcoming strong internal resistance from segregationists, to showcase the United States' commitment to multiracial democracy. These were the only overseas territories the United States has ever admitted into the union, and the only states whose admission was not ultimately dependent on white settlement. They have since been important sources of Native advocacy, anti-imperialism, and racial diversity within US politics; it's telling that the first Black president was born in Hawai'i.[21]

If statehood resolved the predicament of empire by inclusion, independence resolved it by separation. There has been only one clear-cut case of a US territory gaining independence, the Philippines—the most populous territory the United States ever held, relinquished in 1946. Beyond that, a few places that the United States administered for decades—but never annexed—gained independence from US rule. Haiti regained self-government after 19 years of US occupation (1915–1934), Okinawa reverted to Tokyo's control after 27 years (1945–1972), and the US-administered Panama Canal Zone was finally relinquished after more than 7 decades (1903–1979), its land reverting to Panama. In Micronesia, the United States administered the Trust Territory of the Pacific Islands under the United Nations' sovereignty from 1947 until the 1980s and 1990s, when the territory was broken up into the Republic of the Marshall Islands, the Federated States of Micronesia, the Republic of Palau, and the Commonwealth of the Northern Mariana Islands, the last of which became an unincorporated US territory in 1986.

By the "in, out, or in between" analogy between annexation and migration I am proposing, independence corresponds to deportation. This may seem like a strained comparison, but there are important similarities. Both are mechanisms the United States has used to rid itself of unwanted populations, either by retracting its border or pushing people over it. It was largely this exclusionist logic that led US policy-makers to decide to cast off the Philippines in the 1930s. At that time, the economic hardships of the Depression had prompted white workers on the West Coast to turn against job-seeking Filipino migrants and mainland farmers to complain about competition from Philippine produce. Freeing the Philippines would draw an international border between the colony and the US mainland, one that neither migrants nor goods could easily cross. (It would also relieve the US military of the obligation to protect the Philippines if Japan invaded.) Liberation in any broader sense was far from lawmakers' minds at the time. "I want our people to keep out of the Orient and I want the Orient to keep out of the United States," is how one US senator voiced the argument for independence.[22] President Franklin Delano Roosevelt put it more bluntly: "Let's get rid of the Philippines."[23]

The Philippine Independence Act, passed in 1934, did not immediately free the colony. Rather, it cut off unrestricted Filipino migration to the mainland and gradually raised tariff walls while putting the Philippines on a countdown to independence. By the time that countdown ended, on July 4, 1946, World War II had come and gone, leaving the meagerly defended colony in ruins. At that point, US policy-makers gained new reasons for setting the Philippines free, to do with securing legitimacy in decolonizing Asia. This understanding aligned much more closely with the popular Philippine desire for independence. On this logic, the United States denationalized some 19 million people at a stroke.[24]

Nineteen million is far more than the 2.4 million that the United States formally deported in the 20th century. However, historian Adam Goodman has shown that formal deportations accounted for only a small fraction of total expulsions, because the United States also removed people via "voluntary departures." Despite their name, Goodman writes, there was "nothing voluntary about them"; they were just accomplished at a lower administrative level than formal deportations, without court hearings.[25] Adding voluntary departures (counted since

1927) to the tally, de-annexation accounted for roughly a third of 20th-century removals from the United States.[26]

The vast bulk of US territories ultimately became states, though the largest, the Philippines, was set free. Between those two poles lie five overseas territories that remain unincorporated territories, part of the polity but not part of the union: Puerto Rico, Guam, American Samoa, the US Virgin Islands, and the Commonwealth of the Northern Mariana Islands. And within US states—existing as partial legal carve-outs—are more than 300 federal Native American reservations, covering a collective acreage the size of Idaho.

Imminent changes for these spaces seem unlikely, though there is talk of Puerto Rican statehood and, it now appears, a slim majority of support for it on the island (53% expressed a preference for statehood in a nonbinding yes-or-no referendum in 2020). The territories remain, just as the chief justice in one of the turn-of-the-century Insular Cases predicted they would, like a "disembodied shade, in an intermediate state of ambiguous existence for an indefinite period."[27]

That "ambiguous existence" comes with costs. In 2017, a series of deadly hurricanes tore through the Caribbean, striking the US Virgin Islands, Puerto Rico, Florida, and Texas. The damage was general, but the repair wasn't. Federal personnel, charitable giving, and media coverage all privileged the states over the territories. Puerto Rico waited nearly a year before electricity service was fully restored, and the president at the time, Donald Trump, seemed more interested in selling off the territory than helping it.[28] Not "a single dollar" should go to Puerto Rico, Trump privately told his advisers.[29]

Trump's hostility to Puerto Rico was more brazen than the quiet disregard of other US leaders. But it was of a piece with a long tradition of neglect, enabled by the fact that residents of the overseas territories cannot vote in presidential elections, lack effective representation in Congress, aren't covered by the Constitution, and do not count as "Americans" in the popular mainland imagination. Woodrow Wilson, speaking of the overseas territories, described them as lying "outside the charmed circle of our own national life."[30]

He was right. Today, all of the US territories are poorer, per capita, than all of the US states. And most mainlanders are only dimly aware of the territories' existence.

More than a century has passed since the Stars and Stripes went up over the US Virgin Islands, making more than 25,000 people US nationals. In that century, Congress has both extended and retracted US borders; it has set a colony free, annexed new territory, started and ended massive occupations, and made territories into states. The country has not been a fixed location, in other words, but has moved around the map.

These movements are sometimes hard to see. Most people, if prompted to envision the United States, picture a familiar shape: the Atlantic-to-Pacific span of states. They imagine a static and contiguous nation-state, a homeland. In this vision, much of the United States' diversity, laudable or not, stems from outsiders rushing in. If there are too many of them, well, one can always build a wall.

But once you understand the United States as a dynamic empire, talk of "insiders" and "outsiders" makes less sense. The United States, which hasn't been contiguous for more than 150 years, simply isn't the kind of place you can build a wall around. Much of its diversity—including a recent president from Polynesia—comes from its shifting borders. Because it's not only the people who have migrated. The place has, too.

Notes

1. "Took Over Virgin Islands," *New York Times*, April 2, 1917.
2. It should be noted that in many cases that "choice" was made less out of affinity for the United States and more from an urgent need for safety, in some cases from perils exacerbated by US policies. In earlier periods, the notion of those who moved to the United States as "choosing" it breaks down entirely, as hundreds of thousands of people who entered the country did so in chains, as slaves.
3. Much of the following account is based on Daniel Immerwahr, *How to Hide an Empire: A History of the Greater United States* (New York: Farrar, Straus and Giroux, 2019). Other useful recent overviews of the United States' territorial empire are

Julian Go, *Patterns of Empire: The British and American Empires, 1688 to the Present* (Cambridge: Cambridge University Press, 2011), and A. G. Hopkins, *American Empire: A Global History* (Princeton, NJ: Princeton University Press, 2018).

4. *Slave Voyages: The Trans-Atlantic Slave Trade Database*, www.slavevoyages.org /assessment/estimates, accessed February 15, 2020.

5. US Department of Homeland Security, *Yearbook of Immigration Statistics 2019* (Washington, DC, 2020), table 1. Between 1820 and 1899, 18.6 million people legally became permanent residents of the United States, compared with the roughly 9.1 million who became permanent residents by annexation in that same period.

6. Daniel Immerwahr, "The Greater United States: Territory and Empire in U.S. History," *Diplomatic History* 40, no. 3 (2016): 376.

7. Immerwahr, "The Greater United States," 388.

8. David Vine, *The United States of War: A Global History of America's Endless Conflicts, from Columbus to the Islamic State* (Oakland: University of California Press, 2020), 2.

9. US Const. art. I, § 2.

10. Dorr v. United States, 195 US 138, 155 (1904) (Harlan, J., dissenting). See Christina Duffy Burnett and Marshall Burke, eds., *Foreign in a Domestic Sense: Puerto Rico, American Expansion, and the Constitution* (Durham, NC: Duke University Press, 2001); Bartholomew H. Sparrow, *The Insular Cases and the Emergence of American Empire* (Lawrence: University Press of Kansas, 2006); and Gerald L. Neuman and Tomiko Brown-Nagin, eds., *Reconsidering the Insular Cases: The Past and Future of American Empire* (Cambridge, MA: Human Rights Program Series, Harvard Law School, 2015).

11. Eric T. L. Love, *Race over Empire: Racism and U.S. Imperialism, 1865–1900* (Chapel Hill: University of North Carolina Press, 2004); Paul Frymer, *Building an American Empire: The Era of Territorial and Political Expansion* (Princeton, NJ: Princeton University Press, 2017).

12. Immerwahr, *How to Hide*, 422n.

13. Immerwahr, *How to Hide*, 103, 211–212, 421n.

14. Charles A. Willoughby and John Chamberlain, *MacArthur: 1941–1951* (New York: McGraw-Hill, 1954), 56.

15. Thomas Jefferson to John Dickinson, August 9, 1803, in Founders Online.

16. Christina Duffy Burnett, "The Edges of Empire and the Limits of Sovereignty: American Guano Islands," *American Quarterly* 57, no. 3 (2005): 779–803.

17. The extent of local resistance is documented in Noenoe K. Silva, *Aloha Betrayed: Native Hawaiian Resistance to American Colonialism* (Durham, NC: Duke University Press, 2004).

18. James Monroe to Thomas Jefferson, May 11, 1786, Founders Online.

19. Immerwahr, "Greater United States," 384.

20. Immerwahr, *How to Hide*, 38–40.

21. Sarah Miller-Davenport, *Gateway State: Hawai'i and the Cultural Transformation of American Empire* (Princeton, NJ: Princeton University Press, 2019).

22. Statement of Samuel Morgan Shortridge, 72nd Cong., 2nd sess., *Congressional Record* 1930, vol. 72.

23. H. W. Brands, *Bound to Empire: The United States and the Philippines* (New York: Oxford University Press, 1992), 163.

24. Motives and process are discussed in Daniel Immerwahr, "Philippine Independence in U.S. History: A Car, Not a Train," *Pacific Historical Review* 91, no. 2 (2022): 220–248.

25. Adam Goodman, *The Deportation Machine: America's Long History of Expelling Immigrants* (Princeton, NJ: Princeton University Press, 2020), 3.

26. Formal deportations and voluntary departures (or "returns") account for 38.4 million expulsions, 1900–1999, according to DHS, *Yearbook*, table 39. There are three important caveats. First, the DHS figures count total expulsion events, not individuals, so the same person being deported four times will count as four deportations. Second, Goodman found evidence of voluntary departures before 1927, when our numbers are first available. Third, running alongside both formal deportations and voluntary departures were intimidation campaigns causing migrants to "self-deport," and those self-deportations do not count in the tally.

27. Downes v. Bidwell, 18 US 244, 372 (1901) (Fuller, C. J., dissenting). A helpful reflection on the status ambiguities afflicting both immigrants and the colonized (as well as other subordinated groups in US history) is Sam Erman, "Truer U.S. History: Race, Borders, and Status Manipulation," *Yale Law Journal* 130 (2021): 1188–1249.

28. Michael D. Shear, "Leading Homeland Security under a President Who Embraces 'Hate-Filled' Talk," *New York Times*, July 10, 2020.

29. Tracy Jan, Arelis R. Hernández, Josh Dawsey, and Damian Paletta, "After Butting Heads with Trump Administration, Top HUD Official Departs Agency," *Washington Post*, January 16, 2020.

30. Woodrow Wilson, "First Annual Message," December 2, 1913, The American Presidency Project, https://www.presidency.ucsb.edu/documents/first-annual-message-18.

CHAPTER 11

A Nation of Immigrants, a Nation of Refuge

Maria Cristina Garcia

Historians have long debated how and when Americans came to understand themselves as a "nation of immigrants." This narrative, wrote Donna Gabaccia, was an assertion of national pride but one based on two erroneous assumptions: that immigrants have played a larger role in American national life than in other nations and that immigrants have been more easily incorporated into the nation than they have been elsewhere.[1] While the specific origins of this narrative and paradigm have been debated, most historians agree that the "nation of immigrants" narrative, denoting inclusiveness, developed only gradually over the course of many generations. By the final decades of the 20th century, Americans routinely celebrated and commercialized their immigrant heritage in parades, pageants, museums, folklife festivals, and historical monuments; but as Americans celebrated their presumed exceptionality, they also policed borders, built walls and detention centers, and passed legislation to bar entry, revealing the ambivalence and fear of immigrants this narrative obscures.

Among the historians who have challenged the "nation of immigrants" narrative are Roxanne Dunbar-Ortiz and Adam Goodman.[2] Dunbar-Ortiz argues that this "convenient myth," which celebrates a vision of American society as multicultural and diverse, erases the brutal displacement and murder of Indigenous peoples by immigrant settlers and armies. The myth developed, she says, as a reaction to the

1960s movements against colonialism and white supremacy. Goodman, in turn, noted that the "nation of immigrants" paradigm has ignored the wide range of free, forced, and coerced migrations that have shaped American history and society. It gives European immigrants a privileged place in US history, he writes, while treating non-European immigrants as secondary actors and altogether excluding Indigenous and enslaved peoples and their descendants.

Refugees and asylum-seekers are central to this "nation of immigrants" narrative. As one recent study noted, the United States was, from its very foundation, "shaped by the idea that it would be a refuge for the world's oppressed people [and] this concept pervaded the minds of the country's earliest political thinkers."[3] Despite the centrality of refugees to the immigration—and national—narrative, American understandings of who or what a *refugee* is has changed over time. The term has been flexible in both popular usage and legal understanding.[4] Similarly, American attitudes toward refugees—and the protections offered them—have also changed over time. In the late 20th and early 21st centuries, policy-makers have routinely blocked entry to refugee-seekers by claiming that specific groups are *migrants*, not refugees, driven by poverty rather than persecution and thus not eligible for special protection.

In this chapter I offer a brief examination of refugees in the US national narrative, from the earliest expressions of refugee policy in the 19th century to the highly bureaucratic, legalistic, and contested "refugee regime" of the 21st. I conclude with a discussion of some of the humanitarian challenges facing policy-makers in the 21st century and how these challenges both reflect and disrupt not only our understandings of who is worthy of entry and protection, but also our understanding of the United States as a nation of immigrants, a nation of refuge.

Contesting the Origins of the Refugee Narrative

The word "refugee" is derived from the French verb *se réfugier*, which means to seek shelter from danger. Historians of North America have long studied refugee experiences: that is, the experiences of people who have fled the dangers of religious or ideological persecution, political upheaval, famine, or natural disasters and sought refuge in the United States and Canada. Historians of the colonial era, the revolutionary and early national periods, and the long 19th century have studied the refugee experiences of such populations as the Acadians and Huguenots who sought safety in the North American colonies; the British loyalists who resettled in Canada after the American Revolution; the French planters who fled the revolution in Haiti; the Irish who escaped British colonization; the Germans forced to flee the failed revolution of 1848; the enslaved peoples who escaped to Mexico and Canada; and the Cuban workers and revolutionaries who fled Spanish colonial rule, among many other populations.[5] Though these works are not examinations of US refugee policy per se, they discuss the conditions and policies in the countries of origin and destination that directed these populations toward specific locations in North America.

The historiography on US refugee law and policy, in turn, has focused almost exclusively on the decades following the Second World War because it was during the mid-to-late 20th century that a series of statutes defined refugee status and institutionalized a distinct track for entry (and system of resettlement) for refugees and asylum-seekers within the US immigration bureaucracy. The establishment of refugee policy, it was argued, required the existence of federal immigration law as well as a bureaucracy to register immigrants, and these systems were not fully in place until the late 19th century. This is not to say that local, state, and federal actors did not try to regulate the entry and movement of populations prior to 1875, the year the Supreme Court declared the regulation of immigration a federal responsibility; local and state actors did regulate migration, as historians of immigration have demonstrated, but these regulations were largely crafted ad hoc, with great variability across states.[6]

In the 2010s and 2020s, scholars influenced by the interdisciplinary field of critical refugee studies and feminist legal scholarship have challenged this periodization in refugee studies, and have reconceptualized refugees as political actors (and not merely objects of rescue) who make visible the processes of colonization, war, displacement, and citizenship.[7] Scholars of US settler-colonialism, empire, and borderlands have found early expressions of a US refugee policy in the 19th and early 20th centuries that challenge the traditional and triumphalist narrative of the United States as a refuge for the oppressed. Historian Julian Lim, for example, examined the case of the 522 Chinese refugees in northern Mexico who were allowed to accompany General John "Blackjack" Pershing's expeditionary force when it returned from Mexico. Because of the race-based immigration restrictions of the Chinese Exclusion Act, these Chinese refugees were allowed only temporary entry into the United States in 1917, as a humanitarian gesture, to protect them from the anti-Chinese violence generated by the Mexican Revolution; but in 1921, through Public Law 29, the "Joint Resolution [p]ermitting certain Chinese to register under certain provisions and conditions," 365 Chinese men received the right to remain in the country as permanent legal residents. As Lim explains, this case can be analyzed as a precursor to several of today's immigration policies, but perhaps more significantly, it illustrates how immigration law and refugee law can "work dynamically together to produce varieties of second-class citizenship." Though eventually allowed to establish permanent residence in the United States, these Chinese refugees held a liminal legal status, "belonging" in the United States because of a special law Congress passed to accommodate them, but not entirely "belonging" because of the exclusionary immigration laws and court rulings that barred them from full citizenship and participation in American political and civic life.[8]

Evan Taparata, in turn, has examined how political officials, administrative actors, lawmakers, and concerned citizens created a system of "refugee regulation" from the 19th to mid-20th century—that is, "laws, policies, administrative choices, military orders, treaty clauses, and on-the-ground-decisions" that functioned independently of immigration policy. This system of refugee regulation was representative of the settler state, argues Taparata, and subjected Indigenous populations, enslaved peoples, and other marginalized communities to "oppression, displacement and persecution—making them refugees in experience, if not always in name or legal status."

These and other works illustrate the multiple ways Americans understood refugees before Congress codified refugee status and created a distinct administrative track for their admission. The United States became, in myth, "an unassailable refuge for the world's most vulnerable people," but, as Taparata, Lim, Dunbar-Ortiz and Goodman have argued, it was a refuge created only for certain groups and built on the backs of marginalized populations in the United States.[9]

The Cold War Refugee Narrative

Many historians of US refugee policy have traced its political origins to the Second World War and the early Cold War period, when the United States responded to a series of humanitarian crises in Europe. The admission of hundreds of thousands of "displaced persons" and "refugees" during this period reinvigorated the narrative that the United States was a refuge for the oppressed; but this history also reveals that the admission of refugees was never easy nor automatic. Legislators and their American constituents had to be convinced that refugee admissions served the national interest.[10]

During the 1930s and 1940s, as thousands fled fascism, Naziism, and certain death in Europe, immigrants from southern and eastern Europe found their entry to the United States barred because of the racist national origins quotas embedded in immigration law and the overzealous application of those laws by consular officials. Between 1933 and 1945, for example, the United States took in only 132,000 Jewish refugees, or just 10% of the quota allowed by law.[11] The immigration quotas, small though they were, remained unfilled throughout the war. Instead of accommodating those fleeing Europe, American officials bowed to the anti-immigrant pressure at home and focused on trying to resettle refugees in Great Britain and other countries of the Western Hemisphere. Many immigrants already in the United States—Japanese, Italians, and Germans—and their US-born children were interrogated, harassed, fired from their jobs, and, in some cases, sent to internment camps because they were viewed as potential threats to wartime national security.

In the decade following the war, Congress allowed the entry of roughly 600,000 people through the Displaced Persons Act (1948) and the Refugee Relief Act (1953), but these accommodations were controversial and contested. Instead of overhauling the national origins quotas altogether, Congress passed this emergency legislation ad hoc. Legislators understood the destabilizing effect displaced persons could have on Europe's postwar economic recovery, but they also knew that immigration reform was unpopular at home. Despite the hundreds of thousands left homeless and stateless by the war, it took three years for Congress to pass the Displaced Persons Act, and only under sustained pressure from President Harry S. Truman and a co-alition of American political and religious groups. Throughout the 1950s, influential policy-makers blocked any substantial immigration reform to protect the country from "the untold millions . . . storming our gates for admission." As Senator Patrick McCarran (D-NV) said in 1953, "The solution of the problems of Europe and Asia will not come through a transplanting of those problems *en masse* to the United States."[12]

Though the emergency legislation that Congress finally passed was a humanitarian response, it reflected legislators' objections to certain populations. The Displaced Persons Act, for example, established a "maze of technicalities" and restrictions that resulted in few visas for Jews and Catholics, which in the wake of the Holocaust was stunningly callous. Meanwhile, former Nazi scientists were fast-tracked for entry and US citizenship under a separate program so that their expertise would not be used by the Soviet Union.[13] Truman signed the Displaced Persons Act to begin the long-awaited resettlement program, but he acknowledged the "bitter disappointment" this bill was to "the many displaced victims of persecution who looked to the United States for hope; to the millions of our citizens who wanted to help them in the finest American spirit; to the many members of the Congress who fought hard but unsuccessfully for a decent displaced persons bill."[14]

Refugees from Asia were barred from visas altogether until passage of the Refugee Relief Act, when 5,000 visas (out of 214,000) were designated for the Far East; but the 1948 law did allow several thousand Chinese already living in the United States to receive asylum.

Legislative definitions of refugee status changed over the course of the Cold War, reflecting how refugees and refugee policy were often used in support of foreign policy agendas. The Refugee Relief Act, for example, defined a refugee as someone from an area "neither communist nor communist-dominated, who because of persecution, fear of persecution, natural calamity or military operations [was] out of his usual place of abode . . . unable to return . . . [not] firmly resettled, and . . . in urgent need of assistance." An "escapee," on the other hand, was a refugee who "had fled from the Union of Soviet Socialist Republics or other communist, communist-dominated or communist-occupied area of Europe."[15] The Migration and Refugee Assistance Act of 1962, in turn, focused on those fleeing persecution in the Western Hemisphere (and, especially, Cuba).[16] Three years later, the Hart-Celler Act defined refugees as the "oppressed or persecuted . . . because of their race, color, religion, national origin, adherence to democratic beliefs, or their opposition to totalitarianism or dictatorship"; but Congress also included in the definition those "uprooted by natural calamity; those fleeing communist or communist-dominated countries; and those fleeing the Middle East."[17] All these laws created new categories of immigrants such as "displaced persons," "refugees," "expellees," and "escapees," and each category had a precise legal meaning that determined who qualified for admission.

As the Cold War unfolded, US policies signaled a growing recognition that the United States, as a member of an international community and as the presumed leader of the "free world," had a particular responsibility to assist displaced persons. Policy-makers in the executive branch were keenly aware that the national origins quotas (and the segregation of racial minorities at home) undermined American moral authority around the world, just as the United States was competing with the Soviet Union for the "hearts and minds" of those living in the non-aligned developing world. Although the United States had not been a signatory to the United Nations' 1951 Convention on the Status of Refugees, the Lyndon B. Johnson administration signed the 1967 Protocol, thereby officially and symbolically recognizing that refugees were entitled to certain rights and protections, including the rights to education, work, freedom of movement, and non-refoulement—no forced return to dangerous or repressive conditions—which is regarded as the most fundamental of refugee rights.[18] The United States became (and has remained) the principle financial donor to the United Nations High Commissioner for Refugees (UNHCR).

The admission of refugees, then, was a humanitarian response, but it also served foreign policy interests. At times, Congress was a cooperative partner, passing legislation ad hoc to allow the entry and accommodation of groups considered to be "in the national interest"; at other times, the executive branch acted unilaterally, over the objections of many in Congress. During the Cold War, for example, the executive branch drew heavily on the humanitarian "parole" authority granted by the 1952 Immigration and Nationality Act (McCarran-Walter Act), which allowed the entry (outside of established immigration quotas) of people who had been displaced by the postwar communist governments. Between 1956 and 1979, the United States "paroled" 32,000 Hungarian refugees following the failed pro-democracy revolution of 1956; 640,000 Cubans who fled Fidel Castro's communist government; 360,000 Vietnamese after the fall of Saigon; 30,000 Soviet Jews and other religious minorities; and several hundred Chileans following the 1973 overthrow of the Allende government. Because humanitarian parole offered only temporary entry, Congress then had to pass "adjustment acts" to allow these populations to become legal permanent residents.

Over time, members of Congress became concerned by the overuse of the humanitarian parole authority in service of Cold War objectives. Humanitarian parole, they argued, was providing a "back door" to the United States, allowing hundreds of thousands to enter the country without congressional input, on the assumption that those fleeing communist countries were more worthy of admission than other immigrants. These concerns led to the passage of the 1980 Refugee Act, which established a "permanent and systematic procedure for the admission [of refugees] of special humanitarian concern to the United States," but one that that required congressional consultation and based admissions on the United Nations' more ideologically neutral definition of "refugee." The 1980 Refugee Act now defined a refugee as

> any person who is outside any country of such person's nationality or, in the case of a person having no nationality, is outside any country in which such person last habitually resided, and who is unable or unwilling to return to, or is unable and unwilling to avail himself or herself of the protection of that country because of persecution or a well-founded fear of persecution on account of race, religion, nationality, membership of a particular social group or political opinion.[19]

The law also established guidelines for granting asylum to those fleeing persecution who were already physically present in the United States or who were requesting protection at a port of entry.[20] This is the law that has regulated refugee admissions in the United States ever since.

Although the Refugee Act tried to free refugee policy from its ideological uses, over the next decade, most of the refugees admitted to the United States continued to come from communist countries. Fleeing a communist country did not guarantee anyone admission, but it did maximize an applicant's chances for admission because decision-makers operated on the premise that communist states were authoritarian and persecuted its dissidents. By the end of the Cold War, most refugees had come from just three countries: the Soviet Union, Vietnam, and Cuba. Smaller numbers came from communist Hungary, Poland, Czechoslovakia, East Germany, and other countries of the Eastern Bloc, as well as the People's Republic of China, Cambodia, and Laos.

Policy-makers argued that admitting refugees from communist countries served foreign policy interests because they demonstrated to the rest of the world—especially the non-aligned nations in the developing world—the desirability and triumph of democracy and capitalism over communist totalitarianism. Refugees from communist countries had gone to great lengths to escape their homelands, they argued, forfeiting homes, family, careers, and property. When public opinion polls revealed resistance to the admission of more refugees, the executive branch (sometimes with the assistance of Madison Avenue advertising firms and key media personalities) tried to inspire popular support for the admission of refugees. In the White House's narrative, refugees from the communist bloc were the "freedom fighters," worthy of admission to the United States because they were powerful symbols of an innate human need to live in free societies. Their presence legitimized and served the values of American democracy and capitalism.

The United States benefited from refugee admissions in multiple ways. Many were the highly educated of their societies, and their education, skills, and expertise served the US economy; others provided important intelligence that informed US diplomatic, military, and economic policies overseas. Some refugees were drawn into US military missions upon arrival: Jewish refugees, for example, served as spies, interrogators, and soldiers during the Second World War; and Cuban humanitarian parolees served in the Bay of Pigs invasion, in the war in southeast Asia, and in the CIA's "secret war" against the Castro government and in the Congo.[21] When refugees were nonwhite or non-Christian, it was generally harder to convince an ambivalent American public that their entry served the American interest. Some refugees were admitted over protest because of a sense of obligation: after the fall of Saigon in 1975, for example, Vietnamese, Hmong, and other southeast Asians were admitted in ever-growing numbers as the failures of US policies in the region became evident. Many of these refugees had served alongside American soldiers in the war in southeast Asia and now suffered retaliation in their homelands for that association. For many Americans back home, however, these southeast Asian refugees were a painful reminder of an unpopular war.

For over 40 years, then, from the end of the Second World War to the fall of the Berlin Wall, Cold War concerns about the political, economic, and military threat of communism shaped the contours of refugee and asylum policy in the United States. The Cold War provided the ideological prism and rationale through which US policy-makers defined who was worthy of admission as a refugee. The end of the Cold War forced US policy-makers to reevaluate their immigration priorities, and soon other geopolitical concerns began to influence and shape their humanitarian responses.

The Refugee Narrative in the Post–Cold War National Security State

The end of the Cold War created a new set of humanitarian challenges for the United States. Millions of people were displaced from their homes as nations disappeared, reconstituted themselves, and politically and economically realigned. The instability in the former Soviet republics, especially Armenia, Azerbaijan, Tajikistan, and Chechnya, created a large-scale movement of people. In China, hundreds of thousands of protesters at Tiananmen Square tried to bring about reforms only to see their pro-democracy movement crushed and thousands of Chinese forced to take refuge in the West. The political and economic destabilization of the Yugoslav republics resulted in war and genocide that forced more than two million people to flee by 1992. In the Persian Gulf region, over a million Iraqi and Kurdish civilians were forced to cross borders in the early 1990s. In central Africa, the genocide in Rwanda killed over 800,000 and led to the creation of sprawling refugee camps in Zaire and Tanzania. War and civil unrest, as well as environmental catastrophes, poverty, and disease resulted in the forced migration of countless people around the globe, internally within their own countries, and across international borders.

As the 20th century came to an end, US policy-makers could not ignore the complexity and scale of forced migration worldwide, and this forced them to reevaluate the country's role in international peacekeeping and foreign aid as well as its immigration and refugee policies. This reevaluation occurred in tandem with a broader conversation on US support for UNHCR and other humanitarian relief organizations.[22] Since the agency's creation, the United States has been the top government donor to UNHCR, assisting its mission to provide relief to displaced persons worldwide. The United States has also relied on

UNHCR, the International Organization for Migration (IOM), and a handful of other nongovernmental organizations to help identify the populations who will fill the United States' annual refugee quota. The final determination about whom to admit—and in what numbers—has always been made by domestic actors, however—the Department of State, and since 2003, the Department of Homeland Security and its Customs and Immigration Services. In making decisions, these government actors have had to balance geopolitical objectives, humanitarian obligations, and domestic pressures. Convincing legislators and their constituents that the admission of refugees serves the national interest has frequently been difficult but became even more so since the terrorist attacks of 1993 and 2001 changed the political landscape. Though the United States remains one of the top resettlement nations in the world—over three million people have been resettled in the United States since the end of the Second World War—the modest annual refugee quotas have routinely gone unfilled since 2001 and were most dramatically cut during the Trump administration.[23] Meanwhile, millions of people have remained trapped for decades in UNHCR refugee camps around the world. The 37 resettlement nations combined have accommodated less than 1% of the total number of displaced persons.[24]

In response to the terrorist attacks of 1993 and 2001, Congress created the new Department of Homeland Security and restructured the immigration bureaucracy within it. This restructuring had profound consequences for all who have tried to enter the United States as tourists, students, and business executives, but its greatest impacts have been felt by refugees and asylum-seekers. The post-9/11 "war on terror" replaced anti-communism as the new lens through which US policy-makers have interpreted eligibility for admission. The vetting of each refugee applicant now takes on average 18–24 months, with no guarantee of admission; and the surveillance of immigrant communities has increased, especially if they come from countries with large Islamic populations, regarded by some as "incubators" of terrorism. The George W. Bush administration, which implemented these changes, justified them as necessary steps to prevent future attacks on the United

States. Public opinion polls showed that the scaling back of refugee (and immigrant) admissions had significant support.[25] In public debate, immigrants, refugees, and asylum-seekers were increasingly portrayed as threats not only to national security but to the safety and well-being of Americans, regardless of the areas of the world they came from. Threat was defined in social, cultural, and economic terms as well as political. By competing with Americans for jobs, or refusing to culturally assimilate, or entering the country without authorization, immigrants were threats to the American way of life, it was argued—a framing familiar to Americans since the 19th century. Refugees encountered a particularly hostile bureaucracy that viewed them as potential threats, and sometimes not even UNHCR's endorsement could help secure a coveted visa.

As in previous generations, US legislators were sensitive to (and shared) their constituents' fears and concerns about immigrants and refugees, but they were also occasionally responsive to advocacy. Humanitarian aid workers, immigrant rights activists, journalists, clergy, scholars, lawyers, and other political actors called attention to humanitarian crises around the world, framed the issues in ways that were comprehensible to the public, urged action, and reminded legislators of American duties and obligations beyond the borders of the state.[26] They helped secure admission for a wide range of displaced persons, many of whom fell outside the traditional categories of persecution defined by statute. Consequently, political dissidents and pro-democracy advocates have continued to receive protection in the post–Cold War and post-9/11 era, but so, too, have victims of trafficking, forced conscription, coercive population control measures, and restrictive gender and sexuality-based norms. Many of those who have been admitted as refugees (or who have received asylum) would not have been eligible just a few decades earlier, but their advocates mobilized political support for them.[27] In addition to the refugee and asylum tracks, Congress has occasionally created other pathways for admission including the Special Immigrant Visas (for people who have aided the US government abroad) and the "T" and "U" visas (for victims of trafficking and criminal activity). Despite these new pathways, refugee advocates argue that the increased focus on securitization means the United States has not adequately met its humanitarian obligations as a world leader.

The post–Cold War and post-9/11 era has presented policy-makers with yet another challenge: the growing number of people who have applied for asylum on US territory, usually at a port of entry such as an airport, a border checkpoint, or even on a Navy or Coast Guard vessel when picked up at sea. Asylum applications were comparatively few during the Cold War, and the cases that generated the most attention in the news media were the defections of high-profile individuals from communist countries—Russian ballet dancers, Cuban baseball players and jazz musicians, Eastern European athletes and coaches, Chinese physicists—whose celebrity or stature made their defections newsworthy. Asylum-seekers were generally released into society while they waited for a resolution of their case. By the late 1980s, petitions for asylum had increased due to the political turmoil in Haiti and the wars in Central America. Over 400,000 people filed for asylum in the United States between 1980 and 1990 alone, and asylum applications have increased with each subsequent decade, thereby also contributing to the backlog of immigration court cases. By December 2021, the backlog of immigration court cases stood at 1.6 million pending cases, the largest on record.[28] These numbers have reinvigorated the argument that the United States' borders are at once too permeable and under siege. In recent years, videos, and photographic images of "migrants caravans" transiting through Mexico to reach the United States have been the most potent and controversial representations of this argument.

Since 1996, both Republican and Democratic administrations have tried to discourage the filing of asylum claims through such practices as interdiction at sea, "expedited removal" and "metering," the denial of work authorization, indefinite detention in immigration prisons, "safe third country" protocols, the denial of legal representation, and during the Trump and Biden administrations, the "Migrant Protection Protocols" (more commonly called the "Remain in Mexico" program), which forces border-crossing asylum-seekers to wait for a determination of their case in Mexico, and "Title 42" expulsions, which bar entry to those who have been in a country where communicable diseases are present. The use of "Title 42" alone has turned away more than 1.7 million people since the onset of the COVID-19 pandemic.[29] (It was suspended in the spring of 2023.) These polices have raised concerns at home and abroad that the United States has neglected its humanitarian obligations, and through removal and deportation, violated the principle of *non-refoulment.*

Though many refugees and asylum-seekers have found their aspirations thwarted, others have been fast-tracked for entry, once again in support of foreign policy agendas. Shortly after President Joseph R. Biden announced the withdrawal of American troops from Afghanistan in 2021, the administration enacted Operation Allies Refuge and Operation Allies Welcome to airlift Afghan interpreters, embassy employees, and other at-risk personnel and their families from Kabul. By February 2022, the United States had resettled 74,000 Afghans in the United States under the Special Immigrant Visa (SIV) and humanitarian parole programs. After the Russian invasion of Ukraine in February 2022, the 15,000 Ukrainians who requested asylum at the US-Mexico border were fast-tracked for admission. The Biden administration also announced that 100,000 Ukrainian refugees (out of the 5 million who have fled to Poland, Hungary, and other European countries) would be resettled in the United States through a variety of legal pathways including parole, asylum, and temporary protected status.[30]

A Nation of Refuge?

In the 21st century, the term "refugee" continues to be used freely by policy-makers, journalists, and immigrant advocates to refer to a wide range of people of humanitarian concern, but the term's more precise definition in American law today continues to make it difficult for many to be resettled in the United States. Calling a group of people "refugees" does not mean the government will offer them resettlement. Proving a compelling protection need and passing the securitized vetting continue to be the most difficult hurdles for refugees to overcome.[31]

Today's asylum-seekers must meet an even higher burden of proof because their arrival on US territory (usually without authorization) immediately makes them suspect. They must navigate complex legal hurdles without the advice of lawyers or even translators because the federal government is not required by law to provide asylum-seekers with legal representation.[32] Many attorneys, translators, law school clinics, expert witnesses, and immigrant advocates assist asylum-seekers pro bono with their petitions, but the demand for assistance far exceeds the supply. These unofficial actors, when available, are enormously influential in securing a successful outcome. Due to the backlog of cases in immigration courts, wait times for a hearing on an immigrant's asylum claims now average 58 months; many of them must wait in either immigrant detention facilities or in the immigrant shantytowns that have emerged just across the US-Mexico boundary line.[33] Less than a quarter of all asylum cases today have a successful outcome, and success rates vary across groups or nationalities.[34] Because the merits of asylum are always evaluated on a case-by-case basis, identical cases heard by different asylum officers or immigration courts can result in vastly different outcomes.

The difficulties encountered by refugees and the harsh measures directed at asylum-seekers raise important ethical and moral questions. Over the years, Americans of conscience have advocated on the behalf of refugees and asylum-seekers. During the 1980s, for example, both faith and secular communities across the United States, working with their counterparts in Mexico and Canada, created "sanctuaries" for Salvadorans and Guatemalans who fled the brutal wars in the region and were now trying to avoid detention and deportation. With asylum-seekers having a less than 5% chance of securing asylum in the 1980s, sanctuary workers argued that Americans had a moral responsibility to assist Central Americans given the role the Reagan and Bush administrations had played in destabilizing the region.[35] These immigrant advocates also filed class action suits to protest the conditions in immigration detention centers and the lack of due process in asylum hearings.

Since the turn of the 21st century, immigrant advocates have continued to offer sanctuary and other forms of social and legal assistance, not only to the Central Americans who continue to flee the isthmus but also other migrants who are transiting through the region hoping to find refuge in the United States or Canada. To prevent the deaths that are too common along the desert stretches of the US-Mexico borderlands, a new generation of sanctuary workers leaves food, water, and medicine in various locations, even though federal authorities consider such actions "aiding and abetting" potential lawbreakers and thus a violation of US law.[36] These advocates are part of a broader immigrant rights movement that has questioned the militarizing of borders, the inhumane and indefinite detention of migrants, and the development, free trade, energy, and security policies that have left millions of people vulnerable and displaced them from their homes. All these policies, they argue, have prevented people worldwide from exercising the basic human right to stay home.

Other challenges lie ahead. The expanding awareness that societies are accelerating climate change to life-threatening levels must force the United States and other countries to reevaluate the populations they prioritize for assistance and adjust their immigration, refugee, and asylum policies accordingly. Millions of people are being forced to migrate within their own countries and across national borders because of the loss of livelihoods caused by extreme weather events such as hurricanes, earthquakes, and volcanic eruptions, which have become fiercer as the planet grows warmer. They have also been displaced by more slowly developing catastrophes such as drought, desertification, rising sea levels and erosion, the salination of land and water sources, air pollution, and toxic waste. Researchers and humanitarian agencies forecast that several hundred million will be displaced over the next 50 years if climate change is not mitigated and populations helped to adapt.

Those displaced by natural disasters and climate change are often called "climate refugees," but like many other forced migrants, they are ineligible for refugee status under statutory definitions of the term.[37] Some humanitarian activists have urged the United Nations to revise its refugee convention to recognize a wider range of conditions that create vulnerability, including climate change, in order to make those affected juridically visible, as well as to offer countries more substantive guidance in responding to the new realities of forced migration worldwide. UNHCR and other agencies, which receive much of their funding from the United States, have resisted such calls for radical reform for fear that it will "shift attention away from the specific needs of refugees and from the legal obligations the international community has agreed upon to address them."[38] They view such a revision as unnecessary and, instead, have urged countries to offer complementary protection to those who fall outside legal definitions of refugee status.[39] Such complementary protections are necessary to ensure a just and humane response to those made vulnerable by conditions beyond their control. And yet, over the past decade, dozens of bills introduced in the United States Congress to offer complementary protection to multiple types of forced migrants have died in committee.

Refugees and asylum-seekers, like other forced migrants, will remain a challenge for the United States in the decades to come, continually testing our commitment to the country's founding narrative. In a politically divided country, it's unclear who will be prioritized for admission to the United States in the years to come—or in what numbers. The only certainty is that people of conscience will continue to hold their legislators accountable and encourage a recommitment to the noble idea—flawed though the history has shown it to be—that the United States is a refuge for the vulnerable and the oppressed.

Notes

1. Donna R. Gabaccia, "Nation of Immigrants: Do Words Matter?" *The Pluralist* 5, no. 3 (Fall 2010), 5–31. See also Mae Ngai, chap. 9, this vol.
2. Roxanne Dunbar-Ortiz, "Stop Saying This Is a Nation of Immigrants," *Counterpunch*, May 16, 2006, https://www.counterpunch.org/2006/05/31/stop-saying-this-is-a-nation-of-immigrants/; Adam Goodman, "A Nation of Migrants," *Dissent*, October 8, 2015, https://www.dissentmagazine.org/blog/nation-of-migrants-1965-immigration-act-at-fifty.
3. Evan Taparata, "No Asylum for Mankind: The Creation of Refugee Law and Policy in the United States, 1776–1951" (PhD diss., University of Minnesota, 2018), 1.
4. Avidan Kent and Simon Behrman write that the refugee definition is an "evolving concept": the term "refugee" has been around for 500 years, but the experience of seeking asylum reaches very back into history. See *Facilitating the Resettlement and*

Rights of Climate Refugees: An Argument for Developing Existing Principles and Practices (New York: Routledge, 2019), 40–71.

5. See, for example, Jon Butler, *The Huguenots in America: A Refugee People in New World Society* (Cambridge, MA: Harvard University Press, 1983); Maya Jasanoff, *Liberty's Exiles: American Loyalists in the Revolutionary World* (New York: Alfred A. Knopf, 2011); Nathalie Dessens, *From Saint-Domingue to New Orleans: Migration and Influences* (Gainesville: University of Florida Press, 2010); Maria Esther Hammack, "South of Slavery: Freedom Fighters and Block Movement Across a Global Frontier, Mexico, the United States and Beyond, 1790–1868" (PhD diss., University of Texas at Austin, 2021); Harvey Amani Whitfield, *Blacks on the Border: The Black Refugees in British North America, 1815–1860* (Burlington: University of Vermont Press, 2006); Kerby A. Miller, *Emigrants and Exiles: Ireland and the Irish Exodus to North America* (New York: Oxford University Press, 1985); Jesse Hoffnung-Garskof, *Racial Migrations: New York City and the Revolutionary Politics of the Spanish Caribbean, 1850–1902* (Princeton, NJ: Princeton University Press, 2019).

6. See, for example, Hidetaka Hirota, *Expelling the Poor: Atlantic Seaboard States and the Nineteenth-Century Origins of American Immigration Policy* (New York: Oxford University Press, 2017); Tony Allan Freyer, *The Passenger Cases and the Commerce Clause: Immigrants, Blacks, and States' Rights in Antebellum America* (Lawrence: University Press of Kansas, 2014); Anna Law, "The Myth of 'Open Borders,'" *Washington Post*, September 21, 2021, https://www.washingtonpost.com/outlook/2021/09/21/myth-open-borders/.

7. Lan Duong and Yen Espiritu, "Toward Critical Refugee Studies: Being and Becoming in Exceptional States of War, Violence, and Militarism," University of California Humanities Research Institute, https://uchri.org/awards/toward-critical-refugee-studies-being-and-becoming-in-exceptional-states-of-war-violence-and-militarism/, accessed September 23, 2021.

8. Julian Lim, "Immigration, Asylum, and Citizenship: A More Holistic Approach," *California Law Review* 101, no. 4 (2013): 1013–78. See also Julian Lim, *Porous Borders: Multiracial Migrations and the Law in the U.S.-Mexico Borderlands* (Chapel Hill: University of North Carolina Press, 2017).

9. Taparata, "No Asylum for Mankind."

10. Two important works that provide an overview of the Cold War period are Carl J. Bon Tempo, *Americans at the Gate: The United States and Refugees during the Cold War* (Princeton, NJ: Princeton University Press, 2008), and Gil Loescher and John A Scanlan, *Calculated Kindness: Refugees and America's Half-Open Door, 1945 to the Present* (New York: Free Press, 1986).

11. Maddalena Marinari, Madeline Yuan-Yin Hsu, and Maria Cristina Garcia, eds., *A Nation of Immigrants Reconsidered: US Society in an Age of Restriction, 1924–1965* (Urbana: University of Illinois Press, 2019); Peter Schrag, *The World of Aufbau: Hitler's Refugees in America* (Madison: University of Wisconsin Press, 2019); *Treatment of Latin Americans of Japanese Descent, European Americans, and Jewish Refugees during World War II: Hearing before the Subcommittee on Immigration, Citizenship, Refugees, Border Security, and International Law of the Committee on the*

Judiciary, US House of Representatives, 111th Cong., 1st sess., March 19, 2009 (Washington, DC: US Government Printing Office, 2009), https://www.heinonline .org/HOL/Page?handle=hein.cbhear/fdsysakgio001&id=1&size=2&collection =immigration&index=immigration; Steven Mintz, "Immigration Policy in World War II," Gilder Lehrman Institute for American History, https://www.gilderlehrman .org/history-resources/teaching-resource/immigration-policy-world-war-ii, accessed January 16, 2022; Roger Daniels, *Coming to America: A History of Immigration and Ethnicity in American Life,* 2nd ed. (New York: Perennial, 2002).

12. Senator Patrick McCarran speaking on the Walter-McCarran Act, 83rd Cong., 1st sess., *Congressional Record,* 99 (March 2, 1953), S 1518. See Maddalena Marinari, *Unwanted: Italian and Jewish Mobilization against Restrictive Laws, 1882–1965* (Chapel Hill: University of North Carolina Press, 2020).

13. American policies allowed former Nazi scientists to enter the United States and become citizens to prevent the Soviets and Eastern Bloc countries from using their expertise against the United States and its allies during the Cold War. Monique Laney, *German Rocketeers in the Heart of Dixie: Making Sense of the Nazi Past during the Civil Rights Era* (New Haven, CT: Yale University Press, 2015); Annie Jacobsen, *Operation Paperclip: The Secret Intelligence Program that Brought Nazi Scientists to America* (New York: Little, Brown, 2014).

14. Harry S. Truman, "Statement by the President Upon Signing the Displaced Persons Act," June 25, 1948, The American Presidency Project, https://www .presidency.ucsb.edu/node/232598.

15. Refugee Relief Act of 1953, Pub. L. No. 83–203, *U.S. Statutes at Large* 76 (1953): 400–7.

16. Migration and Refugee Assistance Act of 1962, Pub. L. No. 87–510 (1962), https:// www.govtrack.us/congress/bills/87/hr8291/text.

17. Hart-Celler allowed for the "conditional entry" of 10,200 refugees. An Act to Amend the Immigration and Nationality Act, H.R. 2580, Pub. L. No. 89–236 (1965). The numerical allotment for refugees was set at 6% of overall admissions. The Middle East was defined as the territory between and including Libya on the west, Turkey on the north, Pakistan on the east, and Saudi Arabia and Ethiopia on the south.

18. The 1951 Convention limited the focus of assistance to European refugees in the aftermath of the Second World War. The 1967 Protocol removed these temporal and geographic restrictions. "The 1951 Refugee Convention," UNHCR, http://www .unhcr.org/pages/49da0e466.html.

19. 1980 Refugee Act, Pub. L. No. 96–212 (1980), https://www.gpo.gov/fdsys/pkg /STATUTE-94/pdf/STATUTE-94-Pg102.pdf.

20. Since passage of the 1980 Refugee Act, the White House, in consultation with Congress, has set annual limits on the number of refugees admitted from different regions of the world. The president has submitted to the House of Representatives a proposal (known as the consultation document) with the administration's suggested worldwide refugee ceiling and the various regional sub-allocations. Following congressional discussion, negotiation, and approval, the president has then issued the "presidential determination" establishing the official refugee numbers for the upcoming fiscal year. The 1980 Refugee Act also

authorized temporary assistance to refugees to facilitate their cultural integration and economic self-sufficiency in the United States. The goal has been to turn these refugees, who are so central to American immigration mythology, into self-sufficient, English-speaking Americans. The Office of Refugee Resettlement has contracted with national, state, and local agencies to assist refugees find housing, furnishings, food, and clothing, as well as provide language instruction and employment training and placement. After one year in refugee status, refugees have become eligible to adjust their status to lawful permanent resident status; and after five years of residence in the United States, they have been able to apply for citizenship, like other immigrant groups (1980 Refugee Act, 102). See also Andorra Bruno, "Refugee Admissions and Resettlement Policy" (Washington, DC: Congressional Research Service, December 18, 2018), https://crsreports.congress.gov/product/pdf/RL/RL31269/24; "Resettlement Services," Office of Refugee Resettlement, US Department of Health and Human Services, https://www.acf.hhs.gov/orr/programs/refugees, accessed September 18, 2021.

21. Maria Cristina Garcia, *Havana USA: Cuban Exiles and Cuban Americans in South Florida, 1959–1994* (Berkeley: University of California Press, 1996).
22. Michael N. Barnett, *Empire of Humanity: A History of Humanitarianism* (Ithaca, NY: Cornell University Press, 2011). See also Maria Cristina Garcia, *The Refugee Challenge in Post–Cold War America* (New York: Oxford University Press, 2017).
23. Migration Policy Institute, " US Annual Refugee Resettlement Ceilings and Number of Refugees Admitted, 1980 to the Present," https://www.migrationpolicy.org/programs/data-hub/charts/us-refugee-resettlement, accessed July 3, 2023. See also National Immigration Forum, "Fact Sheet: U.S. Refugee Resettlement," November 5, 2020, https://immigrationforum.org/article/fact-sheet-u-s-refugee-resettlement/.
24. National Immigration Forum, "U.S. Refugee Resettlement."
25. This assessment is based on a sample of public opinion polls conducted during 2003–2008 and available at the Roper Center for Public Opinion Research at Cornell University, https://ropercenter-cornell-edu.proxy.library.cornell.edu/.
26. Margaret E. Keck and Kathryn Sikkink, *Activists beyond Borders: Advocacy Networks in International Politics* (Ithaca, NY: Cornell University Press, 1998), 2–3.
27. For a theoretical discussion of framing and communicating human rights norms see Keck and Sikkink, *Activists beyond Borders*; Thomas Risse-Kappen, Steve C Ropp, and Kathryn Sikkink, *The Power of Human Rights: International Norms and Domestic Change* (Cambridge: Cambridge University Press, 1999); Alison Brysk, *Speaking Rights to Power: Constructing Political Will* (New York: Oxford University Press, 2013).
28. "Immigration Court Backlog Now Growing Faster than Ever, Burying Judges in an Avalanche of Cases," Transactional Records Access Clearinghouse (TRAC), January 18, 2022, https://trac.syr.edu/immigration/reports/675/.
29. Ben Fox, "U.S. Launches New Program to Welcome Ukrainian Refugees, But No Longer through Mexico," PBS News Hour, April 21, 2022, https://www.pbs.org/newshour/politics/u-s-launches-new-program-to-welcome-ukraine-refugees-but-no-longer-through-mexico.

30. "What Is Next for Afghans Who Fled to the United States?" Department of Homeland Security, "Operation Allies Welcome," June 6, 2022, https://www.dhs.gov/allieswelcome; White House, "Fact Sheet: The Biden Administration Announces New Humanitarian, Development, and Democracy Assistance to Ukraine and the Surrounding Region," March 24, 2022, https://www.whitehouse.gov/briefing-room/statements-releases/2022/03/24/fact-sheet-the-biden-administration-announces-new-humanitarian-development-and-democracy-assistance-to-ukraine-and-the-surrounding-region/.

31. US statutes impose certain requirements: refugees must have traveled *outside* of their country of origin or of last residence; they must prove that they have been persecuted because of race, religion, nationality, membership in a particular social group, or political opinion; they must demonstrate that they have a reasonable fear of future persecution; they must show that they have failed to receive protection from their state; and they must confirm that they have not inflicted harm on others (only civilians can be refugees) and do not pose a national security threat. In addition to these requirements, the US State Department has categorized refugees according to "processing priorities." Priority One cases, for example, are those refugees with "compelling protection needs" who are referred by the UNHCR, a US embassy, or a designated nongovernmental organization, while Priority Two cases are those of special humanitarian concern to the United States such as persecuted religious minorities whom the White House has singled out for special protection. Priority Three cases have been the spouses, parents, and unmarried children (under the age of 21) of persons admitted lawfully to the United States as refugees, asylees, or green-card holders. See "United States Refugee Admissions Program (USRAP) Consultation and Processing Priorities," available at https://www.uscis.gov/humanitarian/refugees-asylum/refugees/united-states-refugee-admissions-program-usrap-consultation-worldwide-processing-priorities. See also US Department of State, "The United States Refugee Admissions Program: Reforms for a New Era of Refugee Resettlement," 2009, https://2001-2009.state.gov/g/prm/refadm/rls/rpts/36059.htm.

32. Asylum-seekers must maneuver a complex legal bureaucracy that operates on several different "sub-tracks." Those who have legally entered the United States on a temporary visa can apply for asylum at one of the offices of the US Citizenship and Immigration Services (USCIS). These cases are known as the "affirmative" cases for asylum. The asylum officer reviews applications, interviews the applicants, and decides whether the applicants are refugees. An applicant who is an unauthorized immigrant and requests asylum files a "defensive" application (to prevent removal from the United States by securing asylum). Defensive cases are heard by an immigration judge rather than an asylum officer. The same legal test applies to both affirmative and defensive asylum applications: applicants must show they have a well-founded fear of persecution based on race, religion, nationality, political opinion, or membership in a particular social group. However, establishing a well-founded fear is far more difficult in defensive cases—the burden of proof is higher. In both affirmative and defensive cases, applicants

denied asylum can try to request "Withholding of Removal" before an immigration judge but meeting the standard of proof is also difficult.

33. TRAC, "Immigration Court Backlog."
34. For detailed information on asylum cases across immigration courts, consult the records of the Transactional Records Access Clearinghouse (TRAC), https://trac.syr.edu/.
35. Maria Cristina Garcia, *Seeking Refuge: Central American Migration in Mexico, the United States, and Canada* (Berkeley: University of California Press, 2006), 98–108.
36. Carl Lindskoog, "Sanctuary Is Justice: Resilience and Ingenuity in the Sanctuary Movement since 1986," in *Whose America? Immigration Policy since 1980*, ed. Maria Cristina Garcia and Maddalena Marinari (Urbana: University of Illinois Press, 2023), 190–208; Susan Bibler Coutin, "Smugglers or Samaritans in Tucson, Arizona: Producing and Contesting Legal Truth," *American Ethnologist* 22, no. 3 (1995): 549–71; Isaac Stanley-Becker, "An Activist Faced 20 Years in Prison for Helping Migrants. But Jurors Wouldn't Convict Him," *Washington Post*, June 12, 2019, https://www.washingtonpost.com/nation/2019/06/12/scott-warren-year-sentence-hung-jury-aiding-migrants/.
37. In some cases, those displaced by environmental disruptions could be considered refugees *sur place* if they demonstrate a well-founded fear of persecution because human rights violations erupted in their country after they left. UNHCR, "Handbook on Procedures and Criteria for Determining Refugee Status under the 1951 Convention and the 1967 Protocol Relating to the Status of Refugees" (Geneva: UNHCR, 1992), 16, http://www.unhcr.org/4d93528a9.pdf. UNHCR, "UNHCR, Refugee Protection, and International Migration," January 7, 2007, 5, http://www.unhcr.org/4a24ef0ca2.pdf; Norwegian Refugee Council, "Climate Changed: People Displaced," April 15, 2009, 19, https://www.nrc.no/resources/reports/climate-changed—people-displaced/.
38. UNHCR, "'Refugees' and 'Migrants'—Frequently Asked Questions (FAQs)," March 16, 2016, https://www.unhcr.org/news/stories/refugees-and-migrants-frequently-asked-questions-faqs; Essam El-Hinnawi, *Environmental Refugees* (Nairobi: United Nations Environment Programme, 1985); Jodi L. Jacobson, *Environmental Refugees: A Yardstick of Habitability* (Washington, DC: Worldwatch Institute, 1988); Astri Suhrke and Annamaria Visentin, "The Environmental Refugee: A New Approach," *Ecodecision*, September 1991, 73–74; Patricia L. Saunders, "Environmental Refugees: The Origins of a Construct," in *Political Ecology: Science, Myth and Power*, ed. Philip Anthony Stott and Sian Sullivan (London: Hodder Education Publishers, 2000); James Morrissey, "Rethinking the 'Debate on Environmental Refugees': From 'Maximalists and Minimalists' to 'Proponents and Critics,'" *Journal of Political Ecology* 19, no. 1 (2012): 36–49.
39. Dina Ionesco, "Let's Talk about Climate Migrants, Not Climate Refugees," United Nations, June 6, 2019, https://www.un.org/sustainabledevelopment/blog/2019/06/lets-talk-about-climate-migrants-not-climate-refugees/.

CHAPTER 12

Who Supports Immigration Reform?

Ana Raquel Minian

"It's off the Richter scale in terms of importance for the Republican electorate," said John Thomas, a Republican strategist, in June 2021. He was talking immigration—an issue that has divided the nation. In broad strokes, those who identify as conservative seek to rid the nation of unauthorized migrants, while liberals have a seemingly more moderate position, which includes the possibility of legalizing undocumented migrants who are already in the country. These distinct positions on immigration seem as fixed as concrete.

But it was not always so. Curtailing immigration used to be a bedrock goal of groups traditionally associated with the "Left," while "conservatives" sought to allow unauthorized migration to continue uninterrupted. It was only between the 1970s and the 1980s that the anti-immigrant rhetoric changed from "Left" to "Right" on the political spectrum. This chapter traces this change by exploring the history of the Immigration Reform and Control Act (IRCA), which wound its way through Washington from 1972 until its passage in 1986.

In order to understand the views and concerns of those involved in crafting IRCA, one source is especially revealing: congressional hearings. When debating the various immigration bills, Congress held a series of hearings and invited representatives of relevant business groups, Mexican American advocacy organizations, and labor unions to offer testimony. Although the hearings do not demonstrate the full spectrum of political opinions or the actual negotiations that happened behind closed doors, they constitute the key source of formal political discourse. The hearings display the rhetoric that politicians thought would be most convincing, both to each other and to Americans at large.

The hearings show that in the early 1970s it was labor unions and Mexican American organizations, groups generally branded as liberal, which demanded sanctions on employers who knowingly hired unauthorized migrants. For their part, employer lobbies that depended on undocumented workers, and that are generally considered conservative organizations, insisted that migrants were a needed labor force. It was only in the late 1970s and early 1980s that the appeals to curtail undocumented migration came to adopt a more conservative base and international vision. During these years, liberal groups started to support unauthorized workers while conservative ones decided to stop defending migrants, and focused instead on promoting the notion of "law and order."

Along the long and tortured road that culminated in the passage of the 1986 law, policy-makers constantly questioned whether migrants drained the nation's welfare coffers, took jobs away from citizens, increased population growth through their excessive fertility rates, or blurred the nation's boundaries through their illegal entrances. Even though the hearings, to various degrees, all revolved around questions of welfare, unemployment, border permeability, kinship, and population control, policy-makers overlooked how these very issues guided the migratory process and emboldened migrants to live in the United States. Far removed from the world of migrants, those inside the marble and sandstone walls of the US Capitol—from both the "Left" and the "Right"—overlooked one important narrative on migration: that of migrants themselves.[1]

It is thus not surprising that when the law finally passed in 1986, it failed miserably in its intended goals. When Ronald Reagan signed the bill, he hailed it as "the most comprehensive reform of our immigration laws since 1952" and added that "future generation of Americans will be thankful for our efforts to humanely regain control of our borders."[2] His statement accurately predicted the significance of IRCA: the law became the most important legislation regulating immigration to the United States for at least 30 years following its passage. But Reagan's claim that future generations would be thankful for it proved incorrect. Scholars, Mexican American activists, and US politicians from both the left and the right of the political spectrum soon declared the law a failure. Indeed, legislators passed IRCA in order to reduce the number of undocumented migrants living in the United States. But, in the two decades following its passage, the number of unauthorized migrants grew faster than ever. While in 1986, there were 3.2 million undocumented migrants, the number reached 5 million in 1996, and peaked at approximately 11 million in 2006.[3]

The Shifting Views of Labor Unions and Mexican American Organizations

The seeds that grew into IRCA were planted by pro-union politicians who denounced migrants for taking jobs away from citizens and draining state and federal welfare coffers. In 1972, Representative Peter W. Rodino (D-NJ), a strong ally of the AFL-CIO and chair of the House Judiciary Committee's Subcommittee on Immigration, introduced the first bill to impose sanctions on employers who knowingly hired undocumented workers.[4] He argued that employer sanctions would reduce the demand for unauthorized labor, which would, in turn, discourage those who did not have papers from migrating. The bill contained ancillary measures that required the Department of Health, Education, and Welfare to disclose the names of undocumented migrants who received public assistance benefits and amended federal law to prohibit the misuse of entry documents.[5] Pro-union Representative Joshua Eilberg (D-PA) came out in support of the bill, declaring that unsanctioned migration "compromises labor conditions, depresses wages, and deprives Americans of jobs."[6] The AFL-CIO had a similar stance: "With more than 7,500,000 Americans unemployed and joblessness rising, the presence of millions of illegal aliens in this country is an acute and growing problem."[7] The federation condemned "the heavy need of these illegal immigrants for free medical care, unemployment compensation, welfare and social services," which put "heavy burdens on government at every level and on the taxpayers of the nation."[8]

During the early 1970s, mainstream Mexican American organizations—which, like unions, were considered liberal groups—upheld the view that undocumented migrants were contributing to the nation's unemployment rates and welfare problems. The stance of the United Farm Workers (UFW) was particularly strong, in part because it was an AFL-CIO union. But most mainstream Mexican American organizations also sought to increase restrictions against Mexican foreigners, whom they blamed for the denigration that Mexican Americans faced in the United States. In the hearings on the issue of unauthorized migration held in 1975, the National Congress of Hispanic-American Citizens, which was linked to some of the most important Mexican American organizations, defended employer sanctions, claiming that "if the purpose of immigration laws is to protect the domestic work force, it is logical to exercise the most stringent control at the place of work."[9] During these years, only radical Chicana/o organizations, which did not voice their position in Congress, argued against the idea that migrants stole jobs from citizens and drained welfare. The Centro de Acción Social Autónoma (CASA), one of these groups, declared in its pamphlets: "The Rodino bill is not the solution to the growing wave of problems which confront this society and manifest themselves in the growing numbers of unemployed or high prices."[10] In terms of welfare, CASA maintained that because workers were "not to blame for fewer jobs or lower salaries," it was the government's responsibility to provide them with income.[11]

Migrants' need to have basic welfare provisions and access to jobs, did, in fact, influence migratory patterns, but the relationship between these various issues was much more complex than unions and Mexican American organizations depicted. Individuals migrated without authorization because of Mexico's high levels of unemployment and underemployment. In the United States they took poorly paid jobs, often in the service industry, which US citizens did not want. Though migrants were lambasted for stealing welfare dollars, the reality was that they did not qualify for US welfare aid and only a few dared to apply illegally. But their jobs in the United States, however meager, provided them and their families with a "safety net" in the absence of a welfare state that might have supported them. As Adalberto Rodríguez recalls, even though he missed his family tremendously, he migrated continuously between Mexico and the United States because in his hometown there was not enough work to sustain him. "There were times when one would think I'm not coming back [to the United States] because it was so hard. . . . I would even start shivering before my departures, but despite this pain, [economic] need was greater," he explains.[12] Unemployment in Mexico made him return to the fields of Coachella Valley every year. There, he was often paid below the minimum wage and lived in cardboard boxes under trees. While these jobs were undesirable to US citizens, for Rodríguez and other migrants they represented a source of income that allowed them to survive and send money back home without relying on state aid. As Rodríguez snickered in 2015: "In all the years I have living here in the United States, the government has given me nothing, not even a smear of Vaseline."[13]

In the mid-1970s, unions and mainstream Mexican American organizations started tempering—and sometimes even reversing—their anti-immigrant position. The development of a Chicana/o identity, which was inherently political, led many Mexican Americans to start seeing Mexicans as their brethren and to insist that anti-immigrant sentiments and policies translated into discriminatory measures against anyone who looked brown.[14] A Mexican American labor union official articulated this increasingly common position when he claimed that Mexican Americans who still favored anti-immigrant policies "should realize that they would not be here if their fathers had not been illegal aliens."[15] As a result of the new perspective on undocumented migrants among Mexican Americans, the ever visible "Hispanic lobby" composed of the National Council of la Raza (NCLR), the Mexican American Legal Defense and Education Fund (MALDEF), the League of United Latin American Citizens (LULAC), and the UFW began to support Mexican migrants.[16] In 1977, the Hispanic lobby gained the backing of the newly created Congressional Hispanic Caucus, formed by Latino represen-tatives in Congress. The caucus's small numbers meant that it had limited power (as late as 1984, there were only 10 Latinos in Congress, and they were all in the House of Representatives, a small portion of the House's 435 total seats). Still, the caucus represented a part of the growing number of Mexican American groups that advocated for un-documented migrants.

As Mexican American organizations began to defend unauthorized workers, they changed their rhetoric on the impact migrants suppos-edly had on the nation's welfare coffers and unemployment rates. In his 1978 testimony before the United States Commission on Civil Rights, Michael Cortés, then vice president of the NCLR, claimed, "There is a growing body of research that concludes that certain jobs have traditionally been shunned by the domestic labor force. Those jobs have traditionally been filled by immigrants."[17] Cortés refuted the notion that migrants exploited welfare, noting that the press and poli-ticians falsely accused undocumented migrants of "illegally receiving welfare payments and otherwise burdening the public treasury." In-stead, he claimed, "undocumented workers are subject to withholding taxes and social security taxes in most employment settings," but un-like citizens and permanent residents, they "typically do not receive publicly supported protections and services paid for by those taxes."[18] Mexican American organizations also insisted that employer sanctions would increase discriminatory employment practices against brown people. As Vilma Martinez, the president of MALDEF, argued at hear-ings on unauthorized migration held in 1981: "For Mexican Americans and other Americans who share the physical characteristics of persons thought to be undocumented, employer sanctions will exacerbate ex-isting patterns of employment discrimination."[19]

During the late 1970s and early 1980s, several unions also changed their stance. The United Auto Workers, the Longshoremen's Union, the United Electrical Workers, the Hotel Employees and Restaurant Employees, and the International Ladies' Garment Workers Union (ILGWU) came to realize that they could not survive in the long run without recruiting the growing population of Mexican nationals. The case of the ILGWU is illustrative. Between 1948 and 1979, ILGWU's membership fell from 67% to 10% of all of the workers who labored in ladies' garments in Los Angeles.[20] This decline could be partially traced to the growing anti-union sentiments in the United States as well as to the ILGWU's failures to organize undocumented migrants who were a growing proportion of the workers of the garment industry.[21] To counter these patterns, the ILGWU began to hire Mexican migrant organizers so that they would enroll undocumented workers in the union. As ILGWU activist María Elena Salazar explained to fellow union members: "For our own survival we cannot adopt the perspective that it is impossible to unionize them [unauthorized laborers]."[22] The ILGWU, in turn, expanded its recruitment efforts through various means, including by publishing a series of cartoons. One of them (Figure 12.1) challenged Spanish-speaking employees to join the union by asking them: "What Type of Worker Are You?" In it, a janitor complains: "I can't join the union because I am 'illegal' and I don't have rights. . . . Besides I am already going to return to my home country and also I don't have

Figure 12.1. "What Type of Worker Are You?" ILGWU cartoon.
Source: El Centro de Información Para Asuntos Migratorios y Fronterizos Del Comité de Servicio de los Amigos, Boletín Informativo Sobre Asuntos Migratorios y Fronterizos (August–September, 1980): 10. Benson Latin American Collection, LLILAS Benson Latin American Studies and Collections, the University of Texas at Austin.

time and blah, blah, blah and blah, blah, blah." In response, a garment worker scoffs: "It is not illegal to be a worker! We produce much wealth for this country and we have the right to a union. The exploitative employers that steal from us are the illegals. . . . I support the union!"[23]

Cartoons such as this one recognized the exploitation that migrants faced, contested their "illegality," and replaced the traditional union narrative that depicted migrants as draining the US economy for one in which they "created much wealth" for the country. ILGWU organizers like Salazar openly discussed the fact that undocumented migrants were taking jobs that US citizens refused to take. As she explained, employers "don't find [US citizens] who come to work in the garment industry because they pay the minimum wage . . . and they greatly exploit the people. It is hard work."[24] The shift in attitudes could sometimes seem like a contradiction. At the congressional hearings, the ILGWU continued to support employer sanctions and sometimes even offered pejorative stereotypes about the economic effects of undocumented migrants; yet it also began to favor the legalization of those who were already in the United States so that they could become legal permanent residents.[25]

After switching their position, some unions and Mexican American organizations started to argue that migrants who were already in the country should be allowed to become permanent residents. In the hearings held in 1981, the president of MALDEF insisted that lawmakers should adjust "the status of undocumented workers who have equities in our society" given that they worked "in our industries, [paid] taxes, and contribute[d] to our economic welfare."[26] Many undocumented migrants were elated by the possibility that the law being discussed could help them legalize their status and eventually enable them to acquire a green card and even citizenship. Wendy Rodríguez, whose parents had brought her to the United States as a child, recalls that she and her high school classmates, who were "going through the same thing" she was because they were also undocumented, would regularly talk about how the new law might help them gain legal status.[27]

Under pressure from some of its own unions and Mexican American organizations, the AFL-CIO capitulated to calls for legalization, and, even though it continued to call for employer sanctions, it started to insist that a sanctions law include measures to prevent discrimination. In the 1985 hearings, the federation called for "the most generous, practical, legalization program."[28] That stance stood in stark contrast to its position just a decade earlier, when the federation had held that in "the matter of the so-called amnesty," it "opposed [measures that] would sweep into legalization for employment large numbers of aliens who came here illegally in the first place" even while it recognized that "a strong case" could "be made for permitting aliens with family and employment ties going back over a reasonable period of years to become eligible for permanent residency."[29]

The Business Community Weighs In

This decade-long migration of attitudes placed Mexican American organizations and unions closer to the traditional stance of business lobbies. For many employers, unauthorized workers constituted a cheap and exploitable labor force. Research conducted by the Concentrated Enforcement Program, an agency established by the US federal government to protect workers, found that in San Diego, 33% of the companies inspected did not pay undocumented migrants the minimum wage or overtime, while almost none of the farms and ranches in the area did so.[30] Some employers also benefited from deportations as these allowed them to avoid paying migrants the wages they owed them. Rodolfo Rosales, who migrated from Zacatecas in 1978, described a particularly abusive, but not particularly unusual, tactic: one of his employers took him and a group of other workers to a remote place to harvest onions for a week. When the job was done, claimed Rosales, "[the boss] failed to pay me." Rosales could not complain, however, because, as he explained, his employer drove off and "just left me there . . . and immigration officials caught me."[31]

At the hearings, employers defended the practice of hiring undocumented workers by insisting that migrants took jobs US citizens didn't want. Although the United States was facing high unemployment levels, employers held, Americans refused to take hard jobs. This meant that unauthorized workers were needed. The US Chamber of Commerce, for example, maintained: "When unemployment is high, the desire to exclude illegal aliens reaches frustrating levels," but "undocumented workers do not cause unemployment."[32]

Employers also reframed stereotypes about the relationship between migrants and welfare in a way that allowed them to critique federal welfare provision more broadly. The Arizona Cattle Growers' Association explained that few American workers actually wanted to perform the hard jobs needed at ranches. At these sites, employers could not "find many so-called domestic Americans willing to fill this job description." Sarcastically, the association's representatives then asked: "Why should they, when [the] system provides a better life through the various and sundry programs available to American workers. Most unemployment and welfare programs in this country now reward an individual for not working as hard as he has to on an Arizona ranch."[33] The association thus repeated the oft-told link between idleness and welfare but with a particular twist: that state benefits were the actual cause of unemployment among Americans and a reason why employers had no choice but to hire migrants.

Some businesses even upheld the argument posed by Mexican American organizations that employer sanctions would induce them to discriminate against brown people. In their statement, the Arizona Cattle Growers' Association asked, "How does a rancher, for instance, differentiate between a legal domestic worker of Mexican descent and a so-called illegal alien that has somehow managed to acquire a social security card or other identification? Is he supposed to avoid hiring anyone with a Mexican or Spanish name [sic]. I don't have to tell you the discrimination problems associated with this method of hiring."[34]

Internationalizing the Employer Sanctions Debate

Even as groups associated with the Left softened their anti-immigrant stance, and as those from the Right—namely businesses and growers—continued to benefit from undocumented migration, the passage of employer sanctions became ever more likely. In 1981, Ronald Reagan, who had previously backed employers, decided that given his emphasis on "law and order," he could not be seen as defending those who were in the country illegally.[35] After a few key staff members and some Republicans in the Senate urged him to introduce measures to curb unauthorized migration, Reagan conceded.[36]

When employers came to realize that they were going to lose on employer sanctions, they sought to reframe the debate to one that at least served them on other fronts. They thus started to critique undocumented migration, but rather than focusing on the familiar tropes that migration increased unemployment and strained the welfare system in the United States, they adopted an international vision on the relationship between migration, unemployment, and welfare. They argued that supporting free trade, capital investment, and a smaller welfare state in Mexico—which they held was necessary to make the Mexican economy more competitive—would increase the number of jobs available south of the border and curb Mexicans' need to head north. Unions and Mexican American organizations did not respond to these new calls with a unified voice. Some remained quiet, others openly spoke out against international aid and trade, and others spoke in favor. Ultimately, from a stew of different ideas, one vision came to seem natural and inevitable: that national borders should exist to contain the flow of people but not of trade and political power.

As they had done with questions of domestic welfare and employment in the 1970s, in the 1980s, policy-makers overlooked what was actually happening on the ground. In the 1981 hearings, the US Chamber of Commerce argued that the business community was already helping curtail immigration by reducing unemployment in Mexico through capital investment. As it explained, "Over 600 companies have attempted to utilize the large labor force in Mexico by building 'twin plants' along the U.S.-Mexico border."[37] The chamber acknowledged that many of the workers at those *maquiladoras* (assembly plants) would eventually migrate to the United States. But it concealed that the assembly plants employed primarily women while men were the primary migrants. It also failed to disclose that the plants themselves encouraged internal migration to northern Mexico, which, in turn, increased border crossings to the United Sates. Mario Lascaino, one of the men who had migrated to work in this female-dominated industry, described his factory's tantalizing proximity to the North: "I lived for a while working in the assembly plants in Nogales, Sonora . . . that was exactly at the border between Mexico and the United States . . . and there was a small block right there," he said, describing the factory's surroundings, and "every time we went out to eat . . . we went to sit on the block."[38] From that concrete block, Lascaino and his coworkers could see how immigration officials worked. As Lascaino sat and ate his lunch, he figured out how to enter the United States illegally.

Business lobbies also condemned Mexico's economic policies while ignoring migrants' experiences with these policies. In 1980, Mexico's president, José López Portillo, defied expectations when he refused to join the General Agreement on Tariffs and Trade (GATT).[39] To the business community in the United States, this decision seemed to symbolize Mexico's insistence on protectionist and welfare-state policies. The US Chamber of Commerce demanded that the federal government intervene to promote open markets in Mexico in order to curtail undocumented migration, holding that Congress should consider taking "a more international and visionary perspective toward the issue of immigration reform."[40] Migrants came to the United States, it argued, because "true opportunity for advancement" existed there, unlike in their countries of origin, where "high taxes, overregulation, oversized governments and lack of personal freedoms [had] smothered the possibilities for advancement and self-betterment of their people."[41] In other words, the Chamber of Commerce claimed that reducing government spending in migrants' home countries was indispensable. The United States ought to try "convincing the nations of Latin America and elsewhere to free up their economies, respect private property rights, and sell inefficient government-owned companies."[42] The chamber failed to explain how such "convincing" ought to take place, but it did argue that this measure would "do more to slow immigration than any fence along the Rio Grande or any regulation of American hiring practices."[43]

The chamber's investment in curtailing Mexico's public spending meant that it ignored that a larger—rather than smaller—welfare state in Mexico might be a more effective solution. It overlooked the fact that increasing government spending could diffuse migrants' need to go north to provide a safety net and basic resources for their families and communities. In towns of high out-migration individuals regularly complained that government officials ignored their needs. Once in the United States, migrants built organizations that performed some of the activities that Mexican government officials failed to carry out, such as investing money in their communities to provide them with electricity, potable water, and paved roads. They did so without government support. As Gregorio Casillas, who helped build the clubs remembers, "We started [sending money to Mexico] but unfortunately we didn't have the support of the government, not of the state government [of Zacatecas], of the municipal government [of Jalpa] or of the federal government [of Mexico]."[44] When the US Chamber of Commerce held that Mexicans came to the United States because of the "high taxes, overregulation, [and] oversized governments" in their country of origin, it ignored migrants' actual desires and needs. By applying their own perspective of the world onto the realities of migrant life, members of the chamber failed to recognize the complex forces that drove Mexicans to the United States.

For its part, the Reagan administration called for an international approach that focused on sending aid to countries with high rates of out-migration. In the congressional hearings held in July 1981, Attorney General William French Smith, the mouthpiece of the White House, maintained: "The administration recognizes that the causes of illegal immigration are international in scope and require international solutions."[45] The administration planned to design a "hemispheric development plan" with Mexico, Venezuela, and Canada to establish "development projects that would alleviate the factors encouraging illegal migration within the hemisphere."[46] Despite such lofty goals, the attorney general failed to mention that the root causes that led people to migrate to and from the United States, Mexico, Venezuela, and Canada varied widely. He provided no context about migrants' actual lives in any of these countries or explained why the administration thought it was wise to develop a single hemispheric plan.

On the other side of the political spectrum, Mexican American groups began to disagree among themselves. Like employers, some Mexican American groups came to recognize that employer sanctions would pass and decided to use the hearings to impress their input into the law. On October 4, 1985, the NCLR's president issued a confidential memorandum to the Congressional Hispanic Caucus claiming that the organization had decided to espouse employer sanctions as the only "realistic strategy."[47] He explained: "It is widely acknowledged that some type of immigration reform bill is likely to pass—if not this year then next. . . . It is further acknowledged by most observers that any bill that passes both Houses of Congress will contain some form of employer sanctions." According to the NCLR, rejecting the law would simply mean allowing it to pass without Mexican Americans' feedback. Not all Mexican American groups agreed, however. MALDEF continued to insist that employer penalties were indefensible and became known as being "purist" in its politics.[48]

The disagreement among mainstream Mexican American organizations extended to their position on using trade, capital relocation, and, especially, aid, as a means to lower unemployment in Mexico and thus to reduce undocumented migration. Up until the 1970s, only radical Chicana/o organizations, such as CASA, denounced sending aid to Mexico, insisting that "only the total economic independence of Mexico from U.S. [*Yanqui*] imperialism . . . can solve the causes behind the push of immigration."[49] In contrast, during those years most mainstream organizations including MALDEF, the American GI Forum, LULAC, and the NCLR, held that the United States should provide aid to Mexico to curb its rates of unemployment and reduce people's need to migrate.[50] In 1976, the NCLR stated that "no meaningful resolution to the undocumented alien situation will ever be achieved without a thoughtful renovation of the current US foreign policy and foreign aid programs, particularly towards those developing nations known to be large sources of undocumented entrants."[51] The organization suggested that the United States should increase financial assistance to countries of high out-migration through international lending institutions such as the World Bank and the Inter-American Development Bank as well as through the Agency for International Development of the US Department of State.[52]

By the 1980s, however, even some of the policy-oriented Mexican American groups began to doubt that US economic involvement south of the border was helping Mexico, especially when it came to capital relocation and trade. In 1985, LULAC's executive director claimed: "LULAC suggests that at a minimum, the proposed Presidential commission be directed to review immigration trends to establish whether or not a correlation exists between U.S. foreign and trade polices vis-a-vis principal countries of origin and numbers of persons seeking entry into the United States."[53]

The NCLR, in contrast, continued to unquestioningly support US economic intervention in Mexico as a means to reduce migration, even by overlooking how economic support was often accompanied by political control. The organization's leaders focused primarily on the importance of aid. In 1982, they held that "the most significant deficiency" of the proposals for immigration reform was the "lack of any substantial mention of cooperative economic development efforts with countries from which large numbers of immigrants enter the United States. Comprehensive immigration legislation cannot be successful without measures on the scale of the recent Caribbean Initiative."[54] The NCLR's statement disregarded that the Caribbean Basin Initiative sought to use trade and aid to counter the possibility of a communist revolution in the Caribbean and Central America.[55] The NCLR was willing to ignore US political interference in Latin America as long as it came alongside aid.

From Employer Sanctions to Border Control

While calls for a more porous border that allowed for the flow of capital and trade became increasingly audible in the US Congress, so did calls for a more fortified border that stopped the flow of migrants. It was the same politicians and organizations, traditionally associated with the "Right," who made both sets of demands. The new clamor for border fortification, which developed quite quickly and vociferously in the 1980s, made sense alongside Ronald Reagan's valorized vision of "law and order." And yet the belief that fortification would solve the problem of unauthorized migration was shockingly blind to a key fact of migrant life: the existing permeability of the national boundary allowed Mexicans to engage in circular migration rather having to immigrate and settle permanently in the United States. Indeed, before the passage of IRCA most migrants engaged in circular migration: they came to the United States, worked for a short period of time, and then returned to Mexico only to start the process all over again when they needed money again. Circularity meant that the overall number of Mexicans living without papers in the United States did not rise nearly as much as the number of individuals who migrated illegally. Indeed, 86% of all entries were offset by departures.

Had they paid attention to what was happening on the ground, policy-makers could have seen that fortifying the border would lead migrants to settle permanently in the United States. Migrant women, for instance, were already staying in the United States rather than returning to their hometowns because crossing the border was more fraught for women, given the risks of sexual assault. While in the years between 1965 and 1985, 55% to 60% of all migrant men went back to Mexico within two years of arriving to the United States, only 30% to 40% of women did.[56]

The case of Feliciana Ramírez is indicative. When her husband first started migrating, she stayed in Mexico because, as she explained, "The smugglers are not always to be trusted."[57] In her hometown, everyone knew that coyotes regularly raped women. Border bandits and Border Patrol agents were also known to assault female border crossers.[58] After many years of seeing her husband come and go, however, Ramírez decided to risk the border and head north. The crossing was uneventful, but once she made it to South San Francisco, she felt scared to leave again. Unlike her husband, a life in both countries seemed impossible to her, because of the uncertainty of the border in between. She went back to Mexico once twice in the next 20 years: once because she was deported and once because her mother died. Policy-makers overlooked the fact that a dangerous border was already trapping migrants in the United States; their proposed solutions would only exacerbate that condition of entrapment.

The obliviousness of politicians is not surprising, since the demand for a more fortified border was originally set off not by unauthorized Mexican border crossings but by Cuban refugees fleeing by boat to Miami. In April 1980, Fidel Castro's government announced that anyone who desired to leave the island could do so. Cuban refugees immediately fled from the port of Mariel to the United States, where news soon spread that a significant number of them had been released from Cuban jails and mental health facilities. By October, when the US and Cuban officials agreed to end the Mariel Boatlift, 124,776 Cubans had already crossed the Florida Straits and arrived in the United States.[59] The Select Commission on Immigration and Refugee Policy, a congressional group that studied migration, reported: "Nothing about immigration—even widespread visa abuse and illegal border crossings—seems to have upset the American people more than the Cuban push-out of 1980. . . . Their presence brought home to most Americans the fact that U.S. immigration policy was out of control."[60] Policymakers used the sense of crisis that stemmed from the Mariel Boatlift to insist on a more militarized border with Mexico.

Policing the national boundary had not been as prevalent a topic in the hearings held in the early 1970s as it became in the 1980s.[61] The focus of the earlier hearings rested on employer sanctions. The preoccupation with domestic employment, by the AFL-CIO and its supporters, meant that the main goal for many had been to ensure that migrants did not get jobs. As a result, border security was only of secondary importance at the initial hearings (despite the fact that there were a few politicians who made an adamant, though futile, argument for greater policing).[62] During the hearings held in the 1970s, the Immigration and Naturalization Service (INS) itself believed that the solution to undocumented migration lay with employer sanctions rather than border militarization. In 1975, INS Commissioner Leonard Chapman argued that there were three alternatives "in the face of this growing flood" of undocumented migrants.[63] The first option was to do nothing "and watch the flood grow into a torrent." The second choice was to "build a massive Immigration Service to deal with the problem . . . with an army of Border Patrolmen" and investigators working in cities. This course of action was "not only impractical" but also "abhorrent to the American conscience." The "third alternative," Chapman held, "[is] to turn off the magnet that attracts these millions of persons to our country. That magnet, of course, is jobs. Employment of illegal aliens must be prohibited."[64] According to Chapman, this was the correct choice.

In contrast, the hearings held during the 1980s reflected heightened concerns about the need to assert control over the nation's borders. The White House set the tone of this changing rhetoric. After acquiescing to employer sanctions, President Reagan shifted the debate away from the effects that undocumented migrants had on employment and emphasized instead the importance of protecting the nation's boundaries. "We have lost control of our borders," asserted the attorney general at the July 1981 hearings.[65] Consequently, the administration redirected the emphasis away from penalizing private employers and toward painting undocumented migration as a public and foreign policy issue that required policing the country's perimeter with Mexico.

This new rhetoric on border control fit well with US citizens' growing concern that the United States had to reassert its geopolitical influence. Communists remained in control of Eastern Europe and China; the US embassy in Tehran had been taken over by revolutionary Islamic students and US State Department employees had been held hostage; in Latin America and the Caribbean, left-wing guerilla movements were threatening US-backed governments.[66] The need for strong, well-defined national borders seemed urgent. Senator Alan K. Simpson declared in the 1985 hearings that the United States was unable "to fulfill that first test and duty of a sovereign nation—control of our own borders."[67] This posed a foreign policy quandary and was an international embarrassment: "Not only the American people and the American Government are aware of it, but people all over the world are aware that the United States cannot, or does not, control its own borders."[68]

Employers readily backed this new emphasis. Even if penalties were to be imposed against them for hiring undocumented migrants, the focus of the hearings, they eagerly agreed, should be on the border rather than on jobsites. In the 1985 hearings, the Farm Labor Alliance, an umbrella organization representing the interests of growers, processors, and marketers of perishable commodities, embraced the White House's talking points: "The problem of illegal immigration has grown over the years and there is a need for this country to address the problem in a manner that will enable us to regain control of our borders."[69]

In contrast, groups deemed liberal, many of which had been the primary supporters of the Rodino bill in the early 1970s, were ambivalent or silent about increased border patrolling in the 1980s. Unlike most employer lobbies, both the AFL-CIO and most Mexican American groups (including LULAC and MALDEF) tried to avoid the issue in their statements at the 1985 Senate hearings. When they did tackle the question of border regulation, they provided different perspectives. The Arizona Farmworkers Union and the National Hispanic Leadership Conference held that their members were "extremely concerned" about an increase in "border enforcement."[70] For his part, Raúl Yzaguirre, the NCLR's president, did not bring up the topic himself, but when he was asked about it by Senator Simpson, he responded: "We have in the past and continue to believe that the most humane, the most cost effective way to deal with immigration control is to deal with it at the border."[71]

By this point, even the INS had switched its stance. While in 1975, INS Commissioner Chapman had noted the inadequacy of border control measures, in 1985, Commissioner Alan Nelson defended those same measures. Although he called employer sanctions the "cornerstone of this legislation," he also described the new law as "absolutely essential to gaining control of our borders."[72]

The new emphasis on border "control" that was constantly repeated in the hearings served to cast migrants as a horde to be defended against and expunged their humanity. It denied migrants the possibility of belonging to the United States and erased their many contributions to the country. Despite its recurrent use at the hearings, the militarized language of control appears outlandish when placed alongside migrants' actual lives and desires. Mexicans tended to go to the United States to work and support their families; they returned home regularly to see the spouses, children, parents, and friends whom they missed; they built strong communities to support each other; and they longed to be able to reside in Mexico permanently one day. The geopolitical story that was told in Congress did not match up with the very human stories happening on the ground.

Undocumented Mexican Migrants and a "Nation of Immigrants"

Across the rapid shifts in emphasis that occurred between the 1970s and 1980s, one issue remained stable throughout the hearings: a concern over who "migrants" were and where they belonged. Calls to restrain undocumented migration rested on notions about safeguarding the population of the United States, and with it, the very meaning of being American. The AFL-CIO spoke of protecting US laborers, environmentalists of preserving the nation's environment from outsiders, and political conservatives of upholding the nation's identity. To make these claims, policy-makers relied on the notion that there was an intrinsic difference between US citizens and undocumented migrants, as well as on the fear that the growing rates of illegal entry and the purported high fertility rates of those migrants would change the demographic composition of the United States.

When warning about the growth in the number of unauthorized migrants living in the United States, lobbyists typically described only the upward trend in the number of people entering the country but failed to note that most of those who entered the United States eventually left.[73] As a result, fears of population growth rested on wildly high estimates about the number of migrants residing in the United States. For example, the Environmental Fund's strict focus on entrance led it to assert that "illegal immigration" was growing by "an unknown number, but 1 million a year is not an unreasonable guess."[74] This estimate was much higher than even the highest official numbers cited at the 1981 and 1985 hearings, which held that the "illegal population" was growing by "250,000 to 500,000" per year.[75]

Those who believed that migrants did not belong in the nation had to contend with commonly repeated narrative about the United States: that it was, first and foremost, a "nation of immigrants."[76] The apparent contradiction led to a lot of rhetorical gymnastics. The AFL-CIO, for example, used this enduring ideal to portray itself as sympathetic to the plight of migrants, but then immediately sought to distance itself from the migrants themselves. The secretary treasurer of the AFL-CIO declared that "as members of a nation of immigrants . . . we deeply sympathize with those who seek a better life in our country."[77] The federation expressed as well that the exploitation of undocumented workers was an "acute concern to the American labor movement which insists on safeguarding its hard-won standards of life and work."[78] To do so, however, organized labor chose to protect US citizens, not migrant workers. Rather than fighting for better conditions for migrants, the AFL-CIO called for "a strong, fair U.S. immigration policy," which included employer sanctions.[79]

In the hearings held during Ronald Reagan's tenure, conservative politicians addressed the nation's immigrant past by insisting that the character of the nation now depended on protecting US sovereignty. The assumed inclusiveness of the nation's origins was even invoked to reiterate the theme of control. Congressman Hank Brown (R-CO) offered one version of a sentiment echoed throughout the hearings, when he claimed: "We rightly pride ourselves on being what John F. Kennedy called 'a nation of immigrants.' . . . At the same time, we are a sovereign nation and, as a sovereign nation, we have the right—and we have a duty to our own citizens—to control our own borders."[80] Business lobbies claimed that undocumented migration was destroying the United States and the very meaning of being American. In its 1985 statement the US Chamber of Commerce described the country's border as "hemorrhaging."[81] This image depicted the influx of Mexicans as bloodying the territorial boundaries of the United States and thus effacing the definition of the country. The porous border, in turn, was often inextricably linked to fears of a porous American identity. The Chamber of Commerce statement made this link explicit: "Our Nation's ability to control its demographic future is key to retaining the economic and political liberties which we value." Its members feared that the nation's "currently permeable borders," were creating great "social, economic, political, environmental, and cultural" costs.[82]

For Mexican migrants, the rhetoric about their place in the nation was particularly painful because it failed to address their contributions to the United States. While not using the term "nation of immigrants," Mexicans insisted that they were an indispensable part of building the country. Reflecting the perspective held by most migrants, Manuel Jiménez exclaimed: "Mexicans have lifted the U.S. economy."[83] Another migrant wrote to his local newspaper in Jalisco scorning US citizens for believing that there were too many Mexicans in the United States. He argued that migration was "the best business that our neighbors, the gringos, have done because it provides them with a cheap labor force."[84]

Stereotypes about "Mexican families" and their "excessive fertility" haunted the hearings and buttressed arguments that undocumented migration would alter the demographic composition of the United States. In practice, most Mexican women remained in Mexico and raised their children there. Nonetheless, John Tanton, the head of the population control organization Zero Population Growth (ZPG) asserted in 1975 that the "fertility of immigrant women" would increase population growth in the United States.[85] Although ZPG had the reputation of being an extremist organization, others repeated these types of claims. For instance, in 1983 Martin Finn, the medical director for public health for the Department of Health Services of Los Angeles County—the very hospital sued a few years earlier for forcibly sterilizing Mexican American women—told Congress: "I noted that 64 percent of the deliveries in our hospitals were in the undocumented population. This shows the extremely high fertility rate in this population."[86]

For their part, in the 1980s, Mexican American groups and their allies tried to reframe the debate around "the Mexican family" away from its pejorative connotations and to pursue family reunification policies. In the May 1981 hearings, for instance, MALDEF claimed that Mexican migrants should be allowed to bring their relatives because "family reunification" had "for several decades been an underlying theme of American immigration policy."[87] Clergy from a range of denominations— from Catholics and Jews to the African Methodist Episcopal Church— added to this chorus, maintaining that "family reunion has appropriately been the cornerstone of our immigration laws and polices since their beginning."[88]

When focusing on "the family," Mexican American organizations and the clergy emphasized that deportations and employer sanctions would separate families, but ignored that migration itself split Mexican families. After all, most migrants were married men who left their families behind in Mexico. In the 1975 hearings, the secretary for research of the US Catholic Conference maintained that employer sanctions would lead to "the dismissal of untold numbers of workers from their jobs in a short period of time," which would cause "unbelievable havoc among their families and in the communities. . . . In our judgment, it is unconscionable that our Government should even consider separating families by forcing a mass exodus or deportation of literally millions of men, women, and children."[89] By emphasizing the primacy of unbroken families, these groups attempted to protect migrants from deportation, but disregarded the fact that for most migrants the family was a transnational institution.

Repeatedly, the representations of Mexican families at the congressional hearings aimed to convince policy-makers about the need to ease or increase restrictions on migration, but they failed to recognize the intricacies of migrants' family lives. It was a time when the vast majority of Mexican migrants were men who had to live far from their wives and children and forge families across borders in which attachments were shaped through regular visits, love letters, and remittances. Neither the joys nor the hardships of a bi-national family were recognized. Without an adequate analysis of—or even an interest in—the messy complexity of lived experience, it is no surprise that the solutions policy-makers proposed were similarly one-dimensional.

Conclusion: The Voices of Migrants

The voices heard least at these hearings were those of undocumented migrants themselves, although after the mid-1970s Mexican American groups often claimed to speak in their name. In a sense, migrants had already spoken. They had expressed their desires—or their lack of alternatives—with their very movement. They borrowed money to make their first trip, promised their families they would return, and left their hometowns in Mexico with a heavy heart. They willingly put themselves in danger in order to cross the border. They agreed to work long hours in the worst paid jobs and live in fear of apprehension in a country that viewed them only as "illegals." Mexicans chose this path because despite the hardships of migration, no other trajectory offered them better hope. Through these actions, migrants spoke through their feet rather than their voices. But those in Congress failed to take note.

In the rare instances in which unauthorized migrants were allowed to address Congress, they articulated their hopes for a world in which Mexicans could migrate in order to work, make enough money to live decently, and then settle permanently in their home country. Ramón Andrada, an undocumented migrant from Nayarit and a member of the Maricopa County Organizing Project (MCOP), an organization that insisted that migrants be given time to testify at the hearings, held that all Mexicans who wanted to migrate for work should be allowed to do so "because the fact that we live [in Mexico] does not mean that we don't have the right to work. We have the right to work, to support our families."[90] His ultimate goal was to settle down in Mexico: "My solution is come to work here, on a temporary basis, if allowed, because I believe that, with that time that I would be allowed to work here, we can better afford to support our families there, and avoid coming here."[91] Andrada recognized how his settlement in Mexico depended upon his continued ability to migrate and live, for the time being, north of the border.

Andrada's aspirations for a different future never came to fruition. Neither did those of the groups that rallied for more stringent immigration control through IRCA. The law ultimately passed by balancing the interests of the multiple groups concerned with the issue, but ended up satisfying none of them. IRCA introduced employer sanctions and increased the INS enforcement budget with the goal of reducing the number of undocumented migrants who entered and resided in the country. It placated employers in part by establishing the new Seasonal Agricultural Worker (SAW) program: migrants who could prove that they had been in the United States for a minimum of 90 days, during the year ending on May 1, 1986, were offered a path to legal residency.[92] Beyond SAW, the new law allowed those who could prove continuous residence in the United States since January 1, 1982, to become legal resident aliens.[93] Congress agreed to this measure in order to pacify Mexican American groups that had come to support migrants.

After the passage of IRCA undocumented migration grew dramatically. The fortification of the border made it harder for Mexicans to engage in unauthorized, circular migration as entering the United States illegally became more dangerous and expensive because smugglers charged more. Because they could no longer go back and forth across the border between the two countries and because the situation in Mexico hadn't improved, they decided to settle permanently in the United States. In fact, men started to bring their wives and children north with them, which they had previously not done. In turn, this also increased the number of people crossing the border and now settling permanently in the United States.[94]

As seen in this chapter, the narratives that "the Left" and "the Right" told about immigrants and unauthorized migration have changed over time. While calls to curtail undocumented migration would eventually become associated with the Right, in the early 1970s it was labor unions and Mexican American organizations, groups generally branded as liberals that made such demands. For their part, employer lobbies and other seemingly "conservative" organizations viewed such migration with favor. In other words, the bedrock principles of both the Left and the Right regarding migration have changed and can continue to do so. But the history of IRCA also shows us how laws backed by stereotypes and narratives that ignore migrants' views and lives—no matter where they land in the political spectrum—come at a very high price.

Notes

1. "Marble," Architect of the Capitol, https://www.aoc.gov/capitol-hill/architecture /marble, accessed May 27, 2017.
2. Quoted in Robert Pear, "President Signs Landmark Bill on Immigration," *New York Times*, November 7, 1986.
3. Douglas S. Massey and Katherine Bartley, "The Changing Legal Status Distribution of Immigrants: A Caution," *International Migration Review* 39, no. 2 (2005): 479; and Douglas S. Massey, *Immigration and the Great Recession* (Palo Alto, CA: Russell Sage Foundation and Stanford Center on Poverty and Inequality, 2012).
4. *Illegal Aliens: Hearings before Subcommittee No. 1 of the Committee on the Judiciary*, US House of Representatives, Committee on the Judiciary, 93rd Cong., 1973–1974.
5. *Illegal Aliens.*
6. Statement of Joshua Eilberg, *Illegal Aliens*, 2.
7. *Statement of the AFL-CIO, Illegal Aliens: Hearings Before the Subcommittee on Immigration, Citizenship and International Law of the Committee on the Judiciary*, US House of Representatives, Committee on the Judiciary, 94th Cong., 1st sess., February/March 1975, 192.
8. *Statement of the AFL-CIO*, 193.
9. Testimony of Manuel Fierro, President of National Congress of Hispanic-American Citizens, in US House of Representatives, 94th Cong., *Illegal Aliens*, 316.
10. Bay Area Coalition Against the Rodino Bill, "Un Llamado . . . /A Call . . . ," pamphlet, CASA Archive, M0325, Box 32, Folder 12.
11. Bay Area Coalition.
12. Adalberto Rodríguez, interview by author, March 18, 2015, Thermal, California, digital recording.
13. Rodríguez interview.
14. David G. Gutiérrez, *Walls and Mirrors: Mexican Americans, Mexican Immigrants, and the Politics of Ethnicity* (Berkeley: University of California Press, 1995), 179–205.
15. Quoted in Gutiérrez, *Walls and Mirrors*, 199.
16. Christine Marie Sierra, "In Search of National Power: Chicanos Working the System on Immigration Reform, 1976–1986," in *Chicano Politics and Society in the Late-Twentieth Century*, ed. David Montejano (Austin: University of Texas Press, 1999), 131–34.
17. Michael Cortés, Testimony on the Civil Rights Implications of Proposed Federal Policies Concerning Undocumented Workers and Immigrants Before the United States Commission on Civil Rights, November 14, 1978, National Council of La Raza Records, Stanford University, M0744, Record Group 5, Box 58, Folder 2.
18. Cortés, Testimony.

19. Statement of Vilma Martinez, in US Senate and House of Representatives, *Final Report of the Select Commission on Immigration and Refugee Policy: Joint Hearings Before the Subcommittee on Immigration and Refugee Policy of the Senate Committee on the Judiciary and Subcommittee on Immigration, Refugees and International Law*, US House of Representatives, Committee on the Judiciary, 97th Cong., 1st sess. on the Final Report of the Select Commission on Immigration and Refugee Policy, May 1981 (Washington, DC: US Government Printing Office, 1981), 149.

20. Nora Hamilton and Norma Stoltz Chinchilla, *Seeking Community in a Global City: Guatemalans and Salvadorans in Los Angeles* (Philadelphia: Temple University Press, 2001), 83.

21. Hamilton and Chinchilla, *Seeking Community*, 83.

22. María Elena Salazar, quoted in El Centro de Información Para Asuntos Migratorios y Fronterizos Del Comité de Servicio de los Amigos, "Indocumentados," *Boletín Informativo Sobre Asuntos Migratorios y Fronterizos*, 1980, 9.

23. Salazar, 10.

24. Salazar, 9.

25. See, for instance, ILGWU's statements to US Senate and House of Representatives, 97th Cong., *Immigration Reform and Control Act of 1982: Joint Hearings Before the Subcommittee on Immigration, Refugees, and International Law of the Committee on the Judiciary House of Representatives and Subcommittee on Immigration and Refugee Policy of the Committee on the Judiciary of the Senate, United States Senate, Ninety-Seventh Congress, Second Session on H.R. 5872, S2222, Immigration Reform and Control Act of 1982* (Washington, DC: US Government Printing Office, April 1982), 700–705; and to US House of Representatives, 98th Cong., *Hearing on Employment Discrimination and Immigration Reform: Hearing Before the Subcommittee on Employment Opportunities of the Committee on Education and Labor, House of Representatives, Ninety-Eighth Congress, First Session on H.R. 1510, to Revise and Reform the Immigration and Nationality Act and For Other Purposes*, May 1983 (Washington, DC: US Government Printing Office, 1983), 242–43.

26. Statement of Vilma Martinez, in US Senate and House of Representatives, 97th Cong., *Final Report of the Select Commission on Immigration and Refugee Policy*, 156–7.

27. Wendy Rodríguez, interview by author, March 16, 2015, Palm Desert, California, digital recording.

28. Statement of Thomas S. Donahue, Secretary-Treasurer, AFL-CIO, in US Senate, 99th Cong., *Immigration Reform and Control Act of 1985: Hearings Before the Subcommittee on Immigration and Refugee Policy of the Committee on the Judiciary United States Senate, Ninety-Ninth Congress, First Session on S. 1200 Bill to Amend the Immigration and Nationality Act to Effectively Control Unauthorized Immigration to the United States, and For Other Purposes* (Washington, DC: US Government Printing Office, June 1985), 422.

29. Statement of AFL-CIO Executive Council on Illegal Aliens, in US House of Representatives, 94th Cong., *Illegal Aliens*, 197.

30. Rodolfo Rosales, pseudonym, quoted in El Centro de Información Para Asuntos Migratorios y Fronterizos Del Comité de Servicio de los Amigos, "Testimonios," *Boletín Informativo Sobre Asuntos Migratorios y Fronterizos*, 1979, 9.
31. Rosales, 9.
32. Statement by Robert T. Thompson, in US Senate, 97th Cong., *The Knowing Employment of Illegal Immigrants: Hearing Before the Subcommittee on Immigration and Refugee Policy of the Committee on the Judiciary, United States Senate Ninety-Seventh Congress, First Session on Employer*, September 1981 (Washington, DC: US Government Printing Office, 1982), 96.
33. Arizona Cattle Growers' Association, in US Senate, 95th Cong., *S. 2252: Alien Adjustment and Employment Act of 1977: Hearings Before the Committee on the Judiciary, United States Senate, Ninety-Fifth Congress, Second Session on S. 2252 to Amend the Immigration and Nationality Act, and For Other Purposes, Part 2* (September 1978), 200.
34. Arizona Cattle Growers' Association, 201.
35. Kelly K. Richter, "Uneasy Border State: The Politics and Public Policy of Latino Illegal Immigration in Metropolitan California, 1971–1996" (PhD diss., Stanford University, 2014), 1.
36. Richter, "Uneasy Border State," 54. See Nicholas Laham, *Ronald Reagan and the Politics of Immigration Reform* (Westport, CT: Praeger, 2000), 109–10.
37. Statement by Robert T. Thompson, in US Senate, 97th Congress, *The Knowing Employment of Illegal Immigrants*, 112.
38. Mario Lascaino, interview by author, March 17, 2015, Coachella, California, digital recording.
39. For more on Mexico's entrance to the GATT and reactions to it, see Dale Story, "Trade Politics in the Third World: A Case Study of the Mexican GATT Decision," *International Organization* 36, no. 4 (1982): 767–68.
40. Ralph B. Evans, Statement of the Chamber of Commerce of the United States on Immigration Reform, to the Subcommittee on Immigration and Refugee Policy of the U.S. Senate (June 14, 1985), National Council of La Raza Archives, M0744, Record Group 5, Box 400, Folder 3.
41. Evans, Statement of the Chamber of Commerce.
42. Evans, Statement of the Chamber of Commerce.
43. Evans, Statement of the Chamber of Commerce.
44. Gregorio Casillas, interview by author, October 7, 2009, Aguascalientes, México, digital recording.
45. US Senate and House of Representatives, 97th Congr., *Administration's Proposals on Immigration and Refugee Policy: Joint Hearings Before the Subcommittee on Immigration, Refugees and International Law of the House Committee on the Judiciary and the Subcommittee on Immigration and Refugee Policy of the Senate Committee on the Judiciary, Ninety-Seventh Congress, First Session on Administration's Proposals on Immigration and Refugee Policy*, July 1981, 10.
46. US Senate and House of Representatives, 97th Cong., *Administration's Proposals on Immigration and Refugee Policy*, 10.

47. Memorandum from Raul Yzaguirre, president National Council of La Raza to Congressional Hispanic Caucus, "On Immigration Reform Confidential—Not for Distribution," October 4, 1985, National Council of La Raza Records, MO744, Record Group 5, Box 107, Folder 12.
48. Sierra, "In Search of National Power," 148.
49. Handwritten notes, no title, subsection called "Sobre la amnistía—Elementos y Conclusiones," CASA Archives, MO325, Box 31, Folder 9.
50. Michael Cortés, Hispanic Ad Hoc Coalition on Immigration, "Response by Hispanics to Changes in Immigration Law Proposed by President Jimmy Carter," National Council of la Raza Archives, MO744, Record Group 5, Box 58, Folder 2.
51. Raul Yzaguirre, "Guidelines for the Development of a Fair and Just U.S. Immigration Policy on Undocumented Aliens, First Draft," June 1977, CASA Archives, MO325, Box 33, Folder 12. Unable to verify if written correctly by Yzaguirre.
52. Yzaguirre, "Guidelines."
53. Statement of Joseph M. Trevino, "On S. 1200: The Immigration Reform and Control Act of 1985 Before the Senate Judiciary Committee Subcommittee on Immigration and Refugees," June 17, 1985, National Council of La Raza Archives, MO744, Record Group 5, Box 400, Folder 7.
54. Raul Yzaguirre, President, National Council of La Raza, "On Immigration Reform and Control Act of 1982 S. 2222," Before the Joint Hearings of the Senate Subcommittee on Immigration and Refugee Policy And House Subcommittee on Immigration, Refugees, and International Law, April 1, 1982, National Council of La Raza Archives, MO744, Record Group 5, Box 58, Folder 4.
55. Michael Cornell Dypski, "Caribbean Basin Initiative: An Examination of Structural Dependency, Good Neighbor Relations, and American Investment," *Journal of Transnational Law and Policy* 12, no. 1 (2002–2003): 100.
56. Douglas S. Massey, Jorge Durand, and Nolan J. Malone, *Beyond Smoke and Mirrors: Mexican Immigration in an Era of Economic Integration* (New York: Russell Sage Foundation, 2002), 63.
57. Feliciana Ramírez, interview by author, August 6, 2013, South San Francisco, California, digital recording.
58. John M. Crewdson, "Violence, Often Unchecked, Pervades U.S. Border Patrol," *New York Times*, January 14, 1989; Frank del Olmo, "Crackdown on Border Bandits," *Los Angeles Times*, October 26, 1976.
59. María Cristina García, *Havana USA: Cuban Exiles and Cuban Americans in South Florida, 1959–1994* (Berkeley: University of California Press, 1996), 46.
60. US Select Commission on Immigration and Refugee Policy, *U.S. Immigration Policy and the National Interest: The Final Report and Recommendations of the Select Commission on Immigration and Refugee Policy with Supplemental Views by Commissioners* (Washington, DC: US Government Printing Office, 1981), 4–5.
61. For a history of how the border became militarized in practice after 1978, see Timothy Dunn, *The Militarization of the U.S.-Mexico Border, 1978–1992: Low Intensity Conflict Doctrine Comes Home* (Austin: Center for Mexican American Studies, University of Texas, Austin, 1996).

62. For instance, an article from the *Washington Star-News* that became additional material for the 1975 hearings suggested that the border be "tighten[ed] up" by using "the sensors, which are Vietnam war surplus devices planted in the major foot trails to detect movement." Michael Satchell, "The Biggest Hole in the Dike," *Washington Star-News*, November 18, 1972, cited in US House of Representatives, 94th Congr., *Illegal Aliens*, 68.

63. Statement of Leonard F. Chapman, in US House of Representatives, 94th Cong., *Illegal Aliens*, 34.

64. Chapman statement, 34.

65. Statement of William Smith, in US Senate and House of Representatives, 97th Congr., *Administration's Proposals on Immigration and Refugee Policy*, 71.

66. Massey, Durand, and Malone, *Beyond Smoke and Mirrors*, 85.

67. Congressional Record—U.S. Senate, May 23, 1985, cited in US Senate, 99th Cong., *Immigration Reform and Control Act of 1985*, 493–94.

68. Congressional Record—U.S. Senate, 494.

69. Congressional Record—U.S. Senate, 184.

70. Congressional Record—U.S. Senate, 103.

71. Congressional Record—U.S. Senate, 160.

72. Statement of Alan C. Nelson, in US Senate, 99th Cong., *Immigration Reform and Control Act of 1985*, 437 and 442.

73. While seeming ignorance about migrants' actual movement drove much of the congressional discourse on "population," some witnesses did address the circularity of migration as a way of insisting that migrants and their families be excluded from national belonging. See for instance, Statement of Barry Chiswick, in US Senate, 99th Cong., *Immigration Reform and Control Act of 1985*, 40–41.

74. Statement of Dr. M. Rupert Cutler, in US Senate, 99th Cong., *Immigration Reform and Control Act of 1985*, 295.

75. Testimony of William French Smith, in US Senate and House of Representatives, 97th Cong., *Administration's Proposals on Immigration and Refugee Policy*, 7.

76. John F. Kennedy, *A Nation of Immigrants* (New York: Harper & Row, 1964).

77. US Senate and House of Representatives, 97th Cong., *Final Report of the Select Commission on Immigration and Refugee Policy*, 101.

78. US Senate and House of Representatives, 97th Cong., *Final Report*, 102.

79. US Senate and House of Representatives, 97th Cong., *Final Report*, 102.

80. Statement of Hank Brown, in US Senate, 98th Cong., *Immigration Reform and Control Act of 1983: Hearings Before the Subcommittee on Immigration, Refugees, and International Law of the Committee on the Judiciary, House of Representatives, Ninety-Eighth Congress, First Session on H.R. 1510, Immigration Reform and Control Act of 1983* (Washington, DC: US Government Printing Office, 1983), 143.

81. Evans, Statement of the Chamber of Commerce 472.

82. Evans, Statement of the Chamber of Commerce, 472.

83. Manuel Jiménez, interview by author, August 6, 2013, South San Francisco, California, digital recording.

84. P. Lussa, "Charlas de Sobremesa," *El Informador*, February 27, 1980.

85. US House of Representatives, 94th Cong., *Illegal Aliens*, 277–78.

86. Statement of Martin D. Finn, M.D., to United States House of Representatives, 98th Congress, *Immigration Reform and Control Act of 1983: Hearing Before the Subcommittee on Health and the Environment Committee of Energy and Commerce, Committee on Energy and Commerce, House of Representatives, Ninety-Eighth Congress, First Session on H.R. 1510, A Bill to Revise and Reform the Immigration and Nationality Act, and For Other Purposes* (Washington, DC: US Government Printing Office, 1983), 108. See Madrigal v. Quilligan, No. CV 75-2057-JWC (D.C. Dist. Ct., 1978).

87. Statement of Vilma S. Martinez, in US Senate and House of Representatives, 97th Cong., *Final Report of the Select Commission on Immigration and Refugee Policy*, 157.

88. Statement of Religious Leaders on Immigration Reform signed on by Bishop R. Cousin African Methodist Episcopal Church, Bishop Anthony J. Bevilacqua, Rabbi Alexander Schindler, Rev. Dr. Arie Brouwer, Rabbi David Saperstein, Rev. Daniel F. Hoye, Rev. William K Duval, National Council of La Raza Archives, M0744, Record Group 5, Box 340, Folder 10.

89. Statement of George G. Higgins, in US House of Representatives, 94th Cong., *Illegal Aliens*, 300.

90. Statement of Ramon Andrada, in US Senate, 95th Cong., *S. 2252: Alien Adjustment and Employment Act of 1977*, 77.

91. Andrada statement, 77.

92. Immigration Reform and Control Act of 1986, Pub. L. No. 99–603, §302, 100 Stat. 3359, 3417. The new law also provided a program by which replenishment workers (RAWs) could be brought into the United States. However, because there were never labor shortages in the country, replenishment farmworkers were never needed. See Debra L. DeLaet, *U.S. Immigration Policy in an Age of Rights* (Westport, CT: Praeger, 2000), 132; and Laham, *Ronald Reagan and the Politics of Immigration Reform*, 189.

93. Immigration Reform and Control Act of 1986, Publ. L. No. 99–603, § 201, 100 Stat. 3359, 3394.

94. Massey, Durand, and Malone, *Beyond Smoke and Mirrors*, 105–41.

- - - - - - - - -

CHAPTER 13

Between Family Unity and Separation

A History of Gendered Exclusions, Deviance,
and Deservingness in the United States

Wendy Vogt

In November 2018, a photograph of a Honduran woman named Maria
Lidia Meza Castro frantically running with her twin daughters away
from an exploded cannister of tear gas near the US-Mexico border wall
in Tijuana went viral on news and social media. In the photo, Maria is
wearing a t-shirt with the images of Anna and Elsa from the Disney
blockbuster *Frozen*, capped with the innocent phrase "Family Forever"
on the top left corner. Maria and five of her nine children traveled as
part of a migrant caravan in search of asylum in the United States after
one of her daughters started receiving violent threats from gangs in
their hometown of San Pedro Sula. Central American migrants were
increasingly traveling in caravans because the journey across Mexico
had become so dangerous, particularly for women and children. Even
so, it was not until she reached the border and had tear gas shot at her
and her family by US Customs and Border Protection agents, officials
from the country in which she was seeking protection, that she felt her
life was in immediate danger.

The image became instantly iconic, spurring moral outrage across
the political spectrum—the harrowing realities of state-sanctioned
border violence, the fears of invasion at the southern border, the
agonizing choices migrant parents must make for their children. On
his Twitter account, Governor Gavin Newsom of California stated,

"These children are barefoot. In diapers. Choking on tear gas. Women and children who left their lives behind—seeking peace and asylum—were met with violence and fear. That's not my America. We're a land of refuge. Of hope. Of freedom. And we will not stand for this." With these words, Governor Newsom channeled a core myth of the United States, that it is a nation founded upon and welcoming to immigrants and particularly women and children. While Governor Newsom's comment reflects one dominant narrative, on the other side of the political spectrum, people responded to the photograph with skepticism, fear, and hyper-nationalism. Commentaries used the photo as evidence of the hordes of migrants "storming" and "charging" the border, violating the "territorial integrity" of the United States, and cutting in line of other immigrants who "do it right." There were also claims that the photograph was staged, that the children were not actually running away from tear gas, that they were instead running away from the woman because she was, in fact, a sex trafficker. Another common thread of commentary focused on the qualities of the mother herself, blaming her for putting her children in harm's way. Indeed, the hysteria that emerged in the wake of the photograph captured a cultural moment when political polarization around immigration reached a zenith during the Trump administration.

While easy to extract from this image either an opportunistic invader or a deserving victim, I suggest that the image taps into a much deeper history of the gendered and racialized dimensions of belonging and deservingness in the United States. Since the earliest years of state formation, legal frameworks and policies that determine who is included and excluded in the United States have been intertwined with hierarchies based on race, gender, sexuality, nationality, class, and kinship. The 1790 Naturalization Act limited citizenship by naturalization to "free white persons" of good "moral character," thus excluding Native Americans, slaves, indentured servants, and women. During the colonial period, a white immigrant woman could receive the title of US citizen, though without the right to vote, own property, and other political rights, only through marriage to a US citizen. On the flipside, under the Expatriation Act of 1907, an American citizen woman could lose her citizenship if she married a foreigner. Such coverture laws, wherein married women did not possess legal status apart from their husbands, worked to reproduce heteropatriarchal norms and formations.[1]

These are early examples of the ways US immigration law is deeply intertwined with gendered hierarchies and family life. While immigration is often framed through discourses of economics and law, we must also remember that sociocultural politics are always central to political and economic processes, where the personal and political, the public and the intimate cannot be separated.[2] Not unlike the ways colonial power was historically consolidated through the governance of the intimate domains of everyday life, what Ann Stoler calls the "intimacies of empire," gender, sexuality, and family are central to the politics of immigration, citizenship and exclusion.[3]

While it is impossible to offer a comprehensive history here, this chapter reviews the centrality of gender, sexuality and family to US immigration politics and policies. I begin with a focus on the ways race, gender and sexuality intersect in historical exclusions and narratives and then turn to some of the contradictions that have emerged in more contemporary immigration regimes, particularly surrounding the tensions between family unity and separation. Since 1965, the principle of family unity has been the cornerstone of US immigration and visa policy. Whereas other countries prioritize merit-based immigration, the United States gives more family-based visas than any other visa category;[4] these constitute the majority of the more than 700,000 green cards issued each year. At the same time, ideas about what constitutes a family, proper gendered norms and behaviors, and sexual preferences and practices have historically played into the ways certain families and kin relations are favored over others.

Throughout the chapter, I move between historical and contemporary cultural moments to demonstrate the enduringness of gendered narratives within moral imaginaries of welcome and exclusion. Such an approach speaks not only to the ways history is crucial for understanding current trends and politics, but also to the ways different groups have been strategically included and excluded throughout US history based on broader political economic processes. Fears and social anxieties around gender and sexuality play a significant role in political discourse and in media representations of immigration, which not only reflect societal currents and sentiments, but also have profound effects on producing subjectivities and hierarchies of belonging and stigma for immigrant groups.[5] The goal of the chapter is thus to reveal the power and often violent consequences of immigration narratives on people's lives, as well as the ways individuals and communities work to contest these narratives in larger struggles of mobility, solidarity, and justice.

Histories of Exclusion: From the Yellow Peril to Queer Deviants

On March 16, 2021, a 22-year-old white male systematically traveled to three separate spas and massage parlors in the Atlanta area and killed 8 people, 6 of them women of Asian descent, 2 Chinese and 4 Korean women. An eyewitness said the shooter shouted "I'm going to kill all Asians," and yet authorities and, later, the shooter, were quick to state that the violence was in no way racially motivated. Instead, they claimed, the shooter suffered from a "sex addiction" and that the killings resulted from his desire to "eliminate sources of temptation." The spokesperson for the sheriff's office stated during the press conference that it had been "a really bad day for him."[6] This perpetrator of an organized mass murder targeting a specific group of racialized and sexualized immigrant women was constructed as a victim, while the actual victims, about whom we never learned much as individuals, were abstracted into the category of sex workers and dehumanized, if not blamed, for the violence they experienced. During his trial, the shooter's lawyers argued that the crime was not racially motivated. The obvious fallacy in this defense is the assumption that acts of racial violence and gendered violence are mutually exclusive when in fact, race, gender, sex, and immigration status are all significant intersecting factors in understanding this type of intentional violence.

The United States has a long history of scapegoating, demonizing, and exoticizing Asian immigrants and Asian women specifically. In 1875, the Page Act, which was the first US federal law to restrict immigration, barred anyone accused of prostitution, "lewd[,] or immoral behavior" from entering the United States. It was presumed that most working-class Chinese women were migrating to the United States to become sex workers, and the Page Act resulted in a general ban on all Chinese women. Exacerbating already skewed gender ratios among Chinese immigrants, the Page Act created a Chinese American immigrant community that was almost exclusively male. Chinese men, whose labor was valuable to Western expansion of railroad and mining industries, were still allowed to enter until the Chinese Exclusion Act of 1882, the first federal legislation to ban immigrants based on nationality. There were some exemptions to the Exclusion Act—namely, merchants, diplomats, academics, ministers, and the children of US citizens. After the 1906 earthquake and fire in San Francisco and the loss of the state's birth records, Chinese immigrants had an opportunity to claim they were born in the United States and were eligible to bring children from China. This gave rise to the tradition of "paper sons and daughters," Chinese immigrants who entered the United States through falsified documents, claiming they were related to Chinese American citizens. Between 1910 and 1940, 175,000 Chinese immigrants were detained and processed at the Angel Island immigration station off the coast of San Francisco, where they were detained for weeks, months, and even years in harsh and isolating conditions.[7]

At the turn of the 20th century, anti-Japanese exclusionist sentiment was also on the rise. In 1907, the United States and Japan negotiated the Gentleman's Agreement, which excluded the migration of both skilled and unskilled Japanese laborers, but also allowed for Japanese men already in the United States to send for wives, or "picture brides." The arrival of Japanese women substantially transformed the gender composition of the Japanese American community and, as Eithne Luibhéid has argued, demonstrates the privilege of conjugal relations built on heteropatriarchal standards.[8] However, anti-Japanese sentiment continued to grow and targeted Japanese women specifically not only as unassimilable, but as threats to American racial integrity. Propaganda about Japanese women's high fertility rates and their mothering tactics, which allegedly encouraged loyalty to the Japanese emperor, fueled fears of Japanese colonization.[9] As discussed below, similar arguments would be used decades later about the reproductive capacities of Latina women to spread fears of invasion and over-population. The Gentleman's Agreement was ended in 1920, and by 1924, Japanese immigrants were included among other Asian nationalities in a total ban on Asian immigration.

Whereas Asian women were constructed as immoral and/or threats to racial purity, Asian male laborers were also constructed as threats—to white women and to Western civilization more generally. A series of anti-miscegenation laws specifically prohibiting marriage or cohabitation between whites and Asians meant that Asian immigrants were effectively barred from having families, the idealized cornerstone of American morality and cultural life.[10] Monogamous heterosexual Christian white marriage was deemed the norm, and other forms of intimacy engaged by Asian immigrants were constructed as deviant and immoral.[11] Because state and social resources flowed through the channel of the family household, the exclusion of Asian immigrants from family life also limited access to resources, entitlements, and economic and social mobility.

The Page Act served as the blueprint for a US immigration policy that regulated sexuality in addition to gendered, racial, class-based exclusions.[12] As of 1917, queer immigrants were labeled "constitutional psychopathic inferiors" and barred from entering the United States. The 1952 Immigration and Nationality act, also known as the McCarran-Walter Act, was praised for lifting racial barriers to US citizenship dating back to the Naturalization Act of 1790, yet it also barred homosexuals on grounds of mental defectiveness. The act was amended in 1965 to explicitly prohibit the entry of aliens "afflicted with psychopathic personality, sexual deviation or a mental defect."[13] In 1961, a woman named Sara Harb Quiroz, a permanent US resident, was stopped and questioned by Immigration and Naturalization Service (INS) at the border between El Paso and Ciudad Juárez based solely on her short haircut, which officials claimed made her look like a lesbian. Despite her refusals of the label, Quiroz was deported by the INS in a move that signaled the power of the US state to surveil and control immigrant women's bodies and sexualities.[14] Five years later, the 1965 Immigration Act reaffirmed the exclusion of queer immigrants, including gay, lesbian, bisexual, and transgender individuals, who were banned under a category of "sexual deviation." In 1973, the American Psychiatric Association officially declared that homosexuality was not a mental disorder, and throughout the 1970s there were campaigns to end the barring of homosexual would-be immigrants, but the policing of queer bodies continued.

In June of 1979, a British journalist named Carl Hill was denied entry to the United States after landing with his partner to cover the San Francisco Gay Freedom Day Parade for the London-based newspaper *Gay News*. Hill, who wore a "Gay Pride" pin on his jacket, was stopped by immigration authorities at the airport and asked if he had ever had a homosexual experience and/or if he was a "practicing homosexual," to which Hill replied affirmatively. Hill was given two options: voluntarily take the next flight back to London or submit to a psychiatric exam that would almost certainly be used to deport him based on current immigration law. While Hill was eventually released from custody, he worked with a lawyer from Gay Rights Advocates to file a lawsuit against Julius Richmond, surgeon general of the United States and supervisor of the US Public Health Service, which was responsible for conducting psychiatric evaluations of suspected homosexuals at US ports of entry.

In response to Hill's case, on August 3, 1979, Richmond directed the Public Health Service, the Centers for Disease Control, and the Health Services Administration to stop the practice of medical screenings that would expel people based on their sexuality.[15] While this was a significant turning point, it was not until 1990 that exclusions based on sexual orientation were finally removed from immigration law. In 1994, LGBTQ individuals were finally eligible to apply for asylum if they had been persecuted for their sexuality. In 2013, after the Supreme Court ruled that the 1996 Defense of Marriage Act (DOMA) was unconstitutional, same-sex married couples were eligible to apply for family visas.

Blame Game: Bad Mothers and Helpless Victims

Not unlike the racialized and sexualized fears associated with Asian immigrants in the early 20th century, the focus of America's immigration "problem" in the second half of the century largely turned southward. Before 1965, most immigrants from Latin America were from Mexico and were predominately male migrants who found jobs as seasonal farmworkers. Between 1942 and 1964, the US and Mexican governments implemented a temporary worker program known as the Bracero Program to address agricultural labor shortages after World War II. However, attitudes toward Mexican immigration were highly gendered; while men were desired as manual laborers, they were not valued as whole individuals deserving of rights or the comforts of family life in their new communities. During the Bracero Program, efforts were made to intentionally recruit men with families back home so as to discourage permanent family settlement in the United States. The US Postal Service went as far as to intercept and censor letters between male migrants and their families so that they could not make plans for family reunification, keeping men isolated.[16] Despite the barriers to family reunification, Mexican families maintained affective bonds and relationships across borders.[17]

After the end of the Bracero Program, the preoccupation with Mexican migration and particularly the migration of women and families accelerated. In 1986, President Ronald Reagan signed the Immigration Reform and Control Act (IRCA) which regularized the status of close to three million people in the United States, ramped up immigration enforcement, and penalized employers who knowingly hired unauthorized immigrants. The stated goal of the IRCA was to "stem the tide" of immigrants from Latin America, but in fact the reverse happened. Employers were able to bypass sanctions through the use of labor contractors and falsified documents that shielded employers and punished immigrants. New pathways for family unification and increased border militarization actually worked to encourage more permanent settlement in the United States and decrease return and seasonal migration patterns among Mexican immigrants.[18] The family reunification mechanisms of IRCA led to an increase in the Latinx population through births and the legalization of unauthorized parents of US citizens, as well as increased unauthorized migration by family members who did not qualify for family reunification under the law's fairly narrow definition of family.[19]

As the numbers of Latinx immigrants—both authorized and unauthorized—continued to increase in the post-IRCA era, a central narrative emerged that focused specifically on the threat of Latina fertility to the nation and to white supremacy.[20] In his analysis of immigration-related media discourse between 1965 and 1999, Leo Chavez found that Latina women's alleged uncontrolled fertility, along with assumptions that Latinx immigrants refused to learn English and did not want to integrate into US society, were used to support arguments that immigrants sought to "reconquest" the US southwest.[21] Latina immigrant women's bodies were constructed as threats to the body politic, thus becoming an important terrain of government struggle that shaped discourse and policy.[22] The 1994 passage of Proposition 187 in California, which limited unauthorized immigrants from accessing non-emergency healthcare, public education, and other social services was a case in point. The early 21st century saw a new obsession with so-called anchor babies—children born to undocumented parents in the United States and guaranteed birthright citizenship under the Fourteenth Amendment of the Constitution. Anchor babies, who are typically of Latinx or Asian origin, are constructed as "underserving citizens" who do not have legitimate claims to the nation.[23] Their parents, predominantly their mothers, are seen as opportunistic individuals who seek to take advantage of the system, draining resources and opportunities from deserving citizens. Similar rationales have been used against mothers such as Elvira Arellano, who in 2006 famously took sanctuary inside a church in Chicago for over a year to avoid deportation and separation from her young son, and the growing number of Central American mothers arriving to the United States with their children as they seek asylum. Critiques of these mothers claim they are exploiting their children for their own gain.

The negative portrayal of parents also run deep in narratives around DREAMers and recipients of Deferred Action for Childhood Arrivals (DACA), the generation of college-aged undocumented individuals who arrived to the United States as young children. A common argument in defense of DREAMers is that they grew up as Americans and should not be punished for the decisions their parents made to bring them to the United States. In this scenario, children are cast as innocent victims and their parents as perpetrators of illegality. Yet, undocumented and DACA-mented students have started to push back on such narratives. Here is an excerpt from an interview I conducted with a college student and activist in Indianapolis who was arrested during a protest at then-Governor Mitch Daniel's office:

> After years of hiding my identity, I finally came out and told the world
> I was undocumented. Not only did I proclaim that I was undocumented,
> I was unapologetic about it. The way the media portrays us often makes it
> hard for us to embrace our identity. By participating in the civil disobedi-
> ence, I was letting the world know I am not ashamed. I am proud of the
> sacrifices my parents made for our family to have a better future. When
> I told my mother I was getting arrested, she cried. She said, "Esa debería ser
> yo [that should be me]." My mother felt that she should be the one getting
> arrested.

Anti-immigrant rhetoric peddled by politicians and the media to villainize parents and victimize their children has become increasingly common since 2014 and the so-called surge of unaccompanied Central American minors at the US border. In June 2022, Governor Ron DeSantis of Florida was granted permission by the Supreme Court of Florida to impanel a statewide grand jury that would investigate the parents and guardians of unaccompanied children brought to the United States by smugglers and charge them for child endangerment.

The strategy of blaming parents and using fear as a tactic also runs through seemingly humanitarian discourses around immigrants. In order to curb the number of children arriving to the border, the Obama administration launched a media campaign called "Our Children Are the Future: Let's Protect Them," targeting parents in Central America. In one poster a young person sits in a desolate desert landscape looking into the distance with an empty water bottle beside them. The poster reads, "I thought it would be easy for my son to get papers in the north . . . that was not true." In a speech on the so-called crisis, President Obama spoke directly to parents: "Our message absolutely is don't send your children unaccompanied, on trains or through a bunch of smugglers. We don't even know how many of these kids don't make it, and may have been waylaid into sex trafficking or killed because they fell off a train. Do not send your children to the borders. If they do make it, they'll get sent back. More importantly, they may not make it."[24] Such language strips the agency of young people in making decisions to migrate, deflects attention from the fact that both children and adults are fleeing the same conditions of violence and insecurity in their home countries, and washes responsibility for the fact that migrant journeys are so dangerous because of state militarization and border enforcement. Smuggling economies, which, despite political discourse, are not solely comprised of organized criminal groups, but rather local actors who are often acquaintances or other family members,[25] exist only in response to border enforcement. To protect children so that they would not have to risk the violence of the journey, the United States would need to end its restrictive and punitive border enforcement policies, which funnel people into illicit economies and dangerous routes.

While much media attention has focused on Latina women as societal threats through their fertility and reproductive capacity,[26] we have also seen them portrayed as victims within both militaristic and humanitarian responses to unauthorized migration. To this last point, I begin with a quotation:

> There is a humanitarian and security crisis on our southern border that requires urgent action. Thousands of children are being exploited by ruthless coyotes and vicious cartels and gangs. One in three women is sexually assaulted on the dangerous journey north. In fact, many loving mothers give their young daughters birth control pills for the long journey up to the United States because they know they may be raped or sexually

accosted or assaulted. Nearly 50 migrants a day are being referred for urgent medical care.

These words are not taken from an Amnesty International or UNHCR report. This is, in fact, a portion of a speech given by President Donald Trump in January 2019 to ask Congress for $5.7 billion dollars to build his border wall. In this statement, Trump draws on several common themes in narratives about Central American women: the widely circulated statistics on the numbers of migrant women who are sexually assaulted on their journeys north, the probable exploitation of Central American children at the hands of smugglers and criminals, and the desperation of "loving mothers" who willingly give their daughters birth control knowing the likelihood they will be raped. The goal of this statement is to construct migrant women and children as innocent victims who must be protected by the state. The enemy are ruthless and hypersexualized criminals—the smuggler boogeymen—who can be stopped only through increased enforcement. However, despite this seemingly sympathetic language and the large numbers of asylum claims based on gender-based violence, the Trump administration took measures to limit asylum protections, claiming that survivors of domestic violence and gang violence were not a particular social group warranting protection under US asylum law. In 2021, the Biden administration restored the possibility of protection for women and families who are survivors of domestic and gang violence.

Returning to Trump's statement above, we see how borders function as political stages where states demonstrate their power to protect the nation from unsavory, undeserving, and dangerous others.[27] Anti-immigrant activists continued to use the specter of sexual violence to justify both state sanctioned and vigilante violence. In the mid-2000s "rape trees"—trees where the undergarments of migrant women are hung as trophies and warnings to other migrants—were evoked by the border militia group known as the Minutemen in their anti-immigrant propaganda. As Amy Lind and Jill Williams argue, such discourse reinscribes the United States as a space of female chastity that needs to be protected from dangerous others while rendering invisible the role of the state in sexual violence.[28] Narratives of sexual violence work to legitimize more punitive immigration policies and security measures, and the mothers and children who are evoked are nothing more than political pawns, quickly deployed and easily disposed of. Through these examples, we see the contradictions in state and public discourses that demonize immigrant women as threats to the nation through their sexuality and fertility, as irresponsible parents that have put their children at risk, and as victims themselves that need to be rescued through stronger enforcement measures.

The Contradictions of Family Unity

In the mid-20th century, social currents had shifted away from racially based exclusions, and a new era in US immigration emerged that centered on the principle of family unity. In 1965, Senator Robert Kennedy testified to the Immigration and Naturalization subcommittee of the Committee of the Judiciary to end the outdated National Origins Formula (1921–1965), the quota system that sought to limit the number of immigrants from Eastern and Southern Europe, Asia, and Africa. The central talking point in his objection to the quota system was the damage it caused to family configurations. He said, "One of the primary purposes of civilization—and certainly its primary strength—is the guarantee that family life can flourish in unity, peace, and order. But the current national origins system separates families coldly and arbitrarily. It keeps parents from children and brothers from sisters for years—and even decades. Thus it fails to recognize simple humanity."[29] Indeed, the central narrative of the Immigration and Nationality Act of 1965, signed by President Johnson, and much of US immigration policy since then, is that immigration to the United States should prioritize family reunification. And while family unity is considered the cornerstone of US immigration policy, we must also consider some of the intended and unintended consequences of laws based on hierarchies of difference and deservingness. For example, the bill sought to maintain racial hierarchies as the majority of visas were reserved for family reunification, and groups that had been barred, namely Asian and

African migrants, had fewer family ties to make claims.[30] In recent decades, however, some of these dynamics have shifted: as European immigration to the United States has slowed, the majority of family-based visas now go to family members from Latin America and Asia. While the United States has historically denied visas to any person who is likely to become a public charge, the 1965 law perpetuated class inequalities by implementing new income requirements for sponsors while continuing to bar immigrants from many federal support systems.[31]

While the vast majority of visas and green cards issued by the United States, as well as reunification programs for refugees and other vulnerable groups, are based on family relationships, what counts as family remains steeped in specific ideas around gender, biological relatedness, and sexuality, privileging certain familial and kinship configurations over others.[32] The family unification program set by the Immigration and Nationality Act of 1965 (expanded upon in the Immigration Act of 1990) distinguishes between two main categories. The immediate relative category includes the spouses, unmarried minor children and parents of US citizens who can receive a family-based visa with no annual limits. The family preference category allows unmarried adult children of US citizens, spouses, and minor children of lawful permanent residents, unmarried adult children of permanent residents, married children of US citizens, and the siblings of US citizens to apply for a green card with limited numerical and per-country caps each year. These caps have created massive backlogs in the immigration system, forcing many people who have qualified to wait years and even decades before they are issued a green card. This backlog, in turn, has made the family-preference system untenable for many families, particularly those with separated children, where waiting one year, not to mention 20 years, for a green card, is detrimental to the well-being of the child and arguably the entire family. Moreover, the family-preference system does not recognize the complex kinship and care arrangements of many families. Unmarried heterosexual or same-sex partners, children born out of wedlock, informal foster parents, grandparents, cousins, aunts, uncles, and other extended kin members are not recognized as eligible family members.[33]

The family-visa system also creates challenges for mixed-status families with members seeking to adjust their status. To adjust to lawful permanent status in the United States, many unauthorized immigrants seeking family-sponsored visas must leave the United States for consular processing in their countries of origin, where they face 3- to 10-year bars on readmission unless they receive a waiver. This is a risk that many unauthorized parents are unwilling to take. Thus, the current system incentivizes unauthorized immigration for family members who are not recognized in the two categories, those who face decades-long waiting times and those who are likely to endure prolonged family separation in order to receive a family-sponsored visa.

Legacies of Family Separation

This chapter began with the controversial image of a mother running with her two children, sparking national hysteria over the arrival of migrant caravans and the treatment of women and children. Several other photographs captured national and international attention during the Trump era, reflecting outrage over the harsh consequences of the administration's policies on asylum-seeking and (im)migrant families. The first was the nighttime image of a two-year old child crying hysterically as she stood between her mother and a border patrol vehicle. Her mother, whose hands were spread flat against the side of the vehicle, was being physically pat down by a purple-gloved border patrol guard from behind. The photograph, along with images of children wrapped in mylar emergency blankets sleeping on the ground of large warehouses behind chain linked fences, came to symbolize the cruelty of the Trump administration's "Zero Tolerance" policy that systematically separated and detained children of any age, including infants, from their parents at the US-Mexico border. Despite the commonly used defense that family separations were an "unintended consequence" of border enforcement, Zero Tolerance was exposed as an intentionally devised and implemented state strategy of deterrence.[34] The rationale behind the policy was that by prosecuting parents as criminals and taking their children away immediately, families would suffer so much that they would be deterred from migrating. The twisted logic used by some of the early masterminds of the plan was that through the suffering of a few, the plan would keep more families safe in the long run.[35] What was not recognized was that deterrence strategies rarely stop people from trying to cross the border again; they only push people into more dangerous and clandestine routes. Moreover, as was the case with Zero Tolerance, the incompetence and inability of officials to adequately plan and keep track of families within the labyrinth of courts, detention facilities, and children's shelters, as well as of parents deported back to Central America, meant that hundreds of parents were deemed "unreachable." In 2020, 545 parents still could not be located. The policy not only produced orphans and familial trauma, but also exposed children to horrific conditions while in detention. In the 4 years between 2014 and 2018, there were over 4,500 reports of sexual abuse of detained immigrant children, perpetrated by other minors and by adult staff members in detention centers.[36] The public outrage surrounding child separation forced the Trump administration to officially abandon the policy, though the US House of Representatives Committee on Oversight and Reform found that the administration continued to separate families after Zero Tolerance was rescinded.[37]

While family separation is egregious, I want to expand our understanding of it by seeing it not just as a single stain on US policy implemented by a single administration, but instead as a recurring strategy of domination throughout US history. As historians have taught us, such policies and practices are not without precedent and in fact must be read within a longer history of state repression, criminalization of families of color, and the taking of children.[38] Historic examples of systemic and legal forced family separations include enslaved Black families separated and sold in the Antebellum South and the separation of Native American children sent to boarding schools (1869–1960). As Ta-Nehisi Coates has argued, the intentional separation of family units is not simply a marker of cruelty, but a strategy to weaken the core units of social life—the family—within larger structures of capitalism and white supremacy. "The parting of black families was a kind of murder," he writes. "Here we find the roots of American wealth and democracy—in the for-profit destruction of the most important asset available to any people, the family. The destruction was not incidental to America's rise; it facilitated that rise. By erecting a slave society, America created the economic foundation for its great experiment in democracy."[39]

The economic incentives to family separation can also be seen in the practice of orphan trains that ran between 1854 and 1929. As many as 250,00 children from primarily Catholic immigrant families were forcibly removed and relocated from New York and other eastern cities to be placed with families in primarily Anglo Protestant households and farmsteads in the Midwest and American West to work as laborers.[40] While the rationale used was to rescue these children from the squalor and dangerous conditions of urban slums, where indeed many of them had lost parents or their parents surrendered them because they could not afford to support them, the trains effectively shipped them like cattle across the American West. In many cases siblings were separated from one another, and while some found happy homes, others were met with abuse and exploitation.

Family separation has also been historically used as a political tool. In the 1970s and 1980s, in efforts to prosecute suspected smugglers, the United States initiated a policy of incarcerating women and minors to serve as "material witnesses" and testify in immigration courts. This mass imprisonment, up to 5,000 people a year, involved the separation of minors from their parents, including young children, the detention of children on separate floors from their adult relatives, and the placement of children with unrelated foster families. It was not until the Obama administration built family detention centers that the United States even had an infrastructure to be able to keep families together.[41]

In addition to these examples, we might recast other US immigration policies as policies of isolation and family separation. As discussed above, the intentional isolation of braceros from their families or the prohibitions placed on Asian female immigration can also be read as forms of family separation intended to maintain an underclass of racialized labor. Beyond border exclusions, the massive industry surrounding surveillance, raids, detention, and deportation is emblematic of the ongoing and everyday practices that separate families already living in the United States.[42] Mixed-status families, comprised of people who are deemed to both belong and not belong, live with uncertainty in their everyday lives, creating both fractures and solidarities.[43] While children live everyday with the reality that they may not see their parents at home for dinner, the trauma of raids and family separation impact entire communities.[44] Family unity may be the hallmark of contemporary US immigration policy, but we must recognize the ways it favors certain types of families and mechanisms of family unity for some and contributes to ongoing forms of familial distress and separation for others.

On Love and Loss: Migrant Disappearance and Death

On a Sunday afternoon in June 2019, a young couple from El Salvador—25-year-old father, Óscar Alberto Martínez Ramírez, his 21-year-old wife, Tania Vanessa Ávalos, and their 23-month-old daughter, Valeria—hoped to apply for asylum in the United States. They had arrived to the border city of Matamoros, but the international bridge to Brownsville, Texas, was closed until Monday. Moreover, the Trump administration had implemented the Migration Protection Protocols, also known as "Remain in Mexico," earlier that year, which forced asylum seekers to wait in Mexico while their asylum claims are processed. The couple decided to try crossing the Rio Grande on their own. Óscar tucked Valeria under his shirt, and she held onto his back as he swam across. Valeria followed them on the back of a family friend, but the water was getting rough, and she turned around. When she reached the Mexican side, she could see her husband and daughter close to the US side, but her husband was tired, and they were swept underneath. Their bodies were recovered several hundred yards away on Monday by Mexican authorities, father and daughter still embraced. A journalist captured a haunting photo of the pair that was published in the Mexican newspaper *La Jornada* before going viral. The final act of this pair, as they clung together, was an act of love and of defiance against a system designed to separate them.

This reality was made clear to me during fieldwork with the families of missing migrants, including a caravan of Central American families who make an annual trek across Mexico to search for their loved ones. Carrying posters with the photographs of their children, families from El Salvador, Honduras, and Guatemala retrace the movements of their loved ones in migrant shelters and transit spaces to raise awareness of the dangers they face long before reaching the US-Mexico border. They represent the thousands of families across the Americas who experience the ambiguous loss that results from not knowing what has happened to a loved one.[45] What they seek is some sort of closure, even if that means receiving the remains of their loved one in a flag-draped coffin, a common practice among repatriated bodies. Losses like theirs have become naturalized under the continued state of emergency manufactured at the US-Mexico border. The tragic end to the lives of Óscar and Valeria and the ripple effects and trauma that will haunt their family members are not simply the "unintended consequences" of immigration policies and border enforcement. Rather, their deaths must be seen as the predictable result of border enforcement regimes fueled by crisis and spectacle that funnel migrants into dangerous routes. They are also the result of immigration policies, like the Migration Protection Protocols and the COVID-era Title 42 emergency order that immediately expelled asylum seekers without due process, both violations of the United Nations 1951 Refugee Convention and principle of non-refoulement.

Conclusion

Competing narratives of gender and the family in US immigration history demonstrate the central tensions around family unity at the heart of US immigration policy, as well as the ways racism, patriarchy, and capitalism are interconnected and embedded within historical and contemporary immigration and border enforcement. In turn, immigration and asylum regimes are critical to the construction, surveillance, regulation and exclusion of racialized and gendered bodies, identities, and behaviors.[46] The spectacle of the border has provided endless amount of political fodder for drumming up fear and playing on social anxieties to justify punitive immigration policies and solidify racial hierarchies. Gendered narratives around deservingness and belonging, anxieties around sexual deviance, and racialized fears of reproductive others are all integral to the history of inclusion and exclusion in the United States. Rather than compartmentalizing acts of sexism and racism to isolated acts of violence, such as the Atlanta spa shootings or the tear gassing of families at the border, or to individualized tragedies like that of Óscar and Valeria, we must instead interrogate the structures, institutions, and global hierarchies that have historically deemed certain individuals, groups, and families more deserving than others. What is often lost, except for the few glimpses that emerge through the serendipity of images going viral or utter tragedy, are the everyday human consequences of such policies and the ways they impact individuals, families, and communities across the Americas and the world. Scholars, activists, and communities of solidarity work to make these histories and contemporary realities more visible in the pursuit of a more just and humane approach to immigration that more accurately reflects the myth and celebration of the United States as a nation of immigrants.

Notes

1. Susan C. Pearce, Elizabeth J. Clifford, and Reena Tandon, *Immigration and Women: Understanding the American Experience* (New York: New York University Press, 2011).
2. Lauren Berlant, "Intimacy: A Special Issue," *Critical Inquiry* 24, no. 2 (1998): 281–88; Lisa Duggan, *The Twilight of Equality? Neoliberalism, Cultural Politics, and the Attack on Democracy* (Boston: Beacon Press, 2003).
3. Ann Laura Stoler, ed., *Haunted by Empire: Geographies of Intimacy in North American History* (Durham, NC: Duke University Press, 2006).
4. Zoya Gubernskaya and Joanna Dreby, "US Immigration Policy and the Case for Family Unity," *Journal on Migration and Human Security* 5, no. 2 (2017): 417–30.
5. Lee R. Chavez, *The Latino Threat: Constructing Immigrants, Citizens, and the Nation* (Palo Alto, CA: Stanford University Press, 2008).
6. Bill Chapell, Vanessa Romo, and Jaclyn Diaz, "Official Who Said Atlanta Shooting Suspect Was Having a 'Bad Day' Faces Criticism," NPR, March 18, 2021, https://

www.npr.org/2021/03/17/978141138/atlanta-shooting-suspect-is-believed-to-have
-visited-spas-he-targeted.

7. Him Mark Lai, Genny Lim, and Judy Yung, eds., *Island: Poetry and History of Chinese Immigrants on Angel Island 1910–1940* (Seattle: University of Washington Press, 2014).

8. Eithne Luibhéid, *Entry Denied: Controlling Sexuality at the Border* (Minneapolis: University of Minnesota Press, 2002).

9. Luibhéid, *Entry Denied*.

10. Peggy Pascoe, *What Comes Naturally: Miscegenation Law and the Making of Race in America* (New York: Oxford University Press, 2008).

11. Nayan Shah, *Stranger Intimacy: Contesting Race, Sexuality, and the Law in the North American West* (Berkeley: University of California Press, 2011).

12. Eithne Luibhéid and Lionel Cantú Jr., eds., *Queer Migrations: Sexuality, U.S. Citizenship, and Border Crossings* (Minneapolis: University of Minnesota Press, 2005); A. Naomi Paik, *Bans, Walls, Raids, Sanctuary: Understanding U.S. Immigration for the Twenty-First Century* (Berkeley: University of California Press, 2020).

13. *Hill v. United States I.N.S.*, 714 F.2d 1470 (9th Cir. 1983).

14. Luibhéid, *Entry Denied*.

15. Laura A. Belmonte, *The International LGBT Rights Movement: A History* (London: Bloomsbury Publishing, 2020).

16. Ana Elizabeth Rosas, *Abrazando el Espíritu: Bracero Families Confront the US-Mexico Border* (Berkeley: University of California Press, 2014).

17. Rosas, *Abrazando el Espíritu*.

18. Ruth Gomberg-Muñoz, *Becoming Legal: Immigration Law and Mixed-Status Families* (Oxford: Oxford University Press, 2017).

19. Patricia Zavella, "Why Are Immigrant Families Different Now?" Center for Latino Policy Research, University of California, Berkeley, 2012.

20. Jonathan X. Inda, "The Value of Immigrant Life," in *Women and Migration in the U.S.-Mexico Borderlands*, ed. Denise A. Segura and Patricia Zavella (Durham, NC: Duke University Press, 2007), 134. See also Chavez, *Latino Threat*.

21. Leo R. Chavez, "A Glass Half Empty: Latina Reproduction and Public Discourse," *Human Organization* 63, no. 2 (2004): 173–88.

22. Inda, "Value of Immigrant Life."

23. Leo R. Chavez, *Anchor Babies and the Challenge of Birthright Citizenship* (Palo Alto, CA: Stanford University Press, 2017).

24. Kathleen Hennessey, "Obama Warns Central American Parents Not to Send Kids to Border," *Los Angeles Times*, June 27, 2014, https://www.latimes.com/nation/la-na -obama-immigration-20140627-story.html.

25. Gabriella Sanchez, *Human Smuggling and Border Crossings* (New York: Routledge, 2014).

26. Chavez, *Latino Threat*.

27. Peter Andreas, *Border Games: Policing the U.S.-Mexico Divide* (Ithaca, NY: Cornell University Press, 2000); Rebecca Galemba, "Mexico's Border (In)Security," *The Postcolonialist* 2, no. 2 (December 2014).

28. Amy Lind and Jill Williams, "Engendering Violence in De/Hyper-Nationalized Spaces: Border Militarization, State Territorialization, and Embodied Politics at

the US-Mexico Border," in *Feminist (Im)Mobilities in Fortress(ing) North America: Rights, Citizenships, Identities in Transnational Perspective*, ed. Amy Lind, Anne Sisson Runyan, and Marianne H. Marchand (New York: Ashgate, 2013), 156–70.

29. Statement of Sen. Robert F. Kennedy, *Hearings before the Subcommittee on Immigration and Naturalization of the Committee on the Judiciary*, 89th Congr., 1st Sess., on S. 500 to Amend the Immigration and Nationality Act, and for other Purposes, US Senate, Committee on the Judiciary (Washington, DC.: US Government Printing Office, 1965).

30. Luibhéid and Cantú, *Queer Migrations*.

31. Luibhéid and Cantú, *Queer Migrations*.

32. Deborah A. Boehm, *Intimate Migrations: Gender, Family, and Illegality among Transnational Mexicans* (New York: New York University Press, 2012); Gomberg-Muñoz, *Becoming Legal*.

33. Zavella, "Immigrant Families."

34. Caitlin Dickerson, "'We Need to Take Away Children: The Secret History of the U.S. Government's Family-Separation Policy," *The Atlantic*, August 7, 2022, https://www.theatlantic.com/magazine/archive/2022/09/trump-administration-family-separation-policy-immigration/670604/.

35. Dickerson, "We Need to Take Away Children."

36. Matthew Haag, "Thousands of Immigrant Children Said They Were Sexually Abused in U.S. Detention Centers, Report Says," *New York Times*, February 27, 2019, https://www.nytimes.com/2019/02/27/us/immigrant-children-sexual-abuse.html.

37. The committee found that at least 700 children were separated from their parents after the official ending of the zero-tolerance policy in June 2018.

38. Laura Briggs, *Taking Children: A History of American Terror* (Berkeley: University of California Press, 2020).

39. Ta-Nehisi Coates, "The Case for Reparations," *The Atlantic*, June 15, 2014, https://www.theatlantic.com/magazine/archive/2014/06/the-case-for-reparations/361631/.

40. Rebecca S. Trammell, "Orphan Train Myths and Legal Reality," *Modern American* 5, no. 2 (Fall 2009): 3–13.

41. Ivón Padilla-Rodríguez, "Opinion: The U.S. Separated Families Decades Ago, Too. With 545 Migrant Children Missing Their Parents, That Moment Holds a Key Lesson," *Time*, November 2, 2020, https://time.com/5906441/family-separation-immigration-history/.

42. Deborah A. Boehm, *Returned: Going and Coming in an Age of Deportation* (Berkeley: University of California Press, 2016).

43. Gomberg-Muñoz, *Becoming Legal*; Heidi Castañeda, *Borders of Belonging: Struggle and Solidarity in Mixed-Status Immigrant Families* (Palo Alto, CA: Stanford University Press, 2019).

44. William D. Lopez, *Separated: Family and Community in the Aftermath of an Immigration Raid* (Baltimore, MD: Johns Hopkins University Press, 2019).

45. Pauline Boss, "Ambiguous Loss Research, Theory, and Practice: Reflections After 9/11," *Journal of Marriage and Family* 66, no. 3 (August 2004): 551–66.

46. Luibhéid, *Entry Denied*.

CHAPTER 14

A Timeline of Queer Migrations

QUEEROCRACY and Carlos Motta

To highlight the issues faced by queer immigrants in the United States, the grassroots organization QUEEROCRACY in collaboration with artist Carlos Motta presented *A New Discovery: Queer Immigration in Perspective*, a project commissioned in 2011 by Risk + Reward, a program of the Museum of Art and Design in New York.

On Columbus Day (now Indigenous Peoples Day) 2011, QUEERO-CRACY and its allies led a social intervention performance at Columbus Circle, New York City. The intervention included a collective reading of "A Timeline of Queer Migrations."

A New Discovery: Queer Immigration in Perspective attempts to bring attention to the way immigrant and queer politics intersect in the public sphere so as to confront, challenge, and transform the state mechanisms that police borders and bodies in the United States.

"A Timeline of Queer Migrations" (Newsprint, 16 × 22 in.) was compiled by QUEEROCRACY cofounders Cassidy Gardner and Camilo Godoy with artist Carlos Motta. The photograph of the Christopher Columbus statue is by Camilo Godoy.

Figure 14.1. Photograph of the Christopher Columbus Statue in New York City, by Camilo Godoy for "A Timeline of Queer Migrations" by QUEEROCRACY and Carlos Motta, 2011.

1492 — The "Discovery" of America
October 12, 1492, Christopher Columbus "discovered" America.

1798 — Alien and Sedition Acts signed into law
The Alien and Sedition Acts consisted of four laws that increased the residency requirement for US citizenship from 5 to 14 years, authorized the president to imprison or deport aliens considered "dangerous to the peace and safety of the United States," and restricted speech critical of the government.

1857 — Dred Scott decision
Supreme Court's Dred Scott outcome claims Black people are not US citizens.

1867 — Karl-Heinrich Ulrichs
On August 29, 1867, Karl-Heinrich Ulrichs became the first self-proclaimed homosexual to speak out publicly for homosexual rights when he pleaded at the Congress of German Jurists in Munich for a resolution urging the repeal of anti-homosexual laws.

1875 — Page Law passed
In 1875, Congress passed the Page Law, the first immigration law that prohibited immigrants considered to be undesirable, including convicts, contract laborers, and specifically Asian women thought to be prostitutes to enter the country.

1882 — Chinese Exclusion Act
The United States suspended Chinese immigration, a ban that was intended to last 10 years, but was repealed by the Magnuson Act on December 17, 1943.

1882 — The Immigration Act
The first comprehensive federal immigration law called for the return of convicts, idiots, lunatics, and persons unable to care for themselves to their countries of origin. The new federal system was funded by a tax of 50 cents on each immigrant.

1891 — The Immigration Act amended
The 1891 Immigration Act amended the 1882 act to also exclude immigrants considered to be polygamists, to have contagious diseases, and those "likely to become a public charge." A congressional report at the time found "at least 50 percent of the criminals, insane and paupers of our largest cities . . . are of foreign birth."

1910 — Emma Goldman
Political activist Emma Goldman first began speaking publicly in favor of gay rights.

1917 — Immigration Act of 1917
In 1917, US Congress passed the Immigration Act, which required all immigrants to pass a literacy test. It also banned psychopaths, inferiors, and "people with abnormal sexual instincts" from coming to the United States. Lesbian and gay immigrants were officially excluded from coming to the United States until 1990.

1924 — National Origins Act
The Immigration Act of 1924 limited the number of immigrants allowed entry into the United States through a national origins quota. The act excluded from entry anyone born in a geographi-

cally defined "Asiatic Barred Zone" except for Japanese and Filipinos.

1924 — Border Patrol
US Congress passed the Labor Appropriation Act of 1924, officially establishing the US Border Patrol for the purpose of securing its borders between inspection stations.

1924 — Society for Human Rights
The Society for Human Rights, the United States' first gay rights organization, was founded in Chicago. The movement existed for a few months before being shut down by the police.

1933–1945 — Nazi Holocaust
Persecution of homosexuals in Nazi Holocaust.

1937 — Pink Triangle
Twenty-five thousand convicted "gay" offenders were forced into prison and then into concentration camps where they were made to wear a pink inverted triangle on their uniform. During the 12-year Nazi regime up to 100,000 men were identified in police records as homosexuals, with about 50,000 convicted of violating Paragraph 175.

1948 — Forbundet af 1948
The homophile group Forbundet af 1948 (League of 1948) was formed in Denmark.

1950 — Mattachine Society and RSFL
The Mattachine Society, the first American homophile group, was founded in New York and RFSL (Swedish Federation for Lesbian, Gay, Bisexual, and Transgender Rights), the first Swedish homophile group, was formed.

1952 — Immigration and Nationality Act (INA)
Also known as the 1952 McCarren-Walter Act, INA recodified exclusion categories to include a ban on psychopathic personalities in the United States.

1956 — Daughters of Bilitis
The Daughters of Bilitis, a pioneering national lesbian organization, was founded in San Francisco.

1965 — Immigration law banned "sexual deviates"
Immigration law in the United States underwent another revision: lesbian and gay exclusion was again recodified, this time under the ban on "sexual deviates."

1965 — Exclusion by Immigration Reform Act
US immigration laws were amended in 1965 to exclude homosexuals "aliens afflicted with sexual deviation" from admission into the United States.

1965–1967 — UMAP detention camps, Cuba
Gay men were detained in reeducation camps known as Military Units to Aid Production (Unidades Militares de Ayuda a la Producción, UMAP).

1969 — Stonewall Riots
In June 1969, police raided the Stonewall Inn in New York, checked for identification, made homophobic and transphobic comments, and physically assaulted members of the LGBTIQ communities. Rather than quietly taking police abuses, the community fought back. This was one of the first LGBTIQ mass uprisings in the United States, and it lasted for

nearly three days. One of the customers at the Stonewall Inn that night was an immigrant man who later committed suicide. He preferred to die than to be deported for being gay. If people didn't disclose their sexual orientation when they entered the United States, but were later caught by the Immigration and Naturalization Services (INS), they could be deported for perjury (lying to cover up their sexuality).

1970 — First Gay Liberation Days
First Gay Liberation Day March held New York City, First Gay Freedom Day March held in Los Angeles, and first Gay-In held in San Francisco.

1972 — Transgender sex change became legal in Sweden
Sweden became the first country in the world to allow transgendered people to legally change their sex and provide free hormone therapy.

1979 — Bullying by US Border Patrol Agents
The Border Patrol often used stereotypes to decide who was gay or lesbian. If an agent suspected an immigrant of being gay or lesbian, they could deport them or send them to a psychiatrist for a deportation hearing.

1979 — Targeting of male homo-sexuality in Cuba
According to the Cuban 1979 Penal Code, public ostentation of homosexuality was punishable by sentences of three to nine months.

1980 — Refugee Act
The US Refugee Act of 1980 expanded the legal definition of "refugee" to include those fleeing "persecution on account of membership in a particular social group."

1980 — Castro launched the Mariel boatlift
On April 20, 1980, Fidel Castro launched the Mariel boatlift in which he allowed as many as 125,000 "undesir-able" Cubans to leave for the United States.

1981 — Norwegian law against homosexual discrimination
Norway became the first country in the world to enact a law to prevent discrimination against homosexuals.

1986 — Immigration Reform and Control Act (IRCA)
The Immigration Reform and Control Act (IRCA) of 1986 was signed into law by President Ronald Reagan in order to control and deter undocumented immigration to the United States.

1987 — ACT UP
The AIDS Coalition to Unleash Power (ACT UP) staged its first major demonstration in New York City.

1987 — La Frontera/Borderlands
Gloria Anzaldúa, a self-proclaimed "chicana dyke-feminist, tejana patlache poet, writer, and cultural theorist," published the popular book *La Frontera/ Borderlands: The New Mestiza*, highlighting the intersection of material and metaphorical borders within the politics of sexuality, culture, and race.

1987 — United States banned HIV+ visitors from entering the country

1988 — Social services, taxes, and inheritances in Sweden

Sweden became the first country in the world to pass laws protecting social services, taxes, and inheritances of gays and lesbians.

1989 — Registered partnership in Denmark

Denmark became the first country to enact registered partnership laws.

1990 — US laws that banned lesbian and gay immigrants officially repealed

Laws that banned lesbian and gay immigrants were officially repealed in 1990, but LGBT immigrants still face substantial difficulties in obtaining legal immigration status. For example, current immigration policy recognizes only "direct family ties" as heterosexual; same-sex partners are therefore denied such immigration privileges. Transgender immigrants may not be able to have gender changed on official documents from their home country, resulting in enormous, sometimes insurmountable difficulties.

1990 — Homosexual ban disappeared from the United States

Barney Frank, congressman from Massachusetts, drafted the comprehensive immigration exclusion amendment that defined the reasons for denying entry into the United States, and left out the sexual preference exclusion.

1990 — "Toboso-Alfonso" case

The Board of Immigration Appeals (BIA) recognized the need to protect homosexuals as a social group and allows Toboso-Alfonso to remain in the United States through "withholding of deportation," but upheld a lower court's decision to deny asylum because Toboso-Alfonso had a US criminal conviction.

1993 — US HIV ban became law

US Congress placed a ban on immigrants who are HIV+. The Immigration and Nationality Act states that any foreign national with a "communicable disease of public health significance," which includes HIV, is "inadmissible." If you are HIV+ and apply for legal permanent residence and do not qualify for a waiver, your application will be denied, and you may be placed in deportation proceedings.

1993 — "Don't Ask, Don't Tell"

The "Don't Ask, Don't Tell" policy was instituted for the US military, permitting gays to serve in the military but banning homosexual activity. President Clinton's original intention to revoke the prohibition against gays in the military was met with stiff opposition; this compromise, which has led to the discharge of thousands of men and women in the armed forces, was the result.

1994 — "Toboso-Alfonso" case became precedent

US Attorney Janet Reno released Order 1895–94, which made the "Toboso-Alfonso" case a binding precedent for Immigration and Naturalization Services (INS) officials making future immigration and asylum decisions. The order states that "an individual who has been identified as homosexual and persecuted by his or her government for that reason alone may be eligible for relief under the refugee laws on the basis of persecution because of membership in a social group."

1994 — Political asylum

In 1994, gays and lesbians were finally recognized as a social group for purposes of applying for political asylum in the United States. Poor LGBT immigrants are particularly likely to be dismissed simply as "economic migrants," while those from countries with whom the United States has friendly relations are often denied asylum for foreign policy reasons. Few transgender people have ever been awarded asylum, because gender and sexual orientation persecution often operates in ways that are difficult to document.

1994 — Refugee status in Canada

Canada granted refugee status to homosexuals because it fears for their well-being in their native country.

1994 — Lesbian and Gay Immigration Rights Task Force

Lesbian and Gay Immigration Rights Task Force (LGIRTF) was formed in New York to provide support, information, and networking opportunities for gay and lesbian immigrants and their partners.

1994 — Audre Lorde Project (ALP)

ALP was formed in New York City as a community organizing center for lesbian, gay, bisexual, two-spirit, trans, and gender non-conforming (LGBTST-GNC) people of color communities.

1994 — Immigration Equality

Immigration Equality was formed as an independent chapter of the Lesbian and Gay Immigration Rights Task Force under its own name and leadership in Los Angeles.

1996 — Defense of Marriage Act (DOMA)

President Clinton signed DOMA into law: "The Federal Government may not recognize same-sex or polygamous marriages for any purpose."

1996 — IIRIRA

President Clinton signed the Illegal Immigration Reform and Immigrant Responsibility Act (IIRIRA) into law. The new law retroactively expanded the criminal grounds for deportation, created mandatory detention for many immigrants, and authorized more state and local law police participation in immigration enforcement.

1997 — Immigration rights to same-sex couples akin to marriage in UK

1999 — PACS in France

France enacted civil union laws (PACS) for same-sex couples.

2000 — Permanent Partners Immigration Act introduced in the United States

Congressman Jerrold Nadler (D-NY) introduced the PPIA on Valentine's Day. This legislation would allow US citizens and lawful permanent residents to sponsor their same-sex partners for immigration to the United States by simply adding the term "permanent partner" in sections where "spouse" appears in the Immigration and Nationality Act.

2000 — Permanent Partners Immigration Act resolution passed in San Francisco and Los Angeles

2000 — *Hernandez-Montiel v. INS*
In California in August, the US Court of Appeals of the Ninth Circuit held that the petitioner, "a gay man with a female sexual identity, who may be considered a transsexual," was entitled to asylum and withholding of deportation.

2000 — Vermont became first US state to legalize civil unions

2000 — Israel recognized same-sex relations for immigration
Israel recognized same-sex relations for immigration purposes for a foreign partner of an Israeli resident.

2001 — DREAM Act
Introduction of the Development, Relief and Education for Alien Minors Act (DREAM Act), a US legislative proposal that would provide undocumented youth a path to citizenship.

2001 — President Bush signed USA PATRIOT Act
Less than a month after the attacks of September 11, 2001, Congress passed the PATRIOT Act. Among other controversial provisions, it authorized the attorney general to detain noncitizens if they have "reasonable grounds to believe" the person may be a threat to national security. It also called for a system to track international students.

2001 — Permanent Partners Immigration Act reintroduced
Congressman Jerrold Nadler reintroduces the PPIA on Valentine's Day in the United States.

2002 — Sylvia Rivera Law Project (SRLP)
SRLP, a collective organization that brings visibility to low income people and people of color who are transgender, gender nonconforming, or intersex, was formed to fight against all forms of harassment, discrimination, or violence they face.

2002 — Adoption
Sweden legalized adoption for same-sex couples, making Sweden's registered partnership nearly identical to marriage, with the exception of the right to marriage in a church.

2002 — Christina Madrazo
Christina Madrazo, a transsexual, said she was raped by a guard in an Immigration and Naturalization Services (INS) Detention Center. She sued the US government for $15 million.

2002 — Canada Immigration and Refugee Protection Act
Same-sex marriage became officially recognized for the purpose of immigrating to Canada.

2003 — Permanent Partners Immigration Act reintroduced
Congressman Jerrold Nadler reintroduced the Permanent Partners Immigration Act in the House on February 13, 2003, and Senator Patrick Leahy (D-VT) introduced it in the Senate on July 31, 2003.

2003 — Immigration and Customs Enforcement Agency
The Bush administration dissolved the INS and transferred its powers to the Immigration and Customs Enforcement

Agency (ICE) under the newly created Department of Homeland Security. Its mission is to uphold public safety by enforcing immigration and customs laws.

2004 — Marriages with a transsexual spouse invalid

On April 16, 2004, the Bush administration issued a new policy regarding marriages with a transsexual spouse. The policy invalidated all legal marriages "between two individuals where one or both of the parties claims to be a transsexual."

2004 — Permanent Partners Immigration Act in California

The California Assembly passes a resolution in support of the PPIA.

2005 — Lovo-Lara

On May 18, 2005, the Board of Immigration Appeals (BIA) issued an interim decision in the "Lovo-Lara" case in which it upheld the validity of a legal marriage with a transsexual spouse and approved issuing of a green card.

2005 — Church of Sweden's blessings

The Church of Sweden, the former state church, decided to hold blessing ceremonies for same-sex couples, who could already enter into registered partnerships equal to marriage.

2006 — Out4Immigration was founded

On June 22, Out4Immigration formed in San Francisco as an all-volunteer grassroots organization to raise awareness on the plight of same-sex bi-national couples and their families, as well as the HIV ban.

2006 — Same-sex marriage in South Africa

Same-sex marriage became legal in South Africa.

2006 — Yogyakarta Principles

In 2006, in response to well-documented patterns of abuse, a distinguished group of international human rights experts met in Yogyakarta, Indonesia, to outline a set of international principles relating to sexual orientation and gender identity. The result was the Yogyakarta Principles, a universal guide to human rights, which affirm binding international legal standards with which all states must comply.

2006 — For All the Ways They Say We Are, No One Is Illegal

The Audre Lorde Project releases a statement in support of LGBTSTGNC immigrants of color.

2007 — Definition of Marriage

At the time, 26 US states had constitutional amendments restricting marriage to that between a man and a woman. An additional 19 states had laws against gay marriage. Several states extended this to all "similar" unions "for any purpose," including Michigan in February of 2007. In California, a constitutional amendment appeared on the November 2008 ballot.

2007 — Victoria Arellano

On July 20, 2007, Victoria Arellano died while in custody at the San Pedro detention center in California. Victoria, an HIV+ transgender woman who came to the United States from Mexico as a child, was refused medication and medical care despite repeated pleas from the men detained with her. In spite of their care for her, she died shackled to her bed.

2007 — Jorge Soto Vega

An immigration judge denied Vega asylum because Vega didn't appear gay to him. The decision was appealed and asylum was secured on January 30, 2007, with the help of Lambda Legal. Vega said: "The court has awarded me my freedom and the opportunity to spend my life in the country I love with the person I love," referring to his partner of 15 years.

2007 — Uniting American Families Act

Reintroduction of UAFA in the House by Congressman Jerrold Nadler and in the Senate by Senator Patrick Leahy.

2008 — *Bosede v. Mukasey*

HIV-positive Nigerian immigrant Bosede Oriade was denied due process by an immigration judge due to having been convicted for possession of small amounts of cocaine. Bosede argued that if he were sent back to Nigeria, he would be immediately detained because of his HIV status. If imprisoned, he would have no access to doctors, proper nutrition, or medication. The Seventh Circuit disagreed with the immigration judge's decision and declared that all aliens in the United States regardless of immigration status are entitled to due process. Bosede was granted a new hearing.

2008 — Queers and Immigration: A Vision Statement

Queers for Economic Justice released a solidarity statement outlining the political challenges facing queer immigrants. It critiques the discriminatory implications of anti-immigrant legislation and issues practical demands that come to make a profound difference for the lives of all immigrants.

2008–2009 — Proposition 8

California voters support Proposition 8, a ballot that eliminated rights of same-sex couples to marry in California. On May 26, 2009, California's supreme court upheld Proposition 8, but did not overturn previous same-sex marriages.

2009 — Anti-homosexuality bill proposed in Uganda

2009 — US President Obama lifted HIV travel ban

2009–2010 — Norway, Iceland, Portugal, and Argentina legalized same-sex marriage

2010 — Arizona SB 1070 signed into law

This bill deters "the unlawful entry and presence of illegal aliens and economic activity by illegal aliens in the United States."

2010 — Secretary Napolitano announced record deportations

Napolitano held a press conference to announce the "highest number of removals in our nation's history": 392,000 deportations in 2010.

2010 — Switzerland Deportation Referendum

Switzerland gains right-wing support in a referendum that called for the immediate deportation of foreigners who are convicted of any serious crime.

2010 — Phallometric Test

The European Unions' leading human rights agency sharply criticized the Czech authorities for using the "Phallometric Test," a method for testing whether homosexual asylum seekers are genuinely gay by measuring the flow of blood to a man's penis to determine the physical reaction to pornography.

2011 — Obama barred US entry for violators of LGBT human rights abroad

President Obama issued a proclamation that barred entry of immigrants who organized or participated in war crimes or serious violations of human rights, which could include those in Uganda who sought to pass legislation that would institute the death penalty for homosexual acts.

2011 — Human rights abuses at US ICE detention centers

Immigrant advocates filed 13 complaints with the Department of Homeland Security alleging civil and human rights abuses of LGBT immigrants being detained pending removal proceedings.

2011 — New York state passed Marriage Equality Bill

2011 — Australian passport gender/ sex policy change

Australia became the first country in the world to allow gender/sex change in travel passports.

2011 — Official documents

In 2011 only Panama, South Africa, New Zealand, Spain, Australia provided the ability to change gender on official documents.

2011 — Rudolf Brazda

Rudolf Brazda, the last known pink triangle Holocaust survivor, died.

2011 — High Level Meeting on AIDS

The UN General Assembly High Level Meeting on AIDS agreed to advance efforts to reduce sexual transmission of HIV and halving HIV infection among people who inject drugs by 2015.

2011 — Revised detention center standards for trans detainees

On March 1, 2011, Immigration Equality announces that the DHS enacted new standards that pertain to transgender persons in detention. Access to hormone therapy if previously taken, strip searches done in private, and gender self-identification taken into consideration for detention placement were all included within the new revisions.

2011 — International Intersex Forum

The world's first International Intersex Forum took place in Brussels.

2011 — Prohibition

Belize, Lesotho, and Swaziland continue to prohibit LGBT migrants.

2011 — DOMA

The US Department of Justice acknowledged that the federal Defense of Marriage Act (DOMA) is unconstitutional when used against lesbian and gay immigrant couples.

2011 — US discretion and deportation
President Obama laid out a plan to suspend the deportation proceedings of DREAM Act–eligible youth, military family members, crime victims, and immigrants with strong family ties. The new policy established a working group comprised of Department of Homeland Security and Department of Justice officials who would review 300,000 pending deportation cases to determine whether each case fell within the administration's "enforcement priorities." The administration halted cases that it determined merited an exercise of discretion and allowed those individuals whose cases were suspended to apply for work authorization.

2011 — "Don't Ask, Don't Tell" officially repealed in the United States

2011 — Green card moratorium
US Immigration officials said that they lifted the moratorium on green card cases for bi-national married couples and that they would continue to enforce the current law, which did not permit same-sex married couples the same immigration rights as heterosexual married couples.

2011 — US Senator Menendez
US Senator Robert Menendez introduced a comprehensive immigration reform, which included provisions for LGBT bi-national couples.

2011 — Employment Non-Discrimination Act (ENDA)
US Senator Patrick reintroduced the Employment Non-Discrimination Act (ENDA), which would help bi-national LGBT couples.

2011 — Alabama's HB 56 took effect
Alabama's tough immigration legislation, which required police to investigate the immigration status of those pulled over for any legal stops if they had a "reasonable suspicion" that a person was undocumented, took effect.

2011 — Undoing Borders: A Queer Manifesto
Horizontal Alliance of Very (or Voraciously or Vaguely) Organized Queers (HAVOQ) launched the Undoing Borders tour to share stories and thoughts about the intersections of queer and im/migrant experience.

2011 — Scarce immigration benefits
Only 16 countries in the world provided immigration benefits to same-sex couples, and 16 countries in the world allowed sponsorship of same sex partners within their immigration rules.

2011 — Over 1 million deported under President Obama
According to US Immigration and Customs Enforcement (ICE), deportations under President Obama have record levels of over one million, which was more than in any preceding administration.

2012 — Russia's anti-gay law
In St. Petersburg, Russia, displays of homosexuality that could influence children were outlawed, with fines of up to 500,000 rubles for anyone who espoused "public actions aimed at propaganda of sodomy, lesbianism, bisexuality, and transgenderism among minors."

2012 — International AIDS Conference in the United States

In July of 2012, the United States held the International AIDS Conference in Washington, DC, for the first time in over 20 years following the lift of the HIV entry ban. Despite progress, sex workers and drug users, two populations severely impacted by HIV, were excluded from the conference due to US visa procedure, which prohibited them from entering the country.

2012 — UndocuQueer Coming Out of the Shadows week

As part of National Coming Out of the Shadows week the National Immigrant Youth Alliance (NIYA) launched a project in March to highlight the stories and experiences of undocumented queer migrants.

This timeline was compiled by Cassidy Gardner, Camilo Godoy and Carlos Motta for "A New Discovery: Queer Immigration in Perspective," a performative intervention commissioned by the Museum of Art and Design and organized in collaboration with QUEEROCRACY, on Columbus Day (October 10, 2011) at Columbus Circle.

The text of the timeline is based on the second edition printed on the occasion of the exhibition *Museum as Hub: Carlos Motta: We Who Feel Differently* at the New Museum, in New York, May 16–September 9, 2012.

For a list of bibliographic sources please visit: www.carlosmotta.com/project/a-new -discovery-queer-immigration-in-perspective.

CHAPTER 15

Immigration Narratives, Past and Present

The Labor Dimension

Ruth Milkman

The movement of people to the United States has first and foremost been a story of the movement of human labor. From European settlers, indentured laborers, and enslaved people in colonial times and the nation's early years, to the labor migrants who crossed the wide-open US borders during most of the 19th century, and finally to those who arrived in the 20th and 21st centuries (in most cases before immigration was severely restricted in 1924 and after 1965 when new laws reduced those restrictions) people have come to the United States to seek economic opportunities: to work. In every era, they have, in a fundamental sense, built America.

The narrative of this mass movement of people across US borders, despite its manifold benefits for both the nation and the migrants themselves, has not always been a positive one. Indeed, there have been two distinct narratives about labor migration throughout US history. One tells the story of European immigrant workers starting with the initial establishment of the Republic, and especially focusing on the late 19th and early 20th centuries. Coming to the United States in search of a life better—both economically and politically—than what they had at home, these immigrants readily became "Americans" and were part of the fabled US "melting pot." This is the "nation of immigrants" narrative.[1] The other narrative, which dates to colonial times and has periodically surfaced ever since, constructs immigrants as a "threat"—not only to US-born workers but also to American culture and public safety. This notion of immigrants as dangerous has most frequently targeted immigrants of color, especially in recent years, and non-Protestant migrants in the 19th and early 20th centuries.

Both narratives obscure central features of labor migration, past and present. First, neither addresses the critical role of labor demand and employer recruitment as drivers of both authorized and unauthorized migration. Second, both stories take little notice of immigrant "selection": that it is not the most desperate who typically leave their countries of origin, as they are unlikely to have the resources to do so, and that those who do leave are often more desirable from the perspective of the receiving countries. Third, both narratives tend to downplay the super-exploitation that many immigrants experience in US workplaces, especially those without documents. Finally, any narrative of migrant labor should recognize the leading role of immigrants in labor movements. Indeed US labor history is in large part the history of immigrant workers' struggles, and in many periods, US union leaders have been disproportionately foreign-born.

Labor Migration

Employer demand for labor is the primary driver of migration to the United States, past and present. To be sure, the newcomers have always included significant numbers of refugees fleeing oppression, war, or natural disasters in their nations of origin, as well as those joining family members who had migrated previously. But labor demand was the critical magnetic force attracting the vast majority of those who arrived from Europe in the Great Atlantic Migration of the late 19th and early 20th centuries, as well as those who headed to the United States from the global South in the late 1960s and 1970s. In the earlier era, employers actively recruited eastern and southern Europeans into construction, mining, and manufacturing jobs; a century later, immigrants from Asia, Latin America and Africa were typically drawn into the service and agricultural sectors, along with construction and what remained of manufacturing in the post-industrial economy of the era.

As Mae Ngai points out, contrary to conventional wisdom, nativism flourishes less in periods of economic downturn than in eras of massive employment growth and economic restructuring—which often provokes profound anxieties among the native-born.[2] Such anxieties were palpable both during the transition from craft to mass production in the late 19th and early 20th centuries and during the neoliberal transition that began in the 1970s. In both periods, far-reaching economic transformation and expansion sparked massive employer demand for low-wage labor, attracting millions of newcomers to the United States while also engendering a xenophobic reaction among long-settled "white" workers—themselves the product of previous waves of immigration—fearful about their own economic futures.

Crucially, moreover, in both periods most foreign-born workers entered a segmented labor market in which direct competition with natives was extremely limited. Thus, in late-19th- and early 20th-century manufacturing, mining, and construction, southern and eastern European immigrants dominated the ranks of unskilled laborers, while earlier generations of immigrants and their US-born descendants typically occupied better-paid, skilled positions in those industries and also predominated in better-paid sectors such as transportation.[3] Similarly, in the late 20th and early 21st centuries, direct competition was rare between the US-born and the immigrant newcomers from the global South, who flocked to "jobs Americans don't want" in agriculture, domestic service, construction, and low-wage service industries.

After the Civil War, when large corporations first became the dominant force in the US economy, demand for wage laborers swelled to unprecedented heights in the nation's burgeoning mass production factories, as well as in the mines that supplied them with raw materials and on construction sites. Labor demand was the key driver of the Great Atlantic Migration, especially for the young adult males who were its leading demographic. Between 1868 and 1910, 76% of those who entered the United States were between 15 and 40 years old, at a time when only 42% of the US population was in that age group; three-fifths of the newcomers were male.[4]

Young males similarly predominated in the early phases of the post-1965 immigration wave. However, one striking difference was that whereas in the late 20th-century labor demand was driven by economic restructuring predicated on the process of *de*-industrialization and the rise of a service-centered economy, the mass immigration of a century earlier had been fueled by the *rise* of mass production industry. In addition, while the post-1965 immigrant influx took place in the context of de-unionization and *declining* real wages for US-born male workers, in the pre–World War I era real wages for US-born male workers *increased* in the sectors that employed the greatest numbers of immigrants—most notably in the newly created mass production factory jobs. Indeed, the vast bulk the Great Atlantic Migration was comprised of unskilled manual laborers, most of whom had job offers in hand before they left their homes in Europe.[5] Only about 2% of the newcomers in that period found employment in professional occupations, whereas among post-1965 immigrants as many as one-third did do so.

Two Competing Immigration Narratives in US History

The "nation of immigrants" narrative celebrates immigrants as needed workers for a growing country (along with a stunning silence about the millions of enslaved workers forcibly brought to the United States). Emma Lazarus's iconic 1883 sonnet, "The New Colossus," portrayed the nation as a welcoming destination for immigrants and refugees in search of a better life, regardless of their class background or social status. Migrants from China built the transcontinental railroad; migrants from Europe staffed the factories of the Midwest and constructed the New York City subway system; and migrants from Mexico, the Philippines, and elsewhere were crucial to the capitalist agriculture of California and the Southwest.

But this rosy picture of US immigration—still fundamental to many Americans' understandings of the nation's history and that of their own families—faced challenges from the start. The Know-Nothing movement of the mid-19th century explicitly portrayed immigrants as a threat (some questioned whether Catholic immigrants, for example, could be loyal to both the pope and their adopted nation). And in 1882, just a year before Lazarus penned her sonnet, Congress enacted the Chinese Exclusion Act, which severely restricted immigration from China and led to the deportation of many Chinese nationals already residing in the United States. Chinese labor, most European immigrants and their descendants agreed, was no longer needed and constituted a clear and present threat to the rest of the nation's workers.

Similarly, the Great Atlantic Migration of the late 19th and early 20th centuries sparked a virulent backlash. Nativism surged across the United States, and the "new immigrants" (as they were called at the time) were widely portrayed as a threat to the established social order. Many respected elite intellectuals disseminated such views. University of Chicago economist Edward Bemis, for example, claimed in 1888 that the new immigrants were overrepresented among criminals and in poorhouses and that the growing influx of foreign-born workers would lower native-born living standards and wages and lead to increased unemployment.[6] Similarly, a widely-read 1911 report by the US Immigration Commission declared bluntly that "unskilled laboring men . . . from the less progressive and advanced countries of Europe" were "far less intelligent" than their predecessors from northern and western Europe.[7] Many middle-class Americans, unsettled by the dramatic economic transformations underway at the time, also embraced the threat narrative. "Masses of immigrants intensified their insecurity," historian Linda Gordon observes of the native-born citizens who rallied in the 1920s to the Ku Klux Klan's xenophobic platform, which blamed immigrants for "stealing jobs and government from 'true' Americans."[8]

As would be echoed in regard to a different population of newcomers a century later, claims that immigrants "robbed jobs" and lowered wage standards for the US-born proliferated in the late 19th and early 20th centuries, although the vast bulk of the available evidence suggests that such assertions were unfounded in both periods. In fact, immigrants were disproportionately concentrated in regions and industries where economic growth was strongest and where employment was on the rise among US-born and foreign-born workers alike.[9] Nonetheless, after years of political agitation, in 1924 Congress adopted the Johnson-Reed Act establishing a national origin–based quota system, which dramatically reduced immigration from southern and eastern Europe.[10] Migration from the Western Hemisphere was not included in the quota system, largely due to the demands of US agricultural interests. But during the Great Depression, the federal government undertook mass deportations of persons of Mexican descent—including many US citizens—once again justifying the action with an immigrant threat narrative.

The 1965 Immigration Act erased the stain of the 1924 legislation and its discriminatory quota system. In signing the 1965 measure into law at the base of the Statue of Liberty, President Johnson noted: "This bill says simply that from this day forth those wishing to immigrate to America shall be admitted on the basis of their skills and their close relationship to those already here. This is a simple test, and it is a fair test. Those who can contribute most to this country—to its growth, to its strength, to its spirit—will be the first that are admitted to this land."[11] Over the next half century, mass immigration to the United States resumed, but now primarily from Asia and the Western Hemisphere. In 2021, immigrants accounted for 17% of the US labor force—substantially more than their 14% share of the nation's population, in another reflection of the centrality of labor to the dynamics of migration. Even before the COVID-19 pandemic, US birth rates (like those of other rich countries) were stagnating; immigration has consistently been the main source of population growth in the 21st century.

Just like their counterparts arriving from Southern and Eastern Europe a century earlier, Mexicans and other immigrants from the global South in the post-1965 era were greeted with trepidation by many in the US-born population; they soon became the targets of a new immigrant threat narrative.[12] Long before Donald Trump emerged as its most prominent proponent, conservative mass media, including talk radio and, later, Fox News and right-wing websites, beat a steady drumbeat promoting it.. If immigration were curtailed, border security established, and the estimated 11 million "illegals" residing in the United States somehow removed, the narrative suggested, the American Dream and the living standards it once delivered to working people would return, "making America great again."

From the start, the most alarmist rhetoric was directed at unauthorized "illegal aliens" (a category that hardly existed prior to World War I), but those who had entered the United States legally were also rendered suspect. The threat narrative also overtly targeted people of color, who dominated the post-1965 immigrant influx. Indeed, racism was the most formidable obstacle to immigrant rights advocates' sporadic efforts during the late 20th and early 21st century to incorporate the newcomers into the "nation of immigrants" narrative that had already embraced earlier generations of immigrants from Europe. Those efforts repeatedly failed to gain traction in the face of the twin barriers presented by the longstanding ideology of white supremacy and the immigrant threat narrative.

As a result, regardless of their legal status and even after many years of residency in their newly adopted country, immigrants from Latin America, Asia, and Africa were never able to "become white" in the way their southern and eastern European counterparts had managed to do.[13] Whiteness proved elusive even for the many post-1965 immigrants who had settled permanently in the United States and acquired the standard hallmarks of assimilation into their adopted country. Even as they and their children gained proficiency in English, intermarried with the US-born population, and increasingly entered the mainstream of the labor market, most remained racial/ethnic "others." Those who became US citizens—a much more prolonged process than in the pre–World War I era—and moved into the middle class (or beyond) could rarely escape the stigma created by the immigrant threat narrative and the preexisting white supremacist ideology that augmented it. In the Trump years, the threat narrative was further reinforced by explicit white nationalist claims of racial "replacement."

The threat narrative is rooted in the notion that recent immigrants, especially Mexicans and other Latinos/as, inflict economic harm on native-born workers, increase crime, and degrade the nation's cultural life. Economically, as one influential commentary summarizes the narrative's central claim, the US-born population suffers as a result of "immigrants' use of welfare, health and educational services, their propensity to turn to crime, and their tendency to displace native citizens from jobs."[14] But like its 19th-century counterpart, the modern immigrant threat narrative has no evidentiary basis. For example, contrary to what its proponents claim, crime rates are considerably lower among unauthorized immigrants than among other population groups. As one of many such studies recently found, US-born citizens were twice as likely as undocumented immigrants to be arrested for violent crimes and over four times as likely to be arrested for property crime in Texas between 2012 and 2018.[15] Moreover, nearly all experts on the subject agree that the economic benefits of immigration greatly outweigh its costs.[16] Immigrants contribute positively to overall economic growth and to technological innovation. Their presence also benefits consumers, reducing the costs of many goods and services, and increases demand in such key sectors as housing, stimulating the real estate industry and related sectors. Immigrants also contribute more in taxes as well as to Social Security, Medicare, and other government programs than they receive.

Although the threat narrative suggests that the deteriorating situation of the US working class is a result of low-wage immigration, in fact the line of causality runs mostly in the opposite direction. Who could blame immigrants for the evaporation of the manufacturing jobs that once offered high-wage blue collar employment to millions of non-college-educated American workers? Those jobs were either outsourced to other parts of the world or rendered obsolete by new technology; in either case, there was no link to the rise in immigration that took place at the same time as deindustrialization transformed vast parts of the nation into the Rustbelt. In other blue-collar sectors, such as construction and trucking, jobs did not disappear entirely but instead were degraded dramatically by new business strategies such as subcontracting, deregulation, and efforts to weaken or eliminate labor unions.

As those developments unfolded, starting in the 1970s, US-born workers increasingly abandoned the newly undesirable jobs, and that led employers to recruit immigrants to fill the resulting vacancies. In this way newcomers—many of them unauthorized—entered the bottom tier of the labor market to perform "jobs Americans won't take." Demand for immigrant workers also expanded in paid domestic labor, especially childcare and eldercare occupations, driven in large part by rising income inequality. Just when the increasingly prosperous professional and managerial classes began to devote more and more of their income to purchasing such "personal services," the African American women who had formerly been confined to this type of work increasingly abandoned it as the civil rights movement opened up better job opportunities for them.

However, the wider public is poorly informed about these developments. As a result, many US-born workers who have experienced economic reverses in recent years—for reasons unrelated to immigration, such as union decline and outsourcing—have proven highly receptive to demagogues who suggest that immigrants are to blame for their plight. Workers have every reason to be enraged by the degradation of once-desirable types of employment, rising inequality, and declining living standards, but their anger has been tragically misdirected. They should blame employers' new business strategies and public policies promoting the growth of inequality, not immigrants.

The threat narrative has gained even more power and influence simply because most recent immigrants are people of color. As a result, they have been denied access to the process of "whitening" that eastern and southern European immigrants underwent in the past. Instead, late-20th- and early 21st century immigrants from the global South have remained racial/ethnic outsiders, and all too often they have been targets of widespread suspicion, even violence. Resurgent white nationalism has done much to promote this variation of the threat narrative.

Ironically, however, that narrative obscures a key characteristic of the post-1965 immigrant population—namely, the phenomenon of selection mentioned earlier. Indeed, the majority of recent immigrants are distinctly different from their compatriots who did not choose to migrate. Those who make that choice are rarely the most impoverished or desperate populations in their countries of origin (although the story is different in this regard for many refugees). On the contrary, those with sufficient means and motivation to undertake the arduous journey to a new land tend to be younger and better-resourced in many respects than those they leave behind. It is noteworthy that more than one-quarter of all US patents are held by immigrants; the foreign-born also account for a third of all US Nobel Prize recipients in chemistry, physics, medicine, and economics.[17] Those may be extreme examples, but immigrants in general tend to be superior to non-immigrants, especially from the perspective of employers, who often regard them as the "cream of the crop" relative to US-born workers. And although neither the "nation of immigrants" nor the threat narrative explicitly acknowledges its importance, that employer perspective was what often mattered most, in both of the historic waves of mass immigration to the United States.

Labor Movement Responses

The immigrant threat narratives that emerged as an initial response to both major waves of immigration also influenced US labor union leaders, although in the 21st century organized labor would ultimately forge a distinctly different approach. In the late 19th and early 20th centuries, albeit with a few notable exceptions such as the Knights of Labor in the 1880s, the labor movement actively supported immigration restriction and condemned foreign-born workers for undermining the US-born working class and its hard-won labor standards. (Even the Knights of Labor supported the 1882 Chinese Exclusion Act.)

The best-known and most influential example from that era is longtime American Federation of Labor (AFL) president Samuel Gompers—ironically, an immigrant himself—who became convinced that the ready availability of unskilled immigrants facilitated employers' ongoing efforts to degrade skilled labor and break strikes.[18] Gompers was among the leading advocates of the 1882 Chinese Exclusion Act, and under his leadership the AFL went on to strongly support restrictions on European immigration, even as immigrants themselves increasingly participated in strikes and labor protests. A decade after the 1924 Johnson-Reed Act radically restricted immigration, large swaths of organized labor would adopt a more inclusive approach. But at the height of the Great Atlantic Migration most union leaders embraced the immigrant threat narrative vis-à-vis eastern and southern European newcomers.

The tides began to shift with the industrial union upsurge of the 1930s and 1940s, which itself played a significant role in incorporating southern and eastern European immigrant workers and their children into the nation's "white" population. In those decades of union upsurge, labor organizations not only included these groups of workers in their ranks, but they also served as important engines of assimilation and "Americanization." The economic gains won by the industrial unions of this era propelled a critical mass of newly organized first- and second-generation immigrant manual workers and their families into the middle class for the first time. In addition, the rapid growth of labor movement organizations opened up opportunities for individual upward mobility, as immigrant labor activists honed their leadership skills and entered careers as secondary union officials.

Yet, as in the wider society, organized labor's inclusive approach to immigrant workers often did not extend to those of color. Some unions did actively organize Mexican-born workers in the 1930s, but as immigration from south of the border surged in the post-1965 period, most of them reverted to a stance that echoed Samuel Gompers' from decades earlier: embracing the immigrant threat narrative, particularly in relation to the undocumented. Thus, the AFL-CIO stated in 1974 that "illegal immigrants have for years been taking jobs from American citizens and legal immigrants in increasing numbers, often work for substandard wages and accept substandard working and living conditions."[19] Even the United Farm Workers, although in many respects a model of pro-immigrant unionism, tended to view the undocumented as a threat at that time. Cesar Chavez in particular supported proposals for strict border controls and immigration restriction in the 1970s, although a decade later he shifted his stance and threw his support behind the 1986 Immigration Reform and Control Act (IRCA), which provided amnesty to about three million undocumented workers, including large numbers of farm workers.[20] At that time most labor leaders remained wary of immigrant workers and skeptical as to whether they could be successfully recruited into unions, in most cases presuming that their vulnerability to deportation would make that impossible.

In the 21st century, however, organized labor's stance toward foreign-born workers shifted dramatically. After a wave of surprisingly successful immigrant union organizing efforts in the 1990s, some of which involved large numbers of undocumented workers, more and more union leaders began to question the threat narrative. They increasingly recognized that it was impossible to keep unauthorized immigrants out of the US labor force. Indeed, IRCA had failed spectacularly in that respect, leading to rapid growth in the undocumented population, precisely the opposite of what the 1986 law (as its title suggested) had been designed to do. That realization in turn led a number of unions to experiment with recruiting immigrants into their ranks. Organizing campaigns such as "Justice for Janitors," which soon brought thousands of foreign-born building cleaners, including many undocumented, into the Service Employees International Union, began to proliferate.

Those successes led to a gradual abandonment of the previous conventional labor movement wisdom that immigrants were "unorganizable." Instead, it became apparent that foreign-born workers often were more receptive than their US-born counterparts to union overtures. By the 1990s immigrant organizing had emerged as a rare bright spot that suggested the potential to reverse the rapid decline in US unionization rates that had begun in the 1980s. Survey data suggested that immigrant workers' attitudes toward unions were more favorable than the attitudes of the US-born.[21] Those attitudes had concrete results: between 1996 and 2003, the number of foreign-born union members rose 24%, from 1.4 to 1.8 million. In that same period, however, the number of U.S-born union members *decreased* 6%, from 14.8 to 14.0 million.[22]

In 2000, the AFL-CIO announced a sharp reversal of its previous stance on immigration policy, joining the coalition of immigrant rights advocates promoting a path to legalization for the undocumented and other reforms. Yet those new goals were increasingly elusive, especially after the wave of xenophobia that swept the United States in the wake of 9/11. Meanwhile, the traditional constituency of organized labor, namely non-college-educated US-born workers, faced with factory closings and attacks on unions, became more susceptible to the immigrant threat narrative. Although organized labor's political clout in the 21st century has remained greater than one might expect in light of the steady decline in union membership, the labor movement has been unable to neutralize the appeal of the immigrant threat narrative to the white working-class descendants of the wave of European immigrants who had been part of the Great Atlantic Migration and later became the beneficiaries of the "nation of immigrants" narrative.

Future Prospects

At this writing, the political impasse over immigration policy persists, despite the popular repudiation of Donald Trump's xenophobic views in the 2020 presidential election. Unauthorized migration slowed to a trickle in the wake of the 2008 financial crisis, but more recently an influx of asylum seekers at the US-Mexico border, accompanied by renewed economic migration (much of it unauthorized) among those searching for better opportunities, has presented a new set of challenges. The immigrant threat narrative has by no means disappeared, although the Trump administration's overreach, and especially its brutal record of separating families at the border when the surge of asylum-seekers took off, has generated growing public sympathy for immigrants.

Those sympathies were amplified further as the COVID-19 pandemic elevated public awareness of the nation's "essential workers," whose ranks included many foreign-born newcomers toiling in key industries such as meatpacking and agriculture. The pandemic also created acute labor shortages in many sectors, neutralizing (at least temporarily) fears that immigrants would "take jobs" from the US-born. The multiracial support for the Black Lives Matter protests in the summer of

2020 also seemed to present a challenge to the ideology of white supremacy on an unprecedented scale. Perhaps these developments will help to create the conditions under which the "nation of immigrants" narrative can include the millions who arrived in the United States from the global South in the decades since 1965, after all.

Yet new challenges are looming on the horizon. Climate change is already creating growing pressure on US borders (and those of other wealthy countries) as refugees flee regions around the world that are becoming uninhabitable, a trend that will continue and grow in scale in the coming years. Violence and war, in many cases the direct or indirect results of US foreign policy, are also contributing to increased refugee flows. Indeed, those flows may soon eclipse those involving labor migration to the United States, although persistent shortages of workers in sectors such as agriculture and eldercare remain powerful magnets for newcomers. The political task facing those who wish to avoid a resurgence of xenophobia in the aftermath of the pandemic is to forge a humanitarian narrative that not only welcomes immigrants and refugees with compassion but also addresses the urgent needs of ordinary US-born workers. Efforts to facilitate renewed union growth, to reduce inequality, and to improve wages and working conditions in the many jobs that have undergone severe degradation since the 1970s would benefit the US-born and the foreign-born alike.

Notes

1. See Mae Ngai, chap. 9, this vol.
2. Mae Ngai, "American Nativism, Past and Present," in *Immigration Matters: Movements, Visions, and Strategies for a Progressive Future*, ed. Ruth Milkman, Deepak Bhargava, and Penny Lewis (New York: New Press, 2021), 41.
3. For more details, see Ruth Milkman, *Immigrant Labor and the New Precariat* (Medford, MA: Polity, 2020), 39–41.
4. Timothy J. Hatton and Jeffrey G. Williamson, *Global Migration and the World Economy: Two Centuries of Policy and Performance* (Cambridge, MA: MIT Press, 2005), 78–79.
5. Charles Hirschman and Elizabeth Mogford, "Immigration and the American Industrial Revolution from 1880 to 1920," *Social Science Research* 38, no. 4 (2009): 899; Eva Morawska, "The Sociology and Historiography of Immigration," in

Immigration Reconsidered: History, Sociology and Politics, ed. Virginia Yans-McLaughlin (New York: Oxford University Press, 1990), 193, 204.

6. Aristide Zolberg, *A Nation by Design: Immigration Policy in the Fashioning of America* (Cambridge, MA: Harvard University Press, 2006), 209.

7. Hatton and Williamson, *Global Migration and the World Economy*, 81.

8. Linda Gordon, *The Second Coming of the KKK* (New York: W. W. Norton, 2017), 183.

9. Susan B. Carter and Richard Sutch, "Labor Market Flooding? Migrant Destination and Wage Change during America's Age of Mass Migration," in *Border Battles: The U.S. Immigration Debates* Social Science Research Council, 2007, https://items .ssrc.org/border-battles/labour-market-flooding-migrant-destination-and-wage -change-during-americas-age-of-mass-migration/.

10. Gordon, *The Second Coming*, 3, 164.

11. Lyndon B. Johnson, "Remarks at the Signing of the Immigration Bill," Liberty Island, New York, https://www.presidency.ucsb.edu/documents/remarks-the-signing-the-immigration-bill-liberty-island-new-york.

12. Ana R. Minian, *Undocumented Lives: The Untold Story of Mexican Migration* (Cambridge, MA: Harvard University Press, 2018).

13. See Justin Gest, chap. 3, this vol..

14. Marisa Abrajano and Zoltan L. Hajnal, *White Backlash: Immigration, Race and American Politics* (Princeton, NJ: Princeton University Press, 2015): 5.

15. Michael T. Light, Jingying He, and Jason P. Robey, "Comparing Crime Rates between Undocumented Immigrants, Legal Immigrants, and Native-Born U.S. Citizens in Texas," *Proceedings of the National Academy of Sciences* 117, no. 51 (2020): 32340–47.

16. National Academy of Sciences, Engineering, and Medicine, *The Economic and Fiscal Consequences of Immigration* (Washington, DC: National Academies Press, 2017), 11–12.

17. William Kerr, "America, Don't Throw Global Talent Away," *Nature* 563 (2018): 445.

18. Samuel Gompers, *Seventy Years of Life and Labor* (New York: E. P. Dutton, 1925), 2:153–58.

19. Minian, *Undocumented Lives*, 69.

20. For more details, see Milkman, *Immigrant Labor*, 56–61.

21. See Ruth Milkman, *L.A. Story: Immigrant Workers and the Future of the U.S. Labor Movement* (New York: Russell Sage Foundation, 2006): 128–29.

22. Migration Policy Institute Fact Sheet, "Immigrant Union Members: Numbers and Trends," May 2004, https://www.migrationpolicy.org/research/immigrant-union -members-numbers-and-trends.

CHAPTER 16

Religious Diversity and the American Narrative

Eboo Patel and Neil Agarwal

"Is America Still an Exodus Nation?"

In a popular 2022 podcast with *New York Times* host Ezra Klein, that is the question journalist David Brooks takes up with University of Chicago professor Leon Kass.

The Exodus story, Kass insists, is archetypal, relevant not just to the people of Israel but to the American people as well. The three parts hold up a mirror to the state of the soul of our union. First, there is the chapter of slavery and deliverance. Second, the chapter of receiving the divine law and establishing it as normative within a society. And finally, the section about the tabernacle, where the nation finds a way to stay in touch with the divine and align itself with its highest purpose and potential.

Kass worries that America has become unmoored from this narrative. In his view, we have become a people obsessed with personal comfort, economic prosperity, and technological progress rather than collective purpose and national identity. "Can there be a stable and enduring and well-governed nation that lacks a shared story?" he asks. "If our national story is contested, or even despised, if our morals are weakened, if the national fabric is frayed, and if we've abandoned any sense of national dedication, can we endure?"[1]

Brooks agrees that the Exodus story is the animating and binding narrative of the nation—or at least it ought to be. He hits the standard highlights: the Pilgrims saw themselves as reenacting Exodus; the 1776 generation wanted to put Moses on the Great Seal; multiple waves of immigrants have viewed themselves as living proof of the durability of the tale.

But today's college students, Brooks reports, are not buying it. Exodus, for them, is a story of and for privileged white people. The broadness of our multitudes has demonstrated the narrowness of the old narrative.

Brooks finds himself reluctantly agreeing with them. He is convinced that a nation needs a grand narrative, but perhaps Exodus is not it. Perhaps, he suggests, we are a people more in need of confessing our sins and seeking God's forgiveness rather than a people winning its freedom because of divine favor. Either way, Brooks and Kass agree, the "biblical metaphysic" is still present, even if people are neither conscious of it nor especially literate in it.

We found the conversation riveting. And as we were listening, a sly question crossed our minds: What would the Puritans make of this exchange? Would they be moved that they were still considered key players in the national drama 400 years after their ships landed on the Eastern seaboard? Would they be impressed that the biblical story that guided their journey was still considered a candidate for the national narrative? That despite the work of Nikole Hannah-Jones's 1619 Project, many still considered them the original Americans?[2] Or would they be disappointed that the covenant they had so painstakingly established, and which they certainly believed was eternal, appeared to be fraying?

And what would they make of the identities of the individuals in this particular conversation? These were not the Calvinist elect, praying fervently in church every Sunday. Kass, Brooks, Klein (though not personally present on account of parental leave, it was still his show)—all of them are religious minorities, specifically, Jews.

The Puritans left England to escape the impure presence of "strange Gods." John Winthrop warned his compatriots on the *Arabella* of the danger of shipwreck if they were to entangle themselves with outside religious influence. When they established their society in Boston, they took care to banish the likes of Roger Williams and Anne Hutchinson who dared stray even slightly from the straight path. The pope was referred to as "the whore of Babylon."[3] Jesuits were understood to have nefarious designs. And here the Puritans are sharing the stage of national mythmaking with people who consider Jesús not Lord and Savior but rather a good rabbi, maybe.

One wonders what John Winthrop and William Bradford might think if they were privy to other conversations in the United States. If they were in mosques listening to Muslims speak about America as Medina, the city in present-day Saudi Arabia where the Prophet Muhammad established a society in which religious freedom was protected and interfaith cooperation was encouraged. Or if they overheard the conversations of Buddhists wondering aloud about whether a whole nation could be considered a *sangha*, a community seeking to enact the Buddhist practice of loving-kindness. Could our Puritan founders even comprehend the vast and diverse religious topography of today, and would they fret over the subversion of their national symbols?

Civil Religion and Sacred Symbols

Whether or not the reincarnated Puritans would be surprised by the country's current religious makeup (Hindu reference made intentionally), none of us should be. The conversations about which sacred symbols belong in the American narrative continue to evolve with changes in the American landscape. Here are six dynamics that will shape the wars of religious metaphor ahead:

1. "Civil religion," coined by Robert Bellah, is the idea that the nation's artifacts, documents, and rituals are infused with a sense of sacredness.[4] In the United States, reverence for the Constitution, the Declaration of Independence, and the Bill of Rights, combined with a common set of "American values" (liberty, equality, the "American Dream"), create a civil religion

that provides a binding narrative that connects citizens to the nation and one another. Christian references abound in how we describe the nation: "beloved community," "almost chosen people," "cathedral of humanity," "city on a hill." As Jewish scholar of Hinduism Laurie Patton put it, "Pluralism needs myths."[5] Ours have been mostly Christian.

2. The United States is the most religiously diverse nation in human history. More people from more different religious communities have gathered in this political entity than at any other time, ever. There are about as many Muslims and Buddhists as there are ELCA Lutherans (4 million), but the median age of the former is 20 years younger.[6] Just as Brooks, Kass, and Klein fully expect Jews to be part of the conversation of what constitutes the nation's narrative, so will Buddhists, Hindus, and Muslims expect a place in the story, especially as their numbers grow.

3. One especially complicated dimension of American religious diversity is the dramatic growth in what sociologists call the "religious nones"—people who check "none of the above" on the survey question "What religion do you belong to?" While many religious nones say they are spiritual, or even that they occasionally pray, there is every possibility that this group will grow not only in numbers but also in antipathy toward religion. If this happens, will they reject the use of religious symbols in the American narrative altogether?

4. Religion is a preferred identity in American law, from constitutional protections regarding freedom of religion to the Religious Freedom Restoration Act (1993). Furthermore, multiple Supreme Court victories (*Hobby Lobby*, *Masterpiece Cakeshop*, and *EEOC v. Abercrombie & Fitch*) make it clear that American law privileges religious identity, allowing religious communities pride of place in both civic life and public discourse.[7]

5. The United States has seen Christian nationalism grow. Highlighted by rhetoric surrounding the election of Donald Trump in 2016 and brought to wider attention by symbolism at the

January 6, 2021, US Capitol riot, Christian nationalism continues to divide Americans across social boundaries. Survey findings indicate that close to half of Americans support the fusion of Christianity with American civic life, believing Christianity ought to influence public policy and our sense of national identity.[8] How will these attitudes interact with and shape relationships across faith traditions?

6. Discrimination against minorities, particularly religious minorities such as Jews and Muslims will persist.[9] A 2019 Pew study found that 64% of Americans said Jews faced some discrimination—a 20% increase from 2016. Eighty-two percent said Muslims face some discrimination, with 56% responding that Muslims encounter a lot of discrimination. In airports, at job interviews, when going to the hospital—all settings that exacerbate discriminatory behavior for minority religious groups. Will movements such as the anti–Ground Zero mosque movement prevent religious minorities from contributing to civic life and national narratives? Can the spike in anti-Asian hate crimes as a result of the COVID-19 pandemic be battled through exposure to and engagement with practitioners of diverse worldviews?

Put these together and you have a set of fascinating questions: Will the growing numbers of Hindus, Buddhists, Muslims, Sikhs, Jains, Bahai's, among others, begin to weave their religious symbols, language, and imagery into the American narrative? Will the dramatic spike in religious nones start pushing back against the use of religious language in our nation's discourse entirely, telling politicians and pollsters that they are citizens of a nation, not congregants of a church?

What happens if the United States experiences another Great Awakening? There have been several such revivals in American history, and they proved to be tectonic in our culture. And as our civilization evolves through cultural and demographic shifts, mutual language changes over time and American civil religion evolves.

Here is the core question of this chapter: As the American population grows increasingly religiously diverse, will the sacred symbols and myths that constitute American civil religion become more diverse as well? And what role will those myths play in an increasingly polarized nation? The median age of Buddhists, Hindus, and Muslims is mid-30s, compared to mid-50s for white Christians. This demographic fact suggests that these religious minorities are moving into both the prime of their professional lives and the main years for raising families—all of which suggests a greater possible civic influence.

Brooks and Kass both point to Exodus as animating and binding, a myth connecting us. But growing religious diversity can just as easily lead to competing and conflicting narratives. Consider Elijah Muhammad's Nation of Islam, which preached an oppositional and separatist message that galvanized broad swaths of the African American community in the 1960s, including such public figures as Malcolm X and Muhammad Ali. Elijah's son Warith Deen Muhammad preached very nearly the opposite message when he took over his father's community in the 1970s. Not only did he return to a more traditional practice of Islam, but he also encouraged his followers to view the Qur'an's teaching as harmonious with American principles. Such examples highlight just how malleable both religious and national narratives are.

We are hopeful about the prospects of diverse religious groups contributing positively to the nation's narrative. Yes, there are danger signs, such as the manner in which Christian symbols were used during the January 6 insurrection. But by and large the American story about engaging religious difference has been positive, so positive in fact that we rarely mark progress on this front, and instead take it for granted. And yet, as Michael Walzer notes in *What It Means to Be an American*, political philosophers throughout the history of Western civilization viewed religiously diverse democracies as impossible.[10] Participatory societies required religious homogeneity. If you wanted diversity, you needed a dictator.

Not so here. As most of us experience every day, America is a nation where Muslim babies are born in Catholic hospitals, where Buddhist children play in Jewish preschools, where atheists receive doctorates from Methodist universities. What was once considered a fantasy has become unremarkable.

For the purpose of this chapter, we center what we think of as the most positive of the possibilities for the American future: that diverse religious communities do in fact contribute their symbols and interpretations to the national narrative, along the lines of two Jews discussing the continuing relevance of a narrative employed by Puritans. There are of course myriad darker possibilities—that Americans are now too fractured to feel connected through a narrative, that antiminority sentiment lasts for decades or prevents certain communities from making contributions, that religion is effectively ejected from significant dimensions of public life by a growing and increasingly vocal group of religious nones—but we believe that the long arc of history is generally on the side of American inclusiveness. As Ralph Ellison once said, "The irrepressible movement of American culture towards integration of its most diverse elements continues, confounding the circumlocutions of its staunchest opponents."[11]

What follows are three key chapters in the history of America integrating some of its varied religious elements into the mainstream of civic life and national narrative.

The Flushing Remonstrance

While the Massachusetts Bay Colony gets most of the attention in high school history books, the experience of Dutch New Amsterdam sets a far more hopeful template in the area of religious tolerance and interfaith cooperation. Following threats leveled against religious communities by Director-General Peter Stuyvesant in 1656, a group of concerned citizens in Vlissingen (present-day Flushing in Queens, New York) gathered to write a statement of welcome. Despite over a century of religious toleration being practiced throughout the Netherlands, Stuyvesant prohibited the practice of any religion outside the Dutch Reformed Church in the colony. He sought to prevent over 20 Jewish refugees from entering New Netherland, raging that "blasphemers of the name of Christ . . . be not allowed further to infect and trouble this new colony."[12] Stuyvesant prevented the building of a synagogue and refused Lutherans a minister. And when Robert Hodgson, a

Quaker preacher, arrived from Yorkshire and spread his gospel in the streets of Hempstead, Stuyvesant had him beaten for refusing to remove his cap in court.

Thirty Dutch citizens of New Amsterdam gathered in December 1657 to voice their discontent. Penned by Edward Hart in collaboration with magistrates and freeholders of Vlissingen and Rustdorp (Jamaica, Queens), the Flushing Remonstrance offers a striking early example of a powerful civic response to religious persecution. The signees' conscientious objection to Stuyvesant precedes Jefferson's Virginia Statute for Religious Freedom and Madison's "Memorial and Remonstrance against Religious Assessments" by over a century; the foundation was planted by these Dutch settlers' commitment to toleration, grounded in reverence for a forgiving God.

They wrote, "The law of love, peace and liberty in the states extending to Jews, Turks and Egyptians, as they are considered sonnes of Adam, which is the glory of the outward state of Holland, soe love, peace and liberty, extending to all in Christ Jesús, condemns hatred, war and bondage." Note this early linking of Abrahamic faiths: the settlers find solidarity in the "sons of Adam," denouncing violence and discrimination against Jews and the Middle Easterners. "Bound by law," the settlers must treat all men well, "especially those of the household of faith." Respect for God meant respect for oneself. And a fear of karmic forces—punishment for persecuting God's followers—led the settlers to protect other identities. "Our desire is not to offend one of his [God's] little ones, in whatsoever form, name or title hee appears in, whether Presbyterian, Independent, Baptist or Quaker, but shall be glad to see anything of God in any of them, desiring to doe unto all men as we desire all men should doe unto us." The settlers metaphorically equate the religious minorities with God's children, "little ones" who carry the Savior within themselves. And the law must be followed not only because it is morally right, but because God and the prophets say it is the law. "Therefore if any of these said persons come in love unto us, we cannot in conscience lay violent hands upon them, but give them free egresse and regresse unto our Town, and houses, as God shall persuade our consciences, for we are bounde by the law of God and man to doe good unto all men and evil to noe man."[13] Pushed by Stuyvesant's cruelty and the clear divide between persecution of religious minorities and the will of a just God, the signees submitted their document of tolerance to local official Nicasius de Sille for review by Stuyvesant. The director-general immediately had the town schout brought in, two of the signees arrested, and Hart imprisoned (later released after public pressure). No immediate change occurred; Stuyvesant seemed to reign supreme.

Four years later, a Quaker from England named John Bowne began holding prayer meetings in his family home. Banished to Holland by the incensed director-general, Bowne made a successful plea to the directors of the Dutch West India Company based on principles of religious liberty guaranteed by the original Charter of Flushing from 1645 and reinforced by the Remonstrance. In 1663, Stuyvesant was pushed by the Dutch West India Company to end religious persecution in the colony.

The Flushing Remonstrance, which predates the American Revolution by over a century, represents the first foundational example in our democracy of a citizen group organizing to battle oppression. Based in a mutual respect for God's followers, the 30 men in Flushing modeled the ideals of religious toleration espoused by prominent immigrants. They were members of a protected group: none of them were Jews or Quakers, and none had any stake outside of personal conscience. The fundamental right articulated by Hart—"the law of love, peace, and liberty" extending to religious minorities—finds itself paralleled in the writing and action of the Founding Fathers in the late 1700s.

The European Founders Set the North Star

Religious diversity is the dimension of identity that the European Founders of the 1776 generation got mostly right. This group—wealthy, white, mostly Christian, many slaveholding—politicians created a constitutional system protecting the freedom of religious practice, preventing the establishment of a national church, and guaranteeing the rights and liberties of religious minorities. It is worth reviewing some of the highlights.

In 1790, a first generation Jewish-American leader named Moses Seixas from Rhode Island wrote the newly elected president, George Washington, a letter asking about the fate of Jews in the new nation. Seixas passionately argued that the American republic was a government against bigotry and persecution in all forms, instead "affording to All liberty of conscience, and immunities of Citizenship: deeming every one, of whatever Nation, tongue, or language, equal parts of the great governmental Machine." Washington answered back personally to the Hebrew Congregation of Newport, Rhode Island, promising not only tolerance but liberty and safety. In Washington's vision, American citizens possessed both freedom of conscience and immunities of citizenship. He eschewed the concept of toleration, likening it to one class "indulging" another to exercise a natural right. He wrote: "Happily the Government of the United States, which gives to bigotry no sanction, to persecution no assistance requires only that they who live under its protection should demean themselves as good citizens, in giving it on all occasions their effectual support."[14] The message is clear: be a good citizen, and you can believe what you like (within reasonable limits). Washington finds "toleration" paternalistic—he wants equality, independence.

Other founders echoed his focus on nature and conscience. Prior to the Revolution, Jefferson argued for the independence of religious belief from government constraint in the Virginia Statute for Religious Freedom. He wrote: "Almighty God hath created the mind free . . . all men shall be free to profess, and by argument to maintain, their opinion in matters of religion . . . the rights hereby asserted are of the natural rights of mankind."[15] Belief, in Jefferson's mind, was a natural right bestowed by God and could not be regulated. Only when "principles break out into overt acts against peace and good order," he said, may the officers of civil government interfere with religion. The bar remains necessarily high for intervention.

James Madison offered much the same. In his 1785 address "Memorial and Remonstrance against Religious Assessments," offered to the General Assembly of the Commonwealth of Virginia, he wrote: "Religion of every man must be left to the conviction and conscience of every man."[16] Madison believed in the power of letting religious diversity flourish.

Benjamin Franklin contributed financially to each one of the diverse religious communities in Philadelphia. He even raised money for a hall expressly welcoming Muslim teachers and preachers. And John Adams expanded these ethics to apply to international relations in his signing of the Treaty of Tripoli. The Treaty stated, "As the Government of the United States of America is not, in any sense, founded on the Christian religion; as it has in itself no character of enmity against the laws, religion, or tranquility, of Mussulmen [Muslims]; and as the said States never entered into any war or act of hostility against any Mahometan [Mohammedan] nation, it is declared by the parties that no pretext arising from religious opinions shall ever produce an interruption of the harmony existing between the two countries."[17] Religious pluralism was etched into the national fabric by the European Founders of the 1776 generation. They set a north star that we believe is still worth aspiring to today.

Judeo-Christian America and Catholic Achievement

The ideals of the European Founders notwithstanding, anti-Catholicism has long been a part of American life. In the early 17th century, John Winthrop spoke about building a bulwark against "Popery" in his establishment of Puritan Boston. In 1844, anti-Catholic mobs in Philadelphia burned churches and carried out violent attacks that killed dozens. In the 1850s, the anti-Catholic Know Nothing Party elected some 75 people to the US Congress. Governor Al Smith of New York faced virulent anti-Catholicism during his run for president in 1928. Following Smith's nomination, the KKK burned crosses across the country. Anti-Catholics even accused Smith of building the Holland Tunnel in Manhattan as a way to smuggle the pope into the country, where he would establish the Catholic hierarchy as the political ruling class. These accusations effectively torpedoed the Smith campaign.

As a response to this, a civil society organization called the National Conference for Christians and Jews (NCCJ) was formed. Its main purpose was to combat antisemitism and anti-Catholicism, framing such prejudice as un-American, an affront to cherished values of fraternity and liberty. The NCCJ organized trialogue trios—a priest, a rabbi and a Protestant minister—across American cities and towns, seeking to promote harmony and goodwill among faiths. It published books and articles along the same lines. As World War II heated up, the NCCJ saw its breakthrough opportunity—promoting "the brotherhood of man under the fatherhood of God"[18] in its visits to nearly 800 military installations in trios, motivating troops with affirmations that they were fighting for the American way of life.

Through this process of civic inclusion, new language entered American civil religion, specifically, the construct of the "Judeo-Christian." The NCCJ leaders basically invented the term. On theological and historical grounds, "Judeo-Christian" is suspect. Christ, the central figure in Christianity, plays a minor role in Judaism. Modern Protestant Christians balk at supremacy of the Old over the New Testament. Not to mention ethnic conflicts dating back to massacres of Jews during the Black Death in the 14th century and the continuation and eruption of European antisemitism in the 1930s. But "Judeo-Christian" doesn't purport to be theologically or historically airtight—its main function is in the realm of civil religion; it is sacred language that calls for the inclusion of the emerging religious minorities of a particular era, namely the early to mid-20th century. And the phrase did its work beautifully.

Nowhere is the success of "Judeo-Christian" more evident than in the election of John F. Kennedy, the first Catholic president, in 1960. Kennedy faced anti-Catholic attacks, but they did not succeed in killing his candidacy. Moreover, one central way Kennedy responded to the anti-Catholic bigotry was to champion religious pluralism for a range of communities. Speaking to the Greater Houston Ministerial Association, Kennedy said:

> For while this year it may be a Catholic against whom the finger of suspicion is pointed, in other years it has been, and may someday be again, a Jew—or a Quaker or a Unitarian or a Baptist. It was Virginia's harassment of Baptist preachers, for example, that helped lead to

Jefferson's statute of religious freedom. Today I may be the victim, but tomorrow it may be you—until the whole fabric of our harmonious society is ripped at a time of great national peril.[19]

Kennedy believed in an America "where religious intolerance will some-day end; where all men and all churches are treated as equal; where every man has the same right to attend or not attend the church of his choice."[20] He paves the way not only for Catholics, but for all religious minorities seeking the highest office in the land.

Joe Biden is America's second Catholic president. The only anti-Catholicism that Biden faced during his successful campaign came from conservatives in his own church. In his victory speech, President-elect Biden made explicit reference to a Catholic hymn: "And now, together—on eagle's wings—we embark on the work that God and history have called upon us to do." We have come a long way since the Al Smith campaign of 1928.

It is striking to us that in all our public conversation about diversity and prejudice, so little has been said about how Catholics moved from being a group of people who were violently marginalized to being a group at the center of power. The lesson seems simple: America can change, and those on the margins can often reshape society for the better. We think that this portends positively for other dimensions of American religious diversity.

Conclusion: The City on a Hill Is Medina

American Muslims may be walking a similar path as American Catholics. Consider the story of Keith Ellison, an African American attorney from Minnesota, who became the first Muslim elected to Congress in 2006. Ellison chose to use a Qur'an—Jefferson's own translation, in fact—in his private swearing-in ceremony, a decision prompting outrage from certain conservative pundits. Media personalities questioned if Ellison was working for our enemies, or if he planned to institute sharia. But Ellison was coolheaded in his response; he took the doubters' suspicions in stride, staying true to his principles and convictions.

He continued to emphasize that he was an American of Muslim faith and that his Muslim faith made him a stronger American.

There will be more like Ellison.

Picture this: the year is 2036, and there is a plausible Muslim candidate running in the presidential election—a woman from a private Midwestern university, graduate of a southern law school, with a platform built on egalitarian ideals and practices lifted from her faith. She recalls the stories of her grandfather, an immigrant from Sudan in the 1960s, who would tell her the story of Medina. Medina—the second-holiest city in Islam—was originally called Yathrib. When the Prophet Muhammad fled Mecca in 622, fearing for his life, the people of Yathrib welcomed him and renamed the city Medina, "City of the Prophet." Leading the Muhajirun, the Prophet and his followers were housed by the Ansar, the "Helpers" of Medina. The city welcomed all immigrants; immigrants made Medina holy. And one of the Prophet's first actions was to create the Constitution of Medina, which gave diverse communities (Christians, Jews, and pagans among them) rights and liberties previously withheld, along with a mutual pact of defense and loyalty: "The Jews of Banu 'Awf shall be considered as one community [Ummat] along with the believers—for the Jews their religion, and for the Muslims theirs, be one client or patron. But whoever does wrong or commits treachery brings evil only on himself and his household."[21] To her *jiddo* (grandfather), America *was* Medina—a country welcoming refugees, made holy by its internal diversity, protected by a reciprocal relationship between its multiple communities. She read about the "city on a hill" in her high school textbooks. Medina gave specific shape to her vision of an ideal America.

This is just one possibility of how America's religious diversity will impact the American narrative. Consider how the use of the term "city on a hill" has changed over time. Winthrop meant it as a "bulwark against the anti-Christ"—by which he meant the pope. Winthrop's "city on a hill" proactively punished religious diversity, yet American leaders adopted the phrase as a model of diversity. Kennedy, Reagan, Obama, and countless other politicians have reimagined the city as far more diverse and interactional but have stayed within the general

Christian outline. But many religious traditions have holy cities, and as the Muslim presence in the United States grows, it is entirely likely that we will hear Muslim public figures speak of America as Medina. The various elements are there. How will they come together? And how can we as US citizens welcome and encourage the inclusion of minority religious cultures, languages, and symbols into our ever-evolving civil religion?

This is what it means to be a dynamic, diverse democracy.

Notes

1. "Timeless Wisdom for Leading a Life of Love, Friendship and Learning," *The Ezra Klein Show/ New York Times*, December 14, 2021, https://www.nytimes.com/2021/12/14/opinion/ezra-klein-podcast-leon-kass.html.
2. See Nikole Hannah-Jones, Caitlin Roper, Ilena Silverman, and Jake Silverstein, eds., *The 1619 Project: A New Origin Story*, (New York: One World, 2021).
3. See Martin Luther, "On the Babylonian Captivity of the Church" (October 1520), in *Works of Martin Luther with Introduction and Notes*, trans., Albert T. W. Steinhaeuser, ed. Robert E. Smith (Philadelphia: A. J. Holman Co., 1915), https://www.projectwittenberg.org/etext/luther/babylonian/babylonian.htm.
4. Robert Bellah, "Civil Religion in America," *Dædalus, Journal of the American Academy of Arts and Sciences* 96, no. 1 (1967): 1–21.
5. Laurie Patton, "Plural America Needs Myths: An Essay in Foundational Narratives in Response to Eboo Patel," in *Out of Many Faiths: Religious Diversity and the American Promise*, ed. Eboo Patel (Princeton, NJ: Princeton University Press, 2018).
6. PRRI Staff, "The American Religious Landscape in 2020," Public Religion Research Institute (PRRI), July 8, 2021, https://www.prri.org/research/2020-census-of-american-religion/.
7. *Burwell v. Hobby Lobby Stores*, 573 U.S. 682 (2014); *Masterpiece Cakeshop, Ltd. v. Colorado Civil Rights Commission*, 584 U.S. (2018); *Equal Employment Opportunity Commission v. Abercrombie & Fitch Stores, Inc.*, 575 U.S. (2015).
8. "Report on Christian Nationalism and the January 6 Insurrection," Baptist Joint Committee for Religious Liberty (BJC), February 2022, https://bjconline.org/jan6report/. See also Andrew Whitehead and Samuel Perry, *Taking America Back for God: Christian Nationalism in the United States* (New York: Oxford University Press, 2020).
9. See David Masci, "Many Americans See Religious Discrimination in U.S.—Especially against Muslims," Pew Research Center, May 17, 2019, https://www.pewresearch.org/fact-tank/2019/05/17/many-americans-see-religious-discrimination-in-u-s-especially-against-muslims/; Samar Warsi, "Why Muslims Experience More Discrimination than Other Faith Groups in America," *Deseret News*, October 6, 2020, https://www

.deseret.com/indepth/2020/10/5/21497689/muslims-experience-more-religious
-discrimination-than-other-faith-groups-in-america-jews-christians; Alex
Vandermaas-Peeler, Daniel Cox, Molly Fisch-Friedman, and Robert P. Jones,
"Diversity, Division, Discrimination: The State of Young America," Public Religion
Research Institute (PRRI), January 10, 2018, https://www.prri.org/research/mtv
-culture-and-religion/; "Sharp Rise in the Share of Americans Saying Jews Face
Discrimination," Pew Research Center, April 15, 2019, https://www.pewresearch
.org/politics/2019/04/15/sharp-rise-in-the-share-of-americans-saying-jews-face
-discrimination/.

10. Michael Walzer, *What It Means to Be an American: Essays on the American Experience* (New York: Marsilio, 1990).

11. Ralph Ellison, "The Little Man at Chehaw Station: The American Artist and His
Audience," *American Scholar* 47, no. 1 (1978): 25–51.

12. "Pieter Stuyvesant, c. 1612–1672: Director-General of New Netherland, 1647–1664,"
Historical Society of the New York Courts, https://history.nycourts.gov/figure/pie
ter-stuyvesant/#:~:text=Stuyvesant%20refused%20to%20allow%20the,a%20wider
%20concern%20%E2%80%93%20that%20%E2%80%9CJewish.

13. "The Flushing Remonstrance" (1657), Historical Society of the New York Courts,
November 2022, https://history.nycourts.gov/about_period/flushing-remonstrance
/#:~:text=Full%20Text%20of%20the%20Flushing%20Remonstrance&text=Wee%20
desire%20therefore%20in%20this,of%20the%20household%20of%20faith.

14. Moses Seixas, Letter to George Washington, January 1, 1790, Berkeley Center for
Religion, Peace & World Affairs (2022), https://berkleycenter.georgetown.edu
/quotes/moses-seixas-i-letter-to-george-washington-i-on-religious-liberty-in-the
-united-states. See also George Washington, Reply Letter to Moses Seixas.

15. James Madison, Letter, "To Thomas Jefferson from James Madison, with Enclo-
sure," January 22, 1786, Founders Online, 2022, https://founders.archives.gov
/documents/Jefferson/01-09-02-0183.

16. James Madison, "Memorial and Remonstrance against Religious Assessments,"
June 1785, Founders Online, 2022, https://founders.archives.gov/documents
/Madison/01-08-02-0163.

17. Treaty of Tripoli, Article 11, 1797, Avalon Project/Yale Law School, https://avalon
.law.yale.edu/18th_century/bar1796t.asp#art11.

18. Kevin M. Schultz, *Tri-Faith America: How Catholics and Jews Held Postwar America
to Its Protestant Promise* (New York: Oxford University Press, 2011), 65.

19. President John F. Kennedy, "Address to the Houston Ministers Conference" (September 12, 1960), John F. Kennedy Presidential Library, https://www.jfklibrary.org/learn
/about-jfk/historic-speeches/address-to-the-greater-houston-ministerial-association.

20. "Address of Senator John F. Kennedy to the Greater Houston Ministerial Association, September 12, 1960," Rice Hotel, Houston, Texas, https://www.jfklibrary.org
/archives/other-resources/john-f-kennedy-speeches/houston-tx-19600912-houston
-ministerial-association.

21. Constitution of Medina, 622 CE, Constitution Society, November 2022, https://
constitution.org/1-Constitution/cons/medina/macharter.htm.

PART III

ALTERNATIVE NARRATIVES

CHAPTER 17

The Story of a Name

Héctor Tobar

The US-Mexico border was first laid out in the years after the Mexican War, by teams of government surveyors from the United States and Mexico working cooperatively. They used instruments that determined latitude from astronomical observations, and a map of San Diego Bay sketched in 1782 by a pilot of the Spanish Armada. They began their efforts with a three-day shindig of dining and dancing during the Fourth of July weekend of 1849.

For about 100 years the border consisted, mostly, of the 276 marble and steel markers erected by that commission and its successors. In other words, the border was a largely an abstraction, an imaginary line in various desert and mountain landscapes and in the center of the Rio Bravo del Norte. In 1971, when first lady Pat Nixon visited the newly inaugurated Friendship Park on the border at Imperial Beach, south of San Diego, she was able to shake hands with members of a large crowd of Tijuana residents who reached across the few strands of barbed wire that marked the border then.

Some strands of barbed wire, and the kind of hurricane fencing you can buy at a hardware store. That was the border in 1971. It was not enough to stop the immigrants who crossed the US-Mexico frontiers

Adapted from talk at University of California, Berkeley, December 11, 2019.

in increasing numbers in the decades that followed, as economic crises and imperial wars devastated Latin America in the 1980s.

In the mid 1990s, as Latino immigration, especially, brought profound cultural shifts to California, the Clinton administration built a new barrier along the border south of San Diego. This project was called Operation Gatekeeper.

The fence was an improvised construction made of slats of steel used for temporary airport runways during the first Gulf War, and it climbed up from the foamy surf of the Pacific Ocean, on the very spot where a Republican first lady had reached into Mexico. And from there along the wetlands of the Tijuana River estuary, and up into the dune mountains of the Otay Mesa and San Diego County.

When I first traveled to this new fence, in 1996, I sensed I was witnessing the beginning of a quintessentially American undertaking. The ambition of it was familiar to me. Americans like to build big things. I was raised in Southern California during the Vietnam War and the race to the moon, and when Caltrans was still building freeways into the orange groves. My understanding of what it was to be an American growing up was this: we Americans developed these fevers to build and to destroy, and then we poured the country's wealth into these passions, and once we got going, no one could stop us.

Sure enough, over the years, the fence-building project at the border has morphed into a pharaonic project on an ever-increasing scale. After that first 10-foot-high wall and its accompanying seismic sensors and night-vision cameras the barrier underwent several upgrades in the ensuing decades, including the deployment of radar-equipped MQ-9 Reaper drones overhead, and the filling of an entire canyon near Tijuana named Smuggler's Gulch with about two million cubic yards of hard-packed soil.

In 2019, I argued in the pages of the *New York Times* that the expanded 30-foot-high wall President Trump said he would build on the border was an object with more political than practical value. Since there were already so many barriers to illegal entry—barriers that have sent thousands of people to their death in the Sonoran Desert—building a new barrier was really just an act of political theater. I called

Trump's proposed wall a conservative, nationalistic art project. At one point, the administration announced it would place webcams at the site of the new wall so that we could see the construction work in progress, which is precisely the sort of thing an installation artist might do.

The Wall is the climax of a decades' long evolution in the way the ideologues of whiteness (if I may be allowed to use that term) see people of Latin American heritage. The barriers at the border exist to stop this country from turning brown. Or, browner than it already is. They are a nativist response to the growth and spread of Latino communities in every one of the states of the United States in the first decades of the 21st century.

And since people of Latin American heritage are now the nation's largest minority group, The Wall is changing the way United States citizens understand what being an "American" means.

The Wall and the restrictive immigration policies it epitomizes are redefining what "Latino" means to in the American imagination. And to an ever-larger group of people, the Wall is redefining what it means to be "white."

Now, when I say that, I don't mean that every white person carries a wall inside their heads. What I mean is that a certain kind of discourse is trying to communicate a new message about whiteness to people who identify themselves as "white."

Ethnic and race categories in the United States have always been fluid. Every ethnic category is, in part, a collection of stories: the *Mayflower*, the slave trade, Japanese internment, the Trail of Tears. Ethnic categories are social constructions built from our social relationships. The historian Nell Irvin Painter has written that our notions of whiteness in America are tied up with notions of freedom. That's how America's sense of whiteness was built. A country built from many disparate nationalities constructed "white" to mean not Black. Not African. Not a slave, but free.

In California, today, brownness is often synonymous with membership in the lower laboring classes. I know this, in part, because during my 32-year career as a professional writer, while living and working in Los Angeles, I've been mistaken for being a valet who parks cars; a gardener (in front of my own home); a flower delivery man (at the mall); and an ice-cream vendor (at my son's soccer game). Latin American immigrants in Los Angeles serve, and they build order. The order we see in a well-off California suburb is the product of their work. They use electric-powered tools to shape shrubbery into eye-pleasing planes and curves; they scale palm trunks four-stories tall to keep them looking like the icons of sunny Mediterranean living they were planted to be. They keep babies from crying and shuffle soiled diapers into trash cans. This labor has a Sisyphean quality, because despite the order Latino immigrants build, the avenues of class mobility are becoming narrower for them; and for millions, the avenues to full citizenship are completely closed.

Your citizenship means something different when you live among, and work alongside, people who are not citizens. To an increasing number of Americans, to be white means, in part, that you were born without a fear of fences in your life. It means you are part of a country that has to build walls to keep out the barbarous nonwhite peoples of the south.

And if you're a Latino, Latina, or Latinx person . . . well, the existing Fence, and the Wall-to-Be, and the restrictive immigration policies, and the deportations, and the deportation centers: all those things make you a survivor. The Wall oppresses you, it spits in your face, it puts a chip on your shoulder.

Let's remember that Latino, or Hispanic, is, arguably, the most fluid of America's major ethnic categories. You can have blues eyes, be Catholic or Jewish, or be black or Asian, and still be "Latino." You can be Hispanic and not speak a word of Spanish.

These days, I happen to teach at a "Hispanic Serving Institution." The University of California, Irvine, has been designated as such by the federal government because its student body is more than 25% Hispanic or Latino. And by teaching there I know that young Latino people here in California most often respond to questions about their ethnic identity by naming the nation or region of their family roots. They might say "I'm Honduran." Or "I'm from Oaxaca, I'm Zapotec." Or, "My dad is Puerto Rican, and my mother is from El Salvador." A young person with Mexican heritage might say, "My family is from Sonora. I'm from South-Central LA."

"Latino" is too general and too loose a term to adequately describe our cultural roots. Young Latino people are looking for ideas, for stories that will defend them against the things that make them feel small and insignificant, that make them feel they are the sons and daughters of a belittled people. Words that reflect their sense of belonging.

Marketers have helped spread notions of "Latino" identity; but that identity has taken root, in large part, because it expresses the kinship that we people of Latin American descent feel with the various nationalities in our heritage, and with our various border crossing experiences: be it through a fence, across an ocean, or in an airliner.

When I was growing up, long before the Age of the Wall, I did not call myself "Latino." The term was not in widespread usage. If anyone asked me about my ethnicity, I called myself "Guatemalan-American." Hyphens were more popular back then. I grew up with Armenian-Americans and Filipino-Americans and Czechoslovakian-Americans.

I grew up in a sheltered Los Angeles family, unaware of what "race" was, not knowing that racial categories were embedded in the legal and bureaucratic spaces around me and that those categories had shaped how the people around me saw each other. This was in East Hollywood, California, in a neighborhood with a feel of transience about it. A place that was home to people of many different ethnicities.

I had one racist neighbor I never met, but who later became famous. He had escaped from a prison in Missouri in 1967. He was proud to be white and said so to everyone he met. He believed whiteness meant he deserved better than the lot he had in life. He'd been born a few doors down from the biggest brothel in Alton, Illinois, grown up in an abusive family, with an alcoholic father allergic to gainful employment. He looked for enemies who subtracted from the sense of power whiteness was supposed to give him.

During the three months he lived in the apartment building behind my backyard fence in East Hollywood, in 1968, this neighbor began planning to assassinate Martin Luther King. His name was James Earl Ray.

But it was also in East Hollywood that my parents met Booker Wade, a man who was proud to be African American and who became my god-father. As a teenager growing up in Memphis in the early 1960s, Booker had been arrested along with other members of the youth wing of the NAACP for trying to integrate the Memphis Central Public Library. Booker Wade took the bus to Los Angeles in 1962, and moved into an apartment in East Hollywood, where he met two young Guatemalan strangers, my mother and father. He offered my pregnant mother a car ride to the hospital so that I could be born there.

Our neighbor Booker Wade, who put his body on the line to fight segregation, took a bus from Memphis to East Hollywood and became my godfather. Our neighbor James Earl Ray drove his Mustang from East Hollywood to Memphis and assassinated Martin Luther King.

These may seem to be coincidences. But I think that all Latinx kids grow up this way, immersed and surrounded by the artifacts, the witnesses, and the monuments of this country's racialized history. Surrounded by the histories of various Americans and their struggles to be accepted and to understand themselves inside of the unsettled weather of America's ethnic and race relations.

I'm a history nerd, and in one of my many visits to the Civil War battlefield at Gettysburg, I drove into town and stumbled upon a Cinco de Mayo celebration there. Latino people now live in Gettysburg, a few hundred yards up the Emmitsburg Road from marble pillars inscribed with clovers, the symbols of the Irish immigrant soldiers who fended off the desperate charge of an army whose purpose was to establish a new country, the Confederate States of America, founded explicitly on the notion of white supremacy.

During one of my many pilgrimages to the neglected sites of Los Angeles history, I found a group of Latino residents cultivating a garden under the powerlines, growing squash and alfalfa on 116th Street in Watts, 500 feet from the spot where a white police officer pulled over a black motorist in a routine traffic stop that set off the Watts Riots in 1965.

Over at UC Irvine, my students are just starting to see their closeness to American history. But the events of their own lives already feel like history to them, because they've grown up listening to family stories populated with private mythologies and folklore. They might have a great-grandfather who lived through the Mexican Revolution or a father who joined the FMLN guerrillas in El Salvador. They write term papers for me that feature these histories. Tales of Mayan godparents who learned to study the stars to find their way through Guatemalan rain forests at night. Stories that have *brujas* and faith-healers, and a migrant who set off for the north from Mexico with a guitar in hand; and a street-vendor mother who began to build small fortunes playing poker in Southern California parks; and families that are split, and put back together again, and histories that have become intertwined with other families, including families that are Vietnamese, "white," and African American.

They might not say so explicitly, but to me it's clear that many of my Latino students see themselves at the center of a heroic narrative. Their family stories are filled with great dangers and great deeds. But instead of the cyclops and the sirens and Poseidon and the ocean storms of Homer's *Odyssey*, they have had to endure inequality, corruption, the illiteracy of parents and grandparents, smugglers, deserts, immigration courts, and segregated neighborhoods and urban decay and gentrification.

My students tell me stories of undocumented grandparents who have been in the United States long enough to have two generations of American-born, US-citizen progeny. Many are themselves caught in a legal purgatory that shows no signs of ever going away. They have had a variety of immigration categories and classifications attached to them by the Department of Homeland Security: they have learned to say, "I'm DACA," or "I'm from a mixed-status family," or "My father is on a stay from deportation," or "I'm TPS," or "I'm a Dreamer."

Most of these students were born around the cusp of the new century. They were born into a United States with a powerful anti-immigration movement and with a brand-new border fence. So part of my job is to teach them how this came to be. How it is that the story of the ethnicity we today call "Latino," or "Latinx," and specifically of these brown-skinned people of Mesoamerica, came to include this border fence.

I tell them that in the years before Bill Clinton built the first barrier, in the 1990s, we Californians were subjected to media campaigns that focused on the social costs of "illegals," a steady stream of resentment and intolerance on television and radio, climaxing in the campaign for the voter initiative Proposition 187, which would have banned undocumented immigrants from public schools and emergency rooms.

This voter anger was spurred by the transformation of California's demographics: the big waves of immigration of the 1980s and 1990s that changed the feel of California and gave us more Spanish-language media, and day-laborer pickup sites, and fleets of taco trucks, and more waves of white flight. The new border fence was born, in part, from those changes. And from the growth of a new version of the paranoid style in American politics, and from the spread of conspiracy theories and false facts about Latino immigration.

An early conspiracy theory from the early aughts had it that NAFTA was a plot to do away with borders and eliminate the dollar as our national currency, replacing it with the Amero, and to create a NAFTA superhighway connecting Mexico City to Toronto that would give Mexico a "free port" in Kansas City.

At about the same time, conservative activists began circulating a list of ten "facts" about illegal immigration said to have been reported by the *Los Angeles Times*. The list portrayed California as a state being overrun by criminal "aliens" who were filling up the state's prisons and hospitals and draining its public-health funds. For example, the list claimed that "75% of people on the most wanted list in Los Angeles are illegal aliens." And "nearly 35% of all inmates in California detention facilities are Mexican nationals here illegally." But the list was a work of fiction, and its "facts" had never appeared in the *Los Angeles Times*. The author, or authors, had assembled the list, in part, from the conjectures and musings of a conservative writer and a completely fabricated "statistical report on undocumented immigrants" credited to a nonexistent government agency.

I traveled to various communities in the "heartland" of America during just the years when these conspiracy theories and false facts were starting to spread. To Kansas, and rural Alabama, and Idaho. Among the immigrants I met, there was great optimism; I met chicken workers who started newspapers and soccer leagues, and farm hands who organized Cinco de Mayo parades and became radio DJs in places like Rupert, Idaho, and Grand Island, Nebraska. But the arrival of so many immigrant workers to these places led to a certain unease among the locals, as the arrival of newcomers often does. A class of demagogues and pundits monetized this unease on cable television and on syndicated radio programs. Eventually they changed the way mainstream US culture saw people of Latin American descent. The trope of the "illegal" took root. I went from being a Guatemalan American guy from LA, to being an "anchor baby."

In the United States, our ethnic identities have long been shaped by the very real social inequalities produced by global trade and capitalism. By the plantation economy, and by need for cheap labor during the industrial revolution, and to pick crops and pluck chickens in the present day. Today, I'm sorry to say, the public imagination increasingly equates Latino ethnic identity with undocumented status, barbarism, and servility. As a people who will work for cheap, and who crossed a wall or a fence to get here.

At different times in this nation's history, several different groups of people now considered "white" have been assigned outsider status and considered members of a different "race" or "breed" or people. The Irish were often depicted with simian features in 19th-century cartoons, when Irish immigration was changing the face of many American cities; the Jews fleeing the discrimination and the pogroms of central and eastern Europe were greeted with restrictions against their "race."

Faced with the arrival of new groups of outsiders, Americans have long used immigration laws to shape the ethnic makeup of their country. From the Chinese Exclusion Act of 1882 to the 1924 National Origins Formula, which sought to ensure that the United States would retain a white Anglo-Saxon Protestant identity by reducing the number of people admitted from southern and eastern European countries.

America's efforts to stop the flow of immigration and regulate the ethnic makeup of the country mean that millions of Latino kids are growing up deprived of one of their culture's most powerful resources: their extended families.

I was recently in Central America, in Guatemala, in a neighborhood whose residents have been divided by immigration. This is the same neighborhood where my aunt lives, and where my grandfather built the only home he ever owned. It's a neighborhood where many generations of the same family live in constant and intimate contact with one another. A great-grandparent might see his or her great-grandchildren every day. Young mothers live with their mothers. And now this neighborhood is also home to a quiet, painful, domestic drama of family separation.

I met a woman, Carlota, or Loty as she's known to her friends, whose home is a shrine to family that once lived in that home with her—her daughter and grandchildren. Photographs. "These are the things that help fill the void," she told me. "Llenan el vacío." She once lived with them in the cluttered warmth of 800 square feet; but now she's divided from that family by thousands of miles, and by 15 years.

Loty's daughter is an undocumented mother of four and hasn't returned to Guatemala since they left on Valentine's Day 2005, because of the Fence and the Wall-to-Be. Family means everything to Loty and her children, which is why her daughter, Claudia, migrated to central Pennsylvania, to a place not far from Gettysburg. In Pennsylvania, Claudia's four children, now teenagers and young adults, have thrived and learned to speak English, and French and German, too, why not, because education is a beautiful thing. But Loty cannot get a visa to visit her American family, and the guatemaltecos can't return to Central America, because the family is protecting a secret. The secret of their immigration status.

Millions of families in the United States live with these secrets, and with the fear created by the Fence and the Wall and the armies of immigration agents whose job it is to catch and to deport.

This fear changes the way we, as Americans, relate to each other. It means that we have neighbors and coworkers who are less likely to demand fair treatment at work, to protest discrimination. It less likely that any collective grievance we might share as neighbors or as workers will be addressed.

The Fence is a gun pointed at the heads of our neighbors. It sends people into the desert, which is a place of horrors unseen by most Americans; it leads them into the orbit of the criminal bands that have taken over the immigrant smuggling business. It places them inside a murderous ecology that transformed migrants into hostages, and that kills people, and transforms their bodies into carrion for vultures and other scavengers, turning the bones into dust.

In 2017 and 2018, groups of Central Americans started to band together to avoid death in the desert, and to avoid the violations and the assaults and the extortions of criminal smuggling organizations. At a rally in Florida, held after one of these caravans reached the US border, the president of the United States lamented: "How do you stop these people? You can't." A member of the audience shouted back, "Shoot them!" The audience cheered.

Five months later, in August, a man versed in conspiracy theories drove from suburban Dallas, to El Paso, Texas, and shot and killed 22 people, most of them Mexicans and Mexican Americans. He wrote a 2,300-word "manifesto" in which he said he was acting in response to the "Hispanic invasion of Texas."

The image of the Mexican national, or the Latinx American, as a dangerous force of disorder, and violence, is shaping white people's vision of their country. And this image is one sold repeatedly to the American public by Hollywood. At the multiplex, on basic cable, and on Netflix, the cartel operative has become the dominant image of Latino people in American television and cinema.

These onscreen villains are kingpins or hitmen or a small-time drug dealers. And they are the dramatic representation of the dangers said to make the Fence and the Wall necessary. Of "bad hombres." They are armed with replica automatic weapons firing blanks, gallons of stage blood and mangled Mexican accents.

In the odious film *Peppermint*, Jennifer Garner is a suburban mom whose husband and daughter were killed by Latino drug dealers; she becomes a one-woman vigilante army, killing a series of Latino assassins and destroying a piñata warehouse that doubles as a drug lord's secret headquarters.

In the CBS television drama *SEAL Team*, a Mexican cop tells his American counterparts, "We're dealing with a virus," referring to the drug-fueled corruption that has overwhelmed a fictitious Mexican town. "Here," he says, "everyone is born infected."

These media repeat the same tropes: Latino gang members grimacing as they mad-dog confused white people; secret meetings on Mexican haciendas, with tequila served and Latinas in bikinis as poolside eye candy.

In *The Mule*, Clint Eastwood plays an older man filled with regrets after a lifetime of alienating his wife and daughter. He realizes the narcos can make him flush with cash. He travels to a Mexican hacienda, where he's offered tequila by a poolside and the services of two Latinas in bikinis. The narco world is a symbol of his own desires and their potential to destroy him. This is the subtext of most narco films. The drug dealers are really just stand-ins for forces that are eating away at many real-life American families: rampant gun violence and the cruel logic of capitalism.

The bad guys in narco films are always ruthless hyper-entrepreneurs, and in *The Mule*, they tell Eastwood's character, "We own your ass." The real-life threats that hover over white American families—health care costs, corporate outsourcing—aren't quite as photogenic. So, in *The Mule*, as in countless films of lesser quality, Latino stereotypes become symbols of a white man's powerlessness before capitalistic forces no average American feels they can control.

But most often, Latinos' roles in mainstream American media are simply to be what most Americans perceived them to be: people who are quietly in the background, extras to the dramas of Americans whose stories are, in the calculations made by Hollywood studios, more bankable.

In Quentin Tarantino's *Once Upon a Time in Hollywood*, an aging actor (played by Leonardo DiCaprio) begins to weep after leaving a restaurant and realizing his career is on the down swing. His friend and driver (played by Brad Pitt) gets irritated with him. Seeing the valet parkers nearby, he tells DiCaprio: "Don't cry in front of the Mexicans."

Hollywood sees us then as the causes of white suffering, as the symbols of white suffering, and as the witnesses to white suffering.

And how does the American media portray the pathos of Latinx immigrants? Well, in stark terms, of course. In the news media, the most commonly portrayed image of Latino people is of the immigrant facing deportation.

The Latino is a tragic mestizo: the illegal immigrant who will always be denied a share of the "American Dream"; the "conflicted" immigration agent, an officer of the law forced to round up his own people; the bereft boy standing outside a federal building, tears streaming down his cheeks, freshly separated from the father he loves.

By sheer repetition, these images have seeped into our collective national consciousness as the melodramatic essence of the Latino experience.

The full, complex truth of the Latino experience should be coming to you from Latino writers, from Latino directors and screenwriters. But the fact is that even if we had willing buyers for our complicated masterpieces, the existence of The Wall and all is stands for makes us guarded in what we write and produce for you. If I tell you, for instance, something optimistic about the fate of the undocumented in America (and there are many reasons to be optimistic), well, then I'm betraying all the people who have been or are about to be deported by detracting from the hopelessness of *their* situation. And if I tell you a true story about the family dysfunction that leads, say, a Guatemalan kid to migrate (and those migration stories often have more than a little family dysfunction), then I'm tarnishing the reputation of a people who have already been repeatedly slandered. Art is born from ambiguities, from complexities of real-life experience. The existence of the Fence and the Wall-to-Be contributes to the infantilization of Latino people in US drama and literature.

I felt an epic movie, a television series, in the stories of the Oregon State legislator I interviewed recently. She told me about being a young girl in the 1980s, in fields in a town in the northern end of the

Willamette Valley, in a trailer without running water, translating for her parents—stories that still make her weep when she tells them, revealing a sense of humiliation that has never left her. Her career, a long journey through schools and nonprofits and, finally, to the state capitol in Salem, is a response to that humiliation, an answer to it. Her career is a rejection of servility, an embrace of her community.

The roots of this immigrant drama are in economics. In the cold calculations of capitalism. The future legislator's family moved to Oregon and harvested hops, wine grapes, berries, and their work and kept the landowners of the Willamette Valley with their heads above water. I'm also here because of economics. And specifically because US capital has always claimed a moral right to flow across borders, and to defend its interests abroad.

My uncle, who lives in that Guatemala City neighborhood I told you about earlier, is a retired bank employee, and in his home he has a small shrine to Guatemalan history and the role of US capital and the US government in that history. At its center there's magazine clipping with a print of the painting Diego Rivera created in response to the US-backed coup in Guatemala in 1954. This coup overthrew Guatemala's democratically elected government and was instigated by the New Orleans–based United Fruit Company. The painting shows John Foster Dulles, then the secretary of state, at the center of a tableau that's at once satirical and tragic, surrounded by banana workers, and by Guatemalan corpses.

Thanks to this coup, funded by US taxpayers, in the half-century that followed, if you grew up as a person of consciousness in Guatemala, eager to question the status quo, you took your life in your hands. Tens of thousands of peasants, poets, philosophers, social critics, labor activists, lawyers, and assorted rabble-rousers and romantically inclined people were murdered by the military regimes that have ruled Guatemala for nearly a half-century. When my father and mother left that country, they left that enforced silence, that servility, that hopelessness behind.

The mass murder in Guatemala, the death squads in El Salvador of the 1970s, 1980s, and 1990s, the violence in the border crossing in the first decades of this century: all those things have served to create and sustain a social order that keeps our people in an undereducated state, in a desperate state, and in a state of perpetual striving and resistance.

Violence and death are at the heart of this order, although it's a violence that's invisible and unknown to most Americans.

What's also invisible and unknown to most Americans is this: the countless ways that Latino people find to resist the policies of exclusion, marginalization, and ethnic engineering.

Consider the boldness, the vision, and the theatricality of the activists of the National Immigrant Youth Alliance, including the artist Marco Saavedra. In the first years of this decade, they took direct action against the bureaucratic machinery of immigration detention by infiltrating the facilities where Latinx immigrants were being held in order to help the men and women inside win release. By doing so, they directly confronted the system that keeps millions of longtime residents of the United States living as a caste of marginalized, legally "underground" workers.

As one of the activists put it: "'Undocumented,' 'illegal,' I really don't care what you call it . . . they're just different words for 'afraid.'"

Across the United States, in high schools and workplaces and neighborhoods, Latinx youth resist the culture of fear with acts of personal expression, asserting their humanity and their individuality. I know this because, as I said before, I teach writing in a Hispanic-serving institution, and I'm invited to read to accounts of these acts. Each paper is an invitation into a private theater in which great themes of justice and identity are played out.

In a story written by one of my students this year, a young man debates whether he'll be able to take the stage at his high school with his rock band. "His willingness to become the center of attention, even for just a few minutes, felt contradictory to how he had lived his life up to that point," my student writes, describing an undocumented teenage protagonist. Undocumented people in the United States grow up learning to keep secrets and to have ghost identities. They learn to tell made-up stories to strangers about where they were born, what their parents do for a living; above all, they learn not to draw attention to themselves. And so the protagonist of the story worries and vacillates, but finally takes the stage and pronounces: "Today, we'll be playing a cover of 'This Charming Man,' by The Smiths." The first notes of the song play, and the narrator experiences a liberation of the soul and of the mind.

Latino people experience these kinds of personal liberations every day: they come in the form of a cooked meal, a completed school assignment, a courtship story, a break-up story, a coming out story, a confrontation with a parent, an epiphany at the end of a day's work.

These stories are the essence of the present-day United States experience. They are what America is and what it is becoming. They are the stories by which America will know itself in the unfolding century, in the decade to come, and the ones that follow.

Consider the Guatemalan immigrant family I mentioned earlier, the one that's living somewhere in Pennsylvania, in a neighborhood not from a wide and slow-moving river.

During this family's journey to the United States, in 2005, they were detained for some time by smugglers in a house in central Mexico. They were trapped in this house, with lots of other migrants, and one of the boys ended up celebrating his third birthday in that place. When the other migrants heard it was his birthday, they organized a party for him, there, in that house where they were all trapped. That boy graduated from a Pennsylvania high school. One day in the future, that boy and his brother and sisters and parents will feel free to tell that story openly, and then that story will become part of his family lore: "Your grandfather, when he came to this country, they celebrated his birthday in the safe house in Mexico where he was being held by evil men." A story meaningful to them, because it speaks to the strength that carried them through difficult times, a story that will endure for as long as that boy is alive to tell it, and then as long as his children live, in the year 2070 and beyond. A story that, along with millions of others like it, will come to define the emotional universe of the United States of America, in the decades approaching the nation's tricentennial.

CHAPTER 18

Migrant Herbalism

Cinthya Santos Briones

When we migrate, when we move through a territory, our identity, culture, language, and worldview also migrate. The use of herbs and medicinal plants has traveled in space and time, as has knowledge about the uses of traditional Indigenous medicine.

Migrant Herbalism (*Herbolaria Migrante*) is a project in which I investigate the diversity of medicinal herbs that have migrated due to the forced displacement of the Mexican community to the United States. I also reflect on how the use of herbs and traditional medicine, along with its healing practices and rituals, have crossed borders and subsisted through time.

In the Migrant Herbalism archive, I capture in graphic form the soul of each herb and its healing power through historical techniques of camera-less photography and embroidery. Inspired by Anna Atkins' photographs of seaweed, I created a series of cyanotypes on cotton fabric, made from the healing herbs that have migrated with us and that I have collected from Mexican grocery stores in New York City neighborhoods. Each cyanotype archives a variety of diverse components, including barks, pollen, seeds, flowers, petals, leaves, and branches, which can appear alone or assembled in bouquets.

All embroidery and photographs in this chapter by Cinthya Santos Briones.

Quelite

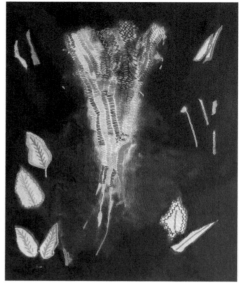

Pericón

In each frame I explore development as a metaphorical, sensory, and alchemical process, in which the character of the brushstrokes of the photosensitive emulsion, the quantity and quality of sunlight, the clouds, and even the exposure time participate in a dialogic process. By macerating the herbs for a few minutes in the light on a cloth impregnated with photosensitive liquid, I am able to capture their figures on the light-sensitive surface, thereby also capturing their essences and auras. On the canvas I record a landscape petrified in an instant.

Subsequently, I narrate the oral histories of plants shared by generations of our mothers and grandmothers through the embroidery done on the cotton fabric of the cyanotypes. Each stitch creates a sensory mosaic of herbs, barks, and seeds that migrated to New York City. The embroidery then takes on a political and resistance dimension, although it is also a metaphor for liberation and healing. In each stitch I return to floral patterns that carry ornamental and functional links of hand embroidery, alluding to the history of traditional women's crafts.

DIENTE DE LEÓN

Sirve Para istimular el apetito
Para Preparar infucion se toman
1-2 cucharaditas finamente
trituramos o en Polvo y se añade
150ml de agua hirviendo se deja
reposar la infusión 10-15 minutos
y se filtra.

Tambien se recoletan las Plantitas
Cuando estan Verdes antes de
floriar y se preparan en
Saladas sele puede poner rabanos
o cebollas las hojas se pueden
Comer en una rebanada de Pan
Con mantequilla mesclados con
requeson y tambien sirve Para
Ponerle a las sopas y tienen un
Sabor aromatico.

Diente de león by Elizabeth Perea

Migrant Herbalism is where I reinterpret our culture and identity through threads that record ancestral knowledge and perpetuate the history of traditional medicine of the Mexican community in the diaspora. This kaleidoscope of images records the soul of herbs and constitutes an archive of collective ethnobotanical memory, in addition to showing the diversity of flora of traditional Mexican medicine used by our ancestors.

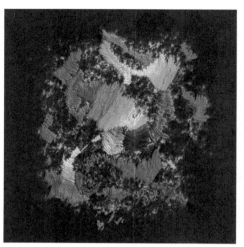

Pipicha   Ruda

Traditional indigenous medicine is a gateway to the diversity of flora, minerals, seeds, and roots used by migrants and their ancestors. Currently, the knowledge and practices related to herbal medicine are in danger of disappearing, due not only to globalization and human displacement, but also to the knowledge not being passed down to newer generations.

Epazote

Employing camera-less photography, ancient codex, oral history, community workshops, DIY books, and embroidery, I document my community's answer to lacking access to the healthcare system. Using ancestral knowledge, we seek to heal physically and spiritually with plant-based medicines and therapies.

Fig leaf

Epazote

El epazote es una planta ancestral tanbien se le conoce con el nombre de Paico El epazote es una yerba medicinal de origen prehispanico, su nombre se deriva del náhuatl que significa zorrillo por el olor fuerte de la Planta.

El epazote es antiparasitorio ya que nos ayuda a eliminar a los parasitos alojados en nuestro sistema digestivo (es un purgante natural) sirve para aliviar el dolor de hemorroides, tambien es antiespasmodico y nos ayuda con los dolores mestruales.

Epazote by Alicia Torres

I began the Migrant Herbalism project as a reflection on herbalism and traditional medicine that migrated with the Mexican community to New York City. Through my own experiences with herbalism as a first-generation Mexican immigrant, I build connections that facilitate intergenerational knowledge-sharing within my community in order to learn about and archive our ancestral, active, and embodied healing practices. I expand this project to the Mexican migrant community by weaving my own visual work with collective narratives and in collaboration with grassroots organizations such as the Mixteca and Voces Ciudadanas Organization in Brooklyn. In the art workshops I share my knowledge of alternative photography, made on different media such as canvas and cotton paper, using the technique of cyanotypes, lumen, and anthotypes. We use embroidery to capture our culture and identity; the threads record our ancestral knowledge and preserve the history of traditional medicine of the Mexican community in the diaspora. Embroidery is a form of political resistance, as well as a creative process of liberation and healing.

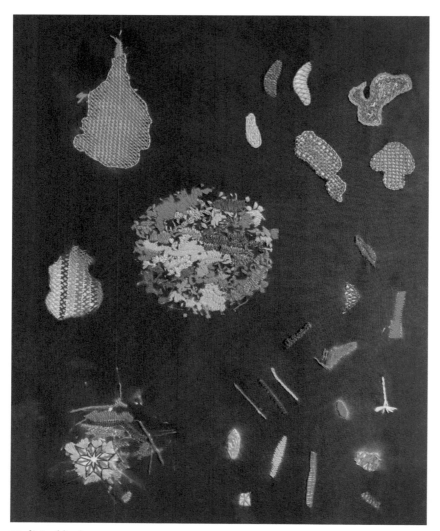

Medicinal herbs

Given migrant communities' limited access to medical services, as well as the economic and linguistic difficulties of navigating a Western health system marked by racism, migrant communities have built, in the transnational space, supportive networks and care through herbalists, midwives, *sobadores*, traditional doctors, and shamans.

Cuando era niña como de 8 años ocurrió el fallecimiento de mi tía Gregoria. Hermana de mi mamá Angela, despues de dejar a mi tía en el cementerio y llegar a la casa mis papas prepararon un baño para la Familia para alejar la tristeza y las malas vibras traidas del cementerio. Para este baño se usa : - Nopal machacado Hojas y Flores de Cempasuchil machacado El Jugo y cascaras de los limones se mezcla con suficiente Agua. Despues del baño Regular se enjuaga con la preparación. Para reconfortar el alma.

Baño para reconfortar el alma by
Antelma Valdez Pérez

Medicinal herbs

For generations, ancestors of contemporary migrants have shared knowledge about traditional medicine through ancient codex and oral history. Through the workshops I hold, I facilitate a collective learning space where participants share memories, poetry, recipes, and narratives linked to the uses and healing properties of herbalism. In these workshops, we create handmade artbooks inspired by the practice of the political movement *cartoneras*, which originated in Argentina in 2003 and spread throughout Latin America, which uses DIY publishing methods, and by illustrations from the Cruz-Badiano codex, the oldest book on medicinal plants in the Americas, written in the Nahuatl Indigenous language in 1552. It describes the healing properties of 227 medicinal plants used by the Aztecs.

In Migrant Herbalism we create a common work of learning and horizontal relationships, where the exchange of experiences allows the construction of new relationships and forms of creation by political actors who exercise their agency and empowerment.

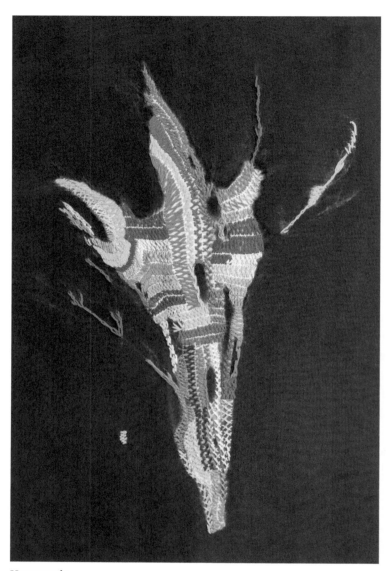

Huauzontle

This project offers a way to think about migrants not just as the country's labor force, but also as contributors of invaluable knowledge and culture. Migrant Herbalism seeks to strengthen the relationships of the community in a landscape riddled with complexity and the tension of belonging and not-belonging by exploring, reinterpreting, and communicating in new terms the importance of our identity expressions linked to medical practices brought from rural México to the urban neighborhoods of New York City.

CHAPTER 19

Reclaiming Humanity

Black History and the Cultivation of Empathetic Imagination

Allison Dorsey

Distancing and denial are strategies some may use to separate themselves from the vicissitudes of life and enable self-satisfaction, but they are not the universal choice. Visionary and multi-award-winning novelist Octavia Butler began to write because, as she said, "When I began reading, heck, I wasn't in any of this stuff I read. I certainly wasn't in the science fiction. . . . I wrote myself in, since I'm me and I'm here and I'm writing. I can write my own stories and I can write myself in."[1] With these few simple sentences, Butler captured the story of the Black experience. Brought to these shores battered, bruised, and in chains, Black people wrote ourselves into the story of the nation and in the process enhanced and redefined democracy in America.

As a historian of American Reconstruction, I remain unrelenting and unapologetic in my commitment to teach Black history: the story of the quest for justice and the development of strategies and hard-earned skills for survival. Knowledge of this history is *essential* for all who wish to understand the American past and present. Contemporary political upheaval demonstrates the need for all participants in American democracy, birthright citizens as well as immigrant populations, to have greater knowledge and understanding of both history and civics. Black history is more than the story of the travails and hardships of the past; it reveals a people who fought for our full humanity, for justice, for freedom for ourselves and our progeny and to claim all the rights of democracy. And in each era, our work and sacrifices forced the nation to confront the dichotomy between democracy on paper and democracy as a lived experience. Indeed, I assert that through our efforts we have made and are continuing to make this a democratic nation.

The Constitution of the United States, the organizing document of American democracy, was "written in 1787, ratified in 1788, and in operation since 1789."[2] That is, existing on paper and in theory. Yet the nation did not approach democracy *in practice* until after the American Civil War, after the passage of numerous amendments, and after the civil rights movement of the mid-20th century. The battle to end chattel slavery began not with white abolitionists but with Black enslaved human beings determined to free themselves and their brethren. The passage and ratification of the Thirteenth Amendment (December 6, 1865) elevated the Constitution, formally making it an anti-slavery document, thereby ending what William Lloyd Garrison called "a covenant with Death and an Agreement with Hell."[3] The Fourteenth Amendment (passed June 13, 1866, ratified July 9, 1868) granted birthright citizenship and establishing equal protection under law. The last of the Reconstruction amendments, the Fifteenth (passed February 26, 1869, ratified February 3, 1870) secured the right of the franchise for men irrespective of "race, color or previous condition of servitude." These changes were forward thinking and potentially revolutionary. Thus empowered, Black men enthusiastically joined the American democratic project as they sat on juries, pursued elective office, and wrote progressive laws, working to make a fuller freedom available to the four million formerly enslaved the nation over. Had their white peers, male and female, shared their radical commitment to a multiracial democracy, Black history and American history would be vastly different.

Sadly, America's devotion to democracy ended on the shores of white liberty. The hope and possibilities of Black Reconstruction were extinguished by white backlash against Black freedom, backlash by the courts (as in the Supreme Court decisions in the *Slaughter-House Cases* in 1873 and *Plessy v. Ferguson* in 1896), and by organized violence by white citizens.[4] Black women who challenged, supported, and cultivated Black male political insurgency in the late 19th century, fought and helped win passage of the Nineteenth Amendment, gaining their right to vote in the 20th. Yet, Black suffragettes, who had first worked for the franchise beginning in the 1830s, discovered gender solidarity was no match for white supremacy after winning their rights in 1919. White women, like white men, used their new voting power to shore up anti-Blackness and suppress Black liberty at every turn. The work of propagandists, spearheaded by the United Daughters of the Confederacy and supported by professional white historians, created and disseminated the mythology of the "Lost Cause," both justifying Southern secession and the Civil War as well as assailing the true character and liberatory power of American Reconstruction. Beginning with Du Bois, historians have worked to challenge the fabrications of the "Lost Cause." Contemporary scholars such as historian Paul Ortiz details the white racial violence and corrupt dismantling of Reconstruction as it occurred in the former states of the Confederacy. His *Emancipation Betrayed: The Hidden History of Black Organizing and White Violence from Reconstruction to the Bloody Election of 1920*, stands out as an example of 21st-century scholarship that centers the history of Black political and social activism while also documenting white opposition to citizenship rights for African Americans.[5]

Full Black liberation, at least as it was tied to American jurisprudence, remained elusive until after World War II. With apologies to those committed to fantasies about "the Greatest Generation"—those men and women who weathered the Great Depression and "saved the world from Nazis," as described by Tom Brokaw and Tom Hanks and Steven Spielberg—it is vital we remember how many of that generation came home after fighting against Hitler and went right back to fighting against liberty, equality, and democracy for Black men and women in America.[6] The true greats of that generation came home from a foreign war, took off their uniforms, and headed to southern court houses to register to vote, where, like civil rights warriors Medgar Evers, Hosea Williams, Amzie Moore, and thousands of others, they were turned away and denied their Fourteenth and Fifteenth Amendment rights, despite the nation's victory over fascism across the sea.

From 1952 to 1968, Black (and Brown and Yellow and Red and yes, some white) men and women engaged in a bloody civil rights struggle that took the lives of more than 100 American citizens and saw hundreds more beaten, injured, and jailed. This was the price paid for the Civil Rights Act of 1964, the Voting Rights Act of 1965 (arguably the most significant piece of civil rights legislation of that era), the Immigration and Nationality Act of 1965, and the Civil Rights Act of 1968. This costly high point of American democracy undid the egregious legal, economic, and social abuses that defined American apartheid, a.k.a. Jim Crow segregation, born in the ashes of Reconstruction. The late 20th-century changes in American society—changes that produced increased access to education, housing, and government services for millions of Americans, and included the election of President Barack Obama—were a direct result of Black activism and devotion to the democratic process.

The ongoing struggle to maintain and grow American democracy continues the reactionary politics of the 2010s and 2020s. We have seen Americans joined in lock step carrying torches, shouting antisemitic slogans, and menacing fellow citizens. Citizens seeking and *elected* to federal office have celebrated the words and deeds of white supremacists who advocate violence against other Americans here at home and debase themselves by endorsing the world view of tyrannical dictators abroad. The nation's highest court has reversed course, acting to undermine voting rights, the rights of privacy, women's rights, and LGBTQIA rights. Federal officials, seemingly forgetful of our stance as a democratic "nation of immigrants," orchestrated policy designed to deny aid to those seeking refuge at our border. Corporate actors continue a nihilistic refusal to acknowledge and take necessary steps to address the global climate concerns though the impact of rising temperatures and sea level change leaves no doubt the planet Earth is in crisis.

Fortunately, a serious study of Black history and a recommitment to democracy has the potential to avert panic in the face of such dire circumstances. Indeed, it can be argued that actors on both sides of our current political divide are aware of the power of the story of the Black past. Histrionics about "Critical Race Theory (CRT) in the schools" reveals nothing if not the deep anxieties of white adults who fear they will be called upon to answer questions about which side of history they were on and why.[7] The effort to efface and erase the experience of generations of nonwhite Americans and their contributions to the building and preservation of our nation depends on the strategies of distancing, denial, and once again, increasingly, denunciation and destruction.

Recent efforts at banning books in classrooms and libraries, which have focused especially on books that teach Black history (as well as books about racism and sexuality), offer a case in point. Ortiz's *An African American and Latinx History of the United States: Revising History* is on a "banned book list" in three states precisely because it celebrates the experiences and activism of Black and Latinx actors in American history. Efforts to ban Ruby Bridges' *This Is Your Time* in elementary schools by the "Moms for Liberty," as well as by various state legislators, brought this repugnant practice to national prominence. The children's book tells the story of Bridges' experience as a 6-year-old confronted by a mob of white angry parents and escorted by armed federal marshals as she became the first Black child to desegregate an all-white school in Louisiana. Those opposed to teaching this story of the inadvertent young activist, argue that her text (and in the case of some lawsuits, the entire history of the civil rights movement) is "anti-American and anti-white," noticeably and exclusively equating the two. Bridges counters this argument, noting that her book provides children of color with an opportunity to see themselves and their contributions to American history. Representative Jaimie Raskin (D-MD), speaking at a congressional hearing on the pressures to ban in the nation's schools, rejected the suggestion that teaching the story of Ruby Bridges might make "white children feel uncomfortable," noting instead the likelihood the tale would speak to "the powers of empathy, compassion and solidarity that all children or most children, have and are capable of developing."[8] For reactionary forces committed to undermining the idea of America as a multiracial democracy, there is great danger in cultivating empathy (and compassion and solidarity) in the nation's children by exposing them to accurate history. Apparently, such ideological descendants of Confederate memorial societies agree with members of the 1950s-era White Citizens' Councils, who feared educating children in integrated environments, arguing that if white children were not inculcated with the belief in white supremacy by age 6, it might be "too late" to teach them bias and prejudice.

The study of a full and inclusive American history with an emphasis on Black history cultivates empathy. There are of course many ways to teach by example and cultivate empathy in learners of all ages. Sociologist Stephanie Medley-Rath focuses on cognitive empathy and the sociological imagination. Musician Terrance Blanchard argues that music and art have "the power to change souls" and tours with visual artist Andrew F. Scott presenting the work of the photographer Gordon Parks" in a show subtitled "An Empathetic Lens." Actor and activist Anna Deavere Smith makes the case that an empathetic imagination is essential for social justice work.[9] All have contributed to the conversation about the need for and the many paths to empathetic imagination. Moreover, hearts and minds are also coaxed toward empathetic imagination by reading fiction. In an interview for *Canada Literature*, Yann Martel, *Life of Pi* author, spoke directly to the significance of empathetic imagination in resolving clashes of cultures: "Yes, the empathetic imagination is the great solution. . . . I strongly believe in the empathetic imagination, in making an effort to understand the other."[10]

Octavia Butler captured and built on this sensibility in *Parable of the Sower*, inviting readers to engage with the idea of empathetic imagination. Lauren Olamina, the protagonist of the novel is a hyperempath, meaning that she feels the pain she witnesses in those around her. Science fiction and fantasy aficionados will have some familiarity with the idea of an empath (see Gene Roddenberry's original TV series *Star Trek* as well as other speculative fiction that challenges the status quo).[11] Butler's Olamina communicates both the danger and the real power of empathetic imagination.

How different is the approach to the world when humans lead with empathy toward their fellows rather than sympathy, suspicion, competition, pity, or contempt? Olamina's "gift" makes her vulnerable to physical and psychic harm from those she would help and those who witness her superhuman trait. Butler, of course, is welcoming readers to think seriously about experiencing and understanding the pain of others, to see others as fully human as we see ourselves. To see others, for example, not as "little black children to be rescued," nor as the "poor" of the "developing world" to be uplifted and transformed through random acts of charity and upper-class philanthropy. Butler's Olamina develops some exciting ideas—"All that you touch you change. All that you change changes you. The only lasting truth is change. God is Change"—but like the rest of humanity, she does not have magical powers.[12] She cannot fix the structural oppression or the personal challenges of others. The problems of the post-apocalyptic moment in which she dwells, like those of the early 21st century, are vast and almost overwhelming. Still, her gift means that she sees and experiences the pain of others almost as a piece of herself and acts compassionately to provide aid and minimize harm.

Historians also work to cultivate empathetic imagination in their scholarship and in the classroom. Thomas Kohut details the importance of empathy and imagination to the work of history in the introduction of his extraordinary text, *Empathy and the Historical Understanding of the Human Past*, where he explains that "the book seeks to establish empathy as a way to know and understand the people of the past by imagining, thinking and perhaps even feeling one's way inside their experience. Although empathizing with past people is to no small degree a rational enterprise, the book seeks to emphasize the vital role that imagination plays in historical knowledge, enabling historians to know and understand past human beings and past experiences that they have not had themselves."[13] Similarly, Amy Stanley speaks of the significance of empathy to her work as a historian:

> Some want to explain how the world we live in came to be this way (and, by implication, how it might be changed). Others want to understand the

past in order to cultivate an empathetic imagination—how can you make sense of people who were very different from you and everyone you know? I think both kinds of historian can be found in every field, geographically and temporally. But I'm definitely the second kind of historian. I'm not as interested in how we got here and more interested in empathy. And I think that's actually more useful than it seems. We're often called upon to understand people who have a radically different worldview from our own—it's a crucial skill, and history is a good place to practice it.[14]

While I agree with Stanley's view of empathy, unlike her, I see it as fundamental to understanding how we as Americans "got here" and where we might go. If we are to address the challenges of our current circumstances, from racial injustice to climate change, empathetic imagination is essential.

I encourage readers to reflect on the 2020 Black Lives Matter protests in response to the killing of George Floyd. The national and global protests, the largest civil rights protests in American history, grew directly from Floyd's murder. Yes, from the sense of horror, but more importantly from the profound sense of *empathy* men, women, and children felt in response to George's deeply human cry for his mother. Those protests brought to mind the words of civil rights icon Ella Baker, "Until the killing of Black men, Black mothers' sons, becomes as important to the rest of the country as the killing of a white mothers' son, we who believe in freedom cannot rest."[15] Americans and others around the world felt and embraced, if only for a moment, the idea that the life of a Black mother's son had meaning, had value, and that we should demand justice for his murder. Empathetic imagination was the necessary first step on a path toward justice.

Growing an empathetic imagination toward our fellow Americans requires knowledge about the experiences of those who are different from ourselves. Here, rapper Kendrick Lamar's call for Black solidarity—"We gon' be alright. Do you hear me, do you feel me? We gon' be alright!"—is instructive, especially when coupled with lyrics from another of his tunes, "Be humble, sit down," ideally, with a book or two to learn more about all these things.[16] Rather than focusing on what each of us can do to help others, and thus make ourselves feel better, as in the "thousand points of light" celebration of individualism and volunteerism advocated by President George H. W. Bush, Americans must be encouraged first to grow their knowledge base and build human connection with others.[17] Rather than presuming what is needed to address a situation affecting others, active citizens must investigate, learn, and then inquire what is needed and how they can assist. The task requires slowing down in order to see and to listen and develop a sense of empathy about the lives of others. During the civil rights movement, Student Nonviolent Coordinating Committee (SNCC) activist Robert Moses helped hundreds of bright, eager college students understand that neither their enthusiasm nor their undergraduate education was as important as what the "local people," those on the ground in Alabama, Mississippi, and Georgia, understood about their needs. A better democracy *requires* that we care about not just our own families but the families of others whether or not they look like our own, have a different point of origin, or speak another language. A better future requires that we understand the ways all our futures are intertwined. Getting to that understanding begins with empathetic connection— actions motivated by an empathetic vibration rather than a sense of superiority rooted in sympathy or pity for those presumed to be somehow "less" than the comfortable, educated, and powerful.

At times, individuals, even groups of individuals, are not able to solve a problem. While Black people devoted time, money, and prayerful energy to end lynching—the violent criminal murder of men, women, and children from the 1870s through the 1950s—despite their best efforts, the practice continued. Nevertheless, Black anti-lynching activists have continued to bear witness, observing and sharing the pain of human suffering and tell the tale via word of mouth, journalism, and documented history. Just as Elie Wiesel called on the world to bear witness to the violence and death of the Holocaust of World War II, James Baldwin demanded the nation bear witness to the brutal murders of those working for civil rights in America.[18] Black Americans have borne witness both to the abuses of the past and our will to survive since the end of slavery. In the early 21st century, when political opportunists are working to sanitize the story of the nation's past and deny the nation's youth the opportunity to learn about the bad and the ugly of America's history along with the good, bearing witness is more vital than ever.

Knowledge of the past is essential to disrupt false narratives about who we are and how we got here and to enhance the possibilities of enabling a democratic future. Make no mistake: new legislative "gag orders" designed to prohibit teaching subjects that allegedly cause someone to feel "guilty or ashamed about the past collective actions of their race or sex" are designed to deflect focus from people who have actually been harmed by racism or sexism and to disrupt the possibility of children, young learners, from developing empathy for human beings who have experienced harm at the hands of others in the past.[19] Such laws are also designed to challenge the memories held by the people who experienced the harm of those past actions. These attempts at gaslighting, made in the spirit of those who promulgated the falsehoods of "the Lost Cause," fail to understand the power and the endurance of memory and storytelling in the Black cultural tradition. Literary genius Toni Morrison made masterful use of this tradition noting, "Memory weighs heavily in what I write, in how I begin and what I find to be significant."[20]

The stories of those who bore witness to the past are the first draft of history, and the early steps toward progressive change often begin with listening to such voices. The 2022 passage of the Emmett Till Federal Antilynching Act, is ultimately the consequence of Ida B. Wells's 1895 *Red Record*, in which she bore witness to and documented the violence of the lynching of Black men and women. Bearing witness, now so often done with a cell phone camera, requires only refusing to look away and instead recording the horrors before us. This is how we begin to breathe life into the struggle against injustice. The process of change enabled by bearing witness is not fast or sure. Please note, the Emmett Till Federal Antilynching Act came 122 years after the first attempt to secure such legislation and after members of the House of Representatives tried some 200 times to criminalize lynching at the federal level. While Ida B. Wells was committed to seeing the crime of lynching end, the current legislation was passed 127 years after her work was first published and 91 years after her death. Her work, her witnessing, informed the work of every legislator and activist who pushed for a federal antilynching law in each era. Her voice challenged the false justifications for public murder of Black men, women, and children and reverberated down through the years. Dynamic American citizens must learn to add our voices to that of others who are acknowledging and objecting to violence and to harm. A chorus of voices, like those who joined Ida B. Wells, can be part of a wave of sound that reverberates and creates small fissures, tiny fractures in the structures of society, new openings for progressive change to take root.

Bearing witness is part of the work of making progressive change. Change that shifts power and access from the comfortable, privileged, and entitled to the vulnerable and marginalized will take more than a single lifetime to achieve, though this should not, must not, encourage Americans to fall into despair or worse to lose interest. That a thing is hard and time-consuming, that the positive results may come not tomorrow or the next year or the next decade, does not make the task unworthy of doing. As attorney Sherrilyn Ifill has said, "I don't know of anything in the history of Black people in this country . . . in which it ended 'and then they gave up.' That's just not what we do. I know we work for the future of our children and our grandchildren and their children."[21]

The truth and wisdom embedded in Ifill's observations is too often lost on Americans who are unfamiliar with the narrative of Black History. Sadly, great swaths of American society have little exposure to it. While the field is vast and deep, courses in Black history, African American history, and Africana studies are still absent in many high schools and colleges. In institutions where the courses are available, there are as many excuses not to seek out and study the Black experience as there are students of all races and ethnicities. Still, as I have gleaned from three decades of undergraduate teaching, there is a common pattern among students who have no interest in the field: many students whose high school preparation did not include the history of

Black Americans tend not to act to rectify this situation in college, having somehow decided that if it was important, it would have been part of their previous curriculum. Some students who have had previous exposure report that Black history is too emotionally difficult, even "traumatic," to study further, and that really is the point. I remind students enrolled in my courses that their task is merely to *study* this "hard history," unlike the people in the past who were forced to live the experiences. Then, too, a number of students, including the history-minded, avoid the study of Black history because they cannot see themselves in the narrative—or they will not see themselves in the narrative, for fear of what such a vision might evoke.

Such resistances are not confined to native-born Americans. As more than one student, not exclusively but especially those who are Black immigrants, has remarked, "After all, this not my story." But nor are the histories of China, Russia, or Early Modern Europe their story. When I have challenged them in this way, and when I have pointed out that Black history is key part to American history, their response has often become more nuanced. As Black immigrants or second-generation immigrant American children most could recognize a shared heritage, but they still rejected any connection to the "shameful" history of slavery and Jim Crow. The resistance to the story of the Black past within the United States is troublesome, for a knowledge and understanding of Black history provides keys to the puzzle of America, a tool for decoding American society, a road map by which to interrogate both the promise and limits of democracy in a raced nation. Although such an understanding is important for all students, I would argue that it is essential for those who are new Americans, especially those who are Black and who will find themselves in a society that continues to grapple with systemic racism. The study of Black history then helps all students develop the empathetic imagination necessary to see the full humanity of people who lived in the past and communicates important lessons for how to live in the present.

In his introduction to *Faces at the Bottom of the Well* (1992), legal scholar Derrick Bell described his experience of "shame" for being a descendant of the enslaved:

When I was growing up in the years before the Second World War, our slave heritage was more a symbol of shame than a source of pride. It burdened Black people with an indelible mark of difference as we struggled to be like whites. In those far-off days, survival and progress seemed to require moving beyond, even rejecting slavery. Childhood friends in a West Indian family who lived a few doors away often boasted—erroneously as I later learned—that their people had never been slaves.[22]

The growing number of Black immigrants from the 1990s onward means that the scenario that Bell describes from the 1940s continues to be replayed. As Ira Berlin argued in a 2010 *Smithsonian Magazine* article on "The Changing Definition of African American," the history that most Black people in mainland North America shared in common—namely, "centuries of enslavement, freedom in the course of the Civil War, a great promise made amid the political turmoil of Reconstruction and a great promise broken, followed by disfranchisement, segregation and, finally, the long struggle for equality"—"has had less direct relevance for black immigrants."[23] Thus, he called on historians to recognize that "new circumstances . . . require a new narrative" and to include in it the life stories of those Black people who emigrated to the United States from the Caribbean, Africa, and South America, especially toward the end of the 20th century.

Berlin was right to call attention to changing demographics of Black America. Due to the Immigration and Nationality Act of 1965, the Refugee Act of 1980, and the Diversity Immigration Visa Program of 1990, the Black immigrant population has grown considerably. According to a January 2022 Pew Research Center report, 21% of the Black people in the United States are immigrants or children of Black immigrants.[24] Voluntary emigrants from Jamaica, Haiti, Nigeria, Ghana, Kenya, Trinidad, Costa Rica, Belize, Liberia, Ethiopia, and elsewhere have both added to the existing narrative of Black history and written their own chapters. Yet as Berlin was well aware, scholars whose work crafts the narrative of the Black past have had no objection to weaving new threads into the tapestry. The story of Haiti and Haitians is deeply embedded in the Black history of the United States. The Haitian Revolution created the first Black republic in the Western Hemisphere and touched the lives of Black leaders from Richard Allen to Frederick Douglass. It is difficult to imagine a serious discussion of the Harlem Renaissance without Jamaican Claude McKay or of Black cinema without Miami-born Bahamian Sidney Poitier. The history of Black politics is incomplete without Jamaican Marcus Garvey, Trinidadian Kwame Ture, or Brooklyn-born Barbadian American Shirley Chisholm, who served as a member of the US House of Representative and ran for United States President in 1972. Articles and monographs that address the history of Black immigrants from the Caribbean, Africa, and South America appear on the reading lists in Black history courses across the nation. Sociologist Mary Waters's *Black Identities: West Indian Immigrant Dreams and American Realities*, historian Irma Watkins-Owens's *Blood Relations: Caribbean Immigrants and the Harlem Community*, cultural anthropologist Zain Abdullah's *Black Mecca: The African Muslims of Harlem*, and others have been added to works by Douglass, Du Bois, and Deborah Gray White, all part of the inclusive process of trying to tell the history of "new African Americans."

The challenge of teaching an expanded history to first- and second-generation Black immigrants has to do with the diversity of the Black students themselves. We must be sensitive to inclusionary and exclusionary narrativizing, which at its worst denied the existence and importance of Black history. In the expanded academic approach, a first hurdle has often been convincing Black immigrant students to take a course in Black History. To my surprise, many such students have reported being discouraged by parents from studying "the history of African Americans," most especially the story of slavery. Once enrolled, Black immigrant students have added as much to the course as any other bright engaged students, though they have often brought new dynamics to the classroom. It is worth considering a few examples. During a discussion of evolving Black identities in late-20th-century America, a Jamaican student, her voice dripping with contempt, explained "I identify as Black, but I absolutely refuse to identify as African American." Her view was immediately challenged by an

Afro-Dominican peer: "Hold up, African Americans have been fighting the fight and holding it down in this country for a long time. Shouldn't new Blacks join the struggle?" A third student, self-described as a white immigrant from eastern Europe, interjected: "Wait, what is all of this about? Won't you all be African Americans over time? In a generation you won't be Jamaican anymore—you, too, will be African American."

In the aftermath of the hullabaloo, the Jamaican student explained she rejected the idea being African American because she had an abundance of "personal observations" and "experiences" with said people. Her hot take emphasized a narrative of broken families and deficient culture; she understood such egregious racial stereotypes as the sum total of the Black American experience. The burning sensation and memory of this discussion remain with me as the episode took place in the final weeks of the term, after students had (supposedly) read monographs and articles about the Black experience for more than three months, taken in numerous lectures, and participated in weeks of discussion. Nevertheless, for at least one student, negative stereotype and bias were more powerful than any lessons to be gleaned from the study of Black history. There seemed little chance of her developing a rich understanding of the Black experience, let alone an empathic imagination.

The next academic year, a trio of Black immigrant students enrolled in the same course. All three young women let me know that in addition to being of West African heritage, they were science majors who had no previous experience of American history beyond high school. I reassured all three that neither their limited exposure to American history nor their majors would be a hindrance or disadvantage. A trip to the National Museum of African American History and Culture proved especially instructive for me and for students enrolled in the class. The journey from the subterranean level of the museum, where the conversation about slavery and the Atlantic Slave Trade begins, to the upper levels, which includes the coffin of Emmett Till, provided much-needed insights for many members of the class. En route I stopped to check on a student (one of the three aforementioned) who stood alone before the wall of placards detailing slave sales. When she finally spoke, her voice was barely above a whisper: "Who would buy a 9-month-old child?" We talked about how the child had been sold away from their mother, about calculating the cost to raise an infant until it was work age (6 years old), and the risks of a young death—all things we had previously discussed in class.

Still, I was unprepared for her response: "This child will never know their family, never know their people, their culture. This is what slavery was." On the return trip to campus, that same student expressed a new understanding that the condition of Blacks in America, from enslavement through Jim Crow, noting perhaps it was "not the fault of Black people," and that maybe stories about the "American Dream" and promises of freedom were not universally true. There was both a confused surprise and disappointment in her voice. Her response revealed assumptions about the Black past in America, assumptions that had been only slightly disturbed by weeks of assigned reading but were not truly shaken free until the personal encounter with the poster advertising the sale of a stolen 9-month-old child. The experience refuted Berlin's suggestion that the history of mainland North American Blacks had "less direct relevance" to Black immigrants. Instead, it reinforced the need to employ a diversity of tools (museum trips, film, novels, and the like) to reach such students. The words on a museum placard created a haunting image of vulnerability of a cruelly enslaved human child and broke open a path to an empathetic understanding of the Black experience.

To be clear, Black American students, descendants of those formerly enslaved in the United States, have no better understanding of the life arc or histories of their Black immigrant peers. Bias and stereotypes about people from foreign climes are alive and well in the consciousness of American students. Those born in the late 20th or early 21st century, have little knowledge of the history of American exploitation and occupation of Caribbean nations. They are unfamiliar with the story of the Liberian Civil War, the brutality of Charles Taylor, and the connection to the emigration of Liberians to the United States. Similarly, they have no historical understanding of the stigma generated by the 1983 federal policy labeling all Haitians as potential carriers of HIV/AIDS and the resulting mistreatment, abuse, and exclusion of immigrants from the island. Black American students have no more understanding of the culture and history of their Black student peers from Ghana, Togo, Nigeria, or Mali than does the average American citizen. Which is to say almost none at all. Sadly, tropes and fantastical stereotypes about endless ethnic warfare, lack of development, and encounters with wild animals—all part of the steady diet of mainstream media reportage about Africa—have as much impact on Black students as they do on the rest of the American population. Exoticization effectively contributes to preventing the recognition of a shared humanity and replaces development of an empathic imagination with a fascinated alienation.

For their own part, US -born Black students have "experiences" and negative bias about urban neighbors from Sierra Leone and Cameroon. I have heard cringe-inducing questions about Ghanaian foodways and seen the wide-eyed surprised in response to learning that a classmate from "the continent" was from a family whose education, wealth, and status mark them as part of the world's "1 percent." There is no reason to assume Black American students have some inborn understanding of the history of their grandparents let alone their enslaved great, great, great grandparents. No one currently enrolled in undergraduate classes has lived the Black experience since 1619, and it is foolish to presume academic knowledge based on heritage.

Political scientist Christina Greer offers important insights in *Black Ethnics: Race, Immigration, and the Pursuit of the American Dream.* Greer analyzes the opinions and worldview of Caribbean immigrant, African immigrant, and Black American union members in New York City in the post–civil rights movement era. Like sociologist Mary Waters before her, she notes the frustration and disappointment of many Caribbean immigrants who presumed they would assimilate into "Americanness" but instead found themselves coded as Black and thus racially discriminated against. African immigrants had a similar experience. Greer invited members of all three groups to assess their work ethic. African and Caribbean immigrants gave themselves high marks for work ethic and pointed to their educational and entrepreneurial success as evidence. Members of both groups ranked Black Americans poorly, citing racial stereotypes about laziness to explain poverty and incarceration of native-born Blacks.[25] It is believed these alleged failings and deficiencies of Black Americans, stereotypes about Black family life, sexuality work ethic, and presumed criminality, negatively influence white American's perceptions of Caribbean and African immigrants, resulting in bias and discrimination against them. It is sad, but not unsurprising that Black immigrants might internalize the anti-Blackness long cultivated in American society—and in its law, economy, and cultural products. Knowledge of Black history in America can help clear up this misguided perception that Black people, rather than white supremacy and racism, are the problem.

Black ethnic tensions in the Black history classroom are one thing. But consider the huge number of students from all backgrounds who graduate from college without having studied Black history or any history. In this, they miss an opportunity to recognize a shared humanity among diverse peoples. While the study of history has so much to offer in practical terms—how to "find the answer" by mastering the use of databases and analyzing documents, how to research and write a persuasive essay, or for that matter, a work of historical fiction—in a democratic nation, the study of history provides necessary lessons about competing ideologies, systems of government, legal freedoms, and civic responsibilities. Perhaps most importantly, the study of Black History has the ability to reconnect us to the humanity of those who came before us. History can jumpstart our empathetic imagination by helping to disrupt negative stereotypes and bias as well as teaching students how to interrogate and understand the evolution of ideas about race and class over time. In an era of dangerous disinformation and political manipulation, all Americans can benefit from having a better understanding of our past. If 21st- century Americans hope to upend the discrimination, economic exploitation, and racial violence that haunted the nation's past and threaten our democratic future, then understanding and confronting white supremacy, especially the ways it has changed over time, is essential. As Octavia Butler sought to teach us with her fantasy novel *Kindred*, we must both acknowledge and confront the past. Learning from the past based on responsible history allows the individual to cultivate habits of both mind and heart that can enable the development of an empathetic imagination. Thus armed, we can acknowledge the pain of the experiences of others, reduce our fear of their "otherness," and reconnect to their humanity and our own.

Notes

1. "VISIONS: IDENTITY; 'We Tend to Do the Right Thing When We Get Scared,'" *New York Times*, January 1, 2020, https://www.nytimes.com/2000/01/01/books/visions-identity-we-tend-to-do-the-right-thing-when-we-get-scared.html.

2. US Senate, "Celebrating Constitution Day," September 17, 2020, https://www.senate.gov/artandhistory/senate-stories/celebrating-constitution-day.htm.

3. Paul Finkleman, "Garrison's Constitution: The Covenant with Death and How It Was Made," *Prologue: A Quarterly Publication of the National Archives and Records Administration* (Winter 2000): 231–45.

4. Examples of this backlash include extra-legal violence, lynching, and the Colfax massacre, as well as the establishment of the Ku Klux Klan (1865), Knights of the White Camelia (1867), and Red Shirts (1875).

5. Paul Ortiz, *Emancipation Betrayed: The Hidden History of Black Organizing and White Violence in Florida from Reconstruction to the Bloody Election of 1920* (Berkeley: University of California Press, 2005).

6. Tom Brokaw, *The Greatest Generation* (New York: Random House, 1998); Stephen Spielberg and Tom Hanks, executive producers, *Band of Brothers* (HBO, 2001). Both Spielberg and Hanks were instrumental in efforts to bring aging veterans to the National Memorial as part of their commitment to honor the "greatest generation."

7. Critical race theory, a legal theory taught in law and graduate schools as explained by Kendall Thomas, Nash Professor of Law at Columbia University Law School, "views race law and policy as tools of power. . . . Critical race theory tells a story about institutionalized racial disadvantage and systemic racial inequality. It highlights the structural harms of the 'colorblind racism' we see at work in laws that don't mention race per se" (Susan Ellingwood, "What Is Critical Race Theory, and Why Is Everyone Talking about It?" *Columbia News*, Columbia University, July 1, 2021, https://news.columbia.edu/news/what-critical-race-theory-and-why-everyone-talking-about-it-0).

8. Ariana Garcia, "Ruby Bridges Speaks Out against Texas Book Bans at Congressional Hearing," *Houston Chronicle*, April 8, 2022, https://www.chron.com/politics/article/Texas-book-ban-Ruby-Bridges-desegregation-17066921.php.

9. Stephanie Medley-Rath, "Becoming Empathetic through Sociology," Learn Sociology Blog, March 10, 2018, http://www.stephaniemedleyrath.com/2018/03/10/becoming-empathetic-through-sociology-repost-from-sif/; Christian Bright,

"Artistic Impulse: Three Artists Speak about the Influence of Gordon Parks," *Mercury News*, April 9, 2022, https://www.themercury.com/news/three-artists -speak-about-the-influence-of-gordon-parks/article_798617ef-c1b7-5ead-aded -f86acb5000d1.html; Anna Deavere Smith, "Toward Empathetic Imagination and Action," Anna Deavere Smith (blog), accessed November 10, 2022, https://www .annadeaveresmith.org/toward-empathetic-imagination-and-action-2/.

10. Sabine Sielke, "'The Empathetic Imagination': An Interview with Yann Martel," *Canadian Literature* 177 (Summer 2003): 25, 20.

11. Esther L. Jones, *Medicine and Ethics in Black Women's Speculative Fiction* (New York: Palgrave Macmillan, 2015).

12. Octavia Butler, *Parable of the Sower* (New York: Four Walls Eight Windows Publishing, 1993), 3.

13. Thomas A. Kohut, *Empathy and the Historical Understanding of the Human Past* (London: Routledge, Taylor and Francis Group, 2020).

14. *Humanities* Staff, "History and the Empathetic Imagination: An Interview with Amy Stanley," *Humanities: The Magazine of the National Endowment of the Humanities* 42, no. 3 (Summer 2021), https://www.neh.gov/article/history-and-empathetic -imagination.

15. Ella Baker, "Address at the Hattiesburg Freedom Day Rally," January 21, 1964, Voices of Democracy, The U.S. Oratory Project, https://voicesofdemocracy.umd .edu/ella-baker-freedom-day-rally-speech-text/.

16. Kawan Prather/Kendrick Lamar Duckworth/Mark Anthony Spears/Pharrell L. Williams, *Alright lyrics* ©BMG Rights Management, Sony/ATV Music Publishing LLC, Universal Music Publishing Group, Warner Chappell Music, Inc.; Asheton Hogan/K. Duckworth/M Williams li *Humble lyrics* ©Hard Working Black Folks Inc., Top Dawg Music, Sounds From Eardrummers Llc, Eardrummers Entertainment Llc, Tde Music Llc.

17. Presidential candidate George H.W. Bush first used the phrase "thousand points of light" at the Republican National Convention in New Orleans in 1988. As president, Bush created the Points of Light Foundation to promote private, volunteer, specifically nongovernmental activism to address the nation's social problems. See https://www.pointsoflight.org/.

18. Asked by President Jimmy Carter to give voice to his vision for the proposed US Holocaust Memorial Museum, Elie Wiesel wrote "For the dead and the living, we must bear witness." Those words now mark the entrance to the US Holocaust Memorial Museum as Wiesel noted in his April 22, 1993 remarks at the opening of the museum. Lovia Gyarke, "James Baldwin and the Struggle to Bear Witness," *The New Republic*, February 3, 2017, https://newrepublic.com/article/140395/james -baldwin-struggle-bear-witness.

19. Jeffrey Sachs, "Steep Rise in Gag Orders, Many Sloppily Drafted," PEN America (Blog), January 24, 2022, https://pen.org/steep-rise-gag-orders-many-sloppily -drafted/.

20. Toni Morrison, "Memory, Creation and Writing," *Thought: Fordham University Quarterly* 59, no. 4 (1984): 385–90.

21. Bill Whitaker, "Sherrilyn Ifill: Why George Floyd's Killing Is a Tipping Point and How America Can Move Forward," CBS News, June 7, 2020, https://www.cbsnews .com/news/naacp-sherrilyn-ifill-george-floyd-donald-trump-response-60-minutes -2020-06-07/.

22. Derrick Bell, *Faces at the Bottom of the Well: The Permanence of Racism* (New York: Basic Books, 1992).

23. Ira Berlin, "The Changing Definition of African-American," *Smithsonian Magazine*, February 2010, https://www.smithsonianmag.com/history/the-changing-definition -of-african-american-4905887/.

24. Pew Research Center, "One-in-Ten Black People Living in the U.S. Are Immigrants," January 2022, https://www.pewresearch.org/short-reads/2022/01/27/key-findings -about-black-immigrants-in-the-u-s/.

25. Gene Demby, "Black Like Who?" NPR Code Switch, April 15, 2020, https://www .npr.org/2020/04/14/834027120/black-like-who.

CHAPTER 20

Unity in the Struggle

Immigration and the South's Emerging Civil Rights Consensus

Hana E. Brown, Jennifer A. Jones, and Taylor Dow

In October 2015, North Carolina Governor Pat McCrory signed a bill into law that banned the state's counties and cities from declaring themselves sanctuaries for undocumented immigrants. Though they take many forms, self-declared "sanctuary cities" typically refuse to allocate municipal funds or resources toward immigration enforcement and decline to prosecute undocumented immigrants for minor offenses. The bill, HB318, mandated local cooperation in federal immigration enforcement efforts and prohibited local authorities from accepting as valid any identification issued by foreign countries or by local governments. Because these forms of identification are the only ones held by many undocumented immigrants, the bill took a direct swipe at the state's growing and largely Latino undocumented immigrant population.

That a Republican governor and Republican-dominated legislature in the South enacted such a bill may seem unsurprising. After all, many southern states have made similar moves in recent years.[1] But while HB318 had significant support, it also encountered widespread censure and resistance. For months leading up to the bill's passage, a coordinated team of immigration activists lobbied for its defeat. Emphasizing the protective effects of sanctuary cities, these advocates argued

An earlier version of this chapter originally appeared in *Law and Contemporary Problems* 79, no. 5 (2016): 5–27.

that HB318 would threaten public safety and strain police budgets. Although this coalition featured a host of immigrant rights organizations and liberal activist groups, some of the most prominent and vocal opponents of the bill were the state's Black civil rights organizations. Calling on its members to protest the bill, North Carolina's NAACP declared, "Our immigrant brothers and sisters are under attack."[2] Governor McCrory signed HB318 at the Greensboro sheriff's office, flanked by local law enforcement officials who vowed the bill would preserve law and order as well as American values. But as McCrory put pen to paper, opponents amassed less than a mile away at Greensboro's International Civil Rights Center and Museum. The museum, designed to commemorate the civil rights struggles of the 1960s and the sit-in movement that began in Greensboro, became a powerful symbol for the immigrant rights movement.

In many ways, Black activists' embrace of immigration is surprising. Media narratives in the United States tend to focus on stories of Black-Latino conflict, not cooperation or solidarity. National histories of the civil rights and immigrant rights movements are typically told in isolation from each other rather than in a way that emphasizes the movements' linkages. The US legal system also treats immigration and civil rights as separate bodies of law. Yet despite these divisions, Black social justice groups around the United States today are taking the precise steps taken in North Carolina in 2015, embracing immigration as a civil rights issue and drawing comparisons between the discrimination Latinos face today and the racism that has long targeted Black communities. These multiracial coalitions are developing new vocabularies, making new collaborative demands, and developing new strategies to upend systemic racism and usher in a new social and political reality.

This chapter documents how immigrant rights became a contemporary civil rights issue, focusing on a particularly compelling case: the emergence of an immigration and civil rights consensus in Mississippi. While Mississippi has proven a trendsetter in Black-Brown alliance building, Mississippians' organizing models have spread across the region and even the nation. The emergent understanding of immigration as a civil rights and racial justice movement is reshaping social justice struggles and encourages us to rethink the narratives we usually tell about race, citizenship, and inclusion in the United States.

The Struggles for Civil and Immigrant Rights

By the time photos of 14-year-old Emmett Till's mangled corpse began circulating in Black news publications during the fall of 1955, the nation was in the midst of a civil rights insurgency. Till's murder occurred less than three months after the Supreme Court's mandate that public schools desegregate "with all deliberate speed."[3] By this time, the civil rights movement had been brewing for decades, but the murder of Emmett Till in Mississippi exposed the racial terror of the Deep South to a nation finally beginning to grapple with its ramifications.

The civil rights protests of the 1950s and 1960s emerged in a region characterized by entrenched racism and white hegemony. The Delta Council, a regional consortium of white business interests, maintained the racial order by combatting burgeoning labor unions' attempts to organize Black workers and undermine the sovereignty of the white plantation establishment. Following the 1954 *Brown v. Board* decision, an array of Citizens' Councils, much like the Delta Council before them, formed across the South to combat school integration and maintain white supremacy.

Civil rights protests grew and expanded even in this context of repression, led by organizations such as the NAACP, the Congress on Racial Equality (CORE), and the Student Non-Violent Coordinating Committee (SNCC). By 1964, Freedom Summer and the brutal beatings of Selma-to-Montgomery marchers exposed Black disenfranchisement and racial terror to a national audience. That exposure would help ensure the passage of the Voting Rights Act of 1965 (VRA) just one year later.

This civil rights history is recounted often in the United States. Indeed, no social movement is as routinely invoked as the civil rights struggle, often mentioned as part of a national narrative of racial uplift and progress toward racial equality.[4] Less often noted, however, is that amidst the sweeping domestic policy change engendered by the civil rights movement, an equally momentous reform occurred in federal immigration law. Until that year, US immigration policy operated according to the Immigration Act of 1924's racially exclusionary immigration regulations, including outright bans on Asian and Arab immigration and severe restrictions on African immigration.

The Immigration and Nationality Act of 1965 (INA) abolished this quota policy just 37 days before the Voting Rights Act. Like the VRA, the INA sought to eliminate explicitly racist policies and practices, in this case by overturning national origin quotas. However, nearly 60 years later, the INA is rarely lauded as a civil rights milestone. This silence reflects a larger decoupling of civil rights and immigration politics in our collective recounting of these movements. Instead, American immigration narratives have historically focused on white immigrants and characterized their experience as one of consistent upward mobility through hard work and dedication to the "American Dream." This recounting understates, and even outright ignores, the role of race and racial dynamics in immigrant integration and immigration enforcement.

Immigration in the United States has long been intertwined with race and racism. Formative immigration laws excluded certain foreigners from entry and citizenship on the basis of race.[5] For much of the nation's history, US politicians, the media, and residents have framed new immigrant arrivals in racialized terms, characterizing early Asian, Mexican, and European immigrants as disease-prone, dirty, and dangerous.[6] Immigration law has also continued to racialize immigrants in more recent decades, limiting opportunities for lawful immigration from Mexico, in particular, and using targeted enforcement along the US-Mexico border to criminalize entrants.

The idea that modern-day immigration politics are not racialized is a ruse. The convergence of ostensibly race-neutral immigration policies disproportionately disadvantages racialized minorities.[7] This is particularly true of Latinos, for whom immigration policies have functioned as a "race-making institution," much the same way as criminal justice policies have etched the racial parameters of Black life.[8] Yet these parallels and intersections go widely unnoticed, whether in policy and law or in our collective recounting of this nation's history.

Policy and Structural Precursors

Given the separation of immigration and civil rights narratives, a campaign like the HB318 resistance in North Carolina seems, at worst, impossible and, at best, an anomaly. However, two major structural shifts set the groundwork for a new civil rights consensus around immigration in the 1990s: demographic change and administrative shifts in immigration enforcement. Both prompted increasing realization among activists of the longstanding linkages between immigrant and native-born Black struggles for justice in the face of entrenched and institutionalized white dominance.

The first of these precursors was a shift in immigrant settlement patterns. Prior to the 1990s, Latino immigrants settled overwhelmingly in traditional gateway cities, such as Los Angeles, New York, and Miami. By mid-decade, economic stagnation on the West Coast and in Mexico, combined with the implementation of the North Atlantic Free Trade Agreement, incentivized migration out of Mexico and away from the West Coast. At the same time, significant economic growth in the South attracted new migrants to the region. By 2000, the population of foreign-born residents in many southern cities and towns increased by as much as three-fold.

The second shift happened between 1980 and 2010, when significant changes also occurred in the administration of US immigration policy. Local and state officials became increasingly involved in immigration politics, proposing and adopting punitive anti-immigration policies.[9] New federal guidelines allowed states to request agreements with Immigration and Customs Enforcement (ICE) using Section 287(g) of the INA to identify unauthorized immigrants for detention. At the same time, growing concerns over terrorism and security led the federal government to expand state and municipal jurisdiction over immigration. The September 11, 2001, attacks had particularly important consequences. The political response immediately targeted Arab Americans as racialized and criminal outsiders,[10] but this characterization quickly expanded to other immigrants. With the restructuring of the US Immigration Service under the domain of the Department of Homeland Security, new immigration initiatives increasingly framed noncitizens as potential threats to American security and culture.

These shifts happened as Latino immigrants migrated in unprecedented numbers to the South. In 2006, at the height of unauthorized immigration to the United States and at the beginning of a nationwide economic crisis, various cities and counties throughout the Southeast enacted laws and ordinances to restrict immigrant access to social, educational, and medical institutions and benefits.[11] These changes occurred alongside other efforts to enforce more punitive measures on a national scale. This political assault and increasingly hostile atmosphere politicized immigrants, particularly Latinos, who quickly became the racialized target of such initiatives.

Throughout this period, anti-Latino racism and discrimination became increasingly difficult for Black civil rights activists to ignore. Efforts to deprive undocumented immigrants of access to education, healthcare, and work are, in principle, the very forms of discrimination that the long civil rights movement has sought to counter. This racism politicized and mobilized Latino immigrants, inspiring a new set of political and social identities closely aligned with Black Americans.[12] In this context, civil rights groups and immigration groups recognized an opening to work together in solidarity and reimagine immigration as a civil rights and racial justice issue.

The Origins of Mississippi's New Civil Rights Consensus

The rise of anti-Latino racism gave rise to the Mississippi civil rights community's embrace of immigration activism. In the 1990s, the state's foreign-born population nearly doubled, with most new arrivals coming from Latin America. In 2000, a group of immigration advocates formed a statewide organization—the Mississippi Immigrant Rights Alliance (MIRA)—to advocate for immigrants' rights. As its executive director, Bill Chandler, explained in an interview, the group arose out of a campaign among former civil rights leaders to unionize Black and Latino casino workers. Recognizing that any progressive coalition in Mississippi required a broad base of support, MIRA's founders intentionally structured the organization around the principle of Black-Brown solidarity. By design, the original board consisted of Latino immigration advocates, Black and white union leaders, and Black civil rights activists. In its 20 years of existence, MIRA's board has maintained this racial composition while regularly collaborating with veteran civil rights activists.

The civil rights community's embrace of immigration emerged over time, sparked by a range of racially motivated threats against Latino noncitizens. One such controversy involved access to public education. As Latino immigrants arrived in larger numbers along the Mississippi Gulf Coast in the early 2000s, Black civil rights leaders soon became aware that local public school officials were unconstitutionally denying Latino children the opportunity to enroll in public schools. Given the state's Jim Crow legacy and racially unequal schooling, many Black leaders viewed these practices as an affront to their decades-long civil rights agenda. Similarly, Black union leaders on the Gulf Coast became increasingly aware of the racial discrimination and wage theft encountered by Latino laborers on the coast and intensified efforts both to recruit Latinos into their ranks and to embrace immigration as an issue.

The brewing sense of linked fate between Mississippi's Black and Latino populations grew following Hurricane Katrina's devastation of the Gulf Coast in August of 2005. In the wake of the disaster, President George W. Bush temporarily suspended wage protections for construction workers on federal contracts.[13] In response, contractors denied wages to undocumented Latino workers who migrated to the region in droves to assist in rebuilding efforts.[14] Recruited with the promise of $15 and $18 hourly wages, guaranteed housing, and other assistance, these Latino workers soon found themselves paid $4 an hour or less and living 20 to a trailer.[15] The Red Cross and the Federal Emergency Management Agency also turned thousands of Latinos away from shelters, even circulating flyers in Latino neighborhoods discouraging Latinos from seeking aid, despite its federal guarantee. MIRA wasted no time teaming up with the Department of Labor, Oxfam America, and other organizations to provide social, legal, and other services to Latino immigrants on the coast. It also filed lawsuits against ruthless contractors, ultimately winning over $1 million in back wages.

As the parallels between Latino racial discrimination and racism against African Americans became increasingly clear, the state's civil rights leaders embraced immigration as a key issue. Bill Chandler, the head of MIRA, recruited to his organization's ranks former leaders from formative civil rights groups including the Southern Christian Leadership Conference, the NAACP, SNCC, and the state's influential Legislative Black Caucus. These groups not only embraced immigration as a civil rights issue but used tactics from the civil rights movement to challenge the growing spate of anti-immigration laws being proposed in the state legislature. Although the ties between the civil rights movement and the immigrant rights movement in Mississippi are deep and multifaceted, we focus on two specific strategies the alliance used to further its cause and recast immigration as a civil rights issue: framing and coalition-building.

Framing Immigration: Race and Civil Rights

MIRA's efforts reflect their understanding that how they frame immigration as a public issue will affect what they are able to accomplish. Their work has, therefore, involved efforts to coordinate their language and framing work to recast immigration as a civil rights issue.

On one front, this framing work targets Latino immigrants who routinely approach MIRA for assistance with visas, family reunification, deportation hearings, and other immigration matters. One of MIRA's goals is to help noncitizens understand their civil rights. These efforts involve introducing Latino immigrants to basic civil rights protections. For example, its April 2008 newsletter included a piece entitled "You Have the Right to Know," which outlined the basic protections included in the Civil Rights Act of 1964. The act, the article explained, prohibits discrimination in areas such as public service or government, education, and employment and covers the protected categories of national origin, race, color, religion, and sex. In addition to outlining the basic provisions of the act, the article provided examples of illegal racial and national origin discrimination that routinely befell Latino noncitizens in Mississippi. The piece concluded with contact information for the federal Equal Employment Opportunity Commission for those interested in filing discrimination claims.

These efforts to recast immigration-related abuses as civil rights issues extend beyond legal advising to activists' public characterizations of immigration as a political issue. Framing immigration has long been a challenge for immigration advocates. Among the most commonly used frames to lobby for noncitizen protections include arguments about human rights, worker rights, and legal status.[16] While not eschewing these frames, Mississippi immigration and civil rights activists have taken a different approach by portraying attacks on immigrants as racial discrimination. MIRA's newsletters demonstrate this blended race-focused approach. In one newsletter, Chandler discussed immigration enforcement as both a human rights issue and a matter of institutional discrimination: in "too many cities across the state of Mississippi, immigrants are being denied their basic human rights," he wrote. "Our experiences with hundreds of immigrants have revealed the countless ways in which they are marginalized and dehumanized. They have been driven from their home countries by American foreign policies, discriminated against in the workplace, forced to live and work in hostile conditions, and often forcibly separated from their families. They are constantly racially profiled by bigoted law enforcement authorities."[17] In addition to identifying immigration enforcement as racial discrimination, MIRA's framing efforts explicitly link anti-Black civil rights abuses of the past with contemporary anti-immigrant activity and legislation. In opposing Arizona's infamous anti-immigrant bill, SB1070, which passed in 2010, leaders of the immigrant rights movement in Mississippi likened the measure to the Jim Crow laws that once dominated the South. Eddie Smith, chairman of the Mississippi NAACP's Labor Committee, compared the present-day exploitation of immigrants to that faced by African Americans in the mid-twentieth century. "They have the same problems we had in the 1960s [such as] finding jobs, living wages and places to live. . . . The only reason immigrants are trying to come here is because we advertise this as the land of opportunity. . . . Once they're here, to me they're Americans."[18]

Immigration supporters also refer to lethal violence against Latinos in the state as "a new kind of Mississippi civil rights murder." Citing local murders of Latinos in the Jackson area, one immigration advocate went to great lengths to draw comparisons between the Latinos of today and Blacks of the 1950s and 1960s. "Both groups were vulnerable, lacked political clout and the public at large seemed not to care about their fate—operating on the skewed logic that the victims somehow 'got what they deserved.'"[19]

Likening anti-immigration efforts to civil rights–era discrimination against African Americans has become a key strategy that immigration advocates in Mississippi use to counter legislation targeting immigrants. When Mississippi legislators considered passing an Arizona-style immigration measure, advocates for immigrants responded by questioning whether Mississippi wanted, once again, to become the scorn of the nation for racist abuses against people of color. An editor for the *Clarion-Ledger* forcefully took this approach, asking, "Is Arizona the new Mississippi? Will Arizona now be the butt of jokes, subject to boycotts, ridiculed as being backward and intolerant? Those are all unfair stereotypes that Mississippi still has to fight today because of events of the 1960s, when Mississippi's backward and intolerant approaches to civil rights earned national ridicule. . . . If Arizona wants to go down that path, so be it. Mississippi should know better." Arguing that the Arizona law would negatively affect business investment, encourage boycotts, and force legal immigrants to leave, he asked, "Sound familiar?" He further suggested that these protests were like those Mississippi encountered in opposition to its civil rights hostility. "Singling out any group of people and blaming social problems on them . . . appeals to fear and prejudice, and it is wrong. But, that is where much of the debate on immigration is headed. We now have Mississippi politicians pandering to the issue, praising Arizona's law and calling on Mississippi to do the same. They should know that it is playing with fire."[20] Hampton's assertions echoed long-standing claims from the immigrant and civil rights community in Mississippi whose leaders routinely portrayed anti-immigrant legislative efforts as strategically "designed to inflame white racism here in Mississippi" and driven by "the same kind of racism that has been perpetuated against African Americans for years."[21] Equating anti-immigrant race-baiting with Nixon's notorious Southern Strategy, which made anti-Black appeals to secure white votes, MIRA leaders accused immigration opponents of capitalizing on white racism for political gain. "It used to be the Black man," wrote journalist and MIRA supporter Bill Minore. "Now it's also the Brown man—Hispanics."[22]

The framing of immigration as a civil rights issue also involves direct comparisons to specific civil rights movement activists and incidents. MIRA's newsletters announce Black History Month and include photos of Dr. Martin Luther King Jr. amid its sea of immigration-related stories. In an interview, Patricia Ice, the director of MIRA's Legal Project, made just such a comparison:

> There appears to be xenophobia in Mississippi, the likes of which we have not seen since the civil rights era of the 1960s. . . . In Mississippi, immigrants have done some of the dirtiest and low-paid jobs, including helping to clean up and rebuild after the Hurricane. Now, many people want to kick them out of our state. Critics argue that undocumented immigrants have "broken the law." They also said that Rosa Parks broke the law when she refused to move to the back of the bus. I say that some laws are unjust.[23]

By equating immigration laws and anti-immigrant discrimination with injustices against African Americans, these immigration activists seek not only to blur the lines between the immigration and civil rights movements but to compel residents to action.

Nowhere are these dual purposes clearer than in a full-page piece published in MIRA's February 2009 newsletter and written by Jean

Damu, a member of the Black Alliance for Just Immigration. Entitled "Immigration Raids Echo History of African Americans," the piece likened raids targeting undocumented immigrants to those targeting fugitive enslaved Blacks fleeing slavery in the mid-1800s.

> The similarities are powerful enough to convince many African Americans that it is in their best interest to support those who struggle against Black people's historic enemies. . . . The current immigration movement is still in its early stages. If it is to achieve the perceived successes of the civil rights movement, it must do a better job of uniting with Black America. . . . African Americans should be sensitive to the current conditions in which many immigrants find themselves. These conditions, after all, are not unfamiliar to us.[24]

Printed in both English and Spanish, the article framed immigration enforcement as a contemporary civil rights struggle and called on African Americans to recognize their linked fate with immigrants and to flex their political muscle to ensure immigrant rights be respected as civil rights.

Unity Conferences

Collaborative work between immigration and civil rights activists has not been restricted to linguistic strategies and appeals. Mississippi immigrant rights and civil rights groups consistently and deliberately gather organizers from prominent and influential organizations for unity conferences. The long-standing Southern Christian Leadership Conference (SCLC) and MIRA annually bring together civil rights leaders and immigrant rights organizers to discuss events and campaigns of shared interest and to build an effective and sustainable coalition. In doing so, Mississippi's activist leaders have achieved a shared language and politics, as articulated in their framing efforts, while simultaneously building a sustainable and mutually beneficial political base.

These unity conferences have been an important space in which the different groups identify and craft shared agendas by anticipating the sustained backlash against immigrants and African Americans. The first such conference occurred in 2005. By the time MIRA and SCLC organized its 2008 Unity Conference, the event was an established space to reinforce framing strategies and shared beliefs and principles.

In addition to ideological continuity, these conferences reinforce organizational continuity. For example, in 2008, State Representative Jim Evans served as MIRA president, president of the Jackson Chapter of the SCLC, and national organizer with AFL-CIO. In his efforts to organize activists for the coming legislative session, Representative Evans argued at the conference that efforts to enforce REAL ID (a federal law that imposed strict requirements on state identification cards and driver's licenses) during the 2009 legislative session must be monitored, as the passage of such a bill would be a disadvantage to many immigrant and African American communities. He contended that the policy would block both groups from voting, obtaining social services, or receiving IDs to travel because many with limited resources would struggle to surmount government bureaucracy in order to get or replace a Social Security card, driver's license, passport, birth certificate, or proof of naturalization. Wade Henderson, executive director of the Leadership Conference on Civil Rights, made similar arguments, suggesting that organizations and their leaders focus on three areas over the coming months: comprehensive immigration reform, K-12 educational reform, and inclusion of all US residents regardless of their citizenship status in the 2010 federal census count.

Beyond outlining a strategic agenda that responded to punitive legislation and planned proactive mobilization, immigration and civil rights groups also created a platform to discuss the challenges faced by both immigrants and African Americans in Mississippi's communities, particularly on the Gulf Coast, where labor abuses were rampant. These conferences successfully fostered a unified consensus that immigration issues and civil rights issues were one and the same. As noted by Eric Ward, an organizer for the Center for New Community in Chicago, "The greatest trick the anti-immigrant movement has played on African Americans is convincing us that [the] anti-immigrant movement is no threat to us."[25] By highlighting their efforts as intertwined, organizers were able to put forth a set of commitments to fostering the incorporation of immigrant rights into their 21st-century civil rights agenda.

These annual unity conferences continued to grow in size and intensity, garnering 160 participants in 2009. The goal of that conference was to discuss the 2010 Census, education, racial profiling, language access, labor rights, and health care. In its February 2010 newsletter, MIRA noted that the ties forged during these conferences have allowed MIRA to work effectively with allied communities of color in the South, progressive whites, and workers of all ethnicities "to understand the complexities and inhumanity of a number of anti-immigrant, anti-worker, anti-poor people policies on the federal, state, and local levels." They also further expanded their base of organizers, joining with unions and legislators to propose an alternative immigration reform bill based on the goal of "human, civil, and labor rights for all."[26]

Indeed, by the time of the 2013 unity conference, the ties between civil rights organizations and immigration organizations were solidified. Titled "Crimmigration: The Tragic Consequences of U.S. Drug Policies on Families and Youth," the SCLC/MIRA conference brought together 250 organizers, as well as keynote speakers Michelle Alexander, law professor and author of *The New Jim Crow*, and Javier Sicilia, the leader of Mexico's Movement for Peace with Dignity and Justice, to discuss the wide-reaching impact of the War on Drugs on Black and Latino communities.[27] This momentum toward a sustained and powerful coalition of immigration and civil rights activists was no accident. As Bill Chandler noted in an interview with the authors, "We made a conscious decision when building MIRA to make our board half Black and half Latino. . . . I think what helps us is that we have relationships we've built up over the years, we have people coming from different struggles. That is the power of the South. . . . And we saw right away the potential for significant political change."[28] In this sense, these unity conferences have been essential not only to building and sustaining the discursive frames that tied immigration issues to civil rights issues but also to these long-term coalitional relationships.

The Trump Era

Legalized racial exclusion has been at the fulcrum of both immigration and civil rights law and activism for centuries. Despite this, our public narratives largely treat these issues as separate, rarely recognizing the inherent links between the struggles for inclusion. With the election of Donald Trump to the presidency in November 2016, however, the intersections between immigrant and racial justice took center stage in US politics. President Trump's verbal broadsides targeting immigrants were explicitly racist, and his administration's immigration policies disproportionately affected immigrants of color. For some around the United States, the brazen racism of his immigration policies proved a shock. But for organizers in Mississippi, these efforts proved what they already knew: immigration is a civil rights and racial justice issue.

Given MIRA's continued boots-on-the-ground work of building a strong Black-Latino alliance, the organization and its allies were well equipped to push back against the Trump administration. Nowhere was this clearer than in summer 2019, when immigration agents carried out the nation's largest immigration raid in history in Mississippi. That summer, ICE agents arrived at a chicken processing plant first thing in the morning and lined up all the workers. They separated the men from the women, the white workers from the Black workers. Seeking out undocumented immigrants, they also separated out the "immigrant-looking" workers, code for Latino or Hispanic. By the end of the day, authorities had taken hundreds of the plant's Latino workers into custody on immigration charges. Children found themselves without a parent or, even worse, alone in an empty house. Local businesses shut down, their clientele now residing in detention centers.

Economically, socially, and personally, the devastation was palpable, but for MIRA the scene was also familiar. ICE had carried out an identical raid back in 2008 in Laurel, Mississippi. Until the 2019 raid, that Laurel raid had been the largest in US history. It left a lasting scar on the community, and not just on Latino families. It also scarred many of the African American employees of the plant who watched their coworkers and fellow union members get taken away from their jobs and families. These workers watched as ICE agents separated out workers by race, deliberately targeting Latinos for apprehension. Recognizing the obvious racism in this act and viscerally understanding racism themselves, many Black employees worked diligently in the coming weeks and months to find the families of those arrested and raise funds to support them, aided in their work by MIRA in what would become a crucial steppingstone in the organization's history.

A red state steeped in a history of racial strife, Mississippi in 2019 may have seemed like a place that would pose little resistance for aggressive Trump administration immigration policies. But what the Trump administration and broader media coverage missed is that events like these raids often serve as flashpoints, sparking activism, advocacy, and coalition-building that can change the face of politics. Thus, public discussions of the raids centered on communities suddenly, dramatically, and unexpectedly at the mercy of a power structure disinclined to protect people of color. In other words, when racism and discrimination have publicly targeted immigrants in Mississippi, such as during the 2008 and 2019 raids, African Americans have deepened their commitment to immigrant rights, growing an influential movement with real political power.

On August 8, 2019, MIRA held a press conference on the raids at the NAACP headquarters in Mississippi. They did so in collaboration with faith-based organizations, the ACLU, the United Food and Commercial Workers, the Southern Poverty Law Center, and others, with the goal of announcing their next steps. Bill Chandler, flanked by a multiracial coalition of organizers across the state, opened the press conference by introducing Nsombi Lambright of the NAACP's One Voice project. After lamenting the terrible impact of the raids, Lambright said, "It's crucial that we start organizing and mobilizing all of our organizations, groups, and churches in solidarity. . . . We want to show Mississippi that there is a strong, *strong*, statewide organizing component, ready to address these issues, and these tragedies, as they happen. . . . We are here to let everyone around the world know that we are going to fight back and make sure that these families are supported."[29] For more than an hour, organizers, clergy, families, and neighbors highlighted the importance of solidarity and unity in the pursuit of justice and social change. This was not a call for tolerance. This was a call for action. As veteran Civil Rights leader, former state legislator, and MIRA co-founder Jim Evans put it, "No más." As this story makes clear, the Trump administration's attacks on immigrants did not stymie the civil rights movement's embrace of immigrants; it furthered that embrace.

While Mississippi established itself as an early leader in the new civil rights coalition, these developments are happening nationally. Organizations around the country have recognized that the lexicon of civil rights can be used to frame and build broad minority coalitions. These state and national organizations have taken a cue from Mississippi to initiate similar changes within their own networks. Thus, for example, hundreds of immigrant rights organizations from across the country gathered in the early months of the 2016 presidential campaign "to build a deeper understanding of institutional racism, and white supremacy, strategizing on how to dismantle it in our local communities and institutions and actively work to build solidarity between the immigrant rights movement and the #blacklivesmatter movement," as the Alabama Coalition for Immigrant Justice (ACIJ) put it.[30]

One need not look far to see evidence of these efforts. The ACIJ joined forces with the Birmingham Black Lives Matter chapter to compel the city of Birmingham to declare itself a sanctuary for all and to commit to police reforms that would broadly reduce mass incarceration, including immigration enforcement. In North Carolina, immigrant rights groups organized with the NAACP and local Black organizations to provide sanctuary to undocumented immigrants in local churches, often drawing parallels between mass incarceration and immigration enforcement as racialized practices of family separation. Mijente, a Phoenix-based immigrant rights organization, has been organizing communities toward avowedly pro-Black policy and electoral outcomes.

Civil rights and immigration groups have also coordinated joint campaigns to replace local sheriffs known for racially targeting Black and

Latino residents. In 2018, immigrant and civil rights organizations in North Carolina successfully campaigned to elect progressive Black sheriffs in five of the state's largest counties, each of whom ran on a promise to limit local cooperation with ICE.

Immigrant rights organizations and Black-led racial justice organizations have teamed up to press for local, regional, and national change, but a series of events in 2020 further amplified their national significance. During months of isolation and death due to the slipshod response to the COVID-19 global pandemic, a young man by the name of George Floyd was murdered in the process of being detained by police, tipping off an unprecedented country-wide series of protests demanding justice, structural changes in law enforcement, including calls to abolish the police, and a real and sustainable commitment to protecting Black lives and eradicating anti-Black racism. This new iteration of the Movement for Black Lives emerged just as the Abolish ICE movement hit the mainstream. Responding to the Trump administration's efforts to restrict refugee admissions, engage in mass deportations, and turn a blind eye to, or in some cases, facilitate ongoing abuses in detention centers, citizens and activists across the country called for the end of ICE as we know it.[31]

Painfully conscious of the connections between Black and Brown marginalization, this contemporary abolition movement has issued broad calls for the liberation of Black and Brown people and an end to white supremacy and racism. Nationally there have been numerous protests calling on the United States to abolish its detention centers, end deportations, stop the policing of its minority communities, and increase political participation among Black and Brown residents.

These calls have echoed across the nation as activists have made abundantly clear that "police brutality is a Black and Brown issue, a poor people's issue."[32] A recent poll conducted by the *New York Times* and Siena College found that nearly 21% of Latino voters said that they participated in Black Lives Matter protests, which is nearly identical to the percentage of Black voters (22%) who did so. This assertion of a shared stance against anti-Blackness and for Black liberation underpins advocates' joint calls to abolish ICE and to abolish the police. As

Silky Shah, executive director of Detention Watch Network, explained, ICE and the police are "built on the same foundation of racism and white supremacy."[33] In Phoenix, activists made the connection overt, marching wearing masks stamped with the message, "Defund the PolICE", with the last three letters marked in red to emphasize ICE— Immigration and Customs Enforcement.[34] As if to confirm these claims, police worked in cooperation with ICE at these very protests, taking protesters into custody in violation of the agency's guidelines.

As this new world of activism builds across the nation, MIRA continues to sustain its work in coalition- and community-building, from actively participating in Black Lives Matter protests to advocating for removing confederate symbols from the Mississippi state flag. MIRA's advocacy work has long been consistent with the values of the abolition movement. As MIRA organizer Melinda Medina noted in 2018, "Policies and programs that exclude, detain, segregate and physically remove immigrants are products of institutionalized racism created by our country and feed racial inequality. We must stop the detention and deportation of immigrants which tears families apart a[nd] harm[s] all our communities."[35]

Conclusion

In recent years, some politicians have used anti-Black racism and xenophobia to stoke fears around demographic change and shifting power relations, drumming up widespread support for a political agenda that continues to marginalize African Americans and immigrants. New coalitions of immigration and civil rights activists recognize the white supremacy inherent in these policies and in their shared oppression. Based on this recognition, they have increasingly engaged in strategic and collaborative efforts to build a new consensus that immigration is fundamentally a civil rights issue.

This trend is particularly visible in the South, with its long and storied history as a civil rights battleground and its ongoing policies of racial exclusion, which continue to target both African Americans and immigrant newcomers. In places like Mississippi, civil rights and immigrant organizations are working together to shift both activist and public understandings of civil rights to a more expansive definition inclusive of the struggles experienced by immigrants. By recasting civil rights as a broad set of challenges to any effort to marginalize and exclude nonwhite peoples, activists have created a new discursive organizing framework to guide future struggles.

Not only are today's activist organizations offering a historical corrective to the division between civil rights and immigration, but they are also promoting a redefinition of immigrant rights as central to the broader goals of the contemporary civil rights movement and newer racial justice movements. For them, the language of civil rights (as well as abolition) may have particular utility in articulating a framework of political change and strategic alliance in the South—a region whose contemporary racial struggles play out in the broad shadow of its racial past.

This coalition-building has not been without its challenges, but these coalitions have been successful both in reshaping actions around immigrant rights and in civil rights advocacy more generally. Black civil rights groups such as the SCLC and the NAACP have also come to identify parallels between the exclusion of noncitizens from the polity and the institutional racism facing African Americans. Broad coalitions have formed in places like Georgia, where Stacey Abrams and others brought together a coalition of activists and advocates, including the Georgia NAACP, Mijente, Southerners on New Ground, and others under the Fair Fight umbrella. In so doing, they united Black and Brown Georgians and their allies, effectively reshaping the outcome of the 2020 elections by sending two Democratic senators from Georgia to Washington in a historic runoff election win.

These outcomes suggest that coalitions built around shared struggle can be highly effective, not only in securing electoral victories, but expanding conceptions of sanctuary and abolition to mean safety and freedom from state-sanctioned violence against all marginalized communities. Efforts by activists in organizations such as Mijente to expand sanctuary city ordinances to include freedom from over policing and surveillance, as well as to make investments in community institutions that serve to provide safety and support for all marginalized people, are evidence of this work. Just as the sanctuary movement traces its origins to the Underground Railroad and efforts to protect slaves from fugitive slave laws, as Naomi Paik notes, "As the multitudinous attacks on indigenous land and life ways, immigrants, Muslims, Jews, women, people of colour, and queer and gender non-conforming people show, the new administration is fortifying the violence tying our fates together and highlighting the urgent need for a multitudinous front of struggle. A radical sanctuary depends on mobilizing these connections that the state has already made and the Trump administration seeks to thicken."[36] A collective recognition of the histories of exclusion and marginalization as distinct but connected serves to build a stronger ideological foundation for the work of making a more just and equitable America. New narratives that continue to recognize those historical and structural truths are essential to make change.

Notes

1. See Tom Crawford, "Tough Immigration Law Hurts Georgia Agriculture," *Augusta Chronicle*, December 21, 2011, 4; Richard Fausset, "Alabama Enacts Anti-Illegal-Immigration Law Described as Nation's Strictest," *Los Angeles Times*, June 10, 2011. http://articles.latimes.com/2011/jun/10/nation/la-na-alabama-immigration-20110610; Monica Varsanyi, *Taking Local Control: Immigration Policy Activism in U.S. Cities and States* (Palo Alto, CA: Stanford University Press, 2010).
2. Heather Travar, "Oppose House Bill 318," North Carolina NAACP, September 28, 2015, http://www.naacpnc.org/oppose_house_bill_318.
3. United States, Supreme Court, *Brown v. Board of Education*, May 17, 1954, *Legal Information Institute*, Cornell University Law School, www.law.cornell.edu/supremecourt/text/347/483.
4. Louise Seamster and Victor Ray, "Against Teleology in the Study of Race: Toward the Abolition of the Progress Paradigm," *Sociological Theory* 36, no. 4 (2018): 315–42.
5. Lucas Guttentag, "The Forgotten Equality Norm in Immigration Preemption: Discrimination, Harassment, and the Civil Rights Act of 1870," *Duke Journal of Constitutional Law & Public Policy* 8, no. 1 (2013); Erika Lee, "American Gatekeeping: Race and Immigration Law in the 20th Century," in *Not Just Black and White*, ed. N. Foner and G. M. Fredrickson, 119–44 (New York: Russell Sage Foundation, 2004); Mae M. Ngai, "The Architecture of Race in American Immigration Law: A Reexamination of the Immigration Act of 1924," *Journal of American History* 86, no. 1 (1999): 67–92.

6. Matthew Frye Jacobson, *Whiteness of a Different Color: European Immigrants and the Alchemy of Race* (Cambridge, MA: Harvard University Press, 1999); Erika Lee, "The Chinese Exclusion Example: Race, Immigration, and American Gatekeeping, 1882–1924," *Journal of American Ethnic History* 21, no. 3 (2002): 36–62; Natalia Molina, *Fit to Be Citizens? Public Health and Race in Los Angeles, 1879–1939* (Berkeley: University of California Press, 2006).

7. Kevin R. Johnson, "The Intersection of Race and Class in U.S. Immigration Law and Enforcement," *Law and Contemporary Problems* 72, no. 4 (2009): 1–35.

8. Douglas S. Massey and Karen A. Pren, "Origins of the New Latino Underclass," *Race and Social Problems* 4, no. 1 (2012): 5–17.

9. Amada Armenta, "From Sheriff's Deputies to Immigration Officers: Screening Immigrant Status in a Tennessee Jail." *Law and Policy* 34, no. 2 (2012): 191–201; Douglas S. Massey and R. Magaly Sanchez, *Brokered Boundaries: Creating Immigrant Identity in Anti-Immigrant Times* (New York: Russell Sage Foundation, 2010).

10. Louise A. Cainkar, *Homeland Insecurity: The Arab American and Muslim American Experience After 9/11* (New York: Russell Sage Foundation, 2011).

11. Daniel J. Hopkins, "Politicized Places: Explaining Where and When Immigrants Provoke Local Opposition," *American Political Science Review* 104, no. 1 (2010): 40–60; Varsanyi, *Taking Local Control*.

12. Jennifer A. Jones, *The Browning of the New South* (Chicago: University of Chicago Press, 2019).

13. Vicki Cintra, "Oral History with Vicki Cintra," University of Southern Mississippi, Center for Oral History and Cultural Heritage, 2006, http://www.usm.edu/oral-history.

14. Hana E. Brown, Zhongze Wei, Michelle Lazaran, Christopher Cates, and Jennifer A. Jones, "Rebuilding without Papers: Disaster Migration and the Local Reception of Immigrants after Hurricane Katrina," *Social Currents* 10, no. 2 (2023): 121–41.

15. Bill Chandler, interview by Jennifer A. Jones, July 28, 2014.

16. Hana E. Brown, "Refugees, Rights, and Race: How Legal Status Shapes Immigrants' Relationship with the State," *Social Problems* 58, no. 1 (2011): 144–63; Hana E. Brown, "Race, Legality, and the Social Policy Consequences of Anti-Immigrant Mobilization," *American Sociological Review* 78, no. 2 (2013): 290–314; Lynn Fujiwara, "Immigrant Rights Are Human Rights: The Reframing of Immigrant Entitlement and Welfare," *Social Problems* 52, no. 1 (2005): 79–101; Kim Voss and Irene Bloemraad, *Rallying for Immigrant Rights: The Fight for Inclusion in 21st-Century America* (Berkeley: University of California Press, 2011).

17. MIRA, "Newsletter: *Mira en Acción*," Mississippi Immigrant Rights Alliance, Jackson, MS, Aug./Sept. 2010, 1.

18. Riva Brown, "Path to Citizenship," *Clarion Ledger*, September 28, 2003.

19. Sid Salter, "Sid Salter," *Clarion Ledger*, April 5, 2006.

20. David Hampton, "Arizona Law Is Nothing to Copy," *Clarion Ledger*, July 17, 2010.

21. Elizabeth Crisp, "Miss. Officials Eye Immigration Policy," *Clarion Ledger*, July 12, 2010.

22. Bill Minore, "Straw Man, Once Black, Now Brown," *Sun Herald*, September 14, 2007.
23. David Hampton, "Sunday Morning with Lois Patricia Ice," *Clarion Ledger*, March 30, 2008.
24. MIRA, "Newsletter: *Mira en Acción*," Mississippi Immigrants Rights Alliance, Jackson, MS, Feb. 2009, 5.
25. Alisha Johnson, "3rd Annual Unity Conference Joins Civil Rights and Immigrant Rights Leaders," "Newsletter: *Mira en Acción*," November 2008, 3.
26. MIRA, "Newsletter: *Mira en Acción*," Mississippi Immigrants Rights Alliance, Jackson, MS, Feb. 2010, 6.
27. MIRA, "Unity Conference a Huge Success," private collection, Mississippi Immigrant Rights Alliance, Jackson, MS, 2013.
28. Bill Chandler, interview by Jennifer A. Jones, July 28, 2014, Jackson, MS.
29. Speech at press conference, August 8, 2019, Jackson, MS.
30. ACIJ, "In Solidarity with The Gulf South on the 10th Anniversary of Hurricane Katrina," Email Newsletter, Alabama Coalition for Immigrant Justice, August 28, 2015.
31. A. Naomi Paik, *Bans, Walls, Raids, Sanctuary: Understanding U.S. Immigration for the Twenty-First Century* (Berkeley: University of California Press, 2020).
32. Jennifer Medina, "Latinos Back Black Lives Matter Protests. They Want Change for Themselves, Too," *New York Times*, July 3, 2020.
33. Nicole Narea, "How 'Abolish ICE' Protests Brought 'Abolish the Police' into the Mainstream," *Vox*, July 9, 2020.
34. Narea, "'Abolish ICE' Protests."
35. MIRA, "MIRA Organizer Melinda Medina Speaks as Part of Poor People's Campaign Rally in Jackson, MS," private collection, Mississippi Immigrant Rights Alliance, Jackson, MS, 2018.
36. A. Naomi Paik, "Abolitionist Futures and the US Sanctuary Movement," *Race & Class* 59, no. 2 (2017): 3–25, 18.

CHAPTER 21

Story-Walking toward Liveable Futures

Jill Anderson and Maggie Loredo

This chapter is a new weaving with threads from the introduction that we co-wrote for the second edition of the book *Lxs Otrxs Dreamers*, available for digital download or print on demand at the website http://lxsotrxsdreamers.oda mexico.org.

The stories of migration and (inter)national borders are intentionally managed, over-simplified, and impoverished within racialized nationalism, capitalism, and colonialism. Not only do we need new narratives, we need a new approach to narrative itself. For example, the Dreamer / American Dream narrative has been practiced to create people power and access to rights, but it has also been fueled by the same system of oppression that continues to reproduce by amplifying the stories of the good, deserving, successful, and individualized immigrant as preferable to the "bad" or expendable immigrants. In this chapter, we re-trace our strategies to step away from the systemic consequences of stories being adapted and managed to sustain oppression. We have lived into evolving and dynamic collective narrative practices in order to hold space for complexity, contradiction, and deep listening. Our collective organizing intertwines with these narrative practices in order to evade and disrupt the repercussions of oppressive systems of meaning-making that seek to co-opt and distort our collective power and vision.

We met in the context of crafting a story, or rather an anthology of stories, called *Los Otros Dreamers* (2014, 2021).[1] Jill, as postdoctoral fellow, voluntary immigrant to Mexico, US-born citizen, white woman in her 30s, Maggie, as young person, forced returnee to Mexico, undocumented in Georgia, *morena* woman in her 20s. We met because Jill was working on a book of photos and stories with photographer Nin Solis, which became *Los Otros Dreamers*, and Maggie was one of several young people who were eager to be heard from the alienation of post return. The beginnings of our friendship were steeped in the unequal power dynamics of our lives and systems. Eight years later our friendship has evolved and continues to evolve within this mesh of privilege and oppression, hurt and healing, learning and unlearning, to support one another with our personal and shared powers to co-create.

When Maggie first came out as a returnee in Mexico and shared her story in public, she felt it as liberating. But later on, it started to feel uncomfortable. Many in the book narrated their stories while still living them in their bodies—living the trauma of deportation, of forced return, of detention and jail, of separation, of isolation, and of exile. It was not easy to share something that has always been intended to be very personal. Often the public perceives forced migrants as victims, or, in the best-case scenarios, as heroes, congratulating them for bravery instead of hearing the collective demands we shared in the book. It was and is exhausting.

The narrative around "Dreamers" to which the book title alludes was also (re)traumatizing for many who participated in the project. We have learned to be very wary when we sense the imposition of One Big Story to explain and obscure our multiplicities, diversities, complexities, tensions, and interconnections. The narrative about "Dreamers" is an example of how toxic even a people-built story can become when it is used as the One Big Story to obscure our many lived realities and relationships. In Mexico, the term "Dreamers," or Soñadores, has been used with little context and in a way that shadows all of the different experiences and needs that deported and returned people face upon arrival to Mexico.

And yet, in reclaiming spaces and speaking stories aloud, showing up alongside one another, insisting on being heard, we create possibilities for collective and individual healing. The Collective of Narrative Practices teaches that a consequence of a generalized simplification of stories is that we have lost our capacity to uphold complexity.[2] Our realities become dichotomous and have little space to shelter difference and nuance. We have a multiplicity of stories in our lives, in which we have the capacity of sheltering big complexities, big enough that they can even contradict each other. As Nin Solis suggests through her photography for the book, return migration is situated in forests that have been growing for hundreds of years, a damp towel just hung to dry, or the corn planted before arrival and harvested in the confusing aftermath. Similarly, the ways we narrate our lives are in constant movement, and our stories must grow and change along with us.

Maggie came across Narrative Practices in Mexico City and has brought this framework to how we understand our work and our impact. She attended an introductory workshop by the Collective of Narrative Practices that sparked her curiosity and offered the tools to explore her story as part of a collective *tejido*. She started to make sense of the narrative metaphor as a way for her to understand the complexity of stories and the possibilities of reflecting on them. Maggie started to explore the effects that her story was having in the way she related with herself, with others, with her territories, with the way she articulated her experiences of growing up undocumented in Georgia and then living in Mexico. She began to see the ways her story was framed within many other stories—stories that included her skin color, her gender, her sexuality, her class, her age, her nationality, her schooling, and her family. By using Narrative Practices, Maggie found that she could tell her story on her own terms from a place of dignity to re-signify the collective power within the stories of illegalized immigration, deportation, and forced return. The injustice and pain that her family and other families continue to endure across borders encourage her and others to continue to be loud, to take up space, to organize, and to use storytelling as one of the most powerful tools that we have to fight back.

In this brief chapter, we would like to share the new narratives about migration, borders, and US/Mexican national identities that are rising up out of our ongoing mutual commitment and learning, as well as two key principles we have learned from the many story-walkers who have come before us: (1) Many stories are always more true than One Story; a "master narrative" always includes a "master" seeking to control the truths, and often the bodies, of others. (2) True stories are embodied and must never travel far beyond those who told them and hold them, even in print, and especially when mobility is being denied. Narrative must be lived, practiced.

This is a lineage of our own story-telling practice and our ongoing search for collective narratives that help us make sense of the experience of deportation and forced return as lived in organized community. We begin with the multi-voiced story of "Los Otros Dreamers" in 2014, out of which we practice another story: "Visa Justice." From there we move to the transgressive story of "Pocha House" in 2018 and then, in 2019, into the story of "Florecer Aquí y Allá," an explicit action to inhabit new narratives of mobility and migration that feels safer than the toxic narratives of "immigration as threat" or "immigration as being saved from third world conditions." Both of these stories are perpetuated by US and Mexican governments and media, and we do not see ourselves or our communities in them. Our Narrative Practices are processes for naming new forms of community (a new "we")— processes of becoming our many-storied selves in relation to one another.

Los Otros Dreamers

Los Otros Dreamers was and is an iterative process, growing and evolving as we've met people and learned more. It is a combination of art, research, and social justice written for a growing bilingual, bicultural audience. The book bears witness to trauma and resilience in the face of immigration policies that have separated families for generations. In the telling and the re-telling, that all-too-familiar "ni de aquí, ni de allá" experience begins to sound a more resonant clamor for belonging and justice "aquí y allá." And now, growing at the pace of trust, this book has evolved into a place, a practice, and a community.

This iterative approach began with the ways Jill and Nin imagined, co-created, and launched the book. Although it wasn't in the budget at first, money was found to pay Indigenous translators in order to include the languages of those who are multilingual: Saúl Rojas Martínez, Rufino Sántiz, and Virgina Pérez. When Claudia Amaro returned to her hometown in Kansas with the Dream9 in the historic Bring Them Home actions, she updated her story, and then Nin went to Kansas. The return after the return. Finally, as the book launch neared, Nin and Jill decided that they couldn't inaugurate the book without everyone there. Teaming up with Maru Ponce, Daniel Arenas, and others, they invited each contributor to come to Mexico City for the weekend of the book launch, all expenses paid. On September 27, 2014, the independent publication was launched with an overflow crowd at the Museum of Mexico City.

It was a whir of exuberant connection. It was also the first time Maggie and I met and that Maggie met other contributors in person. For many, it was the first time they had met others who shared the formative experience of growing up undocumented in the United States and then having to return to Mexico for myriad reasons. The community organizing took many paths, and life-long friendships were forged that weekend.

The fight to end deportations under Obama, also known as the "Deporter-in-Chief," was led by many Dreamers, to whom the title of the book alludes. A brief history lesson: the term "Dreamer" comes from a legislative proposal, the Dream Act, which was first introduced in 2001 and originally consisted of a pathway to citizenship for those who were brought to the United States as children. In the "Dream Act" struggle, "Dreamers" were engaging actively as citizens in a society that still refuses to recognize them as full-fledged members with equal access to rights and opportunities. Although the Dream Act was never passed, and Deferred Action for Childhood Arrivals (DACA) continues

Photos from Nin Solis's photographic archive for the book. Mexico City, 2014.
Credit: Nin Solis

to be precarious and under threat, these young people went on to create United We Dream, the Undocumented and Unafraid campaign, the National Immigrant Youth Alliance (NIYA), and hundreds of important, local community-based organizations. The first edition of this book evolved out of this hopeful but fraught context in which young immigrants were effective in changing US public narrative and public policy.

But for the estimated two million men, women, and children whom immigration policies and the global economic crisis of 2007–2008 forced out of the United States—a majority of Mexican origin—the aftermath of deportation and return was felt to be an afterthought, if considered at all. They were the others, los otros: young people who had also grown up in the United States without papers and who were now on the other side of the border. About half of the people who shared their stories of deportation and return for this book would have qualified for DACA had they still been in the United States when it was announced in 2012. Maggie is one of them. The other half would have never qualified for DACA, or any version of the proposed Dream Act, given their criminal record. Several contributors to the book describe the ways that affiliation with gangs, run-ins with US law enforcement, and drug use were a part of their coming of age too. Racism overlapped with criminalization in their towns and cities.

The title, the overarching story, of the first edition was meant as a response to the movement for and by Dreamers in the United States: regardless of which side of the border you are on, regardless of your criminal history or educational achievements, growing up in a place gives you as much a claim to belonging as being born into one. Due to economic and immigration policies since 1994, an entire generation of immigrant children has been caught in the crucible of growing up in the United States with no path to legal residency or citizenship. Those who have been "othered"—that is, removed and excluded in prisons and across borders—have key insights to contribute to the struggle for justice. "Los Otros Dreamers," as a title, was meant to interrupt and complicate the merit-based definition of a Dreamer that was solidified by DACA in 2012. Looking back, it is clear that much more than the title, the physical presence of those telling their stories was and is the most disruptive force.

The stories of *Los Otros Dreamers* continue to evolve and shift as others respond and tell their own stories. In 2021, we decided to change the title to Lxs Otrxs Dreamers (Les Otres Dreamers) to reflect gender diversity and other radical forms of knowing, being, and relating. In this way and more, the book continues to be an invitation to tell one's story of deportation and return on one's own terms. But whereas the first edition was primarily a tool for awareness-raising and solidarity-building, the second edition has a more intimate and transformational purpose: inviting people who have experienced forced migration to craft and listen and hold their stories alongside others who have also experienced forced migration. These stories are less available for public consumption, and yet more available for personal connection and collective healing.

Visa Justice

The lived experience of insisting on visas and mobility for the book con-tributors was the most challenging and the most radical impulse behind the book. ODA, Otros Dreams en Acción—a community-based organization in Mexico that is dedicated to translocal political action and mutual support by and for deported and returning migrants—was born out of the struggle for "mobility for all" that we began with the book tour. This is a new narrative too—one that sits in uneasy but in-timate contradiction with the US-based immigrant rights movements for papers and citizenship, the equally powerful and necessary narra-tive that illegalized immigrants are "Here to Stay." The embodied sto-ries of "Visa Justice"—stories of forced migration, illegalization, and criminalization reframed as demands for the universal right to safe and dignified movement across borders—lift up a struggle that is often perceived as secondary to or rendered invisible by the struggle for asylum or the struggle for citizenship.

In September 2015, Maggie received an email from Jill inviting her to go with her to California and present the book. She needed to apply for a B1/B2 visa, a painful and emotional process. At that time Maggie was a college student earning a monthly income of 3,000 pesos (~US$150) working at a fast-food restaurant in San Luis Potosí, and with strong ties to the United States. On October 7, she traveled to Mexico City to attend the interview at the United States Embassy, lo-cated a few feet away from the Ángel de la Independencia monument in Paseo de la Reforma. The whole process lasted just one hour and the interview itself didn't take more than 15 minutes. She was told that her visa had been approved for a period of 10 years. Immediately after those words the agent warned her of the consequences of overstaying her visa and also that her parents would never have a chance to go back if they applied. She was right: her mother never went back to meet her grand-kids or hug her son one last time.

ODA has continued to document, accompany, and organize with over 40 people to insist on their right for mobility through applying for B1/B2 nonimmigrant visas. Academic institutions, nonprofit organizations, collectives, and individuals across the United States have supported ODA by allocating resources to organize educational and advocacy delegation groups. During our delegation group trips across the United States we have participated in different spaces to bring awareness of our collective work in Mexico, but also to engage with undocumented and DACA-mented families, students, and youth to discuss our perceptions of mobility, exile, and citizenship.

When people discuss immigration and border issues there is a sense of disconnection from the multiple realities, effects, and consequences that policies such as the Immigration and Nationality Act (INA) and the Illegal Immigration Reform and Immigration Responsibility Act (IIRIRA) have on people's lives. Under current US consular policies, applicants must overcome the presumption of guilt, of lying, of being an "intending immigrant" in order to receive a temporary visa to travel. If applicants have not overcome this burden, it means there is immigrant intent. If a consular officer has any concern or prejudice, they deny the visa application by default. This is an arbitrary and unfair process. In Mexico (prior to COVID), the approval rate at US embassies fluctuated between 60% and 70%. Embassies and consulate offices do not have official visa approval limits, but there is a certain pressure to fit within the general curve among officers. Having a 100% approval rate on any given day is frowned upon.

In the case of returned or deported people after having lived in the United States without documents, often as children, it is clear that their experience of growing up undocumented in the United States and of having family ties there is considered a strong reason for rejection, even after 10 years of successfully establishing a life in their country of origin. In fact, many receive an automatic 10-year bar for any unlawful presence accumulated after a year upon turning 18 years old. Often, people who were forced to return due to the threat of deportation or the deportation of a family member are unaware of this situation until applying for a B1/B2 visa and being completely honest about the experience living without documents in the United States.

Visa Justice has become a demand and search for mobility for all. We are here to hold this country accountable for its implementation

Poster for the April 2022 Visa Justice delegation and campaign that resulted in two people gaining mobility and two people being denied. Mexico City, April 2022. *Credit*: Areli Rema

and toleration of pre–civil rights practices in the form of consular policy across the globe. The rest of our community members who have previously been issued visas also continue to face the abuse of discretionary power, racial profiling, and criminalization at every port of entry to the United States. The targeting of our people doesn't end with just a visa. There is a lot more to keep doing in order to dismantle the systems that oppress, exclude, and dehumanize us. People born with automatic international mobility might never understand—their bodies will never feel what we feel every day. The sleepless nights, the sweaty hands, the tension that transitions into numbness and nauseous and collective anger upon once again experiencing the rampant, indisputable bias and prejudice that racialize and discriminate against certain applicant pools.

Pocha House

Two upside-down flags—one with the stars and stripes of the United States and the other with the eagle and snake of Mexico—hang above the small crowd gathering around the migrant poets who are reclaiming poetry slam in the aftermath of deportation and return. Santiago and Lalo painted those two flags on the white plastic mesh sacks that Immigration and Customs Enforcement agents use to return some, and often not all, of the belongings of the people they detain. In the middle of the upside-down flags, two hands are painted in black with birds flying from their fingertips. Later Guillermo would add a black bow in memory of our *compañero* José Delgado, who died only three months after his deportation due to the binational policies that made his life expendable. Under these flags our poetry slam unrolls in three languages: *español* rooted and finding roots, a Spanglish that delights in itself and owns its *poder*, and the English of first loves and a knowing sense of humor. Indigenous languages such as Ajuuk and Nahuatl have also filled the mic. All our languages are interwoven into poems inflected with liberation and pain and loss and deep recognition.

The community named our alternative cultural space in a reappropriation of the derogatory term *pocho/a* used in Mexican Spanish to describe a person of Mexican origin who seems somehow less Mexican due to the influence of experiences and time spent in the United States. Leni Álvarez, active member of the ODA community, and others held in-person forums and launched informal surveys across Facebook groups in order to name our new space. Deported and returning youth, along with many others on both sides of the border, are reclaiming the word *pocho/a*. Even in the midst of a pandemic, Pocha House became the living sequel of *Los Otros Dreamers* (2014, 2021), and it has created a bigger story than the Dreamer narrative because multiple identities, trajectories, and immigration experiences can co-exist in meaningful, and transgressive, connection.

Pocha House disrupts all dominant narratives of the deported and forcibly returned community in Mexico. It is an alternative *espacio cultural*; a safe-brave space in constant construction; a community in flux; a resource for support, information, connection, and expression; and a *fuente* for transformation (as opposed to integration into the status quo).

Pocha House has changed literally and metaphorically since 2018, from one room on the third floor of a storage building in downtown Mexico City to a two-story house in the heart of Roma Norte, an internationally gentrified neighborhood. Many of our community members live in the outskirts of the city. In Pocha House, the peripheral is al-

Walking and workshopping in Pocha House. Mexico City, May 2022.
Credit: Jeff Valenzuela

ways remapping the center. Now, Pocha House is our space to continue to defy those norms of centralization and gentrification through spoken word, dance, embroidery, film murals, radical love, and collective care.

From the narrative practices of Pocha House and *Los Otros Dreamers*, we have come together to transform trauma, injustice, and alienation into a multiplicity of stories. We have reclaimed the way we want to tell and retell our stories through multiple artistic and narrative projects:

- El Deportee, a deported spoken word artist and filmmaker who grew up in the mountains of Heber City, Utah, and was born in Juárez, Chihuahua. He tells stories of the deported, houseless, exiled, and those separated from community and family.
- Mujer de Tepexpan, a returned young woman who grew up undocumented in Houston, Texas, and now lives in the periphery of Mexico City. She does paste up and street art to tell her

story and the stories of women who constantly experience gender violence and risk being victims of feminicide.

- Deported Artist, a formerly incarcerated man from Oakland, California, and now living in Tijuana, tells his story through artwork and defies the border every day by going against all odds to keep being a family in the midst of their separation.
- Diary of a Native Foreigner is a digital platform created by former DACA recipients who returned to San Luis Potosí because of the exhaustion of always having to live their lives in fear.
- GDL SUR, an organization in Guadalajara, consists of formerly incarcerated, gang-affiliated men who are deported and struggle with drug and alcohol abuse. They tell their stories through their Chicano culture to show that they can also rebuild their lives, deserve second chances, and still belong to their families and communities.
- *Pochas So What*, a podcast that disrupts the notion of borders and of identities, serves as another platform for them to share their stories, the stories of their families and communities from their experiences as two women.
- Lorenzo's Calihtec Restaurant and Art Gallery is a restaurant and art gallery located in Canoa, Puebla, owned by a Nahua/ Tlaxcalteca returned woman who grew up in South Central Los Angeles. Her project is the result of a lot of work, family, and community support and it's a place that continues to tell and uplift her and her community's stories.

These are just a few of the new or lesser known lived-in-stories that have risen up in the aftermath of deportation and forced return. This is not a complete or exhaustive list. There are many of us organizing and making meaning in and around Pocha House. We can and do contradict each other, we can and do complicate each other's stories, *and* we can and do insist on solidarity and community. We insist on narratives that are big enough to hold us all.

Florecer Aquí y Allá

We were co-creating our Pocha House space the same year as the first exodus (or as some call "caravan") from Central America started their journey into México and toward the United States. Migration from El Salvador, Honduras and Guatemala, as well as from many other countries, wasn't something new. The innovative strategy that many couldn't grasp was that oppressed people, most of brown and black skin tones, who were living in extreme poor conditions, threatened by gangs, all rooted in United States interventions and in collaboration with México, had started to organize and to move together as a strong wave that was transformed everywhere it passed through. Their first-person, loud voices demanded an end to the conditions that for decades have forced them out of their towns and countries. Young and elderly, men, women, queer, children, and youth were fiercely organizing and hoping to better their lives or at the very least preserve them.

There were many stories told about this exodus—some more amplified or more mainstream than others—but they all had a clear intention of dismantling and minimizing the self-determination and collective organizing of the exodus. There was also another narrative that criminalized those who put their bodies in the frontlines to observe, denounce, and respond to government inaction and state violence through actions of solidarity and mutual aid. In ODA, we responded alongside with other organized groups in Mexico City and in the midst of all the violence, the trauma, the devastating conditions, and injustice, we also saw crowds coming together to strategize and organize. Migrant communities were taking to the streets, using cameras, and speaking up because this was the only thing they had left to survive. We heard in their prayers a determination to resist and to flourish alongside their families and communities *aquí y allá*. We recognized and felt kinship with the Caravans.

So, in the summer of 2019, we organized an artistic and musical action that positioned migration as a struggle that goes beyond borders and involves all of us, migrants and non-migrants. We named it "Florecer Aquí y Allá," or Flourishing Here and There. It was a call to action in support of public policies that strengthen the right to migrate and not to migrate. It was trans-local, with simultaneous actions in 14 other cities across the continent. It was an intervention that centered the voices of organized migrants, naming the right not only to survive but also to flourish. Florecer Aquí y Allá also allowed us to announce our alternative vision and vocabulary as immigrants. In San Pedro Sula, Honduras, in San Marcos, Guatemala, in Chiapas, Queretaro, Oaxaca, Tijuana, and Mexico City in México, and in Tacoma, Los Angeles, Phoenix, Chicago, Atlanta, Staten Island, and New York City in the United States, we joined together across borders to name and echo the conditions we all demand for our *buen vivir*, the right to live with dignity.

That day, the main square of Mexico City, known as the Zócalo, was dressed in yellow and green. Over 3,000 deportees, returnees, refugees, allies, volunteers, attendees, and passers-by came together, at one point crowding under the big tent as a summer downpour rained around us. The artist Emily C-D co-created with us a stunning 50-foot-wide mandala made of seeds that had six translocal demands: Families Belong Together, Diverse Communities, People before Papers, Safety and Inclusion, Education and Jobs, Abolish Migrant Detention. Six minimum conditions that we all need in order to flourish in our countries of origin and in the communities we join throughout our migration journeys. A seventh condition, Climate Justice and the importance of defending our territories, arose as an overarching message of the artistic action evoked by the corn, beans, and rice making up the mandala. The deported and returned community voiced these conditions through songs, poems, storytelling, and performances, and we were all interconnected across Honduras, Guatemala, El Salvador, México, and the United States.

Florecer Aquí y Allá was a celebration, a demand for the building blocks for dignity, and to demonstrate the power of trans-local organizing. But it was also a tribute to Stephani, a 10-year-old girl who died while held in a Mexico City immigration detention center with her mother a few weeks before the action, and to José Delgado, a recently deported community member, mentioned earlier, who died only three months after his deportation and less than two weeks before our action.

Fifty-foot-diameter mandala made from beans, corn, rice, and painted canvas. Created by Emily C-D in collaboration with ODA. Mexico City, July 2019. *Credit*: Emily C-D

Stephani and Don José didn't have to die. Their passing was the direct result of the deportation machine, of the negligence of nation-states, of a system that needs to be demolished.

We learned more than we ever wanted to know about the deadliness of the multinational deportation regime while accompanying José in his return to México. Mexican consular agents defied José's US-citizen children and his community's wishes when they facilitated his deportation in the midst of chronic kidney failure that required weekly dialysis. José found us as his cash was running out, and he could not figure out how to cover his next dialysis treatment, the only thing that would keep him alive. ODA jumped into action. We helped with his application for his official ID (known as the INE), which was initially denied because it seemed "suspicious" to the government worker that José was born in Michoacán but was applying in Mexico City. We talked to our contacts in the Secretaría de Relaciones Exteriores and the Secretaría de Salud about his dire situation, and we tried to follow the paper trail as to why he was not receiving government care.

In the wake of the inertia and lack of answers on the part of the government, we called on our solidarity networks for donations and contacts with medical professionals willing to provide life-saving treatment at a discount. He was receiving regular dialysis at no cost from Médica Santa Carmen, a justice-oriented and generous private clinic. He was even exploring job options for moving out of the shelter where the government had dropped him off. Complications due to a negligent fumigation of that shelter that affected his already-compromised health conditions, a shelter in no way equipped to respond to people with life-threatening medical conditions, led to his internment and subsequent death in a public hospital known for medical abuse in Iztapalapa, Mexico City. In his name and in his honor, we are even more committed to our collective power, to our resistance, and to our struggle to flourish here and there.

The second Florecer Aquí y Allá is an even more iterative process. (We must be getting more and more comfortable with open-ended, emergent processes.) For it, we initiated a collaboration with Luisa Martínez, a *transfronteriza* artist, also our first "Artivist in Residence" in 2019. We obtained a grant through the National Association of Latino Arts and Culture (NALAC) and have coordinated and organized online spaces with over 40 participants who identify as deported, forcibly returned, refugees, undocumented, displaced, *transfronterizxs*, immigrants, and allies.

For three months, six groups connected virtually on a weekly basis to reflect on borders, territories, and our stories. We came together to listen and co-create alternative narratives that later turned into a powerful cloth zine edition with eight pockets stitched together and in each one of them four more zines that hold the collective narratives together. Many stories within a story. We presented the Florecer Zine during our Artivist Summit, which brought together over 30 artists to share their work in more than 20 workshops, and we hosted the first Zine Fest in Pocha House inviting artists from the periphery to make use of the space for their artistic work and demands. As a collective, we have engaged in radical creativity practices, naming our work "art" and acknowledging ourselves as artists. In 2019, Florecer Aquí y Allá started as a performance, and now it has become a collective process that holds space for new narratives to be created and shared in community.

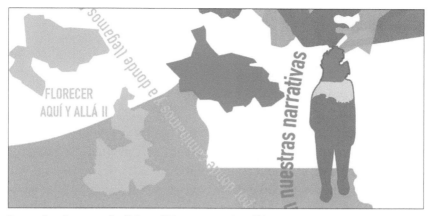

Poster for the second edition of Florecer Aquí y Allá, 2021–2022.
Credit: Qué Gente

Florecer Aquí y Allá is always in a state of becoming. And the path we are walking, the strategy we have chosen, is trans-local organizing. Although it is not a common word, and the definition is a bit hazy even in academic circles, we find the term "trans-local" to be useful as a description for an aspirational practice for deepening collective and individual dignity as migrants with multiple communities of belonging. We are divesting from the toxicity of nationalism and the inadequacy of the nation-state, a political and economic system that has criminalized some of us, racialized some of us, and separated all of us. Geographers use the term to describe networks of cross-border relationships between locally embedded people, relationships often forged via multigenerational migration flows, trade routes, and increasingly rapid technologies for travel and digital communication. Activists and community organizers are taking up the term too, but as a description of a creative practice that addresses and defies the violence and rupture inherent in forced migration. Globalized capitalism, violently defended patriarchy, and unaddressed white supremacy depend upon forced migration to entrench vulnerability and inequality and thereby sustain systems of extraction and exploitation. Not only do we expose and denounce those conditions, but together we are creating alternatives of collective care and dignified conditions.

Conclusion

Living into and inside of these narratives has significant implications for political and economic policy. We trust in the lessons, the worlds, that come from these stories. "Ls Otros Dreamers," "Visa Justice," "Pocha House," and "Florecer Aquí y Allá" are only four of the many narratives that have allowed us to learn and unlearn while sheltering complexity, contradiction, discomfort, fears, and trauma. We have created these narrative practices with intention. As a community, we show up for others so people don't have to go through family separation, exile, and trauma alone. As a community, we are also active and strategic so that these new narratives gain legitimacy in order to contribute to systemic transformation. We tell these stories as concrete possibilities that are based on lived experiences but with very real implications for public policies, laws, and economics.

In the face of the generational and systemic roots of forced migration in our region and learning from decolonizing projects around the globe, we are embracing, articulating, and practicing Abolition, Mobility, and Repair. For "Visa Justice" and to "Flourish Here and There" we require Abolition of the nation-state's supposedly sovereign right to forcefully detain and deport human beings because of a fictional border that has no basis in geography, topography, or ecology. We need Mobility to be widely recognized as a natural and fundamental right that nation-states are undermining with unequal passports, visa regimes, and immigration management models. Finally, we demand political and economic systems focused on Repair of the social fabric and the conditions for local well-being in regions ravaged by (post)colonial exploitation, conditions that are the fundamental causes of the condition of poverty, violence, oppression, and climate change that force migration.

What we can see so clearly now is that immigration policies that depend upon the discretion of authorities are wholly inadequate to protect the human rights of people of color moving across borders. DACA, TPS, and even nonimmigrant visas all depend upon the arbitrary discretion of government agents. The immigrants' rights movement in the United States has organized and won discretionary protections that do not fundamentally challenge the nation-state's authorized use of force to detain and remove people or to control who crosses what borders when. Similarly, in Mexico, the Instituto Nacional de Migración (INM), in collaboration with a newly formed National Guard, deports hundreds of desperate families every month even as it is also charged with receiving citizen-deportees and migrants from other countries under the abominable "Remain in Mexico" and Title 42, COVID-era policies that allowed the US government to refuse asylum and remove non-Mexican citizens to México. This system is a legal and moral schizophrenia because the same agency that deports migrants is also supposed to welcome them and protect their rights. We can unite around the abolition of all national governments' seemingly inviolable rights to deport and to manage the mobility of human beings across borders.

Whatever it is called in legal terms, the body and mind experiences deportation as a kidnapping. State-authorized kidnapping. Immigration and Customs Enforcement officers—as well as other legal enforcement agents under the Department of Homeland Security in collaboration with local police forces—use military equipment and SWAT-team tactics to detain people with civil infractions. Arrests happening while in transit from one state to another are common. Someone is on a bus or driving and then quite suddenly detained; they have just one phone call to pick up the pieces of their sudden disappearance. Trucks left on the side of the road. Mothers who never arrive to pick up their child from school. Once detained, people are moved in the middle of the night from detention center to detention center by bus and by plane with no explanation of where they are going and why. Many times, strip searches are enforced with each entry and departure from the detention center or local jail. Deportees are cuffed at their hands, waists, and ankles before boarding buses and planes. We believe that the detention and deportation regime, one part of the mass incarceration era, will one day be remembered with the same universal reproach as chattel slavery.

Just as detention and deportation are often taken for granted as justified use of force, the ways that national governments control and manage the movement of people across national borders is so normalized that we forget that national territories are human-made, historical constructions. There is nothing sacred or inviolable about them. Global passport inequality and the visa regimes that create quotas and barriers to freedom of movement are part of the laws that "illegalize" people in the first place. What we take for granted—the visa-free travel of US and European citizens to most countries around the world, in contrast to the visa-controlled travel of citizens from México, Central America, the Middle East, and Africa—is a global expansion of the way movement was controlled within colonized countries such as those in British-occupied Africa in the 19th and 20th centuries. More pragmatically, immigrant integration models that do not explicitly take on the state's policies and laws for legal documentation, legal mobility, and identity documents are trying to stop a hole in the dam with their fingers. All institutions, government actors, and advocates invested in "immigrant integration" must unite to advocate for residency-based visas and citizenship that is based on community-embedded trajectories, instead of employment trajectories for those already within the country, and to fully embrace legal mobility for all, independent of the economic and racial status of the person in transit.

The third strategy for migrant justice and well-being that has risen up for us within the narrative intention to flourish is what we are starting to call "repair." A *retorno digno*. Integration defined as access reads as hypocrisy in many developing countries, and increasingly in so-called developed countries as well. Focusing on access to education, labor/employment, social services (health care), and social inclusion in contexts where native citizens do not enjoy full access to basic rights is doomed not only to fail but also to foment xenophobia. For returning and deported immigrants, current immigrant integration models do little to address the conditions for emigration in the first place. After years of organizing around access to rights and services, we have realized that access is one important piece of a much bigger puzzle. The bigger picture leads us to robust programs for trans-local repair that creates the conditions for well-being in the communities forced migrants have to leave behind, as well as the destination communities in which forced migrants seek to rebuild and recover. These conditions for well-being affect all residents, immigrant or not.

In order to take concrete steps towards "Visa Justice" and "Flourishing Here and There," we need specific policies and laws to change. Many of the changes that are urgently needed are well-known and have been articulated by broad, trans-local coalitions for years. They include the adoption of DACA into the law of the land; The legal recognition of 11 million undocumented immigrants living in the US as essential workers, students, and family members of US citizens; the ending of "Remain in Mexico" and more robust and well-funded asylum and refugee programs across the continent. In order to include those who have been deported or forced to return to their home countries across the globe, there are also concrete policy shifts that could create pathways for Mobility and Repair for hundreds of thousands of families: (1) immediate creation of the US embassy and consulate directives that require officers to consider temporary family reunification of returned and deported individuals as a positive discretionary factor at the time of issuing non-immigrant visas and NOT a reason to accuse one of a hidden "immigrant intent"; (2) immediate creation of waivers for automatic bars (e.g., unlawful presence, entry without inspection after a prior removal, multiple deportations, false claims, and misrepresentations, and so on) for those seeking both immigrant and nonimmigrant visas; and (3) Elimination of the 3- and 10-year bars that are in the 1996 Illegal Immigration Reform and Immigration Responsibility Act.

We name these legal and political possibilities even as we also know that the national government leaders in México and the United States do not have the political will to reform or repair inhuman immigration policies. Organizing from the other side of deportation and forced return has long felt like a lost cause we committed to anyway. We committed because life goes on in the aftermath of state violence, and the stories we tell ourselves and one another are creating new possibilities for our lived experiences that current governments refuse to value. Narrative change is not a means to an end. These are the stories that sustain us, and even if governments do not yet make the changes we know immigrant families need and deserve, we are living into these new narratives every day with more and more people who understand themselves to be part of this community of change. Like many others around the globe, we are deep into the exhausting, humbling, and healing work of imagining and articulating and practicing this new vision and related demands for just transfers of resources and power so that we can all *florecer aquí y allá*. We tell our stories to one another so that we can connect more safely inside of them, and maybe, just maybe, walk together into a more livable future for all.

Artists Cited

Instead of a traditional list of works cited, we have chosen to include a list of artists who have made this work possible.[3]

> Areli Rema, Instagram: @areli.rema
> Colectivo de Prácticas Narrativas, www.colectivo.org.mx
> Deported Artist, Instagram: @deportedartist
> Diary of a Native Foreigner, Instagram: @diaryofanativeforeigner
> El Deportee, Instagram: @el_deportee
> Emily C-D, Instagram: @emilycdart
> Guanatos GDL SUR, https://guanatosgdlsur.org/
> Lorenzo's Calihtec Restaurant & Art Gallery, Instagram: @iztakpatchouli / @diekoras
> Luisa Martínez, Instagram: @luisaluisaww
> Mujer de Tepexpan, Instagram: @mujerdetepexpan
> Nin Solis, https://www.nin-solis.net/
> *Pochas So What*, Instagram: @pochassowhat
> Que Gente, Instagram: @que_gente

Notes

1. Even this chapter is an exercise in narrative practice, the active and thoughtful co-creation of a narrative "we." Maggie usually writes from a we that refers to the deported and forcibly returned in México. In this chapter, we are writing together, across our distinct positionalities in relationship to privilege and oppression, and our *nosotras* holds other signifiers of connection: years of solidarity and commu-

nity organizing alongside each other and many others; shared outrage in the face of decades of sanctioned state violence that separates families and can be fatal; common convictions about the urgency and power of trans-local organizing, Visa Justice, and Mobility For All.

2. For more information about the collective's work, see https://www.colectivo.org .mx/.

3. This essay is indebted to the many artists who have collaborated with us and with ODA over these many years. The majority of the artists listed have experienced deportation or forced return. Not only are we telling these stories together, but we are finding these stories with one another.

CHAPTER 22

The Narrative Machine

Profits, Brains, and the Reshaping of Our Public Space

Pireeni Sundaralingam

We can explore the shaping of a national narrative through a variety of lenses, from legal and literary metaphors to historical and sociological models. Yet possibly the most powerful force currently determining the way we construct narratives of national identity is also the most overlooked and the least understood. Few Americans understand the nature of artificial intelligence, let alone how AI algorithms regulate the digital spaces in which we conduct so many of our social interactions these days. Nevertheless, as technological development accelerates at an exponential rate, algorithm-based human-computer interaction is increasingly not only transforming the nature of our interactions as a society but, at a deeper level, reshaping our neural structures, the very interface with which we understand and interact with the world.

This chapter sets out to highlight key processes through which algorithm-driven technology impacts our brains, the resulting fallout in how we construct immigrant and national identities, and, given these factors, what steps we can take to safeguard our ability to continue democratically constructing the experiment of American identity.

The Rise of the Narrative Machine

Evolution has shaped our brains to make sense of our surroundings through patterns and narrative. A complex system of neural networks allows us to test out different hypotheses, different stories, juggling diverse ways of shaping information to find the best fit. It has taken millions of years to evolve such a delicately balanced system, yet in the course of just a few years that balance has become fundamentally disrupted. For the first time in human history, we find ourselves facing a Narrative Machine, a conglomeration of pattern-pushing technological processes of such power that our ability to assess incoming narratives has been fundamentally overwhelmed at a neurological level. It is as if our systems have been so overloaded that we have blown out nearly every possible narrative circuit, leaving only the ability to grasp the most basic of narratives forms—that of threat and survival.

It is all too easy to underestimate the power of the new digital Narrative Machine. After all, sensationalist narratives have been prevalent throughout the history of journalism, from the penny broadsheets of the 18th century to the yellow journalism at the heart of our modern-day gutter press. Nevertheless, the nature of the new digital Narrative Machine is not just quantitatively but qualitatively different from anything the human brain has had to grapple with before. The coming together of four critical phenomena—the increasing power of AI, the development of mobile digital technology, the lure of unprecedented amounts of personal social information, and profit-driven "attention extraction" business models—means that we are now facing the perfect societal storm, one that is leaving us increasingly vulnerable to deep levels of neural rewiring, effectively reshaping the ways that we create our own narratives.

First, there is the rise of machine intelligence and its cyclical interaction with human cognition. As our social interactions progressively move into digital spaces, AI systems (AIs) not only have more and more opportunities to monitor our opinions, choices, and behavior, but also increasingly have the ability to cherry-pick the stories that they decide to show us in our newsfeeds, thereby shaping our perceptions. As a result of AI intervention, the types of narratives that we experience are becoming narrower and narrower, whether in terms of the news articles we see from our favorite newspapers or the images we see in our online photo-streams, such as on Instagram and other photo-sharing platforms. The resulting impact on how we make sense of the world can be profound as we are repeatedly exposed to the same curtailed patterns of information.[1]

Second, there is the development of light-weight mobile devices with massive amounts of computing power that can be effortlessly carried around on our bodies 24/7. As a result, the AIs embedded in our devices have endless opportunities to track and interact with us, progressively fine-tuning their ability to influence our ideas and decisions. Additionally, whether we're using social media or video channels, the third factor in this perfect storm is the Narrative Machine's "lubricant." Our smartphones and their embedded AIs pull us into interaction by offering the most irresistible of human rewards, that of social interaction: we are offered the chance to be part of vast social eco-systems, where we can potentially be noticed or even "liked"; they even offer us the ultimate neurological bait—the ability to signal our social status within the tribe.

Finally, the current business model of every major tech platform revolves around attracting and keeping users' attention, even against their conscious will (the so-called attention extraction economy).[2] The more that users stay engaged on a platform, the more ads can be delivered to them. and the more advertising revenue the platform receives. With Facebook earning $33.67 billion dollars in 2021 and 97% of its revenue coming from advertising,[3] a trillion dollar industry has grown up around being able to identify and implant the exact internal triggers that keep us hooked to their sites.

Taken together, the four factors outlined above interact in a fine-grained, complex interplay that has given rise to the creation of a Narrative Machine of unprecedented power, one that can track the micro-details of our individual emotional landscapes and deliver personally specific packets of information. The precision of this human-computer interaction and the way that it targets specific personal vulnerabilities is what makes the Narrative Machine qualitatively different from past propaganda or marketing initiatives. It takes just 300 clicks for platform AIs to be able to predict our moods and behavior better than even our spouses can.[4] Such detailed "sentiment analysis" allows platform AIs (such as Lumos, Facebook's video analytics AIs[5]) to track when, where, and how we will each be most suggestible to different narratives, whether in terms of buying advertised products or engaging with political campaigns.

The ability to monitor and exploit each individual's weak spots means that the Narrative Machine can profoundly shape the way we each make sense of our environments as individuals. It has the potential to show each of what we most want or dread to see, fundamentally disrupting our understanding of the world around us. According to whistle-blowers at Cambridge Analytica, Facebook effectively exploited private citizens' tracking and personality profiling findings to micro-target them, persuading them to support Donald Trump's 2016 presidential campaign: the platform's AI was able to analyze users' digital footprints, assessing each person's psychological profile (such as their vulnerability to fear) specifically enough to micro-target them with uniquely tailored fear-based messages such as "Secure our Borders!" and "Keep the Terrorists Out!."[6]

The nature of the Narrative Machine, with its powerful, pervasive AIs interacting with us continuously through our various digital social spaces, is qualitatively different from anything humans have encountered before. It has profoundly changed the process of public political discourse, downgrading in-depth discussion in favor of the optics of performative grand-standing, tuning out slow analyses and weighty considerations of human values in favor of sensationalist propaganda and fast-striking fake news. We see the triumph of inflammatory Trumpian tweets over more profound rhetoric. It is no coincidence that populist politicians armed with simplistic polemics would prosper in this new type of public arena.

If we wish to create a flourishing public dialogue around new immigrant narratives, it would be helpful to gather a basic sense of the mechanics of the omnipresent Narrative Machine. The following sections address how the Narrative Machines hooks into our nervous systems, disrupting our own natural narrative-creating processes, as well as how it disrupts our new public spaces, splitting apart our communal dialogue and our ability to explore social narratives as a cohesive, democratic group.

Neural Networks and the Narrative Machine

As the way we gather information increasingly shifts to online spaces, our ability to evaluate material objectively, let alone explore and create abstract models, such as social narratives, is being radically curtailed. Recent neuroscience data demonstrate that the nature of online environments triggers the brain's neural networks for threat via three key channels, in each case leading to the downgrading of our cognitive functioning. In the most direct cases, exposure to negative words and images online can directly induce anxiety, fear, and other negative emotions. In addition (and less directly), our regular exposure to either informational overload or contradictory information can each also trigger a physiological threat response. As a result, our ability to read, work, and interact socially within many online environments becomes compromised, with the underlying milieu of either conscious or unconscious threat tilting us toward fear-based responding and the plethora of cognitive biases and stereotyped thinking that are associated with this emotional state.

Indirect Threats

Evolutionary biologists note that when we experience intense danger, we are often flooded with an overwhelming amount of contradictory information. Over the course of evolution, informational overload has become one of the cues that we subconsciously associate with encountering danger; contradictory information is the other. Either one of these cues sends our bodies into physiological stress. Unfortunately, our online spaces often recreate these conditions, characterized as they are both by vast amounts of information and by the inevitable inconsistencies that emerge from such a smorgasbord of data.

The dizzying range of information available online is so overwhelming that even a few minutes spent on the internet leads to the brain's cognitive field shrinking, focusing on details at the cost of the larger patterns it typically seeks. It's as if, thrown into a seemingly infinite forest, the brain doubles down on trying to make sense of just a few specific trees.[7] In fact, the internet is now associated with such a strong sense of informational overload that simply reading words associated with the internet (such as "website" or "blog") leads to a hyper-focus on small details, with EEG readings demonstrating that trying to look at larger patterns of information under such conditions demands a much higher recruitment of neurological resources than normal.[8] Such conditions make it much more challenging for the human brain to "pan out" and create new narrative patterns for understanding incoming information. As a result, it becomes harder to rethink former stereotypes of immigrants or even immigration as a whole.

Similarly, when we're exposed to contradictory information, our ability to think in a logical, calm way becomes compromised, and instead we tend to make hasty, emotionally reactive decisions, tilted toward a negative bias. Research experiments have shown that when we encounter contradictory social information—such as conflicting descriptions of another person's behavior—those brain areas involved in emotional regulation and impulse control become overburdened.[9] It is as if encountering inconsistent information levies a form of neurological tax on our cognitive resources, short-circuiting level-headed thinking and leaving us prone to bias. Thus, even if we are the type of person who in the real world is comfortable with exploring a range of different migration narratives, when we work in digital spaces, we are likely to become much less flexible in our thinking.

While technological utopians design our digital spaces with the assumption that "more is always better," the reality of our biological selves means that the vast amounts of unconnected data streaming into us in the Information Age simply serves to overload our finely tuned homeostatic systems, sending them into states of defensive tunnel vision. The numerous digital features designed to distract us when reading online, from pop-up windows to flashing banner ads, disrupt our brains' natural regulatory mechanisms,[10] downgrading our power to pay sustained attention and leading to serious side-effects: experiments reveal that exposure to such digital features significantly reduces our ability to retain the information we're reading[11] and can cause us to process all information equally because we are not able to regulate and filter out irrelevant from irrelevant data.[12]

In short, the overwhelming amount of information on many digital platforms, as well as the contradictory nature of so much data that we encounter there, effectively constrains our brain's neural networks, making it much harder for us to grasp new models of social data or even to engage in wider systems thinking: we become mired in emotionally reactive, stereotyped patterns of cognition, struggling to rethink our existing assumptions about social issues such as migration and movement, and we become less and less able to filter, assess, and remember incoming data. Instead of being able to analyze incoming social information in a calm and controlled way, our neural networks tilt us toward biased or negative judgements. The more overwhelmed we are by information, the more we judge others as unpleasant, even dangerous, and the less likely we are to find common ground. Under such conditions, creating a shared sense of nationhood, or even attempting to prompt collaborative models of understanding, becomes even more challenging as our overloaded brains start "othering" those around us.

Direct Effects

The above social effects are largely unintended side-effects of the digital revolution. In contrast, major tech platforms have also explicitly designed processes for triggering our neural networks for threat. These include features such as the flashing red notifications symbol that alerts us that messages are waiting, or the three flashing dots animation in texting apps that indicate that someone is currently typing a message to us. Both features exploit the fact that when we encounter uncertainty (particularly uncertainty about our current social status) in our physical surroundings, our bodies release stress chemicals into our bloodstream, causing our attention to narrow and pinning us down to remain focused on the platform in question.

The more time spent in this fast-moving digital environment, filled with distracting stimuli, the more stress we experience; and the more stress we experience, the more damage we accrue in exactly the brain areas we need in order to take control and put an end to these stressors.[13] Experimental data demonstrate that such stress leads to a significant reduction in the size and connectivity of the regulatory neural networks that would normally override emotional overreaction.[14] As a result, our brains get trapped in negative feedback loops, focusing our attention on potential threat signals, which in turn increases our stress, causing us to focus even more on such signals and leaving us less and less able to pull away and attend to something else.

Our brain has evolved such that at the first sign of threat (whether this is direct danger or indirect signals of potential danger such as informational overload or conflicting information) the neural systems that support our perception changes: all other negative threat-based patterns become exaggerated in our perception, and we find it harder and harder to see positive or neutral patterns in the data around us. The impacts occur at a cellular level: when we experience such threats, emotion-regulating neural centers such the amygdala recalibrate our sensory "threat" neurons, dropping cells' firing thresholds such that they are activated by any stimulus that falls anywhere close to their range—every twig starts to look like a snake when we are in a state of threat.[15] Our neural networks evolved in a world in which dangerous events could happen several times a day and had the potential to kill us; the gift of our technological age, in contrast, has been to immerse us in a digital environment in which, even though there is little real danger to our immediate survival, our threat systems are continuously being stimulated and we end up in a constant state of high alert.

The negative feedback loop between external stressors and our neural networks becomes exponentially more destructive as a consequence of the profit-driven AIs that underlie many of our digital spaces. As previously discussed, the business model underlying most major tech platforms depends on keeping users engaged on their sites as sitting targets for advertisers. Consequently, the AIs underlying such platforms focus on baiting users with the type of material that will keep them stuck to the site in question. Given our biologically determined proclivity for paying attention to threat stimuli, AIs automatically highlight such information. The extraordinary computing power of machine learning systems allows them to monitor whichever words, images, and narrative themes trap human attention most effectively and then act to prioritize and place them increasingly to the center of our view. The toxic interplay between our own threat-oriented neural networks and the profit-driven mission of AIs (continuously monitoring our online interactions in order to pinpoint and deliver whichever sensationalist informational tidbit best hijacks our attention) means that the promised wide-open information landscape that we were promised at the dawn of the internet era has shrunk to a narrow field of focus, overseen by a Narrative Machine that feeds off human anger, fear, and anxiety.

Attempting to find alternative paths through this constrained landscape can be challenging, particularly in the face of AIs that are exquisitely tuned to amplify and exploit our individual worries and vulnerabilities. With the power to test billions of people at any given time by simply changing a few lines of code, major tech companies continue to run the largest social engineering experiments in the history of our species. (A measure of their success is the level of compulsive attachment to mobile phones: 33% of Americans state that they would rather give up sex than relinquish their smartphone.)[16] If we are to create new social narratives, we will, as a society, need to grasp the ways in which the Narrative Machine of digital technology disrupts our information landscape and exploits our biological vulnerabilities.

Social Impact of the Narrative Machine

Our steady migration into digitized social landscapes leaves us vulnerable to a range of ways in which information can be distorted.

The fact that platform AIs exploit our biologically determined tendency to focus on threat has amplified the impact of deliberately constructed disinformation ("fake news"). Our new digital world means not only that false information can be disseminated to millions of people at the touch of a few keys, but, in addition, that the underlying AIs can also rapidly assess which types of information can trigger the most human attention and then duly exploit this. It is no coincidence that fake news contain significantly more words of anger than real news,[17] and each word of outrage added to a post allows it to travel six times faster around the globe.[18] In fact, the greater the amount of emotion in a fake news post, the more likely it is to be believed.[19]

In such conditions, it becomes increasingly challenging to disrupt established social fears and prejudices and disseminate new social narratives. Instead, the nature of our current digital spaces means that fear-mongering narratives about minority groups or immigration will inevitably be picked up and amplified exponentially, thanks to this deadly interplay of our neurological tilt towards danger and attention-extracting AIs. We may aim to search for information about the nutritional benefits of kale, but we only need to show a split-second's interest in a jelly doughnut, and we find ourselves bombarded with an avalanche of images of powdered sugar and fried bread.

The vast social network underlying the Narrative Machine allows it not only to tap into general human vulnerabilities at scale but also to exploit specific human sensitivities around social status. Fake news proliferates in online spaces because users often share posts irrespective of their accuracy, simply because it comes from a friend or a celebrity with whom they want to be associated. As humans, we're more concerned with establishing status and popularity than with maintaining truth. Analysis indicates that people are seven times more likely to share content online when they see it is popular and can get attention.[20] In fact, people share stories even when they do not believe their content.[21]

The existence of the Narrative Machine means that if popular, charismatic figures create antisocial, even violence-inciting, narratives about specific out-groups, anyone who joins the bandwagon and "shares" or "likes" this toxic narrative will dramatically elevate their own status faster and at greater scale than could have ever been achieved in the past:

the user gains social capital and in the meantime the narrative can spread farther, faster, and deeper than ever before.

Moreover, the virality of a given piece of information can dramatically affect how readers perceive its accuracy: encountering a news story multiple times, whether on different platforms or simply different user newsfeeds, makes the story seem more credible. Experimental data indicate that merely reading a fake news headline just once leads people to later judge it as accurate when they next see it—even if the original fake headline had been clearly labeled as an inaccurate by official fact-checkers.[22] Thus not only do the viral actions of the Narrative Machine spread disinformation to a vast audience, but the resulting repetition of the disinformation across different places leads to users encountering it multiple times, which in turn creates a feeling of familiarity with the disinformation,[23] creating a psychological "feeling" of accuracy—the so-called Illusory Truth effect. In neurological terms, our response to repeated misinformation/disinformation is an example of data being assessed at the lowest level of processing, without any deeper critical analysis, due to the sheer speed that the messages are being pumped out by the Narrative Machine.

The Narrative Machine has several digital properties that allow it to dominate the narrative in any given space: both its speed and its ability to spread ideas across multiple different platforms and users allow it to interrupt our normal way of shaping social information into narratives. A third feature that adds to its narrative reach is its ability to create and deliver "snack news" (a headline connected to an image and a brief description). Neuroscientists note that due to the way that our cognitive systems are wired, even seeing just a few examples of snack news can be enough to create the illusion of deep knowledge on that issue.[24]

Given these conditions, it is perhaps not surprising that memes have become one of the most influential formats for political narrative among the digital generation. Just ahead of the Spanish elections in 2019, for example, over a quarter of the voting population were bombarded with misinformation via hate-speech memes on just the WhatsApp text messaging platform. These messages include hard-to-forget captioned images ranging from doctored photos of a Muslim man leading his three veiled wives using what appear to be chains to vintage photos of Black slave children being ridden by white children, framed with a text lamenting the passing of immigrant slave labor.[25]

Hostile, negative memes proliferate on digital platforms, thanks to the fact that they fit in so well with the essential DNA of the Narrative Machine: their stress-inducing messages trigger the negative feedback loops of our threat neural networks, while at the same time, due to their sensationalist content, they also lure the attention of users and activate the algorithms of platform AIs. As a result, the viral nature of such memes, whether or not they are factually accurate, rapidly comes to hold sway over the public's memory and insidiously influences the political narrative for any given set of circumstances.

A case in point: the most prevalent American memes on the subject of immigration focus on migrant criminality, the cost-effectiveness of the US-Mexico border wall, and doctored images of thousands of Hondurans seemingly marching in caravans toward the US border. The majority of Americans have been exposed to these memes, via one digital platform or another, and whether or not they considered these images to be accurate, the images have nevertheless served to shift the goal-posts of the debate and influence the public perception of immigration.

As a result of the dynamics of fake news and memes, the Narrative Machine has the power to activate neural networks for threat, consequently shaping the public debate on a range of political issues. If we are to propagate new national narratives about migration, we will first need to understand and address the existing workings of the Narrative Machine, including creating suitable counterpoints to the places where it undermines the information landscape.

The Split Narrative

As political philosophers such as John Rawls and Jurgen Habermas have noted,[26] a functioning democracy depends on a diverse public dialogue in civic space, creating a sense of the "we, the people." Yet the possibility of such dialogue is increasingly being compromised by the for-profit algorithms that underpin our new digital civic spaces. It is not just a question of snaring us in downward-spinning spirals of threat; the nature of the Narrative Machine also partitions public dialogue, fracturing any shared sense of social narrative or even the awareness that there is a diversity of social narratives. Five key features of the Narrative Machine serve to amplify distinct, mutually irreconcilable social narratives: the filtering of news and creation of separate newsfeeds for each person; the demographic (sometimes ethnic) filtering of basic information; the use of recommendation algorithms for politically charged videos; the artificial engineering of social clusters; and a digital architecture that treats people differently on the basis of ethnicity.

First, our ability to engage in any shared type of public discourse and civic meaning-making is deeply constrained by the fact that platforms feed each of us a different range of news stories. Facebook is currently the biggest news outlet in the world,[27] with 40% of adults getting their news from the tech titan and a total of 68% getting their news from social media in general.[28] Yet the general public has little understanding of the fact that the AIs underlying this platform curate and feed only a select set of news stories to each user. Algorithms set to maximize user attention on screen will always prioritize whichever news stories touch on issues that the user finds alarming enough to click on, as well as themes in which they have already expressed interest. Within the current "attention extraction" business model, there are no profits to be made by an AI using its computational power to present news stories that broaden or even balance people's social perspectives. The full extent of news distortion is greatly underestimated by most users, and while 57% of users acknowledge that the news on social media may have some inaccuracy, they continue to use these platforms to get their news, with 21% citing that the sheer convenience factor overrides the inaccuracy.

Second, aside from filtering of newsfeeds, the Narrative Machine can also distort our social sense-making by selectively filtering information in general. Experiments demonstrate that simply changing the order in which search results are presented such as prioritizing one political candidate versus another can shift voting preferences of undecided voters by 20% or more.[29] Other studies reveal that it is all too easy for society's existing stereotypes to be picked up and amplified by the AIs' underlying search engines: searching for names associated with ethnic minority groups automatically triggered ads suggestive of former arrest records, while white-associated names such as "Jill" did not trigger such ads, even when there were extensive arrest records for people with such names.[30] Similarly, when fed labels of darker-skinned ethnic groups associated with recent immigration (for example, "Mexican American woman"), on the one hand, and labels related to white immigrant groups, on the other (for instance, "Irish American woman"), search engines tend to generate images of hypersexualized or pornographically debased images of Mexican American women but not for Irish-American women.[31]

A third mechanism by which the Narrative Machine fractures our social narrative is through its deployment of attention-extracting recommendation algorithms on video platforms such as YouTube. As demonstrated by former YouTube engineer Guillaume Chaslot, the algorithm "systematically amplifies videos that are divisive, sensational, and conspiratorial."[32] Users watching videos on YouTube are repeatedly lured down rabbit-holes as video after video feeds them increasing levels of violence and threat, which often drive conspiracy thinking. Such conspiracies can serve to partition populations, separating one ethnic community from another, even separating one generation from another. A range of Vietnamese-language YouTube channels, catering to an older generation of Vietnamese Americans, has been found to be promulgating divisive narratives, such as endorsing anti-Black rhetoric or suggesting that the Democratic Party aligns with communism and the Chinese government. This effectively destroys the ability of targeted older Vietnamese Americans to make sense of current American politics, and has not only created tensions between Vietnamese Americans and African Americans, but also sown division between older and younger sections of the Vietnamese community.[33]

It has been estimated that as many as 50% of Americans believe in at least one conspiracy.[34] Cognitive scientists have demonstrated that once people start believing one conspiracy, they are much more likely to believe others,[35] and exposure to just two minutes of a conspiracy video is frequently enough to reduce a viewer's pro-social behavior.[36] Most worryingly, data analyses reveal that these algorithms actively contributed to the rise and unification of right-wing extremists in the United States as platform AIs partitioned and amplified separate siloes of extremist social narrative.[37]

Fourth, probably the most significant way in which the Narrative Machine splits us into distinct, often mutually exclusive narrative groups, is through the fundamental structure of social media networks themselves. As Ugander and his Facebook-based colleagues noted in their 2011 analysis of the network's algorithm, the natural patterns of social connection that occur in real life are deliberately restructured in the online environment in order to maximize profit-driven engagement.[38] The algorithm explicitly determines the specific number and type of people whom we'll meet online and then build into our social network: analysis by Facebook's vice president of engineering, Lars Backstrom, acknowledges that "a significant chunk" of connections that are made on the platform take place as a direct result of the platform's algorithm PYMK ("People You May Know"), a version of which is now found on most platforms.[39] While early social media platforms (such as MySpace) aimed to build social bridges between different social clusters, Facebook out-stripped its competitors by creating algorithms that maximized the chances of people accepting friend recommendations by deliberately recommending only people from the same social cluster.[40] It is no surprise that the degree of clustering on Facebook is five times greater than on other digital social networks (such as MSN messenger) that do not use recommendation algorithms. As a result of such deliberately engineered clustering processes, the social environment online inevitably becomes more and more homogenized, as people are increasingly pushed into forming segregated groups, and then associating only with others of their same group: thanks to the speed and scale of the machine network, a human tendency is picked up and amplified exponentially. Recommending a wide variety of social connections (such as including people from a range of different ethnicities or connecting members of different newer migrant communities with more established historically migrant groups) might build stronger, more multifaceted, and tolerant social systems in the real world, but doing so runs counter to the constraints of current online economies and network engineering. Complexity of connection may be good for society, but in digital network terms, it's bad for business.

The fallout from such artificially induced social segregation appears to be distrust and hostility toward perceived "out-groups." When two people have no direct social connections within their online social networks, they are significantly more likely to infer that there are deep political differences between themselves with no possibility of any overlap in their narratives.[41] Moreover, people who use social media a lot are significantly more likely to perceive deep political divisions in the United States compared with those who use social media less frequently.[42] This may arise, at least in part, from the fact that simply being exposed to hateful content in general leads to an exaggerated sense of outgroup threat to the self and a significantly greater tendency to attribute negative characteristics to members of a perceived out-group.[43] In such environments, even some of the most pro-social narratives can rapidly turn toxic. The "#StopAsianHate" and "#StopAAPIHate" campaigns are a case in point. They appeared to be successful, as measured by a widespread dissemination of posts across the Twittersphere. Nevertheless, closer analysis indicates that many whites who joined this campaign used the opportunity to denounce others, including blaming African Americans for anti-Asian crimes, retweeting news of Blacks targeting Asians, or using their posts as an opportunity to hype the "All Lives Matter" movement.[44]

The dynamics of our new digital public spaces quickly pushes users into alarm-based narratives. Observational data indicates that expressions of moral outrage receive 100% more positive comments and lead to an increase in a user's tendency to post additional extreme content online the next day. Similarly, experimental data show that when people were given the goal of attracting the most likes and were then exposed to outrage-filled Twitter streams, they were significantly more likely to post further statements of moral outrage than people who had been exposed only to neutral tweets.[45] Toxic narratives will always be amplified and promoted farther and faster than more pro-social narratives as a direct result of the engineering design choices made in the construction of our major current platforms.

While early pioneers of the internet celebrated the online environment as a place where humans could at last be free from the trappings of race, ethnicity, and other social markers, this is far from the reality of Web 2.0. A fifth component contributing to the power of the "Splinternet" is that the design features and code underlying digital spaces are written by humans and all too often reproduce and amplify the sociopolitical narratives and biases of those employees. Facebook engineers, for example, have created a database of what they consider to be authentic names belonging to real humans in an attempt to weed out fake accounts. As a result, people whose names do not fit Facebook's biases regularly have their accounts automatically suspended by the machine's protocols. This includes many migrants, African Americans, and Native Americans. As feminist commentator Alli Kirkham has noted, when Facebook says it is checking for "real names" it appears to equate "real" with "traditional European."[46] On October 14, 2014—Indigenous People's Day—the tech titan suspended Shane Creepingbear's account on the basis that "this name does not meet Facebook standards" for "real humans." Suspended users have to go through a long-winded, opaque appeals process to verify that they are, in fact, humans with authentic names. Meanwhile, Mark Zuckerberg's dog has a Facebook account, registered under its own name.[47]

As MIT's Associate Professor of Civic Media, Sasha Constanza-Chock, has pointed out, such design decisions are "hard-coded Euro-centricity" and inevitably perpetuate the biased narratives of society, even making them worse thanks to the nature of algorithmic amplification.[48] Until tech companies deepen their understanding and commitment to algorithmic justice, including employing a greater diversity in their workforce, such systematic bias will continue to be perpetuated, and the daily barrage of design assumptions as to who qualifies as a normative American will continue to undermine any attempt to broaden new narratives of American identity.

Finally, the question arises as to whether the Narrative Machine's ability to split social narratives could serve to amplify pro-social groups. Could its power to strengthen in-group connections lead to an acceleration in the formation of pro-social groups, including those seeking to create more nuanced immigrant narratives? Certainly, the major platforms have been swift to claim credit for the Arab Spring and to suggest that they have been instrumental in the rise of social movements, including recent campaigns that complicate our sense of American identity from #BLM and #MuslimBan to #StopAsianHate. This claim has, in itself, has become a widely distributed social narrative.

However, closer examination indicates a more troubled and complex relationship between current digital platforms and political change in this country. On the one hand, digital spaces such as Facebook and WhatsApp have empowered social movements to mobilize large numbers of people rapidly around a single, broad demand. Digital tools such as email and instant messaging allow campaigners to gather organizational allies, to share messages and images of solidarity, to organize logistical details, and to promote protest events.[49] On the other hand, the profit-driven architecture of these platforms also constrains the development of social movements in important ways. As Constanza-Chock has noted in describing her own experience of organizing the #QTPower campaign in Boston, protest organizers using Facebook and Facebook Events were able to circulate their call to action to thousands and monitor interest via tools such as the RSVP feature, yet the design of these platforms is such that once the event was over, the discussion about what had been learned and what to do next was automatically diluted on these sites: such posts appeared in the newsfeeds of some members but not others "subject to the opaque decision-making of Facebook's News Feed algorithm."[50] Organizers could not even contact event attendees and invite them to the next mobilization unless they were willing to pay to upgrade their services. Although there are high-end digital platforms such as NationBuilder and ActionNetwork that cater to the needs of professional political campaigners, these are too costly and too complex to learn for the majority of Americans attempting to organize social movements; as a result, most users simply default to using the major tech platforms together with all their in-built limitations.

As tech analysts such as Ramesh Srinivasan have noted, social change requires long, nuanced discussion, which deepens the critical consciousness of those involved and allows the slow build-up of the complex knowledge, social processes, and relationships that are necessary to anchor systemic social change.[51] Without it, we are run the risk of fostering "fast food" social actions: scalable, cheap to create, and rapidly assembled but ultimately lacking in substance.

If we are to continue evolving the great experiment of American identity and nurturing the healthy functioning of civic space, it is essential that we counter the toxic inroads of the Narrative Machine. Initiatives such as "New Narratives," of which this collected volume is an example, open the door to deeper, more substantial forms of discussion between our communities. In lieu of mutually exclusive, polarized narratives, they offer a vital chance to engage in comparative perspective-taking and reflection, to promote sustained dialogue and debate rather than the fragmented, performative monologues currently monopolizing our digital civic spaces. Armed with the right tools, as outlined in the next section, projects such as "New Narratives" may provide a much-needed antidote to the social splintering induced by the Narrative Machine.

Strategies for Change

There are four processes through which we can restore balance and reinstate the deep exploration and exchange of social narratives that marks a forward-moving society.

The first and most essential step in halting the progress of the Narrative Machine is to increase awareness that AI algorithms are fundamentally reshaping our neural networks and that much of the information on digital platforms (even on so-called "search engines") is distorted. That in itself could significantly dilute the impact of the Narrative Machine. While 68% of Americans read their news via social media platforms, 53% acknowledged that they did not know how news feeds work.[52] As is the case in tackling any type of pollution, it is vital to understand the nature and pathways of the toxin if we are to take effective action.

Recent experiments indicate that enhancing awareness of the routes through which the Narrative Machine is contaminating social discourse can significantly bolster resistance to its impact. Research at Cambridge University has shown that just 15 minutes of exposure to playing "Bad News," an online game that exposes the nature of fake news tactics, significantly "inoculates" people against online misinformation.[53] Furthermore, watching a 90- second video about the manipulation tactics used on social media (from hyper-emotional messaging to scapegoating of minority groups) also successfully "inoculated" thousands of people from misinformation messages in the subsequent 24-hour period.[54] Even prompting people to spend a few minutes assessing the accuracy of news headlines is enough to more than double their ability to detect fake news.[55]

If we, as a society, are to protect ourselves against the toxic processes of the Narrative Machine, we urgently need to educate ourselves. It is not enough to discuss the impact of algorithm-driven technology in media studies classrooms; this is a conversation that needs to take place in political studies, sociology, ethnic studies, civics and more. It is a conversation that needs to extend across all generations, and for that to happen, we need to reach beyond high school and university curricula to find a range of public spaces, from pop-up installations to podcasts and panels, to proactively engage our population, thereby both preempting and remediating the impacts of the Narrative Machine.

Second, projects such as "New Narratives" broaden the range of different migration narratives we have to hand. Psychological research indicates that under most circumstances, people tend to seek out news and ideas that agree with their existing belief systems.[56] To counter this, in the past, national media policy in the United States promoted a certain level of diversity in broadcast media, leveraging the fact that with very few TV channels available, viewers had little option but to watch one of the three main news programs and would consequently be exposed to ideas with which they might not agree. Additionally, a large portion of the news audience was exposed to news simply because it took place either before or after their favorite programs, the so-called inadvertent audience effect.[57] In contrast, in the current era of practically infinite online choice, viewers can self-segregate according to their own ideologically distinct groups and avoid being challenged by unfamiliar ideas and social narratives.[58] The promise of the Narrative Machine has been to take away the perplexing complexity of different perspectives and replace it with the personalization of news and information. The customer gets what the customer wants, or rather the customer gets what the AI decides the customer wants. As Eric Schmidt argued, during his tenure at CEO of Google, the idea of Google's search engine providing a range of results for a given search is "a bug. . . . We should be able to give you the right answer just once. We should know what you want."[59] In contrast, projects such as "New Narratives" can provide important balance, offering a diversity of perspectives to consider. In place of just one personalized narrative of American identity, it offers up multiple possible answers. It does not seek to give the reader the solution they already know, the one that fits their preexisting frameworks. It offers an incubator where diversity of ideas is not a bug.

Although people often prefer information that tallies with their existing opinions, research indicates that they do seek out new and challenging information either when they are curious about a topic[60] or in response to a fairness norm in situations where equitable discussion is emphasized.[61] For example, when people were given a news topic and offered an additional range of subtopics, reflecting different aspects of the main topic, arranged in the form of a "NewsCube," they willingly read more news stories and explored more aspects of each topic than if they were reading news online listed by personalized preferences or listed in a random order.[62] Other research groups have shown that giving readers visual feedback about the political bias of their online news consumption (in the form of an animated stick figure balancing on a tight-rope) led to an increase in readers seeking out alternative news sources and political perspectives that were ideologically different from their own views.[63] Democracy-minded start-ups are striving to build on this success: for example, the news aggregator site One-Sub uses AI to give news readers dynamic feedback, not only about the political imbalance of their news consumption, but also about its geographical skew.[64] Additionally, in terms of group interaction, organizations such as Living Room Conversations[65] and Search for Common Ground[66] have shown significant success at bringing together people with differing viewpoints to discuss social issues and reach a better understanding of each other in the process. Such findings suggest that there is a genuine hunger among today's public to seek out the types of different perspectives gathered together in "New Narratives" projects, particularly if they are presented in settings that prompt people to consider issues of fairness and balance. As such, initiatives such as "New Narratives" have the potential to play a pivotal role in fostering the type of active inquiry and wide-ranging information-seeking behavior that is presently being eroded by the profit-driven Narrative Machine.

Third, hand-in-hand with expanding the *range* of migration narratives to consider, it is also important to restore our cognitive capacity to be able to move fluidly *between* them. Experiencing threat, as we so often do in our new digital spaces, reduces our cognitive flexibility while increasing our emotional reactivity, our dogmatism,[67] and our susceptibility to bias.[68] Real-world consequences include an increased avoidance of those perceived to be from other ethnic groups and even an avoidance of unfamiliar commercial products.[69] In contrast, the act of considering different viewpoints actively expands human cognitive flexibility, promoting the robustness of exactly those neural networks that are essential for creating breakthrough ideas.[70] Research comparing two groups of medical students has demonstrated that those who were given the chance to spend time studying completely different types of narrative patterns (namely, visual narratives in paintings) were significantly better at medical diagnoses (that is, assessing medical patterns) than those who had been given extra time to study more typical medical narrative patterns (such as in X-rays).[71] Similarly, the process of switching between the different narratives offered within this current volume has the potential to nurture the type of cognitive flexibility needed to find new and better ways of modeling existing information.

We live in an era of increasing dogmatism with cognitive tests indicating that people at either end of the political spectrum show very little cognitive flexibility.[72] Moreover, as a society, we have a tendency to get stuck in just one dominant narrative when it comes to social issues such as immigration, with the drawback that we get trapped into making poor decisions based on the limited perspective of this model, a phenomenon known by psychologists as "confirmation bias."[73] Narrative metaphors can be useful in knitting together data in a coherent way so as to point to a particular set of actions and decisions to make. However, the problem with narrative metaphors is that they can highlight one set of data at the cost of alternative, potentially better patterns in the data. If we, as a society, seek to reduce dogmatism and the type of situational blindness that drives poor social decision-making, it is in our best interests to engage with a range of *different* social narratives, such as those included in this collection. The ability to think flexibly is foundational to human resilience; nurturing the health of the neural systems that support our cognitive flexibility is one of the most vital things we can do to protect ourselves and our society from the incursions of the Narrative Machine and its attempts to shape our neural networks. The "New Narratives" project provides an excellent opportunity to rebuild this essential cognitive capacity in the wake of the Narratives Machine's onslaught. It offers us the opportunity to compare and contrast different perspectives, to experience moving from one viewpoint to another, and to hold the nuances of multiple dimensions in mind at the same time. Set within an educational curriculum that emphasizes active inquiry, for example, "New Narratives" could provide a vital resource for rebooting our sociopolitical brain.

Finally, it is possible to halt the progress of the Narrative Machine directly at source. However, this requires either the good will of the tech companies themselves or the intervention of legislation. Yet creating effective regulatory policy is extremely challenging given the sheer speed of technological progress. Regulation is also stymied by the lack of transparency around AIs, both because of companies being unwilling to share the details of their proprietary algorithms publicly[74] and because of the inherent complexity and opacity of machine-learning algorithms (the black-box problem).[75] In terms of tech companies voluntarily choosing to self-regulate the Narrative Machine, this would involve jettisoning a highly profitable business model. It would require abandoning the network's cluster-driven growth algorithm and promoting ways for users to use the network to form socially heterogenous groups. It would rely on tech companies slowing down online interactions by introducing features such as automatic pauses to force users to reconsider their posts when the platform AI detects emotionally charged exchanges. Furthermore, the tech titans would have to invest significantly more resources in moderating their sites, so as to reduce hate speech and to down-rank misinformation/fake news before it spreads exponentially throughout society. Yet this is not a financial decision that they usually make. Responding to widespread criticism that it was promoting conspiracies, YouTube recently moderated its own algorithms, reducing the recommendations of Flat Earth and Anti-Vaxx conspiracy theories and, in the process, showing that it could, indeed, successfully regulate its deleterious impacts on civic discourse when it so wishes. It should be noted that it did not chose to moderate many of the other conspiracy theories that are regularly promulgated on its platform, including hate narratives around immigrant groups.[76]

We are at a critical time for public dialogue and our social narratives. Thanks to the profit-driven nature of the Narrative Machine—grounded in the compulsive interplay between platform algorithms and our own neurological threat circuits—the stories and metaphors we use to weave together our social fabric have become deeply distorted. We may not have time to wait for either regulators or tech companies to halt the Narrative Machine. Instead, humanities-based initiatives, such as "New Narratives," paired with a basic understanding of the building blocks of the Narrative Machine, have the potential to increase the range of our stories as well as the flexibility with which we grapple with different perspectives. It is through narratives that we determine how we frame our relationship to each other;[77] as cognitive scientists have demonstrated, it is how we understand our own social agency and what actions to take,[78] and which elements we side-line in a given social issue.[79] If we are to have the type of flourishing democracy outlined by Rawls and Habermas, it is vital that we disrupt the Narrative Machine before it further narrows the diversity and the fluidity of the stories we tell ourselves about the nature of our society.

Notes

1. The profits to be reaped from this type of psychological shaping are profound: advertising mandarins have been fast to cash in on this, using AIs not just to monitor which products trigger our individual consumer desires but also testing out which specific types of stories will prompt impulse buys of their products. Thanks to the scaled reach of digital platforms, at any given moment billions of us can be monitored to assess which types of stories prompt our buying behavior and then make sure that these are the stories we see. For example, advertisers can now directly test whether consumers are more likely to buy emergency rations if they see ads portraying people of color engaged in pro-social actions versus ads showing homogenous groups of white people fleeing disaster. As a result, even within advertising spaces, we see a narrowing of the diversity of narrative types to which we are exposed.

2. M. H. Goldhaber, "The Attention Economy and the Net." *First Monday* 2, no. 4 (1997).

3. M. Johnston, "How Facebook (Meta) Makes Money," *Investopedia*, last modified January 10, 2023. https://www.investopedia.com/ask/answers/120114/how-does-facebook-fb-make-money.asp.

4. W. Youyou, M. Kosinski, and D. Stillwell, "Computer-Based Personality Judgments Are More Accurate than Those Made by Humans." *PNAS* 112, no. 4 (2015): 1036–40.

5. S. Aral, *The Hype Machine: How Social Media Disrupts Our Elections, Our Economy, and Our Health—and How We Must Adapt* (New York: Random House, 2020).

6. K. Amer and J. Noujaim, prod. and dir., *The Great Hack*, The Othrs, 2019, Netflix, https://www.netflix.com/Title/80117542.

7. M. Peng, X. Chen, and Q. Zhao, "Attentional Scope Is Reduced by Internet Use: A Behavior and Erp Study." *PLoS ONE* 13, no. 6 (2018): e0198543.

8. M. Peng, L. Zhang, Y. Wen, and Q. Zhao, " Internet-Word Compared with Daily-Word Priming Reduces Attentional Scope," *Experimental Brain Research* 238, no. 4 (2020): 1025–33.

9. H. U. Nohlen, F. van Harreveld, M. Rotteveel, A. J. Barends, and J. T. Larsen, "Affective Responses to Ambivalence Are Context-Dependent: A Facial Emg Study on the Role of Inconsistency and Evaluative Context in Shaping Affective Responses to Ambivalence," *Journal of Experimental Social Psychology* 65 (2016): 42–51; H. U. Nohlen, F. van Harreveld, and W. A. Cunningham, "Social Evaluations

under Conflict: Negative Judgments of Conflicting Information Are Easier than Positive Judgments," *Social Cognitive and Affective Neuroscience* 14, no. 7 (2019): 709–18.

10. M. Moisala, V. Salmela, L. Hietajarvi, et al., "Media Multitasking Is Associated with Distractibility and Increased Prefrontal Activity in Adolescents and Young Adults," *Neuroimage* 134 (2016): 113–21; E. Ophir, C. Nass, and A. D. Wagner, "Cognitive Control in Media Multi-Taskers." *Proceedings of National Academy of Science* 106, no. 37 (2009): 15583–87.

11. K. K. Loh and R. Kanai, " How Has the Internet Reshaped Human Cognition?" *Neuroscientist* 22, no. 5 (2016): 506–20.

12. Z. Liu, "Reading Behavior in the Digital Environment: Changes in Reading Behavior over the Past Ten Years," *Journal of Documentation* 61, no. 6 (2005): 700–712.

13. A. F. Arnsten, M. A. Raskind, F. B. Taylor, and D. Connor, "The Effects of Stress Exposure on Prefrontal Cortex: Translating Basic Research into Successful Treatments for Post-Traumatic Stress Disorder," *Neurobiology of Stress* 1 (2015): 89–99.

14. A. Starcevic, ed. *Chronic Stress and Its Effect on Brain Structure and Connectivity* (Hershey, PA: Medical Information Science Reference/IGI Global, 2019).

15. J. LeDoux, *The Emotional Brain: The Mysterious Underpinnings of Emotional Life* (New York: Simon & Schuster, 1998). Positive feedback loops, or cycles of virtue, are hard to create for exactly this reason: namely, they do not create the type of stress responses that lead to our physiological systems getting increasingly locked in to the original category of stimulus.

16. Staff, "One-Third of Americans Are More Willing to Give Up Sex Than Their Mobile Phones," IT Business Edge, 2011, https://www.itbusinessedge.com/storage/one-third -of-americans-are-more-willing-to-give-up-sex-than-their-mobile-phones/.

17. D. Lu, "Fake News Gets Shared More When It Is Angry and Anxiety-Inducing," *NewScientist*, May 22, 2020, https://www.newscientist.com/article/2242452-fake -news-gets-shared-more-when-it-is-angry-and-anxiety-inducing/.

18. S. Vosoughi, D. Roy, and S. Aral, "The Spread of True and False News Online," *Science* 359, no. 6380 (2018): 1146–51.

19. W. J. Brady, J. A. Wills, J. T. Jost, J. A. Tucker, and J. J. Van Bavel, "Emotion Shapes the Diffusion of Moralized Content in Social Networks." *Proceedings of National Academy of Science* 114, no. 28 (2017): 7313–18.

20. E. Bakshy, I. Rosenn, C. Marlow, and L. A. Adamic, *The Role of Social Networks in Information Diffusion*, Proceedings of the 21st International Conference on the World Wide Web (New York: Association for Computing Machinery, 2012).

21. G. Pennycook and D. G. Rand, "Who Falls for Fake News? The Roles of Bullshit Receptivity, Overclaiming, Familiarity, and Analytic Thinking," *Journal of Personality* 88, no. 2 (April 12, 2020): 185–200.

22. G. Pennycook, T. Cannon, and D. G. Rand. "Prior Exposure Increases Perceived Accuracy of Fake News," *Journal of Experimental Psychology: General* 147, no. 12 (2018): 1865–80.

23. Repeating a statement leads to it becoming etched deeper and deeper in memory, which, in turn, makes it easier and easier to recall—an effect known as the Fluency

Effect. This occurs whether or not a statement is accurate or even whether or not the statement fits in with the participant's prior beliefs. See Pennycook, Cannon, and Rand, "Prior Exposure."

24. Human brains tend to focus on visual images and process them faster than text; additionally, the brevity of the text clipping also elicits rapid processing, rather than deep analysis. S. Schafer, "Illusion of Knowledge through Facebook News? Effects of Snack News in a New Feed on Perceived Knowledge, Attitude Strength, and Willingness for Discussions," *Computers in Human Behavior* 103 (2020): 1–12.

25. A. Legon and J. Deruy, "Whatsapp: Social Media's Dark Web," AVAAZ, 2019, https://avaazimages.avaaz.org/Avaaz_SpanishWhatsApp_FINAL.pdf.

26. J. A. Rawls, *Theory of Justice* (Cambridge, MA: Belknap Press, 1971); J. Habermas, *The Theory of Communicative Action* (Boston: Beacon Press, 1984).

27. S. Aral, *The Hype Machine: How Social Media Disrupts Our Elections, Our Economy, and Our Health—and How We Must Adapt* (New York: Random House, 2020), 84.

28. E. Shearer and K. E. Matsa. "News Use across Social Media Platforms 2018," Pew Research Center, 2018, https://www.pewresearch.org/journalism/2018/09/10/news-use-across-social-media-platforms-2018/.

29. M. S. Epstein and R. E. Robertson. "The Search Engine Manipulation Effect (Seme) and Its Possible Impact on the Outcomes of Elections," *PNAS* 112, no. 33 (2015): E4512–E21.

30. L. Sweeney, "Discrimination in Online Ad Delivery," *Communications of the Association for Computing Machinery* 11, no. 3 (2013), available at SSRN: https://ssrn.com/abstract=2208240 or http://dx.doi.org/10.2139/ssrn.2208240.

31. S. Noble, *Algorithms of Oppression: How Search Engines Reinforce Racism* (New York: New York University Press, 2018).

32. P. Lewis, "'Fiction Is Outperforming Reality': How Youtube's Algorithm Distorts Truth," *The Guardian*, February 2, 2018.

33. K. L. Johnston, "Young Vietnamese Americans Say Their Parents Are Falling Prey to Conspiracy Videos," *BuzzFeed*, April 21, 2021, https://www.buzzfeednews.com/article/katejohnston2/vietnamese-american-youtube-misinformation-covid-vaccine.

34. J. E. Oliver and T. J. Wood. "Conspiracy Theories and the Paranoid Style(s) of Mass Opinion," *American Journal of Political Science* 58, no. 4 (2014): 952–66.

35. T. Goertzel, "Belief in Conspiracy Theories." *Political Psychology* 15, no. 4 (1994): 731–42.

36. S. van der Linden, "The Conspiracy-Effect: Exposure to Conspiracy Theories (about Global Warming) Decreases Pro-Social Behavior and Science Acceptance," *Personality and Individual Differences* 87 (2015): 171–73.

37. J. Kaiser and A. Rauschfleisch. "Unite the Right? How Youtube's Recommendation Algorithm Connects the Us Far-Right." *Medium*, April 11, 2018, https://medium.com/@MediaManipulation/unite-the-right-how-youtubes-recommendation-algorithm-connects-the-u-s-far-right-9f1387ccfabd.

38. J. Ugander, B. Karrer, L. Backstrom, and C. Marlow. "The Anatomy of the Facebook Social Graph." *arXiv* 1111, no. 4503 (2011).

39. S. Aral, *The Hype Machine: How Social Media Disrupts Our Elections, Our Economy, and Our Health—and How We Must Adapt* (New York: Random House, 2020). The algorithm is built to maximize the network's profits, not to support the healthy workings of social networks based on real human dynamics. For the Narrative Machine to function, it needs users to make only a set number of social connections online: a user with too few friends is not contributing optimally to the network's growth, while those with too many friends make the network algorithms unstable. If a user prefers to socialize by having just a few friends, this is counter to the platform's business interests and the algorithm will duly intervene, repeatedly suggesting new possible "friends" to them. Additionally, because the platform ultimately seeks to maximize user engagement time, friend recommendation algorithms like PYMK try to bank on sure bets when they suggest new contacts: the overriding assumption is that users are more likely to accept friend (or work colleague) recommendations for people who are similar to them on social dimensions such as race, ethnicity, socio-economic status, educational attainment, even citizenship status, and are more likely to spend time with such connections, increasing time then spent on these platforms. Online networks thrive financially by making sure that they are too interesting and too socially valuable for users to leave—the so-called "Network Effect."

40. Aral, *The Hype Machine.*

41. J. E. Settle, *Frenemies: How Social Media Polarizes America* (Cambridge: Cambridge University Press, 2018).

42. M. Barnidge, "Exposure to Political Disagreement in Social Media versus Face-to-Face and Anonymous Online Settings," *Political Communication* 34, no. 2 (2017): 302–21.

43. J. Lees, and M. Cikara, "Inaccurate Group Meta-Perceptions Drive Negative out-Group Attributions in Competitive Contexts," *Nature Human Behavior* 4 (2020): 279–86.

44. H. Lyu, Y. Fan, Z. Xiong, M. Komisarchik, and J. Luo, "Understanding Public Opinion toward the #Stopasianhate Movement and the Relation with Racially Motivated Hate Crimes in the US," *IEEE Transactions on Computational Social Systems* (2023).

45. W. J. Brady, K. A. McLaughlin, T. N. Doan, and M. J. Crockett, "How Social Learning Amplifies Moral Outrage Expression in Online Social Networks," *Science Advances* 7, no. 33 (2021), https://doi.org/10.1126/sciadv.abe5641.

46. S. Costanza-Chock, *Design Justice: Community-Led Practices to Build the Worlds We Need* (Cambridge, MA: MIT Press, 2020).

47. A. Holpuch, "Facebook Still Suspending Native Americans over 'Real Name' Policy." *The Guardian*, February 16, 2015; Avianne Tan, "Why Some Native Americans Say Facebook Is Biased against Them," *ABC News*, February 13, 2015, https://abcnews.go.com/Technology/native-americans-petition-facebook-cease-deactivations-names/story?id=28921793.

48. Costanza-Chock, *Design Justice.*

49. Z. Tufekci, *Twitter and Tear Gas: The Power and Fragility of Networked Protest* (New Haven, CT: Yale University Press, 2017).

50. Costanza-Chock, *Design Justice*, 34

51. R. Srinivasan, *Whose Global Village? Rethinking How Technology Shapes Our World* (New York: New York University Press, 2017).

52. A. Smith, "Many Facebook Users Don't Understand How the Site's News Feed Works," PEW Research Center, 2018, https://www.pewresearch.org/short-reads/2018/09/05/many-facebook-users-dont-understand-how-the-sites-news-feed-works/.

53. J. Roozenbeek and S. van der Linden, "Fake News Game Confers Psychological Resistance against Online Misinformation," *Palgrave Communications* 5, no. 65 (2019), https://doi.org/10.1057/s41599-019-0279-9.

54. J. Roozenbeek, S. van der Linden, B. Goldberg, S. Rathje, and S. Lewandowsky, "Psychological Inoculation Improves Resilience against Misinformation on Social Media," *Science Advances* 8, no. 34 (2022), https://doi.org/10.1126/sciadv.abo6254.

55. G. Pennycook, J. McPhetres, Y. Zhang, J. G. Lu, and D. G. Rand, "Fighting Covid-19 Misinformation on Social Media: Experimental Evidence for a Scalable Accuracy Nudge Intervention," *Psychological Science* 31, no. 7 (2020): 770–80.

56. L. Festinger, *A Theory of Cognitive Dissonance* (Evanston: Row & Peterson, 1957); A. Kastenmuller, T. Greitmeyer, E. Jonas, P. Fischer, and D. Frey, "Selective Exposure: The Impact of Collectivism and Individualism," *British Journal of Social Psychology* 49, no. 4 (2010): 745–63.

57. W. I. Bennet and S. Iyengar. "A New Era of Minimal Effects? The Changing Foundations of Political Communication," *Journal of Communication* 58, no. 4 (2008): 707–31.

58. S. Iyengar and K. S. Hahn, "Red Media, Blue Media: Evidence of Ideological Selectivity in Media Use," *Journal of Communication* 59, no. 1 (2009): 19–39.

59. B. Warren, *infowars.com*, August 21, 2019, https://www.newswars.com/flashback-googles-schmidt-calls-multiple-search-results-a-bug-says-company-should-limit-to-single-right-answer/.

60. D. Frey, "Recent Research on Selective Exposure to Information," *Advances Experimental Social Psychology* 19 (1986): 41–80.

61. D. O. Sears, "Biased Indoctrination and Selectivity of Exposure to New Information." *Sociometry* 28, no. 4 (1965): 363–76.

62. S. Park, S. Kang, S. Chung, and J. Song, "Newscube: Delivering Multiple Aspects of News to Mitigate Media Bias," paper presented at the Computer Human Interaction Conference, 2009.

63. S. A. Munson, S. Y. Lee, and P. Resnick, "Encouraging Reading of Diverse Poliical Viewpoints with a Browser Widget," paper presented at the International Conference on Web and Social Media, 2013.

64. OneSub, https://onesub.io/.

65. Living Room Conversations, https://www.livingroomconversations.org/.

66. Search for Common Ground, https://www.sfcg.org/.

67. L. Schulz, M. Rollwage, R. J. Dolan, and S. M. Fleming, "Dogmatism Manifests in Lowered Information Search under Uncertainty," *Proceedings of the National Academy of Sciences* 117, no. 49 (2020): 31527–34.

68. D. Kahneman and A. Tversky, "Choices, Values, and Frames," *American Psychologist* 39, no. 4 (1984): 341–50.

69. Z. Huang and R. Wyer, "Diverging Effects of Mortality Salience on Variety Seeking: The Different Roles of Death Anxiety and Semantic Concept Activation," *Journal of Experimental Social Psychology* 58 (2015): 112–23.

70. C. J. Nemeth, "Differential Contributions to Majority and Minority Influence," *Psychological Review* 9, no. 1 (1986): 23–32.

71. J. C. Dolev, L. K. Friedlander, and I. M. Braverman, "Use of Fine Art to Enhance Visual Diagnostic Skills," *JAMA* 286, no. 9 (2001): 1020–21, https://doi.org/10.1001/jama.286.9.1020.

72. L. Zmigrod, P. J. Rentfrow, and T. W. Robbins, "The Partisan Mind: Is Extreme Political Partisanship Related to Cognitive Inflexibility?," *Journal of Experimental Psychology: General* 149, no. 3 (2019): 407–18.

73. P. Dolan and A. Henwood, "Five Steps towards Avoiding Narrative Traps in Decision-Making," *Frontiers in Psychology* 12 (2021): 694032, https://doi.org/10.3389/fpsyg.2021.694032. At a neurological level, the more confidence we show, the more that key neurons in our centro-parietal region—an area that is active when we seek out information—are deactivated, making it harder and harder to process any new information that does not tally with our original decision. M. Rollwage, A. Loosen, T. U. Hauser, R. Moran, R. J. Dolan, and S. M. Fleming, "Confidence Drives a Neural Confirmation Bias," *Nature Communications* 11, no. 1 (2020): 2634.

74. F. Pasquale, F. *The Black Box Society* (Cambridge, MA: Harvard University Press, 2015).

75. P. B. de Laat, "Algorithmic Decision-Making Based on Machine Learning from Big Data: Can Transparency Restore Accountability?" *Philosophy & Technology* 31, no. 4 (2018): 525–41.

76. E. Hussein, P. Juneja, and T. Mitra, "Measuring Misinformation in Video Search Platforms: An Audit Study on Youtube," *Proceedings of the ACM on Human-Computer Interaction*, Article 48 (2020).

77. G. Ignatow, "Speaking Together, Thinking Together? Exploring Metaphor and Cognition in a Shipyard Union Dispute," *Sociological Forum* 19, no. 3 (2004): 405–33.

78. H. E. Hershfield, H. M. Bang, and E. U. Weber, "National Differences in Environmental Concern and Performance Are Predicted by Country Age," *Psychological Science* 25, no. 1 (2014): 152–60.

79. Dolan and Henwood, " Five Steps."

CHAPTER 23

Elements of a National Narrative on the Peopling of America

T. Alexander Aleinikoff

The Constitution of the United States begins, "We, the People," but it doesn't define who "the People" are. In the 19th century the US Supreme Court issued two important decisions telling us who was *not* included in "We, the People"—at least as that term was understood by the Framers of the Constitution. In the infamous *Dred Scott* case, decided in 1857, Chief Justice Taney wrote that "neither the class of persons who had been imported as slaves, nor their descendants, whether they had become free or not, were then acknowledged as a part of the people."[1] A quarter century later, the Supreme Court reached a similar decision regarding Native Americans: "The Indian tribes, being within the territorial limits of the United States, were not, strictly speaking, foreign states, but they were alien nations, distinct political communities. . . . The members of those tribes owed immediate allegiance to their several tribes, and were not part of the people of the United States."[2]

These decisions have been overturned, *Dred Scott* by the section 1 of the Fourteenth Amendment and *Elk v. Wilkins* by a federal law declaring all Native Americans born in the United States citizens at birth. But who constitutes "the People" is more than fact and history and law—it is also part of the story we tell about America. And in telling the story of America, whose stories do we include and whose stories frequently go untold?

In the pages that follow, I describe three narratives about the peopling of America.[3] I try to provide the best version of each but then examine them from a critical perspective. I close by offering a new narrative, one that draws from the other three, but also sees the past and present differently, as well as providing a way to think about the future.

First, a few words about narratives.

We tell narratives for a reason. We use them to explain our present and our past. And a corollary is that we tell the story of the past from today's perspective. So our Founding Fathers are differently conceived in later historical eras not because *they* have changed but because *we* have changed; we need them for new purposes that speak to our time. And sometimes our focus shifts altogether. Lincoln's Gettysburg Address, receiving little notice at the time, came to redefine the founding of the nation—his "four score and seven years ago" taking us back not to the ratification of the Constitution but rather the signing of the Declaration of Independence. So too the 1619 Project asks us to take as a starting point neither 1776 nor 1789, but rather a much earlier date—the year enslaved Africans arrived on the territory of what would eventually become the United States.

This means that *narratives are not fixed*, they are open to new and revised tellings.

Think of the common description of the United States as a "nation of immigrants." Proponents of maintaining immigration and fighting against anti-immigrant animus rely on the narrative to strengthen their case, to appeal to "who we are" as a nation. At the same time, what a nation of immigrants means is influenced by where the narrative operates. For most of the second half of the 20th century, that narrative brought to mind, primarily, the Statue of Liberty and images of crowds of people on boats approaching Ellis Island. But consider Barack Obama's characterization of the narrative during a major speech on immigration in 2014: "My fellow Americans, we are and always will be a nation of immigrants. . . . And whether our forebears . . . crossed the Atlantic, or the Pacific, or the Rio Grande, we are here only because this country welcomed them in, and taught them that to be an American is about something more than what we look like, or what our last names are, or how we worship."[4] Obama's words, of course, put Asian migration and Mexican and Central American migration (documented and undocumented) on a par with European migration. This is an important shift in the narrative based on the perceived needs of the early 21st century.

I also want to stress *that the construction (or reconstruction) of narratives can involve—indeed, may require—the uncovering of some uncomfortable truths.*

For scholars and students of immigration today, it means finally coming to grips with the fact that the United States is a product of *settler colonialism.*[5] That is, coming to America in the 17th and 18th centuries meant arriving not on an empty, pristine continent—a New World. Rather, it meant conquering, displacing, killing hundreds of thousands of inhabitants living in communities that had existed here for thousands of years. Making that story part of the national narrative—as I will discuss later—might dramatically change how we think about claims of a sovereign power to exclude persons later seeking entry into this land.

Now to the three narratives.

Narrative One: The United States as a Nation of Immigrants

The dominant narrative about US immigration today is that of America as a "nation of immigrants." This has so permeated our culture and politics that we may fail to recognize that this description is of rather recent coinage, which gained currency with the publication of (then Senator) John F. Kennedy's book, *A Nation of Immigrants* in 1958. Kennedy's adoption of the phrase had a political purpose—to spur action on repealing the National Origin Quota system put in place in the 1920s to stem arrivals from Eastern and Southern Europe. In the post–World War II era, those laws were increasingly assailed as contrary to American values and based on bad science, as well as depriving the United States of some the world's best and brightest and undercutting the ideological war against communism. That is, under the National Origins Quota system, the US immigration system was based on race prejudice fundamentally at odds with the values that United States sought to preach to the world.

As historian Mae Ngai has noted:

> *A Nation of Immigrants* tells a simple story about "continuous waves" of immigration since the colonial era and the contributions of immigrants to the building of the nation—contributions they made as farmers, workers, and consumers; as scientists, artists, and writers. Each successive wave faced difficulty and hardship, and occasionally discrimination, but each eventually climbed the ladder of socioeconomic mobility and realized the American Dream. This narrative is familiar to all of us. But it was a new idea in the post–World War II era. (Chap. 9, this vol., p. 146)

Presidents have a particular penchant for affirming this narrative. I have already quoted President Obama's statement that "we are and always will be a nation of immigrants." A decade before, George W. Bush gave an Oval Office address on immigration in which he said, "We are a nation of laws, and we must enforce our laws. We are also a nation of immigrants, and we must uphold that tradition, which has strengthened our country in so many ways." Ronald Reagan, in announcing the conclusions of a review of immigration policies by his attorney general in 1981, started his statement this way: "Our nation is a nation of immigrants. More than any other country, our strength comes from our own immigrant heritage and our capacity to welcome those from other lands." And when President Johnson signed the historic 1965 immigration act at the foot of the Statute of Liberty in New York Harbor—thereby bringing to fruition his predecessor's goal in ending the National Origin Quota system—he declared: "Our beautiful America was built by a nation of strangers. From a hundred different places or more they have poured forth into an empty land, joining and blending in one mighty and irresistible tide. The land flourished because it was fed from so many sources—because it was nourished by so many cultures and traditions and peoples."

The nation of immigrants narrative concedes that in the past there have been moments of discrimination, even xenophobia—against the Irish, the Chinese, the Jews, and the Italians—but overall it is a progressive story, largely affirming American values of tolerance and nondiscrimination. The narrative is decidedly pro-immigration; indeed it makes immigration central to the nation's self-definition. It is at home with Oscar Handlin's observation from his 1952 Pulitzer Prize–winning book, *The Uprooted*: "Once I thought to write a history of the immigrants in America. Then I discovered that the immigrants *were* American history."

Conceiving of the United States as a nation of immigrants—where everyone is said to have come from "somewhere else"—supplies an equality among immigrant groups. It denies that one group has a primordial claim on the United States.[6] (As has been cleverly said, those who missed the *Mayflower* jumped on the first boat they could get.) This was the message of Kennedy's book: the later arriving immigrants came for the same reasons and contributed to the nation in the same ways as earlier groups. It was this commitment that laid bare the central injustice of the National Origins Quota system.

To be sure, the arrival of new groups has altered the culture and character of the nation. But the nation of immigrants story sees this as benefiting America—whether one adopts an assimilationist view (*e pluribus unum*) where the flavor in the melting pot is uniform even if new spices have been added—or a multicultural understanding of the United States (with each new group adding a distinct vegetable to the salad or instrument to the orchestra, which maintains its distinctiveness but contributes to an overall whole).

The nation of immigrants narrative has come under scrutiny and challenge in recent years. It is noted that it tells largely a European story, making Ellis Island the central focus of our immigration history.[7] Barack Obama's speech quoted earlier broadens the narrative's gaze: "whether our forebears . . . crossed the Atlantic, or the Pacific, or the Rio Grande."[8] But even this welcome expansion leaves out the stories of tens of millions of Americans, past, present and future (as well as those denied entry or deported). As Ngai explains, the slogan of nation of immigrants "obscures other dynamics of American history that are not properly explained as immigrations . . . [:] conquest and removal of indigenous peoples, slavery, and the acquisition of colonies" (chap. 9, this vol., p. 157).

The nation of immigrants narrative purports to foster a national community inclusive of immigrants by recognizing that we all share an immigrant past—that we (or our ancestors) all "came from elsewhere." But I wonder whether this metaphor does the work it sets out to do. I find more persuasive Kwame Anthony Appiah's account that

> what unites this country . . . is not that we are all the same, but that . . . so many of us think of America as ours. And that sense of possession comes from our belief that we each have a place in a great national narrative that we are only a part of and whose complete story none of us knows, because each of us is *aware* of only a part of it. Ishmael Reed once wrote of our country, "The world is here"; and he meant that we Americans are almost as diverse in our origins and our ideas as the globe as a whole. But we are all linked, despite that magnificent diversity, through our identification with one thing, America, our country, however differently we imagine it. (Chap. 2, this vol., p. 20)

This is a focus not on where we came from—or the fact that we came from somewhere else—but rather that, again in Appiah's words, "what makes 'us' a people, ultimately, is our everyday commitment to governing a common life *together*" (chap. 2, this vol., p. 24).

A final objection to the nation of immigrants narrative is its Panglossian feature—describing the United States as one big happy, growing family. Ngai notes that the introduction to the latest edition of *Nation of Immigrants* (published in 2018 and with an introduction written by Joe Kennedy III) continues to reiterate "a version of the wave theory and its message that today's immigrants are, in their essential characteristics, like all others who came before, each group a confirmation of America's success" (chap. 9, this vol., p. 157).

This view never attracted universal approval among the American people, as new immigration waves have regularly been regarded as different from those who came before and often as producing ill effects for the nation as a whole. Our most recent history provides examples of xenophobia, laced with racism, that rosy depictions of the American family cannot—and should not be permitted to—cover up.

Narrative Two: The Construction of the American People ("Nation by Design")

Donald Trump occasionally referred to the United States as a nation of immigrants.[9] But it is difficult to believe that he understood the phrase in the way John Kennedy intended. I think the true colors of the administration were made clear when it rewrote the mission statement of office of US Citizenship and Immigrant Services—this is the part of the Department of Homeland Security that approves visa petitions, grants naturalization, and adjudicates refugee cases overseas. USCIS was created after 9/11, when DHS was established. Despite the anti-terrorism fervor and harsh measures taken against Muslims in the United States at that time, overall migration to the United States was not stopped or even reduced. And when USCIS wrote its mission statement it said this: "USCIS secures America's promise *as a nation of immigrants* by providing accurate and useful information to our customers, granting immigration and citizenship benefits, promoting an awareness and understanding of citizenship, and ensuring the integrity of our immigration system."

During the Trump administration, USCIS rewrote its mission statement—*deleting* the reference to "nation of immigrants." Instead the text stated that USCIS "administers the nation's lawful immigration system, safeguarding its integrity and promise by efficiently and fairly adjudicating requests for immigration benefits while protecting Americans, securing the homeland, and honoring our values."[10]

And Trump's actions spoke louder than these words. The administration adopted brutal and cruel policies that separated families, cut refugee admissions by 90%, virtually ended asylum in the United States, and purported to terminate the DACA program (that action was invalidated by the Supreme Court).

This narrative sees America—and the role of immigration—in a very different light than the nation of immigrants narrative: not that we should welcome all who come and recognize that their arrival will change, for the better, our social and economic fabric. Rather, immigrants are figured as guests, invited on our terms and to serve interests defined by the American people, to assimilate to our way of being. Take it or leave it. Trump, during his campaign for the presidency, said, "Immigration is a privilege, and we should not let anyone into this country who doesn't support our communities."[11]

That right to choose who may enter the United States is understood as a part of national sovereignty—a sovereignty over the territory of the United States secured by tight borders. As Trump repeated throughout his presidency, in defending his "Wall" and other harsh measures, "If you don't have borders, you don't have a country."

This view did not begin with Trump. It is, in fact, deeply embedded in international law and US constitutional law and can be traced in the US to Supreme Court cases of the late 19th century. In upholding the Chinese Exclusion acts of the 1880s, the Court put it this way: "That the Government of the United States, through the action of the Legislative Department, can exclude aliens from its territory, is a proposition which we do not think open to controversy. Jurisdiction over its own territory to that extent is an incident of every independent nation. It is a part of its independence. If it could not exclude aliens, it would be, to that extent, subject to the control of another power."[12] It reiterated this view three years later: "It is an accepted maxim of international law that every sovereign nation has the power, as inherent in sovereignty, and essential to self-preservation, to forbid the entrance of foreigners within its dominions, or to admit them only in such cases and upon such conditions as it may see fit to prescribe."[13]

This narrative can be cashed out as rank restrictionism—immigrants out! closed borders!—but it is also possible to see it from another angle. Borders both exclude and admit, and the decision about whom to welcome is a decision about the construction of the American people (literally, the face of America). That is, the idea of a controlled system of immigration creates, to use Aristide Zolberg's phrase, "a nation by design." According to Zolberg, from the outset US immigration policy involved "a combination of disparate elements designed to facilitate or even stimulate the entry of immigrants deemed valuable while deterring those considered undesirable, and occasionally even going beyond this to rid the nation of populations already in its midst."[14]

For its first 100 years, the United States largely designed itself as having open borders (although naturalization was limited to "white" persons, according to a statute adopted in 1790, and states adopted rules that sought to regulate entry).[15] The Chinese Exclusion laws were a product of the late 19th century, and the National Origins Quota system of the first quarter of the 20th. But these restrictive laws eventually gave way to the 1965 Immigration and Nationality Act, the 1980 Refugee Act, and the 1986 Immigration Reform and Control Act, the latter of which provided legal status to three million undocumented immigrants in the United States. The pendulum swung back in 1996, with the Clinton Administration's building up of the Border Patrol and a focus on removal of "criminal aliens." Additional tough laws have followed, including rules adopted during the COVID pandemic that virtually ended asylum at the US border. But this period also saw the addition of 50,000 "diversity visas" annually allocated to persons from countries "underrepresented" in the current immigration flow. And despite much tougher policies at the border, the Deferred Action for Childhood Arrivals (DACA) program has provided protection to more than 700,000 undocumented migrants in the United States.

The crucial idea underlying this narrative, then, is that it is the responsibility of the federal government to design a nation, in part, through immigration policy and to enforce the relevant laws—lest it be "subject to the control" of other states or immigrants themselves.

Perhaps this narrative cures some of the flaws of the nation of immigrants narrative. It appears descriptively accurate, putting government policy front and center in the crafting the immigration rules. And it *could* be normatively attractive, if those rules embraced values of diversity, openness, rescue of the persecuted—something like, say, "Give me your tired your poor."

But I would note that designing the population through immigration regulation is easier said than done. An example: as was repeatedly promised in the legislative debate on the 1965, the new law would not change overall levels of immigration or the demographic make-up of the nation. Both assumptions proved to be dramatically incorrect. So, too, the decision to end the Bracero Program—in part due to the exploitative results it occasioned—did not stop Mexican migration to the United States; it simply shifted legal temporary migration to undocumented migration, as demanded by US agricultural interests. And starting in the 1990s, when border enforcement was significantly increased to stem this flow, it likewise did not end unauthorized migration; rather it turned seasonal migration into a settled population of more than 10 million undocumented persons.[16]

More significant than design failure, however, is the problem is that the narrative is too easily captured by messages of fear and loathing—as recent history has painfully proven. Federal dollars construct walls and detention facilities rather than bridges and welcome centers.

For a deeper critique, I will need to consider the Third Narrative.

Narrative Three: A Nation of White People

Narrative Three is the narrative of critical immigration studies. It objects to the kumbaya narrative of a "nation of immigrants," and it agrees with the idea that the United States is a "nation by design" in which immigration has played an important role. Central to that design, according to this narrative, is race.

The third narrative's origin story is one of *settler colonialism*.[17] The American people do not trace themselves to a native *Volk*, present in the land since time immemorial. Rather, those who arrived in 17th century and beyond came as settlers from Europe—many centuries after other civilizations established themselves here. This was a different kind of colonialism than was imposed in Africa, which was based on the exploitation of resources and the ruthless control of an Indigenous workforce. The settlers came to stay and to develop their own communities, states. Fairly quickly acknowledging that Native Americans could not be forced to work, the settlers pushed Indigenous people out and brought in indentured servants from Europe and enslaved people from Africa.

The settler colonial perspective undercuts the sovereignty claim of Narrative Two. If the United States was established on land taken by force from others—if the settlers, that is, possessed bad title—on what basis do the current inhabitants possess the right to exclude those who seek to enter today? From whence comes their license to design?[18]

Furthermore, this narrative records a history of design that stains and shames our national self-conception. The settlers indeed created a nation by design—it was a white man's nation. Native Americans born into tribes were not deemed to be citizens of the new country. And, as noted, the first naturalization statute, adopted by Congress in 1790, permitted only white people to become citizens. Just before the Civil War, the Supreme Court held in the *Dred Scott* case that Blacks born as *free persons* in the United States were not citizens—they were not part of the original people of the United States, those for whom the nation was established. The Fourteenth Amendment erased the error of *Dred Scott*, and Congress eventually passed legislation granting birthright citizenship to Native Americans, but race-based design—according to the critical immigration narrative—has remained a constant of US immigration policy throughout American history.

The Chinese Exclusion laws of the 1880s were explicitly so, as was the "Gentleman's Agreement" of 1907 restricting immigration from Japan, and the creation of the Asian barred zone by a 1917 act of Congress. Racial ideology lay at the foundation of the National Origins Quota system put in place in the 1920s (Nordics yes, Mediterraneans not so much). Mexican migration was welcomed as cheap labor only, and deportation programs in the 1930s and 1950s forcibly removed tens of thousands when US economic circumstances were deemed to warrant it.

This narrative recasts the 1965 immigration act. It is noted that the law was not intended to dramatically shift the countries of origin of immigrants to the United States (more on that later) and surely not intended to change the racial make-up of the nation. Furthermore, according to Alina Das, "Civil rights reforms may have ended national origins quotas but they did not stop the racism that drove the quotas in the first place. Tools of deportation and incarceration . . . took on heightened importance. And as the next decades of the post–civil rights era would prove, criminality would provide justification for a vast crime-based deportation machine."[19] In this account, the racism of settler colonialism has not been extirpated; rather, it has been transformed, sanitized. The focus is now on "criminal aliens,"[20] yet the results are the same: the United States is figured as a "deportation nation," removing predominantly immigrants of color (many of whom become removable after being victimized by a racist criminal justice system).

Here, again, is Das:

> Criminalization has ensured the deportation of millions of people of color from the United States. Government officials have used public safety grounds to help justify every anti-immigrant measure since the beginning of restrictive federal immigration law. Where such a narrative was permitted to mingle with overtly racist language, it did so. And when overtly racist language was no longer legally or socially acceptable, the immigrant-as-criminal narrative emerged to help justify what the overtly racist narrative once did—the large-scale exclusion and expulsion of communities of color from the United States.[21]

The treatment of Central American asylum seekers by both Democratic and Republican administrations can be seen further evidence of discriminatory treatment for immigrants of color. Those taking dangerous journeys north to the southwest US border are characterized as "illegal aliens" trying to game a humanitarian program, thus warranting their detention and other deterrence measures, including significant payments to Mexico to help stop the flow. The critical perspective argues that these migrants are fleeing conditions—gangs, corrupt and feckless governments, dire economic situations, and climate change—for which the United States shares responsibility.

Of course, during the Trump years, the fig leaf of a non-race-based deportation system was removed. Racial appeals were overt in the call for a "Muslim ban," the description of Mexican migrants as criminals and rapists, and in Trump's labeling of Haiti and other predominantly nonwhite states as "shithole" nations. The long history of US immigration policy began, and continues today, as a fight to preserve a white America.

As Justin Gest's essay in this volume argues:

> Even as its boundaries have shifted, "whiteness" has persistently charac-terized the American self-understanding. Once members of a Northern European and predominantly Protestant plantation society, Americans have come to recognize the membership of people from German, Italian, Irish, Slavic, and Middle Eastern backgrounds along with a variety of religious faiths in a high-technology democracy. But the expansion of America has taken place only with an expanded definition of whiteness. Whiteness *is* the national myth.[22] (Chap. 3, this vol., p. 30)

I have focused primarily on exclusions based on race. But US im-migration law has historically excluded persons on other grounds—poor people (in the words of a law adopted in the late 1800s that continues today: "persons likely to become a public charge"); persons with "foreign" ideologies—predominantly those from the Left: com-munists and anarchists; persons who have been convicted of crimes in their home countries; terrorists; LGBTQ+ individuals; and other categories deemed "undesirable." While US citizens in these catego-ries could not be banished from the nation, immigration laws could be used to keep out noncitizens possessing these disfavored characteris-tics and to exclude them from becoming part of "We, the People."

The analysis of critical immigration scholars produces bold propos-als for change. If liberals want to pass DACA and legalization legisla-tion, curb abusive practices of the Border Patrol and ICE, restore asylum at the border, and provide enlarged grounds for relief from deportation, the critical advocates call to "Abolish ICE," end detention of immigrants, stop all deportations from the United States, use dol-lars currently spent on enforcement for new programs of welcome, and recognize a human right to free movement over borders.

The critical analysis is powerful. To my mind, it corrects America's origin myth, provides new reasons for challenging the "plenary power" of the federal government to control immigration, and shines a crucial light on the link between mass incarceration of those accused and convicted of crimes and the detention of immigrants.

Thus, I credit the arguments that the criminalization of immigration law (through expanding grounds for criminal removals and ending avenues of relief from deportation) has reinforced structural racism in the immigration system, as it has disproportionately affected immigrants of color and has had the effect of equating illegality with "brownness," which has disadvantaged nonwhite citizens and immigrants alike. And I have little doubt that we would be more open to reforms of the system if most of the deportees were white Europeans.

But by focusing primarily on the US deportation system, the critical narrative misses a number of important elements of the US immigration system taken as a whole. The analysis underplays the positive reasons for immigrants' desires to come to the United States: they are not always pushed from home or victims of an unjust global distribution of resources and opportunities (although of course these causes of movement cannot be discounted). The United States remains a destination of choice for tens of millions of people around the world, as it has throughout its history among those seeking the opportunity to flourish.

Thus, the focus of critical immigration studies on the US *removal system* largely ignores the legal immigration system. It is not as if we have closed the door and are now removing nonwhite people to ensure the continuation of a white nation. Under the current system—in place and largely unchanged since 1965—the United States hands out about a million green cards a year.[23] And the vast majority of persons granted lawful permanent resident status are "immigrants of color" (with the top countries of origin being Mexico, India, and China). The establishment and continuation of "diversity visas" has also opened up immigration from Africa, which, when combined with family visa categories and refugee admission, has increased at a higher rate than from anywhere else.[24]

The impact of immigration on the overall make-up of the American people has been dramatic. In 1990, 75% of the US population identified as "white"; today, 57.8% do. According to the 2020 census, the "white" population of the United States dropped by nearly 9% as a proportion of the overall population. The increase in the Hispanic or Latino population (12 million) accounted from more than half of the total growth in US population between 2010 and 2020; Hispanics or Latinos are now 18.7% of the US population. At the same time, persons identifying as Asian (alone) grew by 33% and Asian in combination by 50%; they now constitute 6% of the US population.[25]

While it is accurate to report that the intent of the 1965 law was not to change the racial make-up of the United States, the law's impact has now been apparent for years. Yet there has been no serious attempt in Congress to alter laws that will continue this trend into the future.[26] Thus, taking the US immigration system as a whole, even if race continues to play a role in opposition to legalization programs and to sustaining high levels of removals, it is problematic to claim that the original design of the United States as a white nation is the dominant motif in current immigration policy.

Conclusion: A Narrative on the Peopling of America

I began by saying that we tell narratives for a reason. What reasons lie behind the three narratives I have sketched? For JFK, the nation of immigrants narrative was intended to lay the groundwork for the repeal of the National Origin Quota system. For Donald Trump, the narrative of control of the border was deployed to gain votes (and it did). Critical scholars believe that their narrative will assist the movement to end detention and deportation of immigrants and to move us closer to a world of open borders.

My goal is simply this: to move beyond this moment of anti-immigrant policies and rhetoric that do extreme damage to immigrants and citizens alike and that do not honor American values. As I have tried to suggest, none of the three narratives seems up to the task of moving us far enough forward.

So I offer a new narrative. Like the others, it is grounded in a reading of US history and embodies implicit normative commitments.

My starting observation is that each of the three narratives I have described is *partial*. Each is concerned primarily with immigration to the United States rather narrowly defined (usually as green card holders), focusing on how through law and policy the United States has admitted noncitizens and the impact of those admissions on the make-up—demographically, socially, economically—of the nation.

An alternative narrative would ask the broader question of who is here, from where did they come, and how did they get here—and who is not here, either because they have been denied entry or because they have been pushed out. This more comprehensive narrative is concerned with *the peopling of America*.[27] To be sure, immigration as generally understood, is an important part of that peopling—but it is only one part. The narrative would also examine stories of those who came not as voluntary immigrants but in chains,[28] those who didn't come to America but rather had America come to them (residents of US territories),[29] those whose lands were taken from them and who faced death and relocation,[30] those who were admitted but have been removed,[31] and those who entered without authorization.[32] This fuller narrative includes the stories of tens of millions of persons in the United States left out of the "nation of immigrants" account. It is by taking this broader view that one gets a better picture of who constitutes America—and whether the promises America makes to its people are kept.

The second element of this broader narrative is the recognition that the United States is *provisional*, in terms of both its land and its people. The usual story told is of western expansion across the continent beginning in the 17th century and ending in the 19th.[33] Since then, the story goes, we have been a nation of fixed borders—indeed, ones that many Americans believe should be more rigorously enforced. But the true story is one of fairly continuous territorial shifting, both increasing and decreasing the size of the America. (Donald Trump was mocked for suggesting that the United States buy Greenland from Denmark, but such a purchase would be consistent with practices dating to the beginning of the Republic. And is the secession of one or more American states truly beyond the realm of possibility?)

As the territory of the United States expanded and contracted, so did the definition of the American people. The annexation of Mexican lands in the mid-19th century led to more than 200,000 new US citizens, while the acquisition of the Virgin Islands from Denmark in 1917 imposed US citizenship on another 25,000. The congressional act granting independence to the Philippines in 1946 denationalized 19 million US nationals.[34]

Recognizing "provisionality" lets us take greater notice of historical periods of mass immigration and mass deportations. Indeed, our current moment evidences both. In recent years, the United States has granted around a million green cards annually, while enforcement at the southwest border has shown the highest number of arrests ever recorded. More than two million persons were summarily expelled from the United States, under both the Trump and Biden administrations, pursuant to Centers for Disease Control rules seeking to prevent the spread of COVID. Should a new legalization program (finally) be adopted, 10 million undocumented migrants will become part of the American people.

Nearly all of these stories—showing the dynamic nature of the peopling of America—are left out of the narratives I have previously described.

A third element of this narrative draws our attention to uncomfortable and usually unmentioned truths about our history. The nation of immigrants narrative—and most K-12 accounts of the peopling of America—start with a story of emigrants (or refugees) seeking religious freedom and a new life in the New World. But here the critical narrative provides a necessary corrective: these vaunted original settlers, and the Founding Fathers of 150 years later, took land from those already here and set out to form a nation primarily for white people—built with the coerced labor of Black people. And since the founding, race-based exclusions and enforcement practices have been a persistent part of US history. We will not be able to bind up the wounds of the nation until we face this part of our peopling history.

While respectful of history, a new narrative must be aware that the past is not always prologue—and that, despite our origins, the people of America are increasingly diverse and will continue to grow more diverse into the foreseeable future. It should further tell the story that adding people to the nation, particularly in our current moment, is good for the nation. The data are clear that without immigration, the US population would be declining and that immigrants and their children account for more than 50% of US population growth.

Finally, my narrative would include the recognition that the United States *remains a place people want to come to and, frequently, to remain.* For reasons not immediately apparent, this is usually left out of US immigration narratives (except when used in a negative way by opponents of immigration, who claim the whole world would come here, given the opportunity). Do a thought experiment of imagining yourself a citizen of a country that no one wants to visit or join. Such a country would be dreary, desolate, boring. It is worthy of note that the United States is a nation that attracts people from every other country in the world.[35]

Putting these elements together creates a narrative about the peopling of America that is descriptively accurate and normatively attractive. It is inclusive, open-ended, and optimistic—people want to come and we are better for them coming—and, in these ways, it is, I suppose, classically American. It is also realistic about the past and the work that must be done to overcome it, taking aim at continuing assertions of white supremacy and putting in play policies of reparations for those whose land or labor were stolen. By offering a new way to tell the American story, it provides a way of moving us beyond the current fraught moment, which seems stalled in an unproductive fight between Donald Trump and Emma Lazarus.

This is not to give up on the Statue of Liberty. But it may put that iconic symbol in a new light. It was, recall, a gift from the French to commemorate the centennial of the Declaration of Independence and the then-recent ending of slavery in the United States. Although hard to see in most views of the statue, there are broken shackles and chains at Liberty's feet. From its origin, then, it resonates with a fuller story of the peopling of America that goes beyond characterizing America as a nation of immigrants. Moreover, while we usually see the torch as lighting the way to America, it can be figured another way—as providing light for those seeking to go out from the United States to the world. This recognizes a new role for immigration in America's future. Historians have described immigrants as "uprooted" and then "transplanted" in the United States. But in an increasingly mobile world, immigrants are more than citizens in waiting; they are in fact bridges to the world; they are part of transnational networks[36] that connect us as a planet and will help us face the global challenges before us.

This is a dynamic and unfinished story, as any narrative worth the telling should be.

Notes

1. Dred Scott v. Sandford, 60 US (19 How.) 393, 407 (1857).
2. Elk v. Wilkins, 112 US 94, 99 (1884).
3. There are other narratives than those I describe; but I believe the three I treat here constitute the dominant narratives.
4. Zeke Miller, "Here's Obama's Immigration Speech in Full," *Time*, November 20, 2014, https://time.com/3598756/obama-immigration-action/.
5. Roxanne Dunbar-Ortiz, *Not "A Nation of Immigrants": Settler Colonialism, White Supremacy, and a History of Erasure and Exclusions* (Boston: Beacon Press, 2021).
6. Randolph S. Bourne, *Trans-National America* (n.p.: Cosimo Classics, 2020).
7. See Ngai, chap. 9, this vol.: "Perhaps not surprisingly, *A Nation of Immigrants* focused entirely on European immigrants. There was no discussion of Mexican or Asian immigrations, reflecting the conventional thinking that they were temporary migrants, birds of passage and sojourners" (p. 147).
8. This is a necessary updating, as now 80% of persons entering the United States on green cards come from Latin American or Asian countries.
9. He did so (to my mind, cynically) in his announcement of a Muslim ban just after taking office: "America is a proud nation of immigrants and we will continue to show compassion to those fleeing oppression, but we will do so while protecting our own citizens and border."
10. The Biden Administration again rewrote the USCIS mission statement. It now reads: "USCIS upholds America's promise as a nation of welcome and possibility with fairness, integrity, and respect for all we serve."
11. Susan Jones, "Trump: 'Immigration Is a Privilege," *CNS News*, June 14, 2016, https://www.cnsnews.com/news/article/susan-jones/trump-immigration-privilege.
12. Chae Chan Ping v. United States, 130 US 581, 603–04 (1889).
13. Nishimura Ekiu v. United States, 142 US 651, 659 (1892).
14. Aristide Zolberg, *A Nation by Design: Immigration Policy in the Fashioning of America* (Cambridge, MA: Harvard University Press, 2006), 19.

15. Zolberg, *A Nation by Design*, 19.

16. See Ana Raquel Minian, chap. 12, this vol.

17. See Rogers M. Smith, chap. 4, this vol.

18. Natsu Taylor Saito, "Border Constructions: Immigration Enforcement and Territorial Presumptions," *Journal of Gender, Race & Justice* 10, no. 2 (Winter 2007): 193–244.

19. Alina Das, *No Justice in the Shadows: How America Criminalizes Immigrants* (New York: Bold Type Books, 2020), 57.

20. Coined by Julia Stumpf, the term "crimmigration" is used by scholars to denote the close links between the criminal justice and removal systems. Julia Stumpf, "The Crimmigration Crisis: Immigrants, Crime, and Sovereign Power," *American University Law Review* 56, no. 1 (December 2006): 367–419.

21. Das, *No Justice*, 24. See Carrie L. Rosenbaum, "Crimmigration—Structural Tools of Settler Colonialism," *Ohio State Journal of Criminal Law* 16, no. 1 (2018), 47: "By framing racial disparities and oppression within the settler colonial methodology, it is possible to recognize the systems of power responsible for the oppression in general, and specifically within the context of crimmigration, and the impact of crimmigration's racial biases on the ability of racialized immigrants to either experience equality or the socio-economic status of the settler class. Settler colonialism teaches us that 'racial remedies,' even those entrenched in the Constitution, will continue to be insufficient in achieving equality and integration. Fundamentally, it may be that only the end of race will provide the most complete answer to this problem."

22. Biden has pledged to make policies more humane, and in some instances has done so, but he has not shifted the paradigm: a huge deportation machine removing overwhelmingly immigrants of color.

23. This figure dropped due to the COVID-19 pandemic, of course.

24. Immigration from Africa has doubled every decade since 1970. The largest countries of origin, Ethiopia, Egypt, Ghana, and Kenya, accounted for half of the foreign-born African population in the United States in 2015. See Monica Anderson, "African Immigrant Population in U.S. Steadily Climbs," Pew Research Center, February 14, 2017, https://www.pewresearch.org/fact-tank/2017/02/14/african-immigrant-population-in-u-s-steadily-climbs/.

25. Nicholas Jones, Rachel Marks, Roberto Ramirez, and Merarys Ríos-Vargas, "2020 Census Illuminates Racial and Ethnic Composition of the Country," US Census Bureau, August 21, 2021, https://www.census.gov/library/stories/2021/08/improved-race-ethnicity-measures-reveal-united-states-population-much-more-multiracial.html. See John R. Weeks, chap. 7, this vol.

26. Indeed, given immigration of past half century, there would be continued change in the racial make-up of United States even if immigration were stopped today. Weeks, chap. 7, this vol.

27. See Ngai, chap. 9, this vol.

28. See Allison Dorsey, chap. 19, this vol.

29. Daniel Immerwahr, chap. 10, this vol.

30. Dakota Mace, "*Dahodiyinii* (Sacred Places)," chap. 5, this vol.
31. Jill Anderson and Maggie Loredo, chap. 21, this vol.
32. Minian, chap. 12, this vol.
33. Beyond this period, statehood came to southwestern states, and later Alaska and Hawaii, only in the mid-20th century.
34. See Immerwahr, chap. 10, this vol.
35. This gives us another way to see undocumented migrants—not as criminals or "illegals," but rather as persons drawn to this country, yet for whom the country does not provide adequate admission slots.
36. See Alexandra Délano Alonso, *From Here and There: Diaspora Policies, Integration, and Social Rights Beyond Borders* (New York: Oxford University Press, 2018).

ACKNOWLEDGMENTS

This book was conceived with the guidance and advice of a committee of friends of the Zolberg Institute on Migration and Mobility; thanks to Deborah Amos, Jonathan Fanton, Simone Lässig, Bita Mostofi, Rubén G. Rumbaut, David Scobey for being there at the beginning and throughout the process. Many of the authors in this volume as well as other colleagues participated in preliminary conversations and workshops dating back to 2018. We thank them all for their continued engagement, particularly through the challenging years of the COVID-19 pandemic. Earlier drafts of three chapters in the volume were presented at public lectures by Kwame Anthony Appiah on Ellis Island on October 6, 2019, and by Héctor Tobar and John R. Weeks on December 11, 2019, cosponsored by the Institute of European Studies at the University of California, Berkeley, and the Berkeley Interdisciplinary Migration Initiative, in association with the Pacific Regional Office of the German Historical Institute.

We benefited from discussions with the Zolberg External Advisory committee—Victoria Hattam, Andrew Kaldor, Renata Kaldor, Ira Katznelson, Frances Liu, Doris Meissner, Ilse Melamid, Will Milberg, David Miliband, Robert H. Mundheim, Edafe Okporo, Peter Seligmann, and Joel Towers—and from three anonymous reviewers of the book proposal and manuscript commissioned by Johns Hopkins University Press. Andrew Carr and Begoña Gerling Sarabia provided crucial assistance in preparation of the final manuscript. We thank Laura Davulis, our editor at Johns Hopkins University Press, as well as Ezra Rodríguez and the Westchester editorial team for their support in the various stages of publication. An earlier version of the chapter by Hana E. Brown, Jennifer A. Jones, and Taylor Dow was published in *Law and Contemporary Problems* and is being published here with the journal's permission.

This project was generously supported with funding from Henry Arnhold and the Arnhold family and the Mellon Foundation. The book is part of the New Narratives Curriculum Project, which will be hosted on the Zolberg Institute webpage.

Special thanks to Catherine McGahan, Deputy Director of the Zolberg Institute on Migration and Mobility.

All the royalties from the book will be donated to mutual aid and community-led storytelling projects, and to the New Narratives Curriculum Project.

Neil Agarwal is a 2020 graduate of Washington University in St. Louis, where he studied philosophy, religion, and politics. Agarwal most recently worked as a research fellow at Interfaith America in Chicago studying political polarization in the United States.

T. Alexander Aleinikoff is Dean of The New School for Social Research and Director of the Zolberg Institute on Migration and Mobility at The New School. He writes on migration, refugees, and race.

Jill Anderson is an academic and activist dedicated to interrupting current power dynamics and embodying alternatives. Born in Utah and raised in Texas, she spent 15 years living, loving, (un)learning, and community organizing in Mexico City.

Kwame Anthony Appiah grew up in Ghana and was educated in England before moving to the United States. He now teaches philosophy at New York University.

Hana E. Brown is a sociologist at Wake Forest University. She researches race, immigration, and US social policy.

Alexandra Délano Alonso is a professor of Global Studies at The New School. Living in between Mexico City and Queens, New York, she writes about Mexico-US migration, memory politics, and transnational practices of resistance and solidarity at the intersection of art, activism, and community organizing.

Allison Dorsey, Professor Emerita Swarthmore College, is the author of "'We've taken old gods and given them new names': The spirit of Sankofa in the Daughters of the Dust," "'The great cry of our people is land!': Black Settlement and Community Development on Ossabaw Island, Georgia, 1865–1900" and *To Build Our Lives Together: Community Formation in Black Atlanta*.

Taylor Dow is an attorney in New York. He is a graduate of the University of Pennsylvania Law School and Wake Forest University.

Maria Cristina Garcia, an Andrew Carnegie Fellow, is the Howard A. Newman Professor of American Studies at Cornell University. Her most recent book is *State of Disaster: The Failure of US Migration Policy in an Age of Climate Change*.

Justin Gest is an associate professor at George Mason University's Schar School of Policy and Government. He is the author of six books primarily on the politics of immigration and demographic change including, most recently, *Majority Minority*.

Daniel Immerwahr is a professor of history at Northwestern University. He is the author, most recently, of *How to Hide an Empire: A History of the Greater United States*.

Jennifer A. Jones is an associate professor of sociology at the University of Illinois at Chicago. Her research lies at the intersection of the sociology of race, immigration, and politics with an emphasis on the relationship between categorical ascription and meaning-making. Her publications include *The Browning of the New South*.

Katy Long is the executive director of the California Migration Museum. She works on refugee and migration issues both as an academic researcher and a writer and journalist. She is a senior research associate at the Refugee Law Initiative, University of London, and presented the BBC series *Century of Exile*.

Maggie Loredo grew up undocumented in the United States and was forcibly returned to México 14 years ago. In 2015 Maggie co-founded the Mexican nonprofit Otros Dreams en Acción (ODA) and is currently the executive director. Maggie is also co-creator of the podcast *Pochas So What*.

Dakota Mace is an interdisciplinary artist whose work engages Diné history and culture. Her works have been exhibited internationally and she currently serves as MFA mentor at the Institute of American Indian Arts, in Santa Fe, New Mexico.

Ruth Milkman is Distinguished Professor of Sociology and History at the Graduate Center of the City University of New York and chairs the Labor Studies Department in CUNY's School of Labor and Urban Studies. Her most recent books are *On Labor, Gender and Inequality* and *Immigrant Labor and the New Precariat*.

Ana Raquel Minian is an associate professor of history at Stanford University and a 2020 recipient of the Andrew Carnegie Fellowship. Minian's first book, *Undocumented Lives: The Untold Story of Mexican Migration*, received the David Montgomery Award, among many others.

Carlos Motta is a Colombian-born, New York-based artist. Motta has an interdisciplinary practice making work in film, photography, and sculpture. Motta's practice challenges dominant ideas about sexuality and gender using a myriad of archival material, art historical references, and the body.

Mae Ngai is a professor of history and Asian American studies at Columbia University. She is author the award-winning *Impossible Subjects, Illegal Aliens and the Making of Modern America* and *The Chinese Question: The Gold Rushes and Global Politics*.

Eboo Patel is founder and president of Interfaith America, the nation's largest interfaith organization. He is the author of five books, most recently *We Need To Build: Field Notes For Diverse Democracy*.

QUEEROCRACY is a New York City-based grassroots organization that promotes social and economic justice through direct action, community engagement, and education. Cofounded by Cassidy Gardner, Camilo Godoy, Megan Mullholland, and Michael Tikili, QUEEROCRACY is committed to challenging institutional injustice locally and globally within a queer framework. Since 2013, QUEEROCRACY is co-organized by Jawanza James Williams with Voices of Community Activists and Leaders (VOCAL-NY).

Marco Saavedra is a political refugee and Indigenous Mixteca painter from Oaxaca, Mexico. He works at his family's mutual aid restaurant, La Morada, in the South Bronx, New York, building something that's new.

Cinthya Santos Briones is a visual artist, educator, and cultural organizer with indigenous Nahua roots based in New York. Her work focuses on a multidisciplinary social practice that combines participatory art and the construction of collective narratives.

Rogers M. Smith is the Christopher H. Browne Distinguished Emeritus Professor of Political Science at the University of Pennsylvania. He is the author of many articles and eight books, most recently *That Is Not Who We Are! Populism and Peoplehood*.

Pireeni Sundaralingam, a cognitive scientist, has held research posts at MIT and UCLA, and led research at Silicon Valley's Center for Humane Technology. She is founder and CEO of Neuro-Resilience Consulting and is currently writing a book on how algorithm-driven tech disrupts society and how we can have a more sustainable relationship with digital technology.

Héctor Tobar is the Los Angeles–born author of six books, including the novel *The Tattooed Soldier* and the forthcoming *Our Migrant Souls: A Meditation on Race and the Meanings and Myths of "Latino."* His nonfiction *Deep Down Dark* was a *New York Times* bestseller, and his books have been translated into 15 languages.

Jesús I. Valles is a queer Mexican immigrant, educator, storyteller, and performer based in Austin, Texas, originally from Cd. Juárez, Mexico. Jesús is a recipient of the 2018 Undocupoets Fellowship, a fellow of The Poetry Foundation, and Crescendo Literary's 2018 Poetry Incubator. Their work has been published in the *Shade Journal*, the *Texas Review*, and the *New Republic*.

Wendy Vogt is an associate professor of anthropology at Indiana University-Purdue University, Indianapolis. Her book, *Lives in Transit: Violence and Intimacy on the Migrant Journey*, chronicles the dangerous journeys of Central American migrants crossing Mexico and is based on long-term ethnographic fieldwork in humanitarian aid shelters and other transit sites.

John R. Weeks is Distinguished Professor Emeritus of Geography and Director of the International Population Center at San Diego State University. He is also author of *Population: An Introduction to Concepts and Issues*, a best-selling textbook on demography now in its 13th edition.

Page numbers in *italics* and **bold** refer to figures and tables, respectively.

deportations of, 109, 237–38; economic contribution, 100, 121, 274, 275, 276; education of, 4; exclusion of, 235–38; experience of, 7, 96, 98, 114n7, 391; fates of, 169–70; fear of, 121, 189–90; integration models, 138, 398–99; labor movement and, 277, 278–79; legalization, 113; negative attitudes toward, 109, 119, 182–83, 271–72, 412–13; racial and ethnic groups, 29, 34, 131–32, 133–34, **134**, 155, 156, 273, 275; regional distributions, 272; religious diversity, 31–32; rights activism, 158–59, 194, 360–61, 371–72, 392; sense of belonging, 113; socioeconomic mobility, 150; statistics, 127, 131, 272; status of, 42n1; taxation, 274; travels to home country, 4–5; undesirable categories, 444; unemployment rate, 138; voluntary ethnic associations, 149; *See also* individual groups of immigrants

immigrant threat narrative, 189–90, 273–74, 275, 276, 278, 279, 308, 411

immigration: after World War II, 52; American story and, 97–98, 445–46; Black-Brown solidarity and, 369–72; border control and, 439–40, 441; challenges of, 8, 9, 13; civil rights and, 13, 356, 358–59, 363, 365, 366, 368, 374; class inequalities and, 245; climate change and, 194; colonialism and, 158; conspiracy theories about, 308–9; control of, 105; current trends, 127–29; debates about, 35, 36; future of, 450; gender and sexuality in discourse of, 235; global perspective on, 121; history of, 110–12, 146–47, 148–49, 157–58, 276; illegal, 213, 308; labor movement and, 276–79; as lesson in loss, 96; modernity and, 149; national discourse on, x; new narratives of, 15–16, 279–80; peak of, 126; perspectives on, 64–65; poetic representation of, 270; political debates on, x–xi, 201–2, 369; post-1965, 275–76; queer politics and, 237–38, 254, 256; racism and, 111, 358–59; stories of, 9–10; visa regimes and, 381, 385–87; waves of, ix, 146–47; *See also* US immigration law; US immigration policy

Immigration Act of 1864, 124–25

Immigration Act of 1882, 125, 256
Immigration Act of 1891, 256
Immigration Act of 1917, 256
Immigration Act of 1924 (Johnson-Reed Act), 256, 272, 277, 309, 358
Immigration and Customs Enforcement (ICE), 359, 369–71, 372–73, 397–98
Immigration and Nationality Act of 1952, 126–27, 151, 185, 237, 257
Immigration and Nationality Act of 1965 (INA): Black immigrants and, 346; conditional entry allotments, 197n17; consequences of, 386; definition of refugee in, 184; enactment of, 146, 151, 160n12, 183, 440; exclusion of homosexuals, 257; family reunification programs of, 244, 245; goals of, 272, 440, 446; national origin quotas, 126, 150, 358
Immigration and Naturalization Service (INS), 217, 219, 237, 259, 260
Immigration Equality, 260
immigration narratives: central features of, 268; history of, 267–68; new approach to, 14–15, 279–80, 378; types of, 270–71; *See also* individual narratives
"Immigration Raids Echo History of African Americans" (newsletter), 365–66
Immigration Reform and Control Act of 1986 (IRCA): enactment of, 201–2, 239, 258, 440; failure of, 278; family reunification mechanisms of, 240; goals of, 202–3, 225, 239; labor unions support of, 278; unauthorized migration and, 203, 225–26
inadvertent audience effect, 422
in-betweenness, 5, 7
Indian Nullification, 54
Indigenous people, colonial dispossession of, 52
Indigenous political thought, 54
information: alternative sources of, 422–23; available online, 407; contradictory, 408, 422; emotions and, 411; filtering of, 414–15; importance of balance of, 422; overload, 406–8; perception of accuracy of, 412; personal beliefs and search for, 421–22; repetitive, 427n23; visual images and, 428n24
Instituto Nacional de Migración (INM), 397

integrationist framework, 11, 12
Inter-American Development Bank, 215
International AIDS Conference, 266
International Intersex Forum, 264
International Ladies' Garment Workers Union (ILGWU), 206–7, 208; "What Type of Worker Are You?" cartoon, 207
International Organization for Migration (IOM), 189
Iran hostage crisis, 218
Irish immigrants, 106–7, 124, 133–34, 158, 180, 309
Italian immigrants, 133–34

Jackson, Andrew, 116n30
Jamestown, Virginia: establishment of, 99; immigrants of, 99–100, 101, 115n11; as money-making venture, 99; mortality rate, 115n11; skills shortage, 99
Jamestown's Poles, 98
January 6 US Capitol riot, 286, 287
Japan, US occupation of, 166
Japanese Exclusion Act of 1924, 125
Japanese immigrants, 28, 236–37, 442
Jay, John, 56
Jefferson, Thomas, 23, 102, 104, 169, 289, 291
Jewish refugees, 126, 182, 183, 187, 309
Jim Crow laws, 150, 337
Jiménez, Manuel, 222
Johnson, Lyndon, immigration policy, 62, 146, 244, 272, 435
Johnson-Reed Act. See Immigration Act of 1924 (Johnson-Reed Act)
Jones, Jennifer A., 13
Joseph, Chief, 60, 64
Judaism, 293
Juneteenth, 22
"Justice for Janitors" campaign, 278

Kass, Leon, 282–83
Kearney, Denis, 106
Kennedy, Edward, 146, 147
Kennedy, Joe, III, 157
Kennedy, John F.: assassination of, 146; civil rights policy, 161n16; immigration policy, 145, 146, 154, 221, 438; A Nation of Immigrants, 145–47, 148, 434–35, 436; religious views, 293–94, 295
Kennedy, Robert, 146, 244

Kent, Avidan, 195n4
King, Desmond, 65
King, Martin Luther, Jr., 61, 62, 155, 305, 306, 365
Kirkham, Alli, 418
Klein, Ezra, 282, 283
Knights of Labor, 276
Know-Nothing movement, 32, 60, 271, 292
Kohut, Thomas, Empathy and the Historical Understanding of the Human Past, 340
Ku Klux Klan, 32, 271, 292

Labor Appropriation Act of 1924, 257
labor migration, 268–69, 270, 272, 274
labor unions, 270, 276, 277–78, 279
Lafitte, Jean, 105, 116n30
Lamar, Kendrick, 341
Lambda Legal, 263
Lambright, Nsombi, 370
Lascaino, Mario, 212
Latin American immigrants, 128
Latino identity, 304–5, 309
Latino immigrants: Black solidarity with, 361, 365, 369–71; as cheap labor, 155; civil rights activism of, 360, 361, 362, 374; conspiracy theories about, 240, 311; cultural contribution of, 302; demographics, 34, 35; discrimination of, 358–59, 360, 361–62, 365; family reunification, 240; ICE raids against, 369; labor disputes, 361–62; limits on immigration of, 147; politics and, 38–39; in popular culture, 311–13; relations with extended families, 309–10; settlement places, 303, 359; social status of, 35, 39; stories of, 14, 306–7, 313–14, 315–16; unaccompanied minors, 241–42; violence against, 242–44, 311, 314–15; whiteness ideologies and, 39, 303–4, 305
Lazarus, Emma, xi, 271, 449; "The New Colossus," 153, 161n23, 270
Leadership Conference on Civil Rights, 367
League of United Latin American Citizens (LULAC), 205, 214, 215, 219
Leahy, Patrick, 261, 263
"Learning from the Outsider Within" (Collins), 63
Lehman, Herbert, 151
Lehman-Humphrey bills, 145
Lenape people, xiii, 18–19

of, 179–80, 182, 184, 186, 192, 195n4, 258;
employment of, 187; government policy
on, 180, 188–89; homosexuality and, 258;
humanitarian parole authority, 185–86;
legislation on, 185; natural disasters and,
194–95; path to permanent residency,
185; political ideology and, 185, 187–88;
in post-Cold War era, 188–92; processing
of, 186, 187, 199n31; public opinion
about, 187, 190; reunification programs
for, 245; scholarship on, 180–82; security
concerns, 189–91, 192; special visa
program, 192; in US military missions,
187; War on Terror and, 189–90
religion, nationalism and, 285–86, 288
religious diversity, 289, 290–92, 295
Religious Freedom Restoration Act of 1993,
285
"Remain in Mexico" program, 191, 397, 399
Renan, Ernest, 8, 24, 26, 27n8, 27n9
Reno, Janet, 259
replenishment workers (RAWs), 231n92
RFSL (Swedish Federation for Lesbian,
Gay, Bisexual, and Transgender Rights),
257
Richmond, Jules, 238
Riell, Henry E., 60
Rivera, Diego, 98, 314
Robertson, W. B., 104
Robeson, Paul, 156
Roddenberry, Gene, 339
Rodino, Peter W., 203
Rodino bill, 203, 204, 219
Rodríguez, Adalberto, 205
Rodríguez, Wendy, 208
Roosevelt, Franklin Delano, 173
Roosevelt, Theodore, 33–34, 41
Rosales, Rodolfo, 209
Rove, Karl, 38
Rumbaut, Rubén, 138
Rutledge, John, 56

Saavedra, Marco, 12
Saint-Domingue, 101, 102, 103
Salazar, María Elena, 207, 208
same-sex marriages, 260, 261, 262, 263,
265
sanctuary spaces/cities, 13, 14, 193–94, 355,
371, 374–75

San Francisco, CA: Asian immigration, 98,
106; Gay Freedom Day Parade, 238; gold
rush, 97
Sántiz, Rufino, 382
Santos Briones, Cinthya: embroidery and
photographs by, 318, 322, 324, 326, 328,
330, 332; Migrant Herbalism, 14
Schmidt, Eric, 422
Schmidt, Ronald, Sr., 46, 47, 48, 64, 66n9
Schurz, Carl, 145
Scott, Andrew F., 339
Scott, Dred, 256
search engines, 404, 415, 420, 422
Search for Common Ground, 423
Seasonal Agricultural Worker (SAW), 225
Second World War, immigration during,
182
Seixas, Moses, 290
Select Commission on Immigration and
Refugee Policy, 217
Seneca Falls "Declaration of Sentiments,"
59
September 11 terrorist attacks, 359–60
Service Employees International Union,
278
settler-colonialism, 11, 12, 49, 434, 441–42,
443, 451n21
Shah, Silky, 373
Shaka the Zulu, 22
Sicilia, Javier, 368
Sille, Nicasius de, 290
Simpson, Alan K., 218, 219
Simpson-Mazzoli act, 141
Singh, Nikhil, 150
Slaughter-House Cases, 335
slavery, 102, 180, 335, 346, 348–49
"Sleepy Lagoon" murder case, 152
Smith, Al, 292, 294
Smith, Anna Deavere, 339
Smith, Eddie, 364
Smith, John, 99
Smith, William French, 213
snack news, 412
social inequalities, 309
social media platforms: AI systems and,
405; alarm-based narratives, 411–12,
417–18; artificial social segregation,
416–17; business model of, 404, 414, 416,
419, 423; disinformation on, 410–11;